W9-BTJ-943

THE LIBRARY OF CHRISTIAN
CLASSICS

THE LIBRARY OF CHRISTIAN CLASSICS

VOLUME XVII

LUTHER AND ERASMUS:
FREE WILL AND SALVATION

THE LIBRARY OF CHRISTIAN CLASSICS

Volume XVII

LUTHER AND ERASMUS: FREE WILL AND SALVATION

Erasmus: De Libero Arbitrio

Translated and Edited by

E. GORDON RUPP, M.A., D.D.

Dixie Professor of Ecclesiastical History
in the University of Cambridge

In collaboration with

A. N. MARLOW, M.A.

Senior Lecturer in Latin in the
University of Manchester

Luther: De Servo Arbitrio

Translated and Edited by

PHILIP S. WATSON, M.A., D.D.

Rall Professor of Systematic Theology
Garrett Theological Seminary, Evanston, Illinois

In collaboration with

B. DREWERY, M.A.

Bishop Fraser Lecturer in Ecclesiastical History
in the University of Manchester

Philadelphia

THE WESTMINSTER PRESS

Published simultaneously in the United States of America and in Great Britain
by The Westminster Press, Philadelphia, and the SCM Press, Ltd., London.

Standard Book No. 664-22017-7

Library of Congress Catalog Card No. 76-79870

Printed in the United States of America

GENERAL EDITORS' PREFACE

The Christian Church possesses in its literature an abundant and incomparable treasure. But it is an inheritance that must be reclaimed by each generation. THE LIBRARY OF CHRISTIAN CLASSICS is designed to present in the English language, and in twenty-six volumes of convenient size, a selection of the most indispensable Christian treatises written prior to the end of the sixteenth century.

The practice of giving circulation to writings selected for superior worth or special interest was adopted at the beginning of Christian history. The canonical Scriptures were themselves a selection from a much wider literature. In the patristic era there began to appear a class of works of compilation (often designed for ready reference in controversy) of the opinions of well-reputed predecessors, and in the Middle Ages many such works were produced. These medieval anthologies actually preserve some noteworthy materials from works otherwise lost.

In modern times, with the increasing inability even of those trained in universities and theological colleges to read Latin and Greek texts with ease and familiarity, the translation of selected portions of earlier Christian literature into modern languages has become more necessary than ever; while the wide range of distinguished books written in vernaculars such as English makes selection there also needful. The efforts that have been made to meet this need are too numerous to be noted here, but none of these collections serves the purpose of the reader who desires a library of representative treatises spanning the Christian centuries as a whole. Most of them embrace only the age of the church fathers, and some of them have long been out of print. A fresh translation of a work already translated may shed much new light upon its meaning. This is true even of Bible translations despite the work of many experts through the centuries. In some instances old translations have been adopted in this series, but wherever necessary or desirable, new ones have been made. Notes have been supplied where these were needed to explain the author's meaning. The introductions provided for the several treatises and extracts will, we believe, furnish welcome guidance.

JOHN BAILLIE
JOHN T. MCNEILL
HENRY P. VAN DUSEN

CONTENTS

LUTHER: ON THE BONDAGE OF THE WILL

ABBREVIATIONS

WA   *Weimarer Ausgabe, D. Martin Luthers Werke.* Kritische
        Gesamtausgabe. 90 vols. Weimar, 1883 ff.
WA Bi *D. Martin Luthers Werke, Die deutsche Bibel.*
WA Tr *D. Martin Luthers Werke, Tischreden.*
MPL   *Patrologiae Cursus Completus, Series Latina,* ed. by J. P.
        Migne. Paris, 1844 ff.
⟨ ⟩   denote additional or corrected references; in Luther,
        references to the text of Erasmus are given thus: ⟨E., p. 00⟩.
( )   denote what is in the Latin text itself.

Introduction

THE ERASMIAN ENIGMA

JAMES A. FROUDE ENDED HIS MEMORABLE LECTURES ON ERASMUS at Oxford [1] in 1894 with the declaration that if you would understand the sixteenth century, "I believe you will best see it as it really was, if you will look at it through the eyes of Erasmus." "The eyes of Erasmus"—the pale blue, the frosty twinkle, the hooded reticences—how well we seem to know them, and how much do they proclaim the man!

It would not be fair to Luther to look at him only through the eyes of Erasmus. But it is true of all the great historical controversies—Newman and Kingsley is another case in point—that we do no service to one side by playing down the merits of the other, for this is a sure way to miss the human poignancy, and even the theological nerve of the encounter. We do not illuminate, we obscure the truth when we underrate the religion and faith of Erasmus.

Not that it was a very great debate, even for its day: More and Tyndale, Erasmus and Hutten, Luther and Zwingli, Cranmer and Gardiner, Jewel and Harding, had better knock-down arguments. When somebody gives us a definitive edition of the debate about Free Choice and Grace between John Eck and Andrew Karlstadt, it may very likely turn out to be a better piece of historical theology, and show that these two stuck rather more closely to their subject.

At best, Erasmus prodded Luther into some splendid epigrams and into uttering hermeneutic principles of worth. At the worst, their debate slammed the door on any reconciliation between two

[1] James Anthony Froude, *Life and Letters of Erasmus* (1895).

1

great men, and embarrassed their common friends. To use the image of another day, it was a duel in which the two participants got up at crack of dawn, one armed with a rapier, the other with a blunderbuss, where shaking of fists and mutterings usurped the place of battle, and which ended with the two antagonists going their separate ways, undamaged but shaken, and with a frustrating sense of honor ruffled but unsatisfied.

Satirists are notoriously thin-skinned. They lie awake o' nights, brooding on lesser insults than they have dealt to their opponents. And Erasmus had taken pains to be urbane with Luther, whereas Luther's occasional elephantine attempts to dance tiptoe were outnumbered by his enormous gestures of disgust, so that the first part of Erasmus' reply, the *Hyperaspistes,* does not get much beyond personalities and hurt feelings. The second is much better—but if it is, as M. Renaudet says, "a noble proclamation of eternal humanism," [2] it is, as he admits, a feeble reply to Luther. Luther himself wrote no further answer. But his letters and the gossip of his Table Talk are littered with scorn of Erasmus as a trifler with truth, a scoffer at religion, an unbeliever.

The last was unjust, but Erasmus had asked for it, in his famous sentence about his preference for the "paths of the Skeptics." In the *Hyperaspistes* he put up a convincing defense. He had merely asserted the right of men to be uncommitted, where doctrine had not been thoroughly and formally defined by the Church. But perhaps the charge of skepticism does not rest upon that single passage. His innumerable tilts at authority, the acid of his satire—the widening ripples of gossip that reported his obiter dicta throughout the learned world—his silences: these led many to suspect that he was at heart more radical than he avowed, and is one reason why some have drawn a line of sympathy between him and the Sacramentarians and Anabaptists.

There is, then, an Erasmian enigma. His contemporaries recognized it, and the contradictory verdicts of posterity derive from it. One of Luther's favorite stories was of how Frederick the Wise at Worms in October, 1520, had asked Erasmus for a judgment on Luther's case and got instead an epigram. "What a wonderful little man that is!"—the prince smiled ruefully—"You never know where you are with him." And Luther commented: "Erasmus is an eel. Only Christ can grab him."

The psychologists buzz round Luther; Erasmus they have neglected. Yet of the two, it is Erasmus who offers better materials for a case history: the illegitimacy casting shadows down all his

---

[2] Auguste Renaudet, *Humanisme et Renaissance* (1958), p. 177.

years, his "thing" about his vows, the fantasies about his past that the historians have not finally resolved. There are the obvious ambivalences, one of which Huizinga profoundly noted: "Rest and independence he desired ardently above all things: there was no more restless or dependent creature."

Erasmus has always had friends and lovers: from Sir Thomas More, Beatus Rhenanus, and the customs officer at Boppard down to P. S. Allen, Auguste Renaudet, and J. Huizinga in our day. He has as constantly had critics and enemies: from Zuñiga, Lee, and that "most intimate enemy," Aleander, to Philip Hughes, Josef Lortz, Hubert Jedin. To Lortz as to Aleander, Erasmus represents a worse menace to the Church than Luther: he is the "half Catholic" who spelled the dissolution of faith, whereas Luther called the Church to arms.[3]

Erasmus might have made a fair reply to his modern Catholic critics. He was, as we shall note, more revolutionary than is sometimes supposed. But he kept to his middle way with a stubborn consistency that recalls Newman in the difficult months before and after 1870. Erasmus would never deny the good in Luther however much he deplored Luther's violence, but he also did not cease to attack the bigotry and intolerance of Luther's enemies. If his famous "I'll put up with this Church until I see a better" [4] is something less than the consciously modernist program that M. Renaudet supposed, it at least provides a plausible text for a homily on the theme "Not only Newman but also Erasmus is an ancestor of Vatican II."

Discussion of the spirituality of Erasmus must surely begin with the last moment of truth, his relapse at death into his native Dutch, *"Lieve God,"* and the fevered murmurings of the preceding hours: *"Jesu, misericordia—Domine, libera me"* (one of the great *Anfechtung* texts of the young Luther). We remember how throughout his life at regular intervals he wrote works of piety and edification, from the early *De contemptu mundi* to the last tract on preaching, *Ecclesiastes.* Though many of them had little fresh to say about marriage or the duties of rulers, and justify Luther's malicious insight, "Erasmus contrives his words—they don't grow," their overall impressiveness increases as the number of these tracts mount up.

It has been noted more than once in modern times how persistently his prayers have appeared and reappear in religious anthologies. At least one of his devotional treatises has always been

[3] J. Lortz, *Die Reformation in Deutschland* (1948), Vol. 1, pp. 131, 136.
[4] *Fero igitur hanc Ecclesiam donec video meliorem* (*Works,* X.1258.A).

taken seriously. William Tyndale rated the *Enchiridion* highly enough to make it the subject of his prentice translation, and it may have left a permanent mark on his theology of baptism. The number of editions in the early years of the sixteenth century speak for its popularity. Nobody can read expositions of it by Dr. Mann Phillips [5] or Dr. E. W. Kohls [6] without being impressed, or study the effects of it in Spain and Italy in M. Bataillon's fine volume [7] without realizing that here is one who contributed effectively to the religion of the age.

There is ambivalence, too, in Erasmus' relation to the "modern devotion," though this is aggravated for us by the confusion of historians concerning the relation between the modern devotion and humanism. Certainly where the influence of ideas is concerned, with their background of mysterious moods and tempers of any age, it is precarious to try to solve problems by dates and people and books.

It is noteworthy that in recent days E. W. Kohls and R. R. Post [8] have turned attention to the earliest writings of Erasmus, and startlingly, to the *De contemptu mundi* in their investigation of this problem. Are we to seek the origins of the Erasmian "philosophy of Christ" here in his early studies as a monk? Or are we, with the older historians, to look for it rather as a development from his widening contacts with humanists in following years, in his first visit to England, and in the influence on him of Colet and Vitrier? Certainly there seems in Erasmus something of a love-hate relation to the religion in which he had been schooled, an undoubted influence upon him of contemporary piety, and a growing enmity toward the obscurantisms of the new barbarians in Holland or the Puritanic rigidities of John Standonck in Paris, both of which have some evident relation to the modern devotion at its latter end.

Dr. Gordon Leff [9] in his learned study of late medieval heresy suggests that it arose from the tension between orthodoxy and dissent. He sees the heart of this dissent—and it would be as true of movements of genuine renewal as of eccentric deviationism—in the endemic tension in Christianity between precept and practice. Hence the return to a primitive Christianity—something more

[5] M. Mann Phillips, *Erasmus and the Northern Renaissance* (London and New York, 1949).
[6] E. W. Kohls, *Die Theologie des Erasmus*, 2 vols. (Basel, 1966).
[7] Marcel Bataillon, *Érasme et l'Espagne* (Paris, 1937).
[8] R. R. Post, *The Modern Devotion* (Leiden, 1968).
[9] G. Leff, *Heresy in the Lower Middle Ages*, 2 vols. (Manchester, 1967).

constant, more fundamental than any humanist return *ad fontes,* though no doubt reinforced by it at this point of time. It is the return, as against too intricate ecclesiastical and theological complexities, to Christianity as above all a way of life, a vision of God, and a divine life within the soul. It involves the simplification, almost always the oversimplification, of "the simple gospel," and often, as in the Franciscan movement and the modern devotion, a distrust of learning and of books.

We ought not to underestimate the strength of late medieval piety. We do not necessarily need to look to the direct influence of Ficino, Mirandola, and the Platonic Academy for what was already familiar through Augustine and Dionysius. The so-called Erasmian spiritualism, with its "body-soul" or "body-soul-spirit" anthropology, is to be found in Wessel Gansfort before him and in Cornelius Hoen among his disciples, and when we find it in Oecolampadius and Zwingli, we do not need to look to Erasmus as its author.

In Germany, as the studies of Landeen have shown, the modern devotion flowed into older channels of German mysticism, which produced in Biel and Suso, and through them among the humanists of South Germany and Alsace, a pattern of devotion, a "theology of the cross," of resignation, of suffering with Christ, which is nearer to Luther than Erasmus, despite all the latter's emphasis on the Christian life as a *"militia Christi."*

Nobody can study the early theological writings of Erasmus without observing the extent to which their moral and even their spiritual and ascetic content is steeped in classical literature. When we remember the distaste of Erasmus for Hebrew, his comparative neglect of the Old Testament (Luther's extraordinary sensitivity to Hebraic ways is a great point of contrast), we might suspect that Erasmus was in a fair way to substituting classical morality and spirituality for that of the Old Testament and thereby establishing a Christian Gnosticism that put erudition above piety. But this would be to fail to understand Erasmus' own interests at that point in his life, his devotion to "good letters," his concern to use in the service of Christ writings that were for him a real preparation for the gospel, though always subordinated to revealed truth.

We can therefore sidestep the complex questions of how and when Erasmus turned from "good letters" to "sacred letters" and to the employment of the tools and methods of Biblical humanism in the service of the gospel.

There were first the tools of the revived study of the sacred lan-

guages—Greek, Hebrew, and the new cleaner Latin. There was a
sense of the need to get to the best manuscripts. There was the
important principle, which he owed probably to Valla, that the
exact grammatical and philological context of Scripture has priority. The fruit of this was the publication in 1516 of his edition
of the New Testament. As a gesture by an individual, and as a
challenge to authority, Erasmus' New Testament can be compared
for boldness with Luther's Ninety-five Theses. We remember how
Erasmus was unprepared for the attacks on him that followed, how
under pressure he put back the so-called *Comma Joanneum* of the
"Three Heavenly Witnesses" in the First Letter of John, but we
forget the daring of the original exclusion. The young dons in
Cambridge missed neither the novelty nor the courage, and henceforth whatever else the Cambridge Reformers were or were not,
they were Erasmians to a man.

Then there were the bold Prefaces. The first, the *Paraclesis ad
lectorem pium,* was a manifesto on behalf of the "Open Bible,"
which was echoed in Tyndale's words and deeds, so that the English Bibles of the reign of Henry VIII may properly be regarded
as within the Erasmian program. The *Ratio seu methodus com-
pendio perveniendi ad veram theologiam* enlarges principles already expounded in the *Enchiridion.* Here is the return to Christ
as he becomes contemporary with us in the Gospels, and the insistence on the importance, above all later theologians, of Paul and
John (the Pauline content of the *philosophia Christi* in Erasmus
must never be underrated).

The return to the Bible meant a return to the Old Fathers as
primarily expositors of Scripture, a bypassing of the later Schoolmen and a return to the Biblical theology of the first centuries. At
first, and naturally, the emphasis was on the Western Fathers—
Jerome, Augustine, Ambrose, Cyprian—but as the massive
printed editions of Erasmus and his friends succeeded one another
in the 1520's, a new prominence was given to the Greek Fathers,
with important results. Perhaps neither Erasmus nor his friend
Rhenanus quite reckoned with the explosive possibilities of their
editions of Origen and Tertullian.

The practical emphasis on Christianity as a way of life, and on
the direct simplicities of the "philosophy of Christ," has within it
a further seminal principle, the distinction between the essentials and nonessentials of religion. The Christian faith is not another Torah, where all must be accepted as equally given, things
great and small. There are some truths "which God has willed to
be most plainly evident, and such are the precepts for the good

life." These truths are clear and they are few. Others are to be reverenced as mystery and simply adored (the emphasis on "mystery" is another modern touch). About others Christians may speculate and differ. The distinction between essentials and nonessentials was important for the emperor Charles V, in his delicate maneuverings with Protestants in the 1530's, and he may have learned it from Erasmian counselors. It is a distinction that was important for the two Reformers most inclined to Erasmian irenics—Martin Bucer and Philip Melanchthon—and in one great theological tradition it would persist and be majestically expounded in the writings of Richard Hooker and William Chillingworth. The Second Vatican Council and its aftermath seem to show that its irenic possibilities are not yet exhausted.

Antagonism to that element in late medieval religion which Gilbert Burnet referred to as "superannuated Judaism" was common ground among the humanists of England, Holland, France, and Germany. Here is the importance of satire. Somebody has said in our own century that "satire is the last refuge of those who shrink from taking up their Cross." The writings and paintings of sixteenth-century satirists have darker shadows than the more cheerful bawdy anticlericalism of earlier centuries. There is here something more than poking fun at what is, after all, human and endearing weakness: there is contempt and anger, and to this extent humanist satire ate corrosively into the ideals of the age helping to ripen discontent. The Reformers on the whole distrusted it. "It doth not become the Lord's servants to use railing rhymes," said Tyndale, a little primly. Luther refused to praise the "Letters of Obscure Men" because he felt the hurt of the daughter of Zion lay too deep for tears, let alone laughter.

Like his friends Colet and More, Erasmus was a writer of satires, and like them, too, he kept a special edge for the members of the religious orders. Part of his antipathy to Luther is, surely, because he saw in him a typical mendicant theologian, with all the loud violences of the breed. Whether Erasmus did or did not write the devasting, comic *Julius Exclusus*, few of his contemporaries put it past him, nor does it go beyond his other utterances of disgust and hatred for Julius II, the embodiment of all he most despised. When we add the gentler but always astringent *Praise of Folly*, the extraordinary undertones of the *Colloquies*, and a thousand asides in the vast correspondence, we can understand why Erasmus became a rock of offense and a stone of stumbling for many. When we add this trait to the rest of his ambivalences, we realize that we can never altogether dismiss "Erasmus, the liberal"; from Rabelais and Montaigne to James A. Froude and Mark Pattison,[10] the ancestors and descendants of the "crisis of European conscience" have rightly put him in their pedigree.

How seriously must we take Erasmus as a theologian? This question has an evident bearing on the debate with Luther. Obviously he was not a technical Scholastic theologian in the late medieval manner; he was a man always moved by intellectual appetites and dislikes, and we may suppose he made little effort to understand, for example, the writings of Duns Scotus, or to pursue the intricate systems that had bored and wearied him in Paris. But this does not dispose of the question. In his own blend of modern devotion, of good and sacred letters, in his direct appeal to the Bible and the Old Fathers, is there evidence that this subtle and penetrating intelligence was really at home among the deep imponderables of theology?

E. W. Kohls has put the best case ever likely to be made, and he sees in Erasmus one who at a very early stage in his career had achieved a coherent Biblical theology, a hermeneutic, and a theology of history. This presentation, however, for all its learning and awareness of the whole field of Erasmian literature, has yet to be sieved by the learned world, and one is bound to have reservations about a demonstration taken almost exclusively from the early writings, the *De contemptu mundi,* the *Antibarbari,* and the *Enchiridion.*

The older historians did not lack evidence when they stressed the importance for Erasmus of his visits to England and Italy, of his friendships with More, Colet, Vitrier, and the significance for him of his studies and of the events that opened up after 1517. There have been too many attempts in recent years to dress up the sixteenth-century Reformers—first Luther, then Calvin, then Zwingli—in modern jargon, to show them each in turn to have been theocentric, existential, eschatological. We suspect that Erasmus, too, has been dressed up, and that there is something in the comment of a Dutch theologian: "Erasmus was not a German, and he did not think like this. He was a Dutchman." To find in Erasmus a coherent *exitus-reditus* view of creation and redemption, and anything like a doctrine of justification along Lutheran lines, or a theology of the cross results in a very un-Erasmus-like Erasmus.

In the case of all men at all times, there is, no doubt, a philosophy and theology implicit in their assumptions about life and its

---

[10] Both James Anthony Froude and Mark Pattison (in his article on Erasmus in the *Encyclopædia Britannica*), on the edge of the coming scientific study of Erasmus, have quite astonishing perceptions which come from sympathy.

meaning, and a whole unconscious field of Christian acceptance is
to be posited by all late medieval Christian thinkers. A great deal
of what is given as Erasmus' own original and conscious articula-
tion we may suspect simply reflects this background, and Erasmus
gives it to us at a level that is always edifying and profitable, but
hardly ever profound. Without trying to close a question which
Dr. Kohls has thrown wide open, we may suggest that in this debate at any rate there is no suggestion that Erasmus is the theologian at bay. Erasmus is the Kingsley, not the Newman.

In fact, Erasmus' *Diatribe Concerning Free Choice* has all the
elements that we have already noted. There is the smooth transition from the classical to the Biblical world, from classical to Biblical allusion and illustration. There is the admission of the authority of Holy Scripture, but the recognition of the paramount
authority of the Church. There is the grateful recognition of the
cloud of witnesses, of the Fathers, and interesting material for a
discussion of the *"consensus fidelium."* There is the insistence that
what is essential and worthy of debate in the Christian faith is a
small body of plain and practical truth.

Dr. Ivor Asheim in his brilliant study *Glaube und Erziehung bei
Luther* [11] considers Erasmus as primarily a moralist with no theology, but only an anthropology; and without conceding all his
argument, it is true that practical and moral considerations determined Erasmus' fastening on "Free Choice" for the debate. It
was a great count of Erasmus against the Reformers that they had
not only not strengthened the good life, but that there had been
a decline in moral behavior (the aging Luther would have been
inclined to agree with him). For Luther, "free choice" touched
the nerve of the gospel—the promises, the glory and the grace of
God—whereas for Erasmus, the questions "whether God foreknows anything contingently; whether our will accomplishes anything in things pertaining to eternal salvation; whether it simply
suffers the action of grace," belong as he explicitly says among
"hidden, not to say superfluous" questions which men investigate
with "irreverent inquisitiveness." For Erasmus, the question at
issue exposed Luther's fatalism and antinomianism, with their
disastrous effect upon the behavior of the masses.

Many scholars have emphasized the importance of the lines:

Therefore, in my judgment on this matter of free choice, having
learned what is needful to know about this, if we are in the path of true
religion, let us go on swiftly to better things, forgetful of the things
which are behind, or, if we are entangled in sins, let us strive with all

[11] Heidelberg, 1961.

our might and have recourse to the remedy of penitence that by all means we may entreat the mercy of the Lord without which no human will or endeavor is effective.

The method and scope of the debate had two serious weaknesses. It was the tedious manner of that age to deal with one's opponent line by line or at least paragraph by paragraph. That is how Luther began, and it was fatal. The pressure of events on Luther in 1525, the watershed of his career, was such that he could not possibly hope to complete the debate on this scale, and he himself later admitted that he took no notice at all of the last chapters of Erasmus, which are perhaps the best part of the work.

Second, the attempt to concentrate on Scripture alone, which as Professor Watson demonstrates elsewhere was impossible, since both debaters appealed to other authorities and to reason, was weakened by the fact that the Scriptural texts proved either too much or too little. Thus the Hebrew mind, as displayed in the Old Testament, knew nothing of secondary causes, and its stress on the divine will and action seemed to justify on the one hand complete fatalism, or on the other an extreme Pelagianism.

Modern Catholic scholars have pointed out the weakness of what Erasmus has to say in relation to the doctrine of grace and of divine foreknowledge and omnipotence. We may be content to draw attention to Dr. H. J. McSorley's balanced and learned study, as the outstanding discussion of the subject in the English language.[12]

He points to the defectiveness of Erasmus' very setting of the problem in his definition of "free choice":

By free choice in this place we mean a power of the human will by which a man can apply himself to the things which lead to eternal salvation, or turn away from them.

He shows it to be more defective than the definitions of Peter Lombard and Gabriel Biel in that it defines freedom with regard to salvation, and yet makes no mention at all of grace. It is true, as he goes on to point out, that Erasmus' argument is better than his definition and that he improves as he goes on. Erasmus does not intend at all to disparage grace, but to establish a point of human responsibility.

It is noteworthy, too, that the Acts of the Second Council of

---

[12] Harry J. McSorley, *Luthers Lehre vom unfreien Willen* (Munich, 1967; E. T. *Luther: Right or Wrong? An Ecumenical-Theological Study of Luther's Major Work, The Bondage of the Will,* New York and Minneapolis, 1969).

Orange (A.D. 529), which condemned Semi-Pelagianism, disappeared and were unknown during the Middle Ages and to Erasmus, and only turned up during the Council of Trent.

The reader may care to have two quotations from these Acts, that he may remember how very far the Council of Orange went in an Augustinian (McSorley would say also in a Lutheran) direction.

Canon 5: "If anyone says that not only the increase of faith, but also its beginning and the very desire for belief, by which we believe in Him who justifies the ungodly and come to the regeneration of holy baptism—if anyone says that this belongs to us by nature and not by a gift of grace, that is, by the inspiration of the Holy Spirit amending our will and turning it from unbelief to faith and from godlessness to godliness, it is proof that he is opposed to the teaching of the apostles."

Canon 6: "If anyone says that God has mercy upon us when apart from His grace we believe, will, desire, strive, labour, pray, watch, study, seek, ask or knock, but does not confess that it is by the infusion and inspiration of the Holy Spirit within us that we have the faith, will or the strength to do all these things as we ought, and thus subordinates the help of grace to human humility or obedience, without acknowledging that our very obedience and humility is a gift of grace itself, he contradicts the apostle who says, 'What hast thou that thou hast not received?' (I Cor. 4:7) and 'By the Grace of God, I am what I am' (I Cor. 15:10)." [13]

This doctrine, which was that of St. Thomas, is one to which Erasmus pays lip service as a "more probable" opinion, about which he has not finally made up his mind.

On the other hand those who, at the other extreme from Pelagius, attribute most of all to grace and practically nothing to free choice, yet do not entirely remove it: for they deny that man can will the good without peculiar grace, they deny that he can make a beginning, they deny that he can progress, they deny he can reach his goal without the principal and perpetual aid of divine grace.

The other view Erasmus quite wrongly ascribes to Scotus, for it is more properly akin to that of Gabriel Biel; it asserts that even though a man

has not yet received the grace which destroys sin, he may nonetheless, by his own natural powers, perform what they call morally good works which, not "condignly" but "congruously" merit that grace which "makes acceptable."

The question arises how far words such as "Semi-Pelagian" or "Neo-Semi-Pelagian" can profitably be applied to late medieval

[13] H. Denzinger, ed., *Enchiridion Symbolorum* (Editio 28), pp. 86–87.

theologians or to Erasmus.[14] P. Vignaux in his classical essay on *Justification and Predestination in the Fourteenth Century* showed that, for example, what Peter of Auriol meant by "Pelagianism" had little to do with the fourth- and fifth-century controversy. It is true that grace and salvation lie at the bottom of the medieval, as of the Augustinian, debate, but the whole setting has so changed that we might remember Newman's saying "New questions demand new answers."

The faint praise and indeed the criticism of Erasmus' handling of the debate from his contemporary and his modern Catholic critics must surely dispose of the view that here is a great theologian's presentation of a case. But there is more here than classical moralism covered with a veneer of piety. Erasmus does deeply and sincerely believe that Christianity is a religion of grace. The idea that men can be saved without divine assistance would have been wholly abhorrent to him. It may be that at the end of the day it will be conceded that as against Luther he grasps the importance of human responsibility and of an insistence on grace which yet does not take by storm the citadel of the soul. Yet at the end of the day, too, Luther could maintain the great Anselmian retort: "Thou hast not considered the gravity of sin"—or what it means for man to have his existence *coram Deo*.[15]

E. GORDON RUPP

THE LUTHERAN RIPOSTE

How are we to understand the conflict between Erasmus and Luther? Is it a matter of temperament? Is it a case of the cool (though somewhat testy) philosophical mind over against the rabidity of the dogmatic theologian? or of the rational, ethical concern of the moralist over against the profound intuitions of a passionately religious spirit? Such suggestions have often been

[14] Harry J. McSorley, "Was Gabriel Biel a Semi-Pelagian?" in *Wahrheit und Verkündigung* (Michael Schmaus zum 70 Geburtstag; Munich, 1967).

[15] The difference between Luther's view of man and that of Erasmus is clear in the lines that Luther could never have penned: *"Male habet Lutherus quod Diatribe non tantum exaggerat pronitatem ad malum quantum ipsi commodum est. Fateor in quibusdam ingeniis bene natis ac bene educatis minimum esse pronitatis. Maxima proclinitatis pars est non ex natura, sed ex corrupta institutione, ex improbo convictu, ex assuetudine peccandi malitiaque voluntatis"* (*Works*, X.1454.F). See Auguste Renaudet, *Études Érasmiennes*, p. 350; *Érasme et l'Italie*, p. 177.

made, but they are at best superficial, for Erasmus is by no means irreligious, and Luther is neither an immoralist nor irrational. The two men represent rather two different theological and ethical outlooks, two alternative ways of "thinking together" God and man.

The nature of this difference does not emerge so clearly as could be desired in the two works before us, and that for two main reasons.

To begin with, the *Diatribe* represents a rather one-sided re-action on the part of Erasmus to Luther's position in his *Assertio,* where he states:

> I was wrong in saying that free choice before grace is a reality only in name. I should have said simply: "free choice is in reality a fiction, or a name without reality." For no one has it in his own power to think a good or bad thought, but everything (as Wyclif's article condemned at Constance rightly teaches) happens by absolute necessity.[1]

Erasmus' argument concentrates on the last part of this statement (concerning "necessity"), and never really comes to grips with Luther's essential concern. For Luther, it is vitally important to know "whether the will does anything or nothing in matters pertaining to eternal salvation," and he thinks Erasmus ought to be aware that

> this is the cardinal issue between us, the point on which everything in this controversy turns. For what we are doing is to inquire what free choice can do, what it has done to it, and what is its relation to the grace of God.[2]

On this subject, however, Erasmus is far from clear.[3]

Then, secondly, the situation is complicated by the fact that in the *De servo arbitrio* Luther accepts Erasmus' choice of the battle-ground, so to speak. That is, he takes the argument of the *Diatribe* and sets out to answer it point by point, instead of giving a systematic clarification of his own position. It is of course true that Erasmus has accepted Luther's proviso that the whole argu-ment should be brought to the test of Scripture; but this, as he points out, scarcely helps, since they disagree about the meaning of Scripture. He accuses Luther with some justice of interpreting

---

[1] *Assertio omnium articulorum M. Lutheri per Bullam Leonis X novissimam damnatorum* (December, 1520), Article 36 (*WA* 7, 446). The German version in *Grund und Ursach* reads more moderately, making no mention of "necessity" (*WA* 7, 446). It was, however, the Latin of the *Assertio* that Erasmus had read, and he quotes it. See below, pp. 64 ff.

[2] *WA* 18, 614; below, p. 116.

[3] Cf. McSorley, *Luther: Right or Wrong?* p. 284.

Scripture to suit his own ends; but the same charge might very well
be brought against Erasmus. The fact is that neither man sticks
faithfully to the plain, literal meaning of Scripture, or simply to
Scripture at all. Each appeals in his own way to "reason" and "experience"; and each exhibits a concern for the practical implications of their debate, both with regard to the welfare of men and
the honor of God. Unfortunately, they come to different conclusions because they start from different premises.

To put it very succinctly: Erasmus thinks essentially along traditional Scholastic lines, while Luther does not. In spite of his
well-known distaste for Scholastic subtleties, Erasmus presupposes
the metaphysical dualism of "nature" and "supernature" on which
all Scholastic thinking rests, and in terms of which the relation
between man and God, human nature and divine grace, is con-
strued. Luther, on the other hand, takes much more seriously a
quite different dualism, namely, that of God and the devil. The
significance of this can best be illustrated by contrasting his view
of the basic human situation with that of the Schoolmen.

According to the latter, man before the Fall was endowed with
certain natural powers (especially reason and free will), together
with a supernatural gift of grace. This gift was necessary if man
was to attain his true end, namely, eternal life and blessedness,
which was beyond the powers of mere nature. But since by these
powers (aided by grace) man was able to know and to do the good,
he could by doing it merit glory. He was, however, under no compulsion, but had freedom of choice between good and evil; he
could obey or disobey God. At the Fall he chose to disobey, and
in consequence lost his supernatural gift and was left simply in
a state of nature.

What effect the Fall had on man's natural powers was a matter
of debate, but most of the Schoolmen agreed that they were weakened, and some that they were considerably impaired—a view
which Erasmus shared. Yet nature remains nature even in fallen
man. His reason and will may be "wounded," even "corrupted,"
but they are not destroyed. His passions, the lower ingredients of
his nature, may be deeply disordered, so that he is a constant prey
to carnality, yet he is not wholly carnal. His nature remains compounded as it always was of animal "flesh" and that rational
"spirit" which is the mark of humanity, with the soul in between
and capable of leaning toward either.[4] Fallen man therefore still

---

[4] Cf. below, p. 76, and Erasmus, *Enchiridion* 7 (*Advocates of Reform: From
Wyclif to Erasmus*, ed. by Matthew Spinka [The Library of Christian
Classics, Vol. XIV; Philadelphia, 1953], pp. 318 ff.).

possesses some capacity for the knowledge of and obedience to God.

But what is this capacity worth as regards the attaining of salvation? Can man do anything toward his salvation without the help of grace? If he can, how much can he do? If he cannot, what measure of grace is needed to enable him? On these questions there were widely divergent views, especially in late Scholasticism, and Erasmus reflects the prevailing uncertainty of his time. He himself inclines to the "probable opinion" (as he calls it) that man can take no steps whatsoever toward salvation without "peculiar" grace; yet he does not reject the opposing view as untenable. Indeed, he rather vacillates between them, being evidently unaware that his "probable opinion" represents the mainstream of Catholic tradition.[5]

What Erasmus does reject is the idea that man has no active part to play in securing his own salvation, for at least man has freedom of choice. That is to say, he has in his will the power to "apply himself to the things which lead to eternal salvation or to turn away from them." It is true that, as Luther observes, Erasmus never quite specifies what those "things" are; but his general argument suggests that he has in mind obedience to God's commandments. It is also true that in the course of the argument man's power to apply himself becomes subject to considerable qualification. Nevertheless, Erasmus continues to maintain that, however little man can do, yet if he "does what in him lies," God will assist him with his grace, for divine grace "always accompanies human effort." Indeed, according to the "probable opinion" the very possibility of such effort depends on prevenient grace, without which the will of fallen man is "compelled to serve sin."

But it is up to man to respond to the divine initiative. Nature must cooperate with grace, the human will with the divine, and this is a matter for man's own choice, so that he is himself responsible for his own eventual salvation or perdition. Salvation is a cooperative enterprise (*synergismos*) of God and man, to which both partners make their contribution, even though man's share in it is so small that it is an excusable and even praiseworthy exaggeration when everything is attributed to God.

Turning now to Luther's view, we find a situation that is both more complex and more dramatic. Before the Fall, as Luther sees it, man's relation to God was characterized by his total dependence on God, whose grace or unmerited love evoked in man the response of faith, that is, trust and obedience. This relationship was and is the truly natural relationship of man as creature to God

[5] Cf. above, p. 11, and McSorley, *Luther: Right or Wrong?* pp. 288 ff.

In this regard he is not free, though he can be set free; hence what he calls his "free will" would more properly be called "self-will," which means bondage to Satan.[11]

There is, however, one respect in which neither fallen nor unfallen man ever had or can have freedom; that is, in relation to "things above him," as Luther calls them, which pertain to eternal salvation or perdition. This means—to put it in its simplest terms—that whatever else man might be free to choose, he can never in the nature of the case choose the motivation of his choice. All choices are determined by some ultimate principle, and in the final analysis there are only two possibilities: man is governed either by the Spirit of God or by the Evil Spirit. There is no neutral ground on which he can stand between these while he makes up his mind to which he will submit. Man is not capable of freedom in this sense; he has no liberty of indifference. Hence, although his eternal destiny depends on whether he is ruled by Satan or God, yet between these he is not free to choose. He is always governed by one or the other—or buffeted between the two, like a beast over which two would-be riders contend.

Luther's famous—or infamous!—simile of the beast and its riders was not, of course, his own invention. There was a long tradition of its use.[12] But it cannot be claimed that Luther uses it in the traditional way, for he equates the beast simply with the will (instead of free will), makes the riders God and Satan (instead of sin and grace), and gives the beast no option as to which rider it shall have. This undoubtedly raises difficulties, but in mitigation of them the following points may be borne in mind. First, neither God nor Satan is conceived here as acting exteriorly and coercively on man's will, but is thought of as a spiritual power operating inwardly, so that all man's consequent action is quite voluntary and uncoerced. Secondly, God and Satan are not equal contenders for the mastery of man. God is the Creator, to whom man as his creature properly belongs, and to whose sovereign sway both sinful man and his "rider" Satan are ultimately subject. (In other words, Luther's dualism is religious, not metaphysical, and relative, not absolute.)

God as the Creator is in Luther's thought the incessantly active source of all activity, and all his activity is absolutely righteous and

---

[11] *WA* 7, 450.
[12] It appears to be derived from the Pseudo-Augustinian *Hypomnesticon* (III.xi.20), where it is connected as Luther connects it with Ps. 73:22 f. (p. 140 below). But as McSorley shows (*Luther: Right or Wrong?* pp. 335 ff.) it has antecedents as far back as Origen, and it was widely used among the Schoolmen.

good. Yet the results of God's activity are not invariably good, for when "by the general motion of his omnipotence" he activates the wills of sinful men and devils (including Satan himself), these act in accordance with their character, which is bad. Even a master craftsman cannot do a perfect work with an imperfect tool, and even God's omnipotence can only move evil wills to evil acts. But the evil of man's or Satan's will is not to be ascribed to God as its cause. Here Luther is entirely in accord with the traditional Scholastic teaching that God is the cause of sinful acts but not of their sinfulness. But he cannot agree with the Schoolmen in attributing this to man's free will or freedom of choice, for it is plain evidence that man is not free but in bondage to Satan. Even with regard to man's original fall into this bondage, he will not admit that it was a matter of free choice; and as to how Satan himself became evil, that is a question he will not discuss. There can be no rational explanation of evil.

It is, however, God's purpose to save man from his evil bondage, and to this end he works by means of his Word and his Spirit. That is how he contends with Satan for the control of man. By his Word he confronts men outwardly, and by his Spirit inwardly, first in the form of law, then of gospel. We have not space here to elaborate on this aspect of Luther's thought, and two observations must suffice. First, it is the function of the law, in what he calls its spiritual use, to bring home to men their sinful plight and their inability to save themselves from perdition. In this way, men are made ready for the gospel and its message of grace. Although, therefore, Luther repudiates the Scholastic idea that man can prepare himself for grace by "doing what in him lies," he does not deny that there is a preparation for grace; he affirms it, only as God's doing, not man's.[13] Secondly, it is the function of the gospel, in what Luther calls its proper office, to bring home to man the grace and love of God and evoke in him the response of faith. Where and insofar as this happens, man is restored to his true and natural relationship to God, and thereby enters into the fullest freedom of which he is capable. This is the liberty of the children of God, in which men can freely cooperate with God, not for the achieving of their own salvation, but in the fulfilling of God's purposes in the world with respect both to its spiritual and temporal welfare.

For Luther, man's cooperation with God is not a precondition

---

[13] It is true that for Aquinas man's "doing what in him lies" depends on prevenient grace, which is God's doing; but for the later Schoolmen it is a matter of man's own efforts. For Luther, however, it is God's doing through his law.

of salvation as it is for Erasmus; it is rather a consequence of salvation. And salvation itself is differently understood. For Erasmus, salvation calls for a "supernaturalizing" of human nature by divine grace in order that man may become acceptable to God and a rightful claimant to the eternal life and blessedness of heaven. For Luther, it means the liberation of man from an unnatural bondage, so that he lives a truly natural life in trustful obedience to God, and can look forward to the heavenly reward, not as in any sense his right, but as the sure and certain promise of God's gracious Word.

Unfortunately, however, the effect of God's Word is not always salvific. It can in fact "increase sin," making bad men worse by hardening them in their resistance to God. As spoken to Pharaoh through Moses, for example, it simply stiffened his self-will and provoked him to open defiance. It can also harden men in self-righteousness, as it hardened the Pharisees when they encountered it in Christ. Why should this be so? In wrestling with this question Luther is led to propound his distinction between the "hidden" and the "revealed" will of God, and his doctrine of double predestination—a subject we shall consider later. Erasmus, however, is satisfied to explain the diverse effects of God's Word on men by attributing them to human freedom of choice, and he finds the problem of divine predestination easily solved by reference to God's foreknowledge of men's merits.

Erasmus knows, of course, that his position is open to the objection (which Luther does not fail to bring) that divine foreknowledge imposes necessity on man, leaving no room for contingency or free choice. He tries to forestall this objection by alluding to the Scholastic distinction between two kinds of necessity: that of "the consequent" *("consequentis")* and that of "consequence" *("consequentiae")*. In Scholastic thought the former represents absolute necessity, the latter conditional necessity, and the former excludes while the latter includes contingency. For example, whatever God wills necessarily happens—with conditional necessity, inasmuch as God is under no necessity to will it; but it happens also in the way he wills it to happen, whether necessarily or contingently (that is, with absolute or conditional necessity).[14]

It is along such lines as these that Erasmus discusses the case of Judas and the foreknowledge of God, about which his argument can be summarized as follows: Undoubtedly God foreknew that Judas would betray Christ; yet Judas was not forced (by absolute necessity) to do this, for he could have changed his mind. Hence

[14] Cf. Aquinas, *Summa theologica* I, q. 14, a. 13 and q. 19, a. 8.

his action was only conditionally necessary, being contingent on his not changing his mind, though of course if he had been going to change his mind, God would have foreknown this as well. To which Luther makes the obvious reply that in that case the change of mind must have been necessary—absolutely and not just conditionally necessary.

As Luther sees it, to say that God's foreknowledge of man's actions leaves room for the contingency of man's free choices is to make it no knowledge at all. It is to say that God foreknows, but he may be mistaken. For choices that are "free" in the sense of "not necessary" are a matter of sheer unpredictable chance. Consequently, Luther dismisses the Scholastic distinction as a mere play on words, and offers an alternative of his own. He is not speaking, he says, of the necessity of force or coercion, but of immutability. Certainly, Judas was not forced to betray Christ, he did it voluntarily; but his will being what it was he could not do otherwise, for the will cannot change itself. Hence he acted as he did of necessity—the necessity of immutability; he certainly did not act freely, for he was under the control of Satan.

But now, if men like Judas cannot change themselves, why does not God so act as to change them? Why does the Holy Spirit not oust the Evil Spirit from their lives? Luther's answer is, not that God cannot because men will not let him, but that for reasons known only to himself he does not so choose. It is in this connection that Luther introduces his distinction between the "hidden" and the "revealed" or "preached" will of God. According to the latter, God does not desire any man to perish, but all men to be saved. Yet it is clear that by no means all men receive salvation, even when the saving will of God as revealed in the gospel is preached to them. The reason for this we do not and cannot know; it has not been revealed to us; it lies in the hidden will of God.

Luther here appears to be saying that there are two contrary wills in God, and a virtual self-contradiction in the divine nature. But that is certainly not his intention. What God contradicts is not himself, but fallen man's distorted picture and false notions of him. The plainest evidence of this, as Luther sees it, is in the incarnation and cross of Christ, where God acts in ways precisely opposite to man's common expectations of him, and not at all in the ways in which unregenerate man would act if he were God. It is therefore far from obvious, not only to physical sight, but also to rational insight, that "God was in Christ." God is in fact profoundly "hidden" in Christ, in whom Christian faith declares him supremely "revealed." [15] Hence, it is only by faith, which is God's own gift, that a man comes to recognize God in the crucified Man of Nazareth.

Now, it is precisely in line with his understanding of the "hiddenness" of God in Christ, when Luther affirms that God "hides his eternal goodness and mercy under eternal wrath, his righteousness under iniquity." Nor is it difficult to accept this idea when wrath has the effect of preparing men for grace and so plays a part in their salvation. But what are we to say when it simply hardens men and ensures their damnation? Luther's answer in brief is this: Admittedly we cannot see *how* God can be righteous and good, let alone merciful, when he "saves so few and damns so many"; but in faith we can and must maintain *that* he is. Judged by the light of nature (the rationality of fallen man), such an assertion may well seem nonsense, but in the light of grace (the revelation of God in Christ) it makes believable though not demonstrable sense; and in the light of glory (God's perfected Kingdom in the life beyond this life) we shall see the unquestionable truth of what here we can only believe.

Clearly, Luther does not mean to assert any will in God that could supersede or override the will revealed in Christ, although in some of his statements he comes perilously close to it. He had had enough of that sort of duality in the Ockhamist theology of his monastic days, with the use it made of the Scholastic distinction between the absolute and the ordained power of God (*"potestas absoluta et ordinata"*). The idea was that God by his absolute power could have done everything, both in creation and redemption, quite otherwise than he has; and even now he is not bound, as his creatures are, by the order he has in fact established. For although by his ordained power he upholds the laws both of the world of nature and the realm of grace, yet by his absolute power he interrupts the former by working miracles, and severely limits the latter by the mystery of predestination. When, therefore, Luther sought to work out his salvation in terms of God's ordained will, he became obsessed by the terrifying fear that he might be among those predestined by God's absolute will, not to salvation, but to damnation.

In this situation Luther had been pointed toward the cure for his anxiety by his Superior, Staupitz, who told him:

In the wounds of Christ is predestination understood and found, and nowhere else; for it is written, "Him shall ye hear" (Matt. 17:5).

[15] *WA* 1, 112 f. Cf. P. S. Watson, *Let God Be God* (London, 1960), p. 103; H. Bandt, *Luthers Lehre vom verborgenen Gott* (Berlin, 1957), pp. 24 ff.

The Father is too high, therefore he says, "I will give a way by which men may come to me . . . in Christ you shall find who and what I am, and what I will; otherwise you will not find it either in heaven or on earth." [16]

These words Luther never forgot; they are echoed again and again in his writings; and years later we find him giving essentially the same counsel to souls distressed as he himself had been. He is convinced that if only a man can be persuaded to turn to Christ and the unfathomable grace of God in him, he can know beyond all doubt that, far from being among the reprobate, he is assuredly among the elect.[17]

With this, Luther furnishes a practical, pastoral solution of the problem of predestination, which theoretically and doctrinally he cannot solve. His doctrine of predestination, like Calvin's after him, is from one point of view a confession of ignorance and a very proper piece of Christian agnosticism. It might be called a "no throughway" sign, indicating that here all attempts to explain and understand come to an end. At the same time it is a confession of faith and an affirmation of entirely legitimate Christian certainty. It expresses the conviction that man's destiny is ultimately determined, not by his own fallible choices, and much less by luck or chance or arbitrary fate, but by the infallibly wise and good will of the gracious God revealed in Christ.

The idea of predestination had of course been a continual topic of debate ever since Augustine's time, and in Scholastic theology it had been variously interpreted. By some it had been rationalized, as Erasmus would rationalize it, in terms of God's foreknowledge of man's merits. Men were predestined to salvation or damnation according to what God foresaw they were going to deserve as a result of their cooperation or noncooperation with his grace. By others, including the greatest of them all, Aquinas, it had been held in as uncompromising a form, if not given as prominent a place, as it ever was afterward by Luther or Calvin.[18] It then furnished an antidote to the pride and presumption of supposing that man by his merits was the final arbiter of his own destiny. For while the Scholastic theologians could never conceive of God as accepting a man without merit, they could and sometimes explicitly did teach that he was not bound to give a man the grace to acquire

[16] *WA Tr* 2, 112, 9.
[17] *Luther: Letters of Spiritual Counsel,* ed. and tr. by Theodore G. Tappert (The Library of Christian Classics, Vol. XVIII; Philadelphia, 1955), pp. 115 ff., 122, 130 ff., 137 f.
[18] See *Summa theologica* I, q. 23, esp. aa. 3, 5, 6.

merit, nor even to accept the merit a man might acquire by grace given. No man therefore could ever be sure of his acceptance with God—unless, as Aquinas suggests, he were granted a special (private) revelation, which was very rare and generally undesirable.[19]

By contrast, both Luther and Calvin find in the idea of predestination a firm basis for the Christian's confidence regarding his salvation—and that on the ground of no other "special" revelation than that given publicly to all the world in Christ. There were subtle and important differences between them in their ways of doing this, but the fact that they did it indicates a much more significant difference between them and their predecessors, which frequent similarities of language should not be allowed to obscure. For them the doctrine of predestination furnished an antidote, not only to pride and presumption, but also to the doubt and despair into which a man might fall (as Luther had done in the monastery) through uncertainty as to God's goodwill toward him.

It does not seem to have occurred to the Reformers that even their versions of the doctrine might become a ground for uncertainty and a threat to the doctrine of grace itself. Yet in the eighteenth century (to mention only one instance) we find John Wesley attacking the Calvinism of his time as constituting just such a threat. The controversy centered on the Calvinists' concept of a limited atonement, according to which the saving work of Christ was directed, not to all men, but only to those already predestined to salvation by an eternal divine decree. To this, Wesley opposed his Arminian conviction that God's grace in Christ was intended for all men without exception; that by the prevenient operation of this same grace a measure of the freedom lost at the Fall was restored to every man; and that there was therefore no man who could not, if he would, accept the salvation offered in the gospel.

The situation in Wesley's time was similar to that in the Early Church, when Gnostic determinism divided mankind into two or more classes on the theory that some men were incapable of salvation and the rest capable in differing degree. Against this, men such as Origen and Irenaeus had asserted human freedom of choice as a means of maintaining the universal scope of the gospel of God and the grace of the Lord Jesus Christ. Man's free will meant for them the possibility of man's receiving God's salvation.

The situation Luther faced, however, was of a different sort. In his time the freedom of the human will was understood, not simply in terms of receptivity, but as an ability in man to make an active contribution to his salvation in the form of merit. The Augustin-

[19] *Summa theologica* I, q. 23, a. 1.

ian aphorism that "when God crowns our merits he crowns but his own gifts" had been replaced by the Semi-Pelagian position aptly stated by Erasmus when he says: "If man does nothing, there is no room for merits; if man does everything, there is no room for grace." Hence it was commonly taught that if a man would only do "what in him lay," however little that might be, God would reward him with a gift of grace, enabling him to do more and yet more until he had enough to qualify for glory. In this connection the Scholastic distinction between "congruous" and "condign" merit, or the merit of "fitness" and of "worthiness" should be noted. The former was ascribed to man's well-intentioned efforts, which, although they were not strictly meritorious, it was "fitting" that God should reward with his grace. The latter, as resulting from good works done with the aid of grace thus received, was regarded as meritorious in the strict sense of the term. Such at least was the late Scholastic view known to Erasmus and Luther, although Aquinas taught somewhat differently.[20]

But all this, as Luther saw it, meant an intolerable cheapening of grace.[21] It was worse even than thoroughgoing Pelagianism, which at least did not pretend that salvation could be purchased at such low cost. The fact is, however, that saving grace is not for sale; it is priceless—and free. It is God's free gift to men, given at the immeasurable cost to God of the death of his Son. Hence the idea that man can merit it by exercising his freedom of choice and doing what in him lies is nothing short of blasphemous.

Nevertheless, it could be argued that Luther's thought does not necessarily exclude every possible idea of human freedom in relation to things pertaining to salvation. We have seen that he distinguishes—as Erasmus does not—between different kinds or levels of freedom; and another might conceivably be added to his list without violating his principles. He acknowledges, for example, that even fallen man possesses a capacity for response to God's grace—a "dispositional quality" or "passive aptitude" he calls it in Scholastic terms—which animals and inanimate objects do not; and he repeatedly insists that the response man makes to the divine initiative is in no way coerced but entirely voluntary. What is more, in reply to a question as to why God elects this man and not that, he can say:

[20] Aquinas holds that man can make no effort toward the good, and therefore can acquire no merit, apart from grace; and that any such effort inspired by grace carries both kinds of merit—congruous inasmuch as it is a work of man's free will, condign inasmuch as it is a work of grace.
[21] See below, p. 321.

This difference is to be ascribed to man, not to the will of God, for the promises of God are universal. He will have all men to be saved. Accordingly it is not the fault of our Lord God, who promises salvation, but it is our fault if we are unwilling to believe it.[22]

By most ordinary standards it would not seem unnatural to speak of a real element of freedom here: not the absolute freedom which belongs to God alone, and not the liberty of the children of God, nor yet the freedom of action man has in relation to "things beneath him," but perhaps (if we may put it so) a freedom of responsible reaction to the "things above him."

Granted, a man completely untouched by the grace of God would have no choice but to sin, being under the undisputed control of Satan. but when men are in the position of the beast between two contending riders, it seems reasonable to think them capable of showing a preference for one rider rather than the other—especially as they are not beasts, but men. We may recall here the analogy of a slave and his master, which both Erasmus and Luther use. A slave may obey or disobey his master's commands; in that sense he has freedom of choice, and that is enough for Erasmus. But for Luther this means only freedom with respect to "things beneath" man, and the analogy must be differently applied with respect to "things above" him. A slave is not his own master, and even if he would much prefer a different master from the one he has, yet between masters he is not free to choose.

Nevertheless, we might insist, he is free to have and express his preferences. But then Luther in turn would insist on our facing the question: What reason can be given for such preferences? The significance of this can be illustrated with regard to the debate between Erasmus and Luther which we are at present discussing, for in that debate readers of the present volume will find themselves taking sides. They will be drawn to this side and perhaps driven from that, according as they are moved by what each man says, being persuaded or dissuaded or even repelled by it. Or, to put it another way, they will take sides according as they approve of the one and disapprove of the other, judging the one to be better or truer than the other. Both ways of putting it are legitimate, and to do justice to the situation both are necessary. Yet neither of them nor both together suffice to explain why any man is on either side. Perhaps the only answer to that question ultimately is that, being the sort of person he is, and therefore look-

---

[22] *WA Tr* 4, No. 4665 (quoted from *Luther: Letters of Spiritual Counsel,* p. 130).

ing at things in the way he does, a man cannot help preferring the side to which he is drawn—or being drawn to the side he prefers. He may of course be open to conviction by stronger arguments for the other side if any can be produced, but apart from such conviction he is not free to change his mind or change sides. A man is not at liberty to determine how he will think.

It is in a similar vein that Luther denies man's liberty to determine whose "arguments" he will believe, and consequently whom he will serve in the conflict between God and Satan. It is only when God produces arguments that prove stronger and more convincing to him than Satan's that a man becomes able to change his mind and change sides. Yet Luther is clear that it is a man's own fault and not God's if he is not convinced by God's arguments. For it goes without saying that the arguments on God's side are in the nature of the case immeasurably stronger than Satan's, so that anyone genuinely open to conviction must be convinced by them and believe them. Unbelievers therefore are without excuse; and believers have nothing to boast about, since apart from the convincing power of God's Word they would be unbelievers still. There are, it is true, moments in the heat of his controversy with Erasmus, when Luther seems to suggest that God has deliberately not pressed his arguments as strongly as he might; yet as a rule, and especially in his preaching and pastoral counseling, Luther certainly regards man as responsible. He knows, moreover, that even when God does press his arguments, unbelief sometimes becomes only the more stubborn. God's Word can repel as well as attract.

Why God's Word evokes in some cases a positive and in others a negative response remains a mystery however we look at it. The postulate of human "free will" no more explains it than does reference to the "hidden will" of God. It is a mystery to which there are analogies in other areas of life, and especially in personal relationships,[23] but analogies can at most help us to accept the mystery, not to fathom it. We are here at a point where life is only too plainly larger than logic, and conceptual analysis is entirely out of its depth. To do justice to the situation we must be content with a paradox, affirming both divine predestination and human responsibility. Which is not to say that both Erasmus and Luther have won and that both shall have prizes, for it commits us neither to Luther's overconfident statements about predestination nor to Erasmus' much too naïve view of free will. What it means is that we are willing to recognize the limits of our own understanding

[23] Cf. P. S. Watson, *The Concept of Grace* (London, 1960), pp. 98 ff.

and to believe that things beyond our comprehension may make perfectly good sense to God.

PHILIP S. WATSON

THE LANGUAGE OF THE DEBATE

Luther in this volume is translated from the Weimar Edition, and Erasmus from the edition of Jean Le Clerc, *Des. Erasmi Opera Omnia,* ed. by J. Clericus (Petrus Vander, Lugduni, Batavorum), Vol. IX (1706), columns 1215–1248, although the first edition printed by Frobenius at Basle in 1524 has been consulted throughout. Unfortunately, this first edition has neither pagination nor paragraphing, so that it is useless for the purposes of reference. The paragraphing, headings, and the subheadings are entirely our own, and in the case of Erasmus constitute pioneering work, whereas of course Luther's *De servo arbitrio* has received much more attention from editors and translators such as Packer and Johnston (J. Clarke, London, 1957).

Our problems begin with the titles of the two works. Erasmus calls his a *Diatribē* or *Collatio,* and these two words are in medieval usage virtually Greek and Latin equivalents. "Discourse" is more closely connected with *Collatio,* and therefore the word "diatribe" has been left to render the Greek word; and indeed there is much in the work to justify the term "diatribe" in both the narrower and the wider implications of the term. *Collatio* was used in special senses in medieval universities, and particularly at Paris, to denote expositions of set texts by candidates for degrees, and also discourses on the *Sentences* of Peter Lombard over which the candidate for a Doctorate in Theology was required to spend two years of his course. It also denoted the conference held every Sunday afternoon, at which the preacher was required to expound the theme of the morning sermon.[1] The common feature here is that of an exposition or discourse. At the end Erasmus says, *"Contuli,"* i.e., "I have completed my discourse," and Luther in his reply plays on the literal sense of *contuli,* "I have compared," by saying that he himself has made assertions, not comparisons. He regards it as his mission, not to complete a discourse on the subject, but to proclaim to Erasmus and the world the great truth of salvation as he sees it.

The word *assertio* is itself loosely used by Erasmus at p. 35 and

[1] See Hastings Rashdall, *The Universities of Europe in the Middle Ages,* ed. by F. M. Powicke and A. B. Ernden, 3 vols. (Oxford, 1936), Vol. I, pp. 402n, 449, 450, and 467n.

p. 37 in reference to a previous thesis by Luther, and each author makes continued use of the literal meaning of the word in order to criticize the other's attitude.

The word *arbitrium* is itself a problem. It has hitherto usually been translated "will," but at p. 47 Erasmus defines *"liberum arbitrium"* as *"vim humanae voluntatis, qua se possit homo applicare ad ea quae perducunt ad aeternam salutem, aut ab iisdem avertere"*; "a power of the human will by which a man can apply himself to the things which lead to eternal salvation, or turn away from them." Here at any rate *arbitrium* cannot be equated with *voluntas,* and it has been decided to sacrifice tradition and a certain measure of euphony on the altar of accuracy, and to translate *arbitrium* throughout by "choice." The phrase *"servum arbitrium"* is of course taken from Augustine, *Contra Iulianum* II.viii.23, which is quoted by Luther himself (p. 174, and n. 13) in the great argument which forms the very core of his treatise.

Certain key words are always a difficulty to the translator. *Pietas,* for instance, does sometimes mean "piety" but more often "godliness" or "holiness," and sometimes what we mean by "goodness" or even "religion." *Carnalis* does mean "carnal," but words like "carnal" and "piety" have acquired the religious flavor of a certain period, and can no longer be used without recalling the beliefs of that period. *Carnalis* does not always refer directly to what we should call the sins of the flesh, though the root meaning is of course never absent and never wrong—merely partial or inadequate; so *carnalis* has been rendered by "sensual," "worldly," "secular," "mundane," or "material," though warning is always given in a footnote that *carnalis (caro)* is in the original. (Cf. also Luther's discussion of "the flesh," pp. 263 ff.)

Erasmus was steeped in classical Latin, and his prose has an easy, sometimes even a free-and-easy, Ciceronian quality that contrasts with the occasionally cryptic syntax of Luther, though Luther too is a first-rate Latinist. Luther's obscurity stems in part from the ineffable things he is trying to say about grace and free will, and in part from his passionate vehemence which does not stop to verify references or to render the nuances of his meaning. He will use a participial or ablatival phrase in puzzling opposition to, or description of, his main subject, or a temporal clause that obviously means something a little different from what he intended. or he will even tolerate an apparent contradiction. in respect of which he would probably have agreed with Walt Whitman in being quite unrepentant.

A specially noteworthy device of Luther's is his use of hendiadys. There are several passages where the sense is made clear if one as-

sumes the use of this device. Thus at p. 107 occurs the phrase
"tanta querulari et exaggerari," which is best translated by some
such phrase as "a mass of complaints." Again at p. 112 the words
"non sine suspitione et aculeo" seem to mean "not without a suspicion of sarcasm"; at p. 145 *"multitudine, authoritate"* is best
translated by "the number of authorities"; at p. 159 *"in iis quae
pertinent ad salutem vel necessitatem"* means "things that are
necessary to salvation"; and at p. 234 *"cum securitate quadam et
contemptu"* is best rendered "with a kind of contemptuous self-
confidence." At p. 316 the problems of perhaps the most difficult
sentence in the whole treatise are eased by taking *per contentionem
et partitionem* as "through a polemical partition."

It is true of both Erasmus and Luther that *"le style, c'est
l'homme-même"*: Luther a daring, subtle, passionate logician in
the medieval manner, for all his advanced thinking; Erasmus a
cool, dexterous logical fencer but not committed so deeply.

It is most instructive to compare the two men in the frequency
and range of their references to classical authors. Here the result
is the reverse of what one might have expected, and it is Luther
who makes by far the more frequent classical allusions. Erasmus
quotes very rarely and even then from obscure authors—Pomponius Mela, for example, several editions of whose work on geog-
raphy were published between 1498 and 1520—and his mytho-
logical allusions are very obscure, as for example the reference to
"Diomedean necessity" at p. 83. Few people without previous acquaintance with Erasmus' own *Adagia* would be likely to recognize
the significance of the allusion. There are so many places where
the *Adagia* throw light on a sentence or phrase in the *De libero
arbitrio* that a short appendix has been included to deal with this
topic.

Luther, on the other hand, abounds in Latin quotations, and
it is possible to deduce his favorite reading from these. He is particularly fond of quoting the *Epistles* and the *Ars poetica* of Horace, and he also has several references to Terence, though none in
this work to Plautus. We also encounter Sallust, Cicero, Vergil,
Livy, Ovid, Quintilian, Juvenal, and even Manilius, though the
line he quotes from Manilius (*Astronomica* iv.14, at p. 121, n. 30)
has a Vergilian ring and may have come to Luther in a collection of
maxims, for we find him also quoting one of the couplets known
as the *Disticha Catonis,* probably from a similar source.[2] He treats

---

[2] The excellent translation of Packer and Johnston is somewhat marred by
the inaccuracy of the classical references in their footnotes. For example, on
p. 83 there are five references in footnotes to *The Aeneid;* of these three are

the elder Pliny as a philosopher, which sounds a little strange to us, but in those days all classical authors were felt to have a kind of blanket authority by virtue of being from the classical period.

We find the familiar but baffling *"vox et praeterea nihil,"* which we all think we can locate until we come to make the attempt; and in at least one place Luther either quotes an unidentified hexameter or unconsciously creates one when he writes *"ante suum clauso componit tempore finem"* (p. 133). In another place the cryptic words *"velut ille ad rhombum"* are most probably an obscure allusion to the fourth satire of Juvenal.

The list of Luther's references to Greek authors is also impressive. He quotes Homer, Heraclitus, Anaxagoras, Leucippus, Plato, Aristotle, and Lucian. Turning to postclassical writers, we find references to Origen, Porphyry, Justinian, Hilary of Poitiers, Augustine, and Jerome. It is interesting that although Luther professes disgust and contempt for Jerome, he has been unconsciously influenced by the latter's style, for such rare words as *andabata* (p. 171), though they do occur in classical authors, were revived by Jerome, and there is little doubt that Luther remembered them from Jerome's polemics; in fact, at p. 237 Luther coins a word *tropologus* from Jerome's use of the adjective *tropologicus,* and similarly at p. 264, n. 60 *Vergilicentonae* is another word coined by Jerome. The extent of Jerome's influence on Luther would repay futher study.

Erasmus tells us that he wrote his discourse in a few months, and the only difficulties for a translator, apart of course from the theological terms, are places where his fluency has led to an awkwardly placed phrase that he has not revised. A good example is at p. 90, where he is discussing the first cause in relation to fire: *"Quemadmodum vis ignis urit, et tamen principalis causa Deus est, qui simul per ignem agit, quae vel sola sufficeret, et sine qua nihil ageret ignis, si se subduceret illa,"* "Just as the power of fire burns, yet the principal cause is God, who acts at the same time through the fire, and this cause would of itself be sufficient, without which fire could effect nothing, if it [i.e., the divine cause] removed itself." Here the clause *"quae vel sola sufficeret"* refers back to *"causa"* and is itself the antecedent of *"illa."* Cicero would probably have written a tidier sentence. Throughout the discourse

---

wrong (one passage is not even from Vergil at all, being the Manilian verse referred to above), while the first four are in the wrong order so that in fact one of the two references correct in number is to the wrong passage anyway. There are also omitted or wrong references in the notes on pp. 237 and 267, and omissions in several other places.

there are occasional problems arising out of what seems to be hurried writing, evidenced in the strung-together style of certain sentences. These problems are discussed in their place.

A difficulty arose in deciding how to translate the numerous passages from Holy Scripture. No modern version could be consistently used, because both Erasmus and Luther base arguments on the very points where ancient and modern translations differ. For example, at p. 47 Erasmus quotes Ecclus. 15:15: *"Si volueris mandata conservare, conservabunt te"*; literally, "If thou shalt be willing to keep the commandments, they shall keep thee." The RSV has: "If you will, you can keep the commandments, and to act faithfully is a matter of your own choice." Yet at p. 54 Erasmus discusses his Latin text, remarking that the Greek has not the addition *"conservabunt te,"* so that it is essential to keep this point in our translation. Similar care must be taken in the Scriptural passages at pp. 56 and 57, where Erasmus in the latter case quotes the Vulgate, and particularly in the long quotation from Deut., ch. 30, at pp. 54 f.

Classical Greek and Roman authors were at no pains to quote correctly, and Luther in particular is their true disciple, going straight for the substance rather than the detail. As he himself remarks, "What is the good of giving a stiff and strict rendering, when the reader can make nothing of it?" Yet he likes to appear in control of his material, and with a typical impatience will give chapter and verse that are quite wrong rather than pause to verify them. In spite of this carelessness, he will base whole arguments on manuscript readings that are not only wrong but nonsensical, as for example, *militantibus* for *ministrantibus,* at p. 268, of the serving women at the door of the tabernacle in I Sam. 2:22. Like Molière, he would have said, *"Il m'est permis de reprendre mon bien où je le trouve."* It does not appear that Luther was so acute a textual critic as Erasmus or he could hardly have failed to make the obvious emendation here.

Each Scriptural quotation has therefore been treated on its merits, and in some few cases Luther's renderings have been corrected where this seemed necessary. As a rule the term *"sacrae litterae"* has been translated by "Holy Scripture," but occasionally it is in opposition to some such phrase as *"bonae litterae"* in the sense of "literature," and here again, we have treated each case on its merits.

A. N. Marlow
B. Drewery

ERASMUS

De Libero Arbitrio
Diatribe Seu Collatio

On the Freedom of the Will[1]

A Diatribe or Discourse

by

Desiderius Erasmus of Rotterdam

THE TEXT

PREFATORY OBSERVATIONS

*Erasmus Acknowledges His Limitations and States
His Point of View*

In the Name of Jesus.

Among the difficulties, of which not a few crop up in Holy Scripture, there is hardly a more tangled labyrinth than that of "free choice," for it is a subject that has long exercised the minds of philosophers, and also of theologians old and new, in a striking degree, though in my opinion with more labor than fruit.

More recently, however, it has been revived by Carlstadt and Eck,[2] in a fairly moderate debate, and now it has been more violently stirred up by Martin Luther, who has put out an *Assertion* about "free choice" and although he has already been answered by more than one writer, it seemed good to my friends that I should try my hand and see whether, as a result of our little set-to, the truth might be made more plain.

Here I know there will be those who will forthwith stop their

---

[1] *"Arbitrio."* See Introduction, p. 29.

[2] Johann von Eck (1486–1543), a German Catholic theologian and opponent of Luther, challenged Andreas Carlstadt (1480–1541) to a public disputation on Luther's Thesis of 1517. This took place in June, 1519, at the University of Leipzig.

ears, crying out, "The rivers run backward" [3]—dare Erasmus attack Luther, like the fly the elephant? [4] To appease them, if I may be allowed to ask for a little quiet, I need say no more by way of preface than what is the fact, that I have never sworn allegiance to the words of Luther. So that it should not seem unbecoming to anybody if at any point I differ publicly from him, as a man surely may differ from another man, nor should it seem a criminal offense to call in question any doctrine of his, still less if one engages in a temperate disputation with him for the purpose of eliciting truth.

Certainly I do not consider Luther himself would be indignant if anybody should find occasion to differ from him, since he permits himself to call in question the decrees, not only of all the doctors of the Church, but of all the schools, councils, and popes; and since he acknowledges this plainly and openly, it ought not to be counted by his friends as cheating if I take a leaf out of his book.

Furthermore, just in case anyone should mistake this for a regular gladiatorial combat, I shall confine my controversy strictly to this one doctrine, with no other object than to make the truth more plain by throwing together [5] Scriptural texts and arguments, a method of investigation that has always been considered most proper for scholars.

So let us pursue the matter without recrimination, because this is more fitting for Christian men, and because in this way the truth, which is so often lost amid too much wrangling, may be more surely perceived.

To be sure, I know that I was not built for wrestling matches: there is surely nobody less practiced in this kind of thing than I, who have always had an inner temperamental horror of fighting, [6] and who have always preferred to sport in the wider plains of the Muses rather than to brandish a sword in a hand-to-hand fight.

[3] This quotation is from Euripides, *Medea*, 410, and is a commonplace metaphor for a prodigy in classical literature. See "Appendix: On the *Adagia* of Erasmus."

[4] In his *Adagia*, Erasmus quotes a saying from Lucian: *"Elephanta ek muias poieis,"* "You are making an elephant out of a fly," and paraphrases it thus: *"Id est, res exiguas, verbis multis attollis atque amplifices."* Here he makes a different use of the metaphor, referring not to rhetorical amplification but to a combat between a pygmy and a giant, though no doubt there is a satirical thrust at Luther's verbosity. For Erasmus' use of his *Adagia*, see Appendix.

[5] The word *collisio* is a very strong one, and is used later (p. 47) of striking fire from flint.

[6] *"Ut qui semper arcano quodam naturae sensu abhorruerim a pugnis,"* a phrase Erasmus repeats in the *Hyperaspistes*.

His Dislike of Assertions

And, in fact, so far am I from delighting in "assertions" that I would readily take refuge in the opinion of the Skeptics, wherever this is allowed by the inviolable authority of the Holy Scriptures and by the decrees of the Church, to which I everywhere willingly submit my personal feelings, whether I grasp what it prescribes or not.

Moreover, I prefer this disposition of mine to that with which I see some people endowed who are so uncontrollably attached to their own opinion that they cannot bear anything which dissents from it; but they twist whatever they read in the Scriptures into an assertion of an opinion which they have embraced once for all. They are like young men who love a girl so immoderately that they imagine they see their beloved wherever they turn, or, a much better example, like two combatants who, in the heat of a quarrel, turn whatever is at hand into a missile, whether it be a jug or a dish. I ask you, what sort of sincere judgment can there be when people behave in this way? Who will learn anything fruitful from this sort of discussion—beyond the fact that each leaves the encounter bespattered with the other's filth? There will always be many such, whom the apostle Peter describes as "ignorant and unstable who twist the Scriptures to their own destruction." [7]

As far as I am concerned, I admit that many different views about free choice have been handed down from the ancients about which I have, as yet, no fixed conviction, except that I think there to be a certain power of free choice. For I have read the *Assertion* of Martin Luther, and read it without prejudice, except that I have assumed a certain favor toward him, as an investigator may toward an arraigned prisoner. And yet, although he expounds his case in all its aspects with great ingenuity and fervor of spirit, I must say, quite frankly, that he has not persuaded me.

If anybody ascribes this to my slowness or inexperience, I shall not quarrel with him, provided they allow us slower ones the privilege of learning by meeting those who have received the gift of God in fuller measure, especially since Luther attributes very little importance to scholarship, and most of all to the Spirit, who is wont to instill into the more humble what he denies to the wise.[8] So much for those who shout so loudly that Luther has more learning in his little finger than Erasmus in his whole body, a view that

[7] II Peter 3:16. On the question of translations of the Scriptures, see Introduction, p. 32.
[8] Erasmus here lapses into Greek, *"sophois."*

I shall certainly not attempt to refute here. I simply ask from such, however ill-disposed they may be, that if I grant to Luther in this Disputation that he be not weighed down by the prejudgments of doctors, councils, universities, popes, and of the emperor, they will not damage my cause by mere snap judgments.

For even though I believe myself to have mastered Luther's argument, yet I might well be mistaken, and for that reason I play the debater, not the judge; the inquirer, not the dogmatist: ready to learn from anyone if anything truer or more scholarly can be brought. Yet I would willingly persuade the man in the street that in this kind of discussion it is better not to enforce contentions which may the sooner harm Christian concord than advance true religion.[9]

The Obscurity of Scripture

For there are some secret places in the Holy Scriptures into which God has not wished us to penetrate more deeply and, if we try to do so, then the deeper we go, the darker and darker it becomes, by which means we are led to acknowledge the unsearchable majesty of the divine wisdom, and the weakness of the human mind.

It is like that cavern near Corycos of which Pomponius Mela tells, which begins by attracting and drawing the visitor to itself by its pleasing aspect, and then as one goes deeper, a certain horror and majesty of the divine presence that inhabits the place makes one draw back.[10] So when we come to such a place, my view is that the wiser and more reverent course is to cry with St. Paul: "O the depth of the riches and wisdom and knowledge of God! How unsearchable are his judgments and how inscrutable his ways!" and with Isaiah: "Who has heard the Spirit of the Lord, or what counselor has instructed him?" [11] rather than to define what

---

[9] On this meaning of *pietas,* see Introduction, p. 29.

[10] The cave of Corycos, now Khorgos, in Cilicia, was renowned in ancient times as being one of the entrances to the underworld. Its gradually increasing awesomeness was described at length by the medieval geographer Pomponius Mela, in a work *De chorographia,* an edition of which was printed by Singrenius at Vienna in 1518. Mela (*op. cit.,* i. 72–75) vividly describes the height of the cliff, the rough path beautiful with trees and plants, the stupendous sight of a torrential river that bursts forth from the rocks only to disappear again underground. His description is one of the most vivid in any ancient author of a rocky grotto and cavern and its sense of the ruminous.

[11] Rom. 11:33; Isa. 40:13. Erasmus reads *audivit* for *adiuvit* in the passage from Isaiah. Is this due to Erasmus' own carelessness, or a printer's error?

passes the measure of the human mind. Many things are reserved
for that time when we shall no longer see through a glass darkly or
in a riddle, but in which we shall contemplate the glory of the
Lord when his face shall be revealed.

Therefore, in my judgment on this matter of free choice, having
learned what is needful to know about this, if we are in the path
of true religion, let us go on swiftly to better things, forgetful of
the things which are behind, or if we are entangled in sins, let us
strive with all our might and have recourse to the remedy of
penitence [12] that by all means we may entreat the mercy of the
Lord without which no human will or endeavor is effective; and
what is evil in us, let us impute to ourselves, and what is good, let
us ascribe wholly to divine benevolence, to which we owe our very
being, and for the rest, whatever befalls us in this life, whether it be
joyful or sad, let us believe it to be sent by him for our salvation,
and that no harm can come to us from a God who is by nature just,
even if some things happen that seem to us amiss, for none ought
to despair of the pardon of a God who is by nature most merciful.
This, I say, was in my judgment sufficient for Christian godliness,
nor should we through irreverent inquisitiveness rush into those
things which are hidden, not to say superfluous: whether God
foreknows anything contingently; whether our will accomplishes
anything in things pertaining to eternal salvation; whether it
simply suffers the action of grace; whether what we do, be it of
good or ill, we do by necessity or rather suffer to be done to us.
And then there are certain things of which God has willed us to
be completely ignorant—such as the hour of death or the Day of
Judgment: "It is not for you to know times or seasons which the
Father has fixed by his own authority," Acts 1⟨:7⟩; and Mark
13⟨:32⟩: "But of that day or that hour no one knows, not even the
angels in heaven, nor the Son, but only the Father." There are
some things which God has willed that we should contemplate, as
we venerate himself, in mystic silence; and, moreover, there are
many passages in the sacred volumes about which many commen-
tators have made guesses, but no one has finally cleared up their
obscurity: as the distinction between the divine persons, the conjunction [13] of the divine and human nature in Christ, the unforgivable sin; yet there are other things which God has willed to be

---

[12] *"Poenitentia."* Does Erasmus mean "repentance" simply, or "penance"?
The word can mean either or both. This whole passage is very loosely con-
structed.

[13] *"Conglutinatio,"* literally, "sticking together" or "adhering." Here, as in
several places, Erasmus uses a direct and forceful word to express a spiritual or intellectual conception.

most plainly evident, and such are the precepts for the good life. This is the Word of God, which is not to be bought in the highest heaven, nor in distant lands overseas, but it is close at hand, in our mouth and in our heart.[14] These truths must be learned by all, but the rest are more properly committed to God, and it is more religious to worship them, being unknown, than to discuss them, being insoluble. How many questions, or rather squabbles, have arisen over the distinction of persons, the mode of generation, the distinction between filiation and procession; what a fuss has been raised in the world by the wrangle about the conception of the virgin as Theotokos! [15] I ask what profit has there been so far from these laborious inquiries, except that with the loss of harmony we love one another the less, while seeking to be wiser than we need.

Some Truths Are Not for Common Ears

Moreover, some things there are of such a kind that, even if they were true and might be known, it would not be proper to prostitute them before common ears. Perhaps it is true, as the Sophists are given to blather, that God, according to his own nature, is not less present in the hole of a beetle (I will not use the more vulgar expression that they are not ashamed to use) than in heaven, and yet this would be unprofitably discussed before the common herd. And that there are three Gods might be said truly according to the rules of dialectic, but would certainly not be spoken before the untutored multitude without great scandal. Even if I were convinced, which is not the case, that this confession which we now use was neither instituted by Christ nor could have been founded by men, and for this reason ought not to be required of any, and further that no satisfaction should be demanded for offenses, yet I should fear to publish this opinion because I see so many mortals who are wonderfully prone to offenses, whom the necessity of confessing either restrains altogether or at least moderates. There are some bodily diseases that are less evil to bear than their removal,[16] as though a man were to bathe in the warm blood of murdered babes to avoid leprosy, so there are some errors that it would cause less damage to conceal than to uproot. Paul knew the difference between what things are lawful and what are expedient. It is law-

---

14 A paraphrase of Deut. 30:11-14.
15 "*Theotokos*," literally "God-bearing." The allusion is to the doctrine of the virgin birth.
16 "*Minore malo tolerantur quam tolluntur*," a play on words of the kind beloved by Augustine.

ful to speak the truth; it is not expedient to speak the truth to everybody at every time and in every way. If I were convinced that at a certain council some wrong decision or definition had been made, I should have the right to proclaim the truth, but it would not be expedient, lest wicked men be given a handle to scorn the authority of the Fathers, even in those decisions which they have taken in a godly and devout spirit. I would rather say that they took a decision that seemed reasonable from the point of view of their own times which present needs suggest should be repealed.

The Dangers Inherent in Luther's Teachings

Let us, therefore, suppose that there is some truth in the doctrine which Wyclif taught and Luther asserted, that whatever is done by us is done not by free choice but by sheer necessity. What could be more useless than to publish this paradox to the world? Again, suppose for a moment that it were true in a certain sense, as Augustine says somewhere, that "God works in us good and evil, and rewards his own good works in us, and punishes his evil works in us"; what a window to impiety would the public avowal of such an opinion open to countless mortals! Especially in view of the slowness of mind of mortal men, their sloth, their malice, and their incurable propensity toward all manner of evil. What weakling will be able to bear the endless and wearisome warfare against his flesh? What evildoer will take pains to correct his life? Who will be able to bring himself to love God with all his heart when He created hell seething with eternal torments in order to punish his own misdeeds in his victims as though he took delight in human torments? For that is how most people will interpret them. For the most part, men are by nature dull-witted and sensual, prone to unbelief, inclined to evil, with a bent to blasphemy, so that there is no need to add fuel to the furnace. And so Paul, as a wise dispenser of the Divine Word, often brings charity to bear, and prefers to follow that which is fitting for one's neighbors rather than the letter of the law: and possesses a wisdom that he speaks among the perfect, but among the weak he reckons to know nothing, save Jesus Christ, and him crucified. Holy Scripture has its own language, adapted to our understanding. There God is angry, grieves, is indignant, rages, threatens, hates, and again has mercy, repents, changes his mind, not that such changes take place in the nature of God, but that to speak thus is suited to our infirmity and slowness. The same prudence I consider befits those who undertake the task of interpreting the Divine Word. Some things for this reason are harmful because they are not expedient, as wine for a fevered patient. Similarly, such matters might allowably have been treated in discussion by the learned world, or even in the theological schools, although I should not think even this to be expedient save with restraint; on the other hand, to debate such fables before the gaze of a mixed multitude seems to me to be not merely useless but even pernicious.

I should, therefore, prefer men to be persuaded not to waste their time and talents in labyrinths of this kind, but to refute or to affirm the views of Luther. My preface would rightly seem too verbose if it were not almost more relevant to the main issue than the disputation itself.

Introduction to the Disputation

Luther Is Opposed Not Only by Scripture but Also by Weighty Authority of the Church Fathers

Now, since Luther does not acknowledge the authority of any writer, of however distinguished a reputation, but only listens to the canonical Scriptures, how gladly do I welcome this abridgment of labor, for innumerable Greek and Latin writers treat of free choice, either as a theme or incidentally, so that it would be a great labor to collect out of them what each one has to say either for or against free choice, and to explain the several meanings of each individual opinion, or to resolve or approve their arguments—a tedious and long-winded affair, and as regards Luther and his friends, quite useless, especially as they not only disagree among themselves, but often contradict their own doctrine.

Yet in the meantime let the reader be admonished that if we shall seem to give equal weight with Luther to the testimonies and solid arguments of Holy Scripture, he should also bear constantly in mind so numerous a body of most learned men who have found approval in so many centuries down to our own day, whom not only their skill in divine studies but also godliness of life commend. For some of them gave testimony with their blood to that doctrine of Christ which they defend with their writings; such among the Greeks were Origen, Basil, Chrysostom, Cyril, John of Damascus, Theophylact; among the Latin Fathers, Tertullian, Cyprian, Arnobius, Hilary, Ambrose, Jerome, Augustine, to say nothing meanwhile of Thomas, Scotus, Durandus, Capreolus, Gabriel, Aegidius, Gregory, Alexander, the skill and force of whose dialectic, in my opinion, no one can afford to despise, not to mention the authority of so many universities, councils, and supreme pontiffs.

From the time of the apostles down to the present day, no writer has yet emerged who has totally taken away the power of freedom of choice, save only Manichaeus and John Wyclif. For the authority of Laurentius Valla,[17] who comes nearest to agreement with them, has not much weight among theologians. The doctrine of Manichaeus, indeed, though it has long been exploded and repudiated by common consent of the whole world, yet I am inclined to think less useless to piety than that of Wyclif. For Manichaeus ascribes good and bad works to two natures in man in such a way that we owe good works to God in consequence of our condition, and yet against the power of darkness he leaves cause for imploring the aid of the Creator, that with this aid we may sin more lightly, and more easily do good works. Wyclif, however, ascribes all things to sheer necessity, and what room does he leave either for our prayers or for our endeavors?

So to return to my first theme. If the reader shall see that my own argument meets the other side with equal weapons, then let him also consider whether more weight ought not to be ascribed to the previous judgments of so many learned men, so many orthodox, so many saints, so many martyrs, so many theologians old and new, so many universities, councils, so many bishops and popes— or to trust instead the private judgment of this or that individual.

Not that, as in human assemblies, I would measure my opinion by the number of votes or the status of the speakers. I know how frequently it happens that the greater part overcomes the better: I know those are not always the best things that are approved by the majority. I know that nothing ever does harm to the investigation of truth, which is added to the industry of one's predecessors. I confess that it is right that the sole authority of Holy Scripture should outweigh all the votes of all mortal men. But the authority of the Scripture is not here in dispute. The same Scriptures are acknowledged and venerated by either side. Our battle is about the meaning of Scripture.

But if in this matter of interpretation some weight is to be given to learning, what minds are sharper and more perceptive than those of the Greeks? Who are more versed in Holy Scripture? Nor among the Latins was insight lacking or skill in interpreting Scripture, for if they have yielded pride of place to the Greeks in natural felicity, they have surely been able, building on their

[17] See p. 145, n. 2.

achievements, to equal the industry of the Greeks. And if in this point of judgment we have regard rather to holiness of life than to learning, you will see the caliber of the champions in the party that defends free choice; but, as the lawyers say, comparisons are odious! For I should not like to have to compare the heralds of this new gospel with these veterans.

How Can Inspiration and Authority Be Tested?

I hear the objection, What need is there of an interpreter when the Scripture itself is crystal clear? But if it is so clear, why have so many outstanding men in so many centuries been blind, and in a matter of such importance, as these would appear? If there is no obscurity in Scripture, what was the need of the work of prophecy in the days of the apostles? You say, "This was the gift of the Spirit." But I have the suspicion that just as the charismata of healings and tongues ceased, this charisma ceased also. And if it did not cease, then one must ask to whom it has been passed on. If to any Tom, Dick, or Harry, all interpretation is uncertain. If to nobody, since even now so many obscurities puzzle learned men, no interpretation will be certain. If to those who have succeeded to the place of the apostles, they will object that for many centuries many have succeeded to the office of the apostles who have nothing of the apostolic Spirit. And yet of these men, other things being equal, it may be concluded as more probable that God has infused his Spirit into those whom he has ordained, just as we may more probably believe grace to be given to the baptized than to the unbaptized. But let us grant, as indeed we must, that it is possible that the Spirit might reveal to a single humble and unlearned man what he has not revealed to the wise and prudent, seeing that Christ thanked his Father for this, that what he had concealed from the wise and prudent, namely, scribes and Pharisees and philosophers, he had revealed to babes,[18] that is, to the simple and foolish according to this world. And perhaps such a fool was Dominic, such was Francis, if it had been permitted to them each to follow his own spirit.[19] But if Paul in his time, in which the gift of the Spirit was in full force, orders spirits to be tested whether they be of God, what ought to be done in this carnal age? How, then, shall we prove the Spirit? By learning? On both sides there are scholars. By holiness of life? On both sides are sinners. On the other hand, there is a whole choir of saints who support free

---

[18] Erasmus uses the Greek *"nēpiois,"* literally, "infants."
[19] This sentence, here literally translated, is obscure.

choice. True, they say, but these are only men. But I am now comparing men with men, not men with God. I hear you say, "What has a multitude to do with the meaning of the Spirit?" I reply, "What have a handful?" You say, "What has a miter to do with the understanding of Holy Scripture?" I reply, "What has a sackcloth or a cowl?" You say, "What has the knowledge of philosophy to do with the knowledge of sacred letters?" I reply, "What has ignorance?" You say, "What has an assembled synod to do with the understanding of Scripture, in which it may be that there is nobody who has the Spirit?" I reply, "What, then, of private conventicles of the few, of whom it is much more likely that none has the Spirit?" Paul cries, "Do you wish for proof of Christ who dwells in me?" ⟨II Cor. 13:3⟩. The apostles were not believed unless miracles created belief in their doctrine. Now every Tom, Dick, and Harry claims credence who testifies that he has the Spirit of the gospel.

Seeing that the apostles shook off vipers, healed the sick, raised the dead, and by laying on of hands bestowed the gift of tongues, they were at length believed, but they were scarcely believed for teaching paradoxes! But now these people bring forth what common opinion accounts as more than paradoxes,[20] yet not one of them has so far appeared who can cure even a lame horse! [21] And miracles apart, would that they could equal the sincerity and simplicity of the apostolic character which for us slow of heart would suffice instead of miracles.

I do not intend this to refer specifically to Luther, whom I do not know personally, and from whose writings I get a mixed impression. I say it rather of certain others better known to me who, if there is any controversy concerning the meaning of the Scriptures, when we bring forward the authority of the Early Fathers, chant at once, "Ah! but they were only men." And if you ask them by what argument the true interpretation of Scripture may be known, since both sides are men, they reply, "By the sign of the Spirit." If you ask why the Spirit should rather be absent from those who have illuminated the world by their published miracles than from themselves, they reply as though for thirteen hundred years there had been no gospel in the world. If you seek of them a life worthy of the Spirit, they reply that they are just by faith, not by works. If you look in vain for miracles, they say that the age of miracles is past, and that there is no need of them now that we

[20] *"Paradoxotera."* Erasmus forms a comparative from the adjective *paradoxon.*
[21] See Appendix.

have so much light in the Scriptures. And if you deny the Scriptures to be clear in such a point about which so many great men have stumbled in darkness, the argument returns full circle.

Moreover, if we grant that he who has the Spirit is sure of the meaning of the Scriptures, how can I be certain of what he finds to be true for himself? What am I to do when many bring diverse interpretations, about which each swears he has the Holy Spirit? And since the Spirit does not furnish the whole truth to anyone, even he who has the Spirit may be mistaken or deceived in some single point. So much for those who so easily reject the interpretation of the Fathers in Holy Scripture and oppose their views to ours as if delivered by an oracle. Finally, even supposing that the Spirit of Christ could have allowed his people to err in trivial matters on which the salvation of men does not greatly depend, how can it be believed that for more than thirteen hundred years he would have concealed the error in his Church and not have found anybody among so many saintly men worthy to be inspired with the knowledge of what these people claim to be the chief doctrine of the whole gospel?

Truly—to conclude this argument—what such people choose to claim for themselves is their own affair. I claim for myself neither learning nor holiness, nor do I trust in my own spirit. I shall merely put forward with simple diligence those considerations which move my mind. If anybody shall try to teach me better, I will not knowingly withstand the truth. If they prefer to rail at one who treats them with courtesy and without invective, rather discoursing than disputing, who will not find them lacking in that spirit of the gospel which is always on their lips? Paul cries, "As for the man who is weak in faith, support him" (Rom. 14:1). And Christ did not extinguish the smoking flax, while Peter the apostle says, "Always be prepared to make a defense to all who call you to account for the hope that is in you, yet do it with gentleness and reverence" (I Peter 3:15). So that if they reply that Erasmus is an old vessel, and is not capable of the new wine of the Spirit which they offer to the world: if they really rate themselves so highly, let them at least treat us as Christ treated Nicodemus and the apostle Gamaliel. Although Nicodemus was ignorant, the Lord did not repulse him, because he desired to learn; and the disciples did not reject Gamaliel because he would suspend his judgment until the outcome of the matter should reveal by what spirit it had been done.

PART I. SCRIPTURE PASSAGES THAT SUPPORT FREE CHOICE

I have completed half of this book, in which, if I do but persuade the reader that it would be better not to contend too super-
stitiously about things of this kind, particularly before the multitude, there is no need for the kind of argument for which I now
gird myself, in the hope that truth may everywhere prevail, by
comparison of Scriptures, as fire comes from striking flint.

Definition of Free Choice and Discussion
of Ecclesiasticus 15:14-17

In the first place, it cannot be denied that there are many places
in the Holy Scriptures which seem to set forth free choice. On the
other hand, others seem to take it wholly away. Yet it is clear that
Scripture cannot be in conflict with itself, since the whole proceeds from the same Spirit. First, then, we shall survey those passages which confirm our position; then we shall try to resolve those
which seem to make for the opposite point of view. By free choice
in this place we mean a power of the human will by which a man
can apply himself to the things which lead to eternal salvation, or
turn away from them.[22]

Among the texts that support free choice, priority is usually
given to a passage in the book called Ecclesiasticus, or the Wisdom
of Sirach, ch. 15⟨:14-17⟩:

> "God made man from the beginning, and left him in the hand
> of his own counsel.
> He added his commandments and precepts. If thou wilt ob-
> serve the commandments, and keep acceptable fidelity for-
> ever, they shall preserve thee.
> He hath set water and fire before thee; stretch forth thine
> hand for which thou wilt.
> Before man is life and death, good and evil; that which he
> shall choose shall be given him."

I do not think anyone will object against the authority of this
work that, as Jerome points out, it was not formerly received into
the canon of the Hebrews, since the Church of Christ has received
it into its canon with common consent, nor do I see any reason

---

[22] "*Vim humanae voluntatis, qua se possit homo applicare ad ea quae
perducunt ad aeternam salutem, aut ab iisdem avertere.*" This is a key passage, for it shows that *arbitrium* involves the action of *voluntas,* and therefore cannot be simply translated "will."

ment. It doubles sin and engenders death, not that it is evil, but because it commands actions which we cannot perform without grace. The law of faith commands more arduous things than the law of works, yet because grace is plentifully added to it, not only does it make things easy which of themselves are impossible, but it makes them agreeable also. Faith, therefore, cures reason, which has been wounded by sin, and charity bears onward the weak will. The law of works was like this: "You may freely eat of every tree of the garden, but of the tree of the knowledge of good and evil you shall not eat, for in the day that you eat of it you shall die" (Gen. 2:16-17). This law of works was further revealed by Moses: "You shall not kill: if you have killed, you shall be killed"; [25] "You shall not commit adultery" (Ex. 20:13-14). But what says the law of faith, which orders us to love our enemies, to carry our cross daily, to despise our life? "Fear not, little flock, for yours is the kingdom of heaven" (Luke 12:32). And "Be of good cheer, I have overcome the world" (John 16:33). And "I am with you always, to the close of the age" (Matt. 28:20). This law the apostles showed forth when, after being beaten with rods for the name of Jesus, they went away rejoicing from the presence of the Council. Thus Paul: "I can do all things in him who strengthens me" (Phil. 4:13). And no doubt this is what Ecclesiasticus had in mind in saying: "He established with them an eternal covenant, and showed them his judgments" (Ecclus. 17:12). For whom? In the first place, for those two founders of the human race in person, then the Jewish people by Moses and the prophets. The Law shows what God wills, sets out the penalty to him who disobeys and the rewards to the obedient. For the rest it leaves the power of choice to the will that was created in them free and able rapidly to turn to one or the other. And, therefore, it says: "If you will keep the commandments, they shall keep you" (Ecclus. 15:15). And again: "Stretch out your hand to whatever you wish" (v. 16). If the power to distinguish good and evil and the will of God had been hidden from men, it could not be imputed to them if they made the wrong choice. If the will had not been free, sin could not have been imputed, for sin would cease to be sin if it were not voluntary, save when error or the restriction of the will is itself the fruit of sin. Thus the responsibility for rape is not imputed to the one who has suffered violence.

Although this quotation from Ecclesiasticus seems peculiarly suited to our first parents, yet in a certain sense it is relevant to all the posterity of Adam, but it would be irrelevant if there were no

[25] *"Si occideris occideris,"* a pun impossible to translate.

strength of free choice at all in us. For although free choice is damaged by sin, it is nevertheless not extinguished by it. And although it has become so lame in the process that before we receive grace we are more readily inclined toward evil than good, yet it is not altogether cut out, except that the enormity of crimes which have become a kind of second nature so clouds the judgment and overwhelms the freedom of the will that the one seems to be destroyed and the other utterly lost.

Different Kinds of Grace, and Three Views of Its Relation to Free Choice

What, then, is free choice worth in us after sin and before grace? About this point ancient and modern writers differ amazingly, as each is concerned with a different aspect of the problem. Those who would avoid despair and complacency, but who would inspire men to hope and endeavor, attributed more to free choice. Pelagius taught that once the human will was freed and healed by grace there was no need of new grace, but that with the help of free will a man might attain to eternal salvation, but that man owed his salvation to God, without whose grace the will of man was not effectively free to do good. And this very power of the soul, with which a man embraces good when he knows it, and turns away from its opposite, is a gift of the Creator who might have made him a frog instead of a man.

Those who profess the doctrine of Scotus are still more in favor of free choice, for they believe it to have such power that even though a man has not received the grace which destroys sin, he may nonetheless, by his own natural powers, perform what they call morally good works which, not "condignly" but "congruously," [26] merit that grace which "makes acceptable," for so they speak.

Diametrically opposed are those who argue that all these works, even though morally good, were detestable to God, no less than crimes of the order of adultery and homicide, since they did not proceed from faith and love toward God. This view seems too severe, especially since, if certain philosophers have had some knowledge of God, they might also have had faith and charity toward God, for they did not act out of vainglory, but from a love of virtue and goodness, which, according to their teaching, is to be embraced for no other reason than that it is good. Whether the case of a man who, on behalf of his country, exposed himself to

[26] See Introduction, p. 25.

perils for the sake of vainglory is good in itself or morally good I
do not know. St. Augustine and those who follow him, considering
how harmful to true godliness it is for a man to trust in his own
powers, are more inclined to favor grace, which Paul everywhere
stresses. For this reason, he denies that man liable to sin can turn
to amend his life by his own powers, or do anything which will
bring him to salvation unless he is moved by the free gift of God
to desire those things which lead to eternal life. This grace which
others call "prevenient," Augustine calls "operative." For faith,
which is the doorway to salvation, is the free gift of God. To this,
charity is added by the more abundant gift of the Spirit, which he
calls "cooperative grace," which is always present in those who
strive until they attain their end, but on condition that at the
same time and in the same work both free choice and grace operate; grace, however, as the leader and not as a companion. Some,
however, make a distinction at this point, saying: "If you consider
the work according to its nature, its principal cause is the will of
man; if according to what is merited, grace is the more powerful."
Nevertheless, faith which makes us will the things that belong to
salvation, and love which sees that we do not desire them in vain,
are distinguished not so much in time as in nature. They both
can be increased in successive degrees. Since grace signifies a benefit freely given, we may speak of three or, if you prefer, four graces.
The first is implanted by nature and vitiated by sin (but, as we
said, not extinguished), which some call a natural influx. This is
common to all, and remains even in those who persist in sin: they
are free to speak, be silent, sit down, get up, help the poor, read
Holy Scripture, listen to sermons; but these things, in the opinion
of some, in no way conduce to eternal life. Nor are there lacking
those who, bearing in mind the manifold goodness of God, say that
man can so far make use of benefits of this kind that he may be
prepared for grace and so call forth the mercy of God. On the
other hand, there are those who deny that this can happen without
peculiar grace. Since this grace is common to all, it is not called
grace, though it really is grace, just as God every day works greater
miracles by creating, preserving, and ordering all things than if
he healed a leper or liberated a demoniac, and yet these things
are not called miracles, because they are offered to all men alike
every day.

The second is peculiar grace, with which God in his mercy
arouses the sinner wholly without merit to repent, yet without in-
fusing that supreme grace which abolishes sin and makes him
pleasing to God. Thus the sinner assisted by a second grace which

we called operative grace begins to be displeased with himself, although he has not yet put off all the desire of sin, yet by his alms and prayers and his devotion to sacred studies, and by listening to sermons, as well as by appeals to good men for their prayers and other deeds morally good, as they call them, he behaves as a candidate for the highest grace. They consider that this grace, which we call the second grace, is, by the goodness of God, not denied to anyone, for the divine benevolence supplies sufficient opportunities to each in this life by which he may recover, if he will, the use of the free choice that remains to him and put his powers at the disposal of that divine will which invites but does not constrain him forcibly to higher things.[27] And this they consider to be within the power of our own choice—that we may apply our wills to grace, or turn away from it, just as we can open our eyes to the light that is borne in upon them or close them again. Since, then, the immense love of God toward the race of men does not suffer men to be cheated, so also by that grace which they call pleasing grace, if he seeks it with all his powers, no sinner ought ever to be secure, yet on the other hand, none ought to despair; and, moreover, no man perishes save by his own fault. There is, therefore, a natural grace; there is a stimulating grace (albeit imperfect); there is the grace that makes the will effective, which we called cooperating, which allows us to perform that which we have undertaken to do; there is a grace that carries things to a conclusion. These three they think to be one, although they are called by different names according to what they effect within us. The first arouses, the second promotes, the third completes.

On the other hand, those who, at the other extreme from Pelagius, attribute most of all to grace and practically nothing to free choice, yet do not entirely remove it, for they deny that man can will the good without peculiar grace, they deny that he can make a beginning, they deny that he can progress, they deny he can reach his goal without the principal and perpetual aid of divine grace. Their view seems probable enough in that it leaves man to study and strive, but it does not leave aught for him to ascribe to his own powers. But harder is the opinion of those who contend that free choice is of no avail save to sin, and that grace alone accomplishes good works in us, not by or with free choice but in free choice, so that our will does nothing more than wax in the hand of the craftsman when it receives the particular shape that pleases him. These seem to me so anxious to avoid all reliance on human merit that

[27] There is an abruptness in this sentence which suggests that Erasmus unconsciously changed the construction in the middle.

they pass *praeter casam*,[28] as we say. Hardest of all seems the view of all those who say that free choice is a mere empty name, nor does it avail either in the case of the angels or in Adam or in us, either before or after grace, but it is God who works evil as well as good in us, and all things that happen come about by sheer necessity. My dispute will be most concerned with the two last positions.

These things we have treated at some length for the sake of the inexpert reader (for I write as a plain man to plain men) that he may more easily understand the rest of the argument. That is why we considered first the passage from Ecclesiasticus, in which he seems to point out most clearly the origin and power of free choice. Now, let us resume more rapidly the other testimonies of Scripture. But that we may do this, let me first point out that this place is otherwise expounded in the Aldine edition than by modern Ecclesiastical Latinists. For in the Greek there is not added *"conservabunt te,"* nor does Augustine add this in citing this text. I myself judge that *poiētai* was written for *poiēsai*.[29]

Further Old Testament Passages Implying Free Choice

Just as God, therefore, set forth in Paradise the choice of life and death, "Obey my commandment and you shall live; if not, you shall die"; "Beware of evil, choose what is good," so in Gen. 4⟨:6-7⟩, God said to Cain: "Why are you angry, and why has your countenance fallen? If you do well, will you not be accepted? And if you do not do well, sin is couching at the door; its desire is for you, and you must master it." He sets before him a reward if he wills to choose what is good and punishment if he prefers to follow the evil. And he shows that the movement of the will toward evil can be overcome, nor does it bring a necessity to sin. And with these texts agrees what God said to Moses: "I have set before your face the way of life and the way of death. Choose what is good and walk in it." What could be put more plainly? God shows what is good, what is evil, shows the different rewards of death and life, leaves man freedom to choose. It would be ridiculous to say, "Choose," if the power of turning one way or the other were not present, as though one should say to a man standing at a crossroad: "You see these two roads, take which you like" . . . when only one was open to him! Deuteronomy 30⟨:15-19⟩, adds: "See, I have set before you this day life and good, death and evil. If you obey the commandments of the Lord your God which I command you this day, by loving the Lord your God, by walking in his ways, and by

28 For this proverb, see Appendix.   29 See above, p. 32.

keeping his commandments and his statutes and his ordinances, then you shall live and multiply, and the Lord your God will bless you in the land which you are entering to take possession of it. But if your heart turns away, and you will not hear, but are drawn away to worship other gods and serve them, I declare to you this day, that you shall perish; you shall not live long in the land which you are going over the Jordan to enter and possess. I call heaven and earth to witness against you this day, that I have set before you life and death, blessing and curse; therefore choose life, that you and your descendants may live."

Here again you hear the words "set before you," you hear the word "choose," you hear the words "turns away," which would be quite inappropriate if the will of man were not free toward the good, but only toward evil. Otherwise, it would be as if one were to say to a man so bound that he could only raise his hand to the left: "See, you have the best wine at your right hand, you have poison on your left—choose which you will"!

Nor is that word inconsistent with these which the same Lord speaks in Isaiah ⟨1:19-20⟩: "If you are willing and obedient, you shall eat the good of the land; but if you refuse and rebel, you shall be devoured by the sword." If there really is no power in man of free choice toward good, or, as some say, no freedom either for good or ill, what do these words mean: "if you are willing"; "if you refuse"? It would be more consistent to say, "if I am willing"; "if I refuse," and, as most of these things are said to sinners, I do not see how one can avoid attributing to them also a will in some way free to choose good, unless we prefer to call this an action of thought or a movement of the soul rather than will, since the will implies decision and is born from the judgment. Thus it is said in the same prophet: "If you will inquire, inquire; turn and come" (Isa. 21⟨:12⟩). What would be the point of such an exhortation, to turn and come, if those who are in question have no such power in themselves? Would it not be like saying to one bound in chains which he [30] would not break: "Bestir yourself and come and follow me."

So also in the same prophet, ch. 43⟨45:20, 27⟩: "Assemble yourselves together and come. . . . Turn to me and be saved," and also in ch. 52⟨:1-2⟩: "Awake, awake . . . shake yourself from the dust . . . loose the bonds from your neck . . . ," and Jeremiah says, ch. 15⟨:19⟩: "If you return, I will restore you, and you shall stand before me. If you separate what is precious from what is worthless,

[30] The subject of *"nolit"* is the imaginary speaker, who refuses to break the fetters yet calls on the prisoner to follow him.

you shall be as my mouth"; when he says, "If you separate," he indicates a liberty of choice. Still more clearly Zechariah shows the effort of free choice, and the grace which responds to this effort: "Return to me, says the Lord of Hosts, and I will return to you, says the Lord." In Ezek. 18⟨:21⟩, God speaks thus: "But if a wicked man repents of all his sins which he has committed and does what is right." And farther on: "But if a righteous man turns away from his righteousness and commits iniquity"; in every case the words: "turns away . . . has done . . . has performed . . ." are repeated again and again in the matter of doing good or evil, and where are those who deny that man can do anything, but must only suffer the action of grace? "Cast away from you all transgressions," says God ⟨Ezek. 18:31⟩. And again: "Why will you die, O house of Israel?"; "I desire not the death of the wicked; return and come" ⟨Ezek. 33:11⟩. Does the good Lord deplore the death of his people which he himself works in them? If he does not will our death and if we nonetheless perish, it is to be imputed to our own will. But what can you impute to a man who can do nothing either good or ill? For those who have no kind of control over their actions, the psalmist sings his mystic chant in vain ⟨Ps. 34:14⟩: "Depart from evil, and do good; seek peace, and pursue it."

But to what use is it to rehearse so many texts of this kind, when the whole of the Holy Scriptures sets forth this kind of exhortation?

⟨Joel 2:12⟩	"Return to me with all your heart."
⟨Jonah 3:8⟩	"Let everyone turn from his evil way."
⟨Isa. 46:8⟩	"Recall it to mind, you transgressors" (*"Prevaricatores reddite ad cor"*) .
⟨Jer. 26:3⟩	"Let everyone turn from his evil way, that I may repent of the evil which I intend to do to them because of their evil doings."
⟨Jer. 26:4⟩	"If you will not listen to me, to walk in my law."

Thus almost the whole of Scripture speaks of nothing but conversion, application, and striving after better things. All these go for nothing if once you admit that doing good or bad comes by necessity.

Not less vain will be all those promises, all those threats, all those expostulations, all those reproaches, exhortations, blessings, and curses to those who have turned to better things or who have refused them.

⟨Ref. uncertain⟩ "The sinner shall have groaning at all times."

⟨Ex. 32:9⟩ "I have seen this people, and behold, it is a stiff-necked people."

⟨Micah 6:3⟩ "O my people, what have I done to you? My people have cast away my judgments."

⟨Ps. 81:13⟩ "O that my people would listen to me, that Israel would walk in my ways!"

⟨Ps. 34:12-13⟩ "Who would see good days, let him refrain his lips from evil."

The expression "Who would see" connotes free choice. If it were not so, would not such texts force the reader to ask: "Why do you promise upon condition, what is decided by your own will? Why do you expostulate when whatever is in me of good or evil you accomplish in me willy-nilly? Why do you reproach, when it is not in my power to guard what you have given me, or to exclude the ill which you send into me? Why do you entreat, when it all depends on you and turns on your good pleasure? Why do you bless, as though I had performed a good work when whatever is done is your work? Why do you curse if I have sinned by necessity? What end do all the myriad commandments serve if it is not possible for a man in any way to keep what is commanded?"

There are those who deny that man, although justified by the gift of faith and love, is able to fulfill any precepts, but that all good works, since they are done in the flesh, would lead to damnation if God did not pardon them through his mercy, for the sake of their faith. Yet the word that the Lord spoke through Moses declares that not only what is commanded is implanted in us but that it is like going downhill, as he says:

"This commandment which I command you this day is not above you, neither is it far off. It is not in heaven, that you should say, 'Who can go up for us to heaven, and bring it to us, that we may hear it and do it?' Neither is it beyond the sea, that you should say, 'Who will be able to go over the sea for us, and bring it to us, that we may hear it, and do it?' But the word is very near you; it is in your mouth and in your heart, so that you can do it." (Deut. 30:11-14.)

And yet there he is speaking of the greatest commandment of all: "That you turn to the Lord your God with all your heart and with all your soul," and what does this mean: "If, however, you will hear"; "if you will keep"; "if you will return" if none of these things is in any way in our power?

I will not bother to go on with more copious citations of this kind, since the books of both Testaments are so amply filled with such that he who labors to find them out will, as they say, be looking for water in the sea.[31] Thus, as I said, the greater part of Scripture will seem to lose its force if you take the last or the penultimate opinion I have been discussing. It is true that there are some passages in the Scriptures which seem to attribute a certain contingency and even mutability to God. Of such is that of which we read in Jer. 18⟨:8-10⟩:

> "And if that nation, concerning which I have spoken, turns from its evil, I will repent of the evil that I intended to do to it. And if any time I declare concerning a nation or a kingdom that I will build and plant it, and if it does evil in my sight, not listening to my voice, then I will repent of the good which I had intended to do to it."

But we must not forget that here the Holy Scripture is speaking after the manner of men, as in other places also it does quite often, since there is no mutability in God. But he is said to become propitious after being angry, when he honors us with grace upon our return to better things, and, on the other hand, after being propitious he becomes angry, when he punishes and afflicts those who fall back into evil ways. Again, in II Kings 20⟨:1⟩, Hezekiah hears: "For you shall die, you shall not live," and then, after his tears, he hears by the same prophet: "I have heard your prayer, I have seen your tears; behold, I have healed you" ⟨II Kings 20:5⟩. Similarly, in II Sam. 12⟨:10⟩ David hears through Nathan from the Lord: "Now therefore the sword shall never depart from your house," but when he has said: "I have sinned against the Lord," he hears the milder judgment: "The Lord also has put away your sin; you shall not die." In passages like this a figurative use of language excludes mutability from God, so it is impossible to avoid the conclusion that there is in us a will that can turn one way or the other: or, if of necessity it is bent toward evil, why is sin imputed? If of necessity it is turned toward the good, why should God from being angry become propitious when there is no further grace due to us?

[31] Another proverb expounded in the *Adagia*. See Appendix.

New Testament Texts Examined. Matthew 23:37 and Other Words of Christ

Hitherto we have taken examples from the Old Testament and one might perhaps complain about this, did not the light of the gospel, far from eclipsing such manner of argument, rather establish it still more strongly.

Let us turn then to the books of the New Testament, and in the first place to the Gospel ⟨of Matthew, ch. 23:27⟩ where Christ, in weeping over the fate of Jerusalem, speaks thus:

> "O Jerusalem, Jerusalem, killing the prophets and stoning those who are sent to you! How often would I have gathered you together as a hen gathers her brood under her wings, and you would not!"

If all is determined by necessity, could not Jerusalem rightly reply to the Lord who weeps over it: "Why do you torment yourself with vain tears? If you did not wish us to listen to the prophets, why did you send them to us? Why impute to us what has been done by your will and our necessity? You wished us to gather together, but at the same time wished us not to do so,[32] for you have worked in us what we did not wish ourselves."

But it is clear that in these words it is not necessity which the Lord arraigns in the Jews, but a reprobate and rebellious will: "I wished to gather you together . . . you refused."

Again, elsewhere: "If you would enter into life, keep the commandments." With what effrontery would it be said: "If you will . . ." to one whose will is not free? Again: "If you would be perfect, go, sell what you possess" ⟨Matt. 19:21⟩. Again ⟨Luke 9:23⟩: "If any man would come after me, let him deny himself and take up his cross daily and follow me." Despite the difficulty of this precept, you have the mention of our will. And then: "For whoever would save his life will lose it" ⟨Luke 9:24⟩. Are not all these clear precepts of Christ pointless if nothing is attributed to human will?

"But I say unto you . . . But I say unto you . . . And if you love me, keep my commandments" ⟨John 14:15⟩. Think how much is there in John which stresses the commandments! How inapposite the conjunction "if" when all was necessity! "If you abide in me, and my words abide in you" ⟨John 15:7⟩; "If you would be perfect . . ." Now, where there is such frequent men-

---

[32] The Latin is *"in nobis nolebas,"* which may govern the accusative *"quod noluerimus"* and mean "Your refusal was manifest in our own refusal."

tion of good and bad works, where there is mention of reward, I do not see how the text can be interpreted of mere necessity. There is nothing meritorious about nature or necessity. And yet our Lord Jesus says in Matt. 5⟨:12⟩: "Rejoice and be glad, for your reward is great in heaven." What does the parable of the laborers in the vineyard mean? What kind of laborers are they, who do nothing? A penny is given, the agreed wages for work. You say, "It is called a reward because in some way it is owed by God, who has pledged his word to the man who believes his promises. But this very believing is in some respect a function of free choice as it turns to, or away from, believing. Why is the servant who has increased his fortune by industry praised by the Lord? Why is the lazy and unprofitable servant condemned if we are good-for-nothing? Again in ch. 25, when He invites all to partake of the eternal Kingdom, he does not call to mind necessity but good deeds: "You gave food, you gave drink, you gave shelter, you clothed the naked"; again to the goats, the accursed on the left hand, he reproaches not necessity, but the voluntary omission of works: "You saw the hungry, you had the opportunity to do good, but you gave no food," etc.

And in fact are not the Gospels and Epistles full of exhortations? "Come to me, all who labor and are heavy laden" ⟨Matt. 11:28⟩. "Watch, pray, ask, seek, knock, see, beware . . ." What do so many parables mean about keeping the Word of God, about meeting the bridegroom, about the thief in the night, about the house built upon a rock? Are they not intended to incite us to striving, to endeavoring, to industry, lest we perish by neglecting the grace of God? These seem empty and vain if they all refer to necessity. The same is true of the threats in the Gospels: "Woe unto you scribes, woe unto you hypocrites, woe unto you Chorazin." And these reproaches also lose their meaning: "O faithless generation, how long am I to be with you? How long am I to bear with you?" ⟨Mark 9:19⟩. "You serpents, you brood of vipers, how are you to escape the damnation of hell?" ⟨Matt. 23:33⟩. "You will know them by their fruits," says the Lord ⟨Matt. 7:16⟩. What he means by fruits are works, and he calls them ours. But they are not ours if they all happen by necessity. He prays on the cross: "Father forgive them; for they know not what they do" ⟨Luke 23:34⟩. How much more justly should he have excused them, since their will was not free, nor could they do otherwise! Again, in John ⟨1:12⟩: "But to all who received him, who believed in his name, he gave power to become children of God." How can power to become children of God be given to those who are not yet children, if there is no liberty in our will? Again, when some were offended at the words of the Lord, and went no more with him, he said to his closest disciples: "Will you also go away?" ⟨John 6:67⟩. But if those others went away not of their own will, but by necessity, what is the point of asking them whether they also wished to go?

St. Paul Also Is a Champion of Free Choice

But we will not weary the reader by going over all the passages of this kind, since they are so countless that they will readily catch the eye of any reader. Let us rather look at Paul, the assiduous champion of grace, and the constant opponent of the works of the law, and see whether one can find that he, too, assumes freedom of choice. And first we are confronted by Rom. 2⟨:4⟩: "Or do you despise the riches of his kindness and forbearance and patience? Do you not know that God's kindness is meant to lead you to repentance?" How can contempt of the commandment be brought against anyone when the will is not free? Or how does God invite to penitence, if he is the author of impenitence? Or how is condemnation just, when the judge himself enforces wrongdoing? And yet Paul himself said shortly before this: "We know that the judgment of God rightly falls upon those who do such things" ⟨Rom. 2:2⟩; you hear of a deed, you hear a judgment according to truth; then where is mere necessity? Where is a will that is merely passive? See to what Paul imputes their wickedness: "But by your hard and impenitent heart you are storing up wrath for yourself on the Day of Wrath when God's righteous judgment will be revealed. For he will render to every man according to his works." And here you have just judgment of God and works deserving punishment. If God were only imputing to us his good works which he works through us to glory, honor, and immortality, his benevolence would be praiseworthy (note here, however, that Paul adds a condition: "For those who persevere in good works," and again: "For those seeking eternal life"). But in the name of what kind of justice does he make his wrath and his indignation and tribulations and anguish fall on a man who is judged to have done ill when in fact he has done nothing of himself, but from simple necessity? Again, what do those analogies of Paul mean, of runners in the games, of the prize, of the wreath, if nothing is to be attributed to our endeavors? First Corinthians 9⟨:24-25⟩: "Do you not know that in a race all the runners compete, but only one receives the prize?

So run that you may obtain it. Every athlete exercises self-control in all things. They do it to receive a perishable wreath, but we an imperishable." A victor's crown is not given save to contestants, and is given in place of a reward to those who have deserved this honor. Again, I Tim. 6⟨:12⟩: "Fight the good fight of the faith; take hold of eternal life." Where there is a contest, there is a voluntary striving; there is the danger that if you stop you lose the reward. It is not the same when all things happen from necessity. Again, the same point is made in the same epistle, II Tim. 2⟨:5⟩: "An athlete is not crowned unless he competes according to the rules." And a little higher up: "Labor as a good soldier of Christ Jesus" (II Tim. 2⟨:3⟩) . He recalls also the work of a laborer in the field; to him who runs a wreath is given; to the soldier his wages; the farmer gets his fruits. And in the same epistle, II Tim. 4⟨:7-8⟩: "I have fought the good fight, I have finished the race, I have kept the faith. Henceforth there is laid up for me the crown of righteousness, which the Lord, the righteous judge, will award to me on that Day." It seems to me difficult to associate the words "contest," "crown," "righteous judge," "giving," "fighting," when all things happen from mere necessity with our will doing nothing, but merely passive. James also does not attribute sin to necessity, and to God working in us, but to our own depraved lusts: "God," he says, "tempts no one; but each person is tempted when he is lured and enticed by his own desire. Then desire, when it has conceived, gives birth to sin." Paul calls transgressions works of the flesh, not works of God, and he calls "flesh" what James calls "concupiscence." And in Acts, Ananias hears: "Why has Satan filled your heart?" Paul again in Eph., ch. 2, attributes evil works to the spirit of the air, who works in the sons of disobedience. "What accord has Christ with Belial?" ⟨II Cor. 6:15⟩. Either plant a good tree and gather good fruits or plant a bad tree and gather evil fruits. With what impudence do we attribute the worst fruits to God, than whom nothing can be better? For although human lust is enticed by Satan, or by outward things, or sometimes by what lies within a man, yet the enticement does not bring with it a necessity of sinning if we will to resist it with the help of God which we have besought, just as the Spirit of Christ, summoning us to welldoing, does not bring necessity, but help. Ecclesiasticus, ch. 15, agrees with James: "He has not commanded anyone to be ungodly, and he has not given anyone freedom to sin," but he who compels does more than if he simply orders. Plainer still is what Paul writes in II Tim. 2⟨:21⟩: "If anyone purifies himself from what is ignoble, then he will be a vessel for noble use."

How can a man keep himself clean when he does nothing at all? I know there is a figure here, but in the present instance it is enough for me that this word contradicts those who would attribute everything to sheer necessity. With this I John 5⟨:1⟩ agrees: "Everyone who believes that Jesus is the Christ is a child of God." I will admit that there is a figure here if in return they will allow us to take refuge in figures in other places, and yet this figure would be too extravagant if anybody translated "sanctifies himself" as "is sanctified by God willy-nilly." "Let us," says Paul, "then cast off the works of darkness" ⟨Rom. 13:12⟩, "despoiling the old nature with its practices" ⟨Col. 3:9⟩. How are we commanded to cast off or put on anything if we do nothing? So in Rom. 7⟨:18⟩: "I can will what is right, but I cannot do it." Here Paul seems to confess that it is in the power of man to will what is good, and this willing good is itself a good work, since otherwise there would be no evil in evil will. And it is beyond controversy that the will to slay is evil.

Again in I Cor. 14⟨:32⟩: "And the spirits of prophets are subject to prophets"; if the leadership of the Holy Spirit is of such a manner that those whom he leads are free to be silent if they will, much more is the will of a man in his own power. For those whom a fanatical spirit leads cannot keep silent even if they wish, and often do not understand what they themselves are saying. His admonition to Timothy is relevant here: "Do not neglect the grace that is in you" ⟨I Tim. 4:14⟩. For he declares it to be in our power to turn away from grace when it is given. So elsewhere: "And his grace toward me was not in vain" ⟨I Cor. 15:10⟩; this means he did not fail divine grace, but how could he not fail it if he did nothing? II Peter 1⟨:5⟩: "For this very reason make every effort to supplement your faith with virtue, and virtue with knowledge," etc., and then: "Therefore, brethren, be the more zealous to confirm your call and election" ⟨II Peter 1:10⟩. He wishes our care to be joined with divine grace, that through the stages of virtue we arrive at perfection.

But I am afraid lest I seem to some to have gone beyond bounds in heaping together so many texts from the Scriptures. For as Paul writes in II Tim. 3⟨:16⟩: "All Scripture is inspired by God and profitable for teaching, for reproof, for correction, and for training in righteousness." None of these things seem relevant where all things happen by sheer and inevitable necessity. What purpose is served by so many praises of the saints in Ecclus., ch. 44, and following passages if nothing is due to our industry? What is the point of praising obedience if in doing good or evil works we are the kind of instrument for God that an ax is to a carpenter? But such a tool are we all if Wyclif is right. All things before and after grace, good equally with ill, yes even things indifferent, are done by sheer necessity. Which opinion Luther approves. That nobody may suppose me to have invented the charge, I will cite his own words from his "assertions": [33] "Wherefore," he says, "it is needful to retract this article. For I was wrong in saying that free choice before grace is a reality only in name. I should have said simply: 'free choice is in reality a fiction, or a name without reality.' For no one has it in his own power to think a good or bad thought, but everything (as Wyclif's article condemned at Constance rightly teaches) happens by absolute necessity." These are Luther's actual words. I prudently pass over many texts which are in The Acts and in the Apocalypse lest I tire the reader. These many texts have induced learned and holy men not to take free choice entirely away. So far from the truth is it that they were provoked by the spirit of Satan, to prepare damnation for themselves by trusting in their own works.

PART II. SCRIPTURE PASSAGES THAT SEEM TO OPPOSE FREE CHOICE

Now it is time to look at certain texts of Scripture that make for the other side, and seem to take away free choice entirely. There are indeed not a few of these which meet us in the sacred volumes, but there are two in particular which stand out from the rest. Paul deals with them in such a way that at first sight he seems to attribute absolutely nothing either to our works or to the powers of free choice.

Exodus 9:12; Romans 9:17: The Hardening of Pharaoh's Heart

One passage is Ex. 9⟨:12⟩, and this is handled by Paul in Rom. 9⟨:17⟩: "But the Lord hardened the heart of Pharaoh, and he did not listen to them," and again: "But for this purpose I have placed you there, to show you my power, so that my name may be declared throughout all the earth" ⟨Ex. 9:16⟩. Paul expounds it thus, bringing forward a similar text, which is Ex. 32⟨33:19⟩; for He said to Moses: "And I will be gracious to whom I am gracious, and will show mercy on whom I show mercy." The other passage is in Mal., ch. 1, and it is treated by Paul in Rom., ch. 9: " 'Was he not Jacob's brother?' says the Lord. 'Yet I have loved Jacob but I have hated Esau,' " which Paul explains thus: "Though they

[33] Erasmus uses the word with a capital letter.

[the children] were not yet born and had done nothing either good or evil in order that God's purpose of election might continue, not because of works but because of his call, she was told, 'The elder will serve the younger.' As it is written, 'Jacob have I loved, but Esau have I hated' " ⟨Rom. 9:11-13⟩. Since, however, it seems absurd that God, who is not only just but good also, should be said to have hardened the heart of a man, so that by the man's misdeeds He might display his own power, Origen, in the third book of his work *Peri archōn* ("On Beginnings") , thus explains the difficulty, and declares that an occasion of hardening was given by God, but he would throw back the blame on Pharaoh who, by his evil deeds, was made more obstinate through those things which should have brought him to repentance, just as by the action of the same rain cultivated land brings forth excellent fruit, and uncultivated land thorns and thistles, and just as by the action of the same sun, wax melts and mud hardens, so the forbearance of God that tolerates the sinner brings some to repentance and makes others more obstinate in wrongdoing. He has mercy, therefore, on those who recognize the goodness of God and repent, but those are hardened who are given an opportunity to repent but who, by neglecting the goodness of God, persist in evil courses. Such a figure, by which he is described as the agent who merely provides an opportunity, is in agreement with usage, as when a father says to his son: "I spoiled you," reproaching himself for not having at once punished his faults. Isaiah has used a similar trope, Isa. 63⟨:17⟩: "O Lord, why hast thou made us err from thy ways and hardened our heart, so that we fear thee not?" Jerome expounds this text according to the interpretation of Origen; God hardens when he does not at once punish the sinner, and has mercy as soon as he invites repentance by means of afflictions. Thus he speaks in anger in Hosea: "I will not punish your daughters when they play the harlot" ⟨Hos. 4:14⟩; on the other hand, he chastises mercifully in Ps. 88⟨89:32⟩: "Then I will punish their transgression with the rod and their iniquity with scourges." With the same figure, Jeremiah says ⟨Jer. 20:7⟩: "O Lord, thou hast deceived me, and I was deceived; thou wert stronger than I, and thou hast prevailed." He is said to seduce when he does not at once recall from error, and this is Origen's opinion conduces meanwhile to a more perfect health, just as experienced surgeons prefer a wound not to scar too quickly in order that, when the corrupting matter is brought out of the open wound, a permanent healing may take place. And Origen notes that the Lord says: "But for this purpose have I raised you up," not "For this purpose I made you." Otherwise, Pharaoh would not have been wicked if God had made him like that: "Who saw everything that he had made, and behold, it was very good" ⟨Gen. 1:31⟩. Now, in truth Pharaoh was created with a will that could turn either way, but of his own wish he turned to evil, and with his own mind preferred to follow evil rather than obey the commandments of God. God, however, turned this malice of Pharaoh's to his own glory and the salvation of his people that thereby it might be made more plain that men strive in vain when they resist the will of God, just as a clever king or master uses the cruelty of those whom he hates to punish the wicked. Nevertheless, violence is not therefore done to our own will if the course of events is in the hand of God, or if he turns the endeavors of men in another direction than they had intended, in accordance with his secret purpose.

So just as he turns the efforts of the wicked to the benefit of the godly, so the efforts of the good do not attain the end they seek, unless they are aided by the free favor of God. Without doubt this is what Paul meant by: "So it depends not upon man's will or exertion, but upon God's mercy" ⟨Rom. 9:16⟩. The mercy of God preveniently moves the will to will, and accompanies it in its effort, gives it a happy issue. And yet meanwhile we will, run, follow after—yet that which is our own let us ascribe to God to whom we wholly belong.

They sufficiently explain the difficulty about foreknowledge by saying that it does not impose necessity on our will—but nobody to my mind more happily than Laurentius Valla. For prescience is not the cause of things which happen, for it befalls us to foreknow many things which do not happen because we foreknow them, but rather we foreknow them because they are going to happen. Thus the eclipse of the sun does not happen because astrologers predict its occurrence, but they predict its occurrence because it was bound to happen. On the other hand, the question of the will and the determination of God is more difficult.

The Problem of the Will and Foreknowledge of God

For God to will and foreknow are the same thing; in some way it must be that he wills what he foreknows as future, and that which he does not hinder, though it is in his power to do so. And this is what Paul means by "Who can resist His will" if he has mercy on whom he wills and hardens whom he wills? Truly, if there were a king who carried into effect whatever he willed, and nobody could resist him, he could be said to do whatever he willed.[34] Thus the will of God, since it is the principal cause of all things that take place, seems to impose necessity on our will. Nor does Paul solve the question, but simply rebukes the questioner: "But who are you, a man, to answer back to God?" (Rom. 9:20). Indeed, he rebukes the impious complainer as if the master of a house should say to a froward slave: "What business is it of yours why I give this order? Just do what I command!" He would reply very differently to a prudent and faithful servant, modestly seeking to learn from his master why he wished a thing to be done which at first sight seemed useless. God willed Pharaoh to perish miserably, and he willed it rightly, and it was right for him to perish. Yet he was not forced by the will of God to be obstinately wicked.

It is as though a master, knowing the depraved mind of a servant, should commit to him a task, in which an opportunity to sin would be given, in which he might be taken and punished as an example to others. He foreknows that he will follow his inclinations and sin, and wills him to perish, and even wills him in some way to sin. Yet the servant is not thereby excused, since he sins from his own wickedness. For he has already previously deserved punishment and is to be publicly punished now that his wickedness is exposed. For what will you take to be the origin of merits where there is perpetual necessity and where there never was free will? What we have said, however, of events, which God often makes to turn out differently from what men had intended, though true in many cases, is not always true, and in fact happens more frequently with evil things than with good. The Jews crucifying the Lord intended to destroy him entirely; this wicked design God turns to the glory of his Son and the salvation of the whole world. But the centurion Cornelius, who sought with good works the favor of the Divine Being, obtained his wish. And Paul, at the end of his course, gained the crown that he sought.

Here I am not discussing whether God, who is without any argument the primary and highest cause of all things which are made, so acts in some cases by secondary causes that he himself meanwhile does not intervene at all, or whether he so works all things that secondary causes only cooperate with the principal cause, without being otherwise necessary. Certainly it cannot be doubted that God can, if he will, turn the natural issue of secondary causes in another direction. So he can make fire grow cold

[34] This sentence seems so tautologous that one must assume carelessness on the part of Erasmus.

and moist, and water to harden and dry up, the sun to be darkened, rivers to freeze, rocks to melt, poison to heal, and food to kill, just as the same fire from the Babylonian furnace revived the three children and burned the Chaldeans. Whenever God acts like this, we call it a miracle. So he can take away taste from the palate and judgment from the eyes, stun the powers of the mind, memory, and will, and make them do what seems good to him. Just as he did with Balaam who came intending to curse, but could not. The tongue spoke one thing, the soul willed another. Besides, what rarely happens does not make a general law. And yet in these cases, whatever God wills, he wills for good reasons, even though they are sometimes hidden from us. This will none can resist, but his ordained will, or as they say in the Schools, his will signified, men often do resist. Did not Jerusalem resist when it refused to be gathered together when God willed?

Two Kinds of Necessity: The Case of Judas

But one may object that there is necessity of a double kind involved in the outcome of things, since the prescience of God cannot be deceived nor can his will be hindered. Not all necessity excludes free will, since God the Father necessarily begets the Son, and yet begets him freely and willingly, for he is not forced to do so. Some necessity can also be posited of human affairs which nonetheless does not exclude a liberty of our will. God foreknew (and what he foreknew he in some way intended) that Judas would betray the Lord. Thus if you look at the infallible foreknowledge of God, and his immutable will, Judas was necessarily going to turn traitor to his Lord, and yet Judas could change his intention, and certainly he had it in his power to refuse to undertake his treacherous design. You say, "What if he had changed his mind?" The foreknowledge of God would not have been falsified, nor his will hindered, since he himself would have foreknown and intended beforehand that Judas should change his mind. Those who argue such things with Scholastic subtlety admit a necessity of consequence, but not of the consequent (for with these terms they are wont to expound their view). For they have it that it must necessarily follow that Judas should betray the Lord if God willed this to happen with his eternal will, but they deny that it follows that Judas therefore betrayed necessarily, since this wicked business originated in a perverse will.

But it is not part of my purpose to pursue such subtleties any further. The passage quoted already: "God hardened Pharaoh's heart" can be taken in the same sense as the saying of Paul: "God gave them up to a base mind and to improper conduct" (Rom. 1:28), and the same deed is sin and the penalty of sin. But whomsoever God delivers over to a reprobate mind, he delivers on account of previous desert, like Pharaoh who, though challenged to do so by so many signs, refused to let God's people go, or the philosophers who, though they knew the deity of God, worshiped wood and stone. Truly where there is sheer perpetual necessity there can be no desert good or bad. And it cannot be denied that the divine action concurs with every act, since every action has something real in it, and is even good in a certain sense, as for example embracing an adulteress or desiring to do so. Certainly the malice of action does not come from God, but from our will, unless God, as some say, can be said in some sense to cause a malice of will in us, letting it go where it wills, without recalling it by his grace. Even so, he is said to have caused man to perish because he suffered him to perish when he might have saved him. But that is enough about that particular passage, at least in this context.

Jacob and Esau

Now, let us look at the other passage about Esau and Jacob, of which an oracle had spoken before they were born, "The greater shall serve the less" as Gen., ch. 25, has it. But this does not properly apply to the salvation of man. For God can will in fact that a man, willy-nilly, be a slave or a pauper, and yet not so as to be excluded from eternal salvation. Besides, as regards the first chapter of Malachi: "Yet I have loved Jacob but I have hated Esau," if you press it literally, God does not love just as we love, nor does he hate anybody, since he is not subject to affections of this kind. Besides, as I said at the beginning, it seems that the prophet is speaking there not of the hate whereby we are damned eternally, but of temporal misfortune, as when one speaks of the wrath and fury of God. Accordingly, those are reprimanded who thought to reestablish Idumaea,[35] which God willed to remain in ruins.

Moreover, as concerns the tropological interpretation, God did not love all the Gentiles or hate all the Jews, but chose some out of both nations, and this testimony in Paul does not champion the

---

[35] On account of Edom's refusal to give Israel passage on their journey to the Promised Land (Num. 20:21), it had been the subject of many curses (Ps. 60:8; Jer. 9:26; 25:21; 49:17; Ezek. 25:14; Joel 3:19; etc.).

cause of necessity, but is to repress the arrogance of the Jews who believed that the grace of the gospel was their especial due, since they were the posterity of Abraham, and that the Gentiles were abominated and could not be suffered to receive the comfort of gospel grace.

Paul shortly afterward explaining this says: "Even us whom he has called, not from the Jews only" ⟨Rom. 9:24⟩. Thus those whom God hates or loves, he hates or loves for just reasons, and the hatred and the love are not more opposed to free choice than the hatred and love with which he pursues those who are to be born and those who are actually born. He hates the unborn because he surely knows that they will commit deeds worthy of hatred; he hates the born because they do commit deeds worthy of hatred. The Jews, who were a chosen people, are rejected; the Gentiles, who were not a chosen people, are received. Why are the Jews plucked from the olive tree? Because they refused to believe. Why are the Gentiles grafted in? Because they obeyed the gospel. This is what Paul himself argues: "They were broken off because of their unbelief" ⟨Rom. 11:20⟩. That is undoubtedly in either case because they refused to believe. To those plucked off he gives a hope that they may again be grafted in if, abandoning their unbelief, they choose to believe, and to those grafted in he instills fear lest they may fall if they turn themselves from the grace of God. "You," he says, "stand fast only through faith. So do not become proud, but stand in awe" ⟨Rom. 11:20⟩. And later on: "Lest you be wise in your own conceits" ⟨Rom. 11:25⟩. All this shows clearly that Paul's sole object here is to repress the arrogance at once of the Gentiles and of the Jews.

The Potter and the Clay

The third passage is Isa. 45⟨:9⟩: "Woe to him who strives with his Maker, an earthen vessel with the potter! Does the clay say to him who fashions it, 'What are you making?' or 'Your work is without hands'?" And still more clearly, in Jer. 18:6: " 'O house of Israel, can I not do with you as this potter has done?' says the Lord. 'Behold, like the clay in the potter's hand, so are you in my hand, O house of Israel.' " These passages have more polemic force in Paul than in the prophets from whom they are taken.[36] For Paul comments on them thus: "Has the potter no right over the clay, to make out of the same lump one vessel for beauty and another

[36] Possibly an echo of Jerome's criticism of Paul, "Things have a force in Paul which they did not possess in their original context."

for contempt? What if God, desiring to show his wrath and to make known his power, has endured with much patience the vessels of wrath made for destruction, in order to make known the riches of his glory for the vessels of mercy, which he has prepared beforehand for glory?" ⟨Rom. 9:21-23⟩. In both these passages the prophet rejects the complaint of the people against God, since they are afflicted in order that they shall be amended. The prophet beats down the impious voices, just as Paul beats down the impious complaint: "But who art thou, O man?" In these things we are to submit to God as a vessel to the hands of the potter. Yet in truth this is not to take away free choice wholly, nor does it exclude our will from cooperating with the divine will in order to attain eternal salvation. For in Jeremiah there soon follows an exhortation to penitence which we have already quoted. There would be no point in such statements if all things happen by sheer necessity.

I should say, moreover, that here the word of Paul is not whether free choice is entirely excluded, but to repress the wicked murmuring of the Jews against God, who on account of their obstinate unbelief were rejected from the grace of the gospel, while the Gentiles were received on the ground of their faith, as II Tim. 2:20-21 sufficiently explains: "In a great house there are not only vessels of gold and silver but also of wood and earthenware, and some for noble use, some for ignoble. If anyone purifies himself from these, then he will be a vessel for noble use, consecrated to honor and useful to the master of the house, ready for any good work." Such illustrations are adduced in the Scriptures for the sake of their teaching, but not in such a way as to be always consistent. Otherwise, what could be more stupid than to address a Samian pot [37] and say, "If you make yourself clean, you will be a useful and honorable vessel"? Yet this could well be said to be a vessel endowed with reason which, when admonished, can conform to the Lord's will. Besides, if a man is simply to God as clay in the hands of a potter, whatever shape the vase takes must be attributed to no one but the potter, especially if the potter is the one who first created the clay and molded it by his own choice. Yet here a vessel which has been guilty of nothing because it is not its own master is thrown into eternal fire. Let us interpret the parable in the sense in which it was intended. For if we were to press the comparison into the tiniest details, we should be forced to say some preposter-

[37] "Matulae Samiae." A matula is a vessel for holding liquids, in particular a chamber pot or urinal. Samian ware was made of very fine clay, and to say "Samian pot" is rather like saying "Wedgwood pot."

ous things. This potter makes a vase for dishonor not on account of preceding merits, just as he rejects some Jews, but on account of unbelief. Again, of the Gentiles he makes a vessel of honor on account of their belief. Why do those who urge on us the literal words of Holy Scripture, and wish the parable of the potter and the vessel to be taken as it stands, not allow us an equally literal interpretation of that other passage: "If anyone purifies himself"? On this interpretation Paul will be found to contradict himself, for in the former passage he puts everything in the hands of God, but here he puts it all in the hands of man. And yet each passage is right, though each makes a different point. The first shuts the mouth murmuring against God, the other incites to endeavor and is a warning against complacency or despair. Not very different from this passage is Isa. 10⟨:15⟩: "Shall the ax vaunt itself over him who hews with it, or the saw magnify itself against him who wields it?" As if a rod should wield him who lifts it, or as if a staff should be raised, though made of wood. These things are said against a wicked king, whose cruelty God had used to chastise his own people. But those things which he did by divine permission he attributed to his own wisdom and strength, when he was simply the instrument of the divine wrath. An instrument he was indeed, but a rational and living one. And if an ax or saw had been such, it would not have been absurd to say that they had shared in the action of the craftsman. Aristotle teaches that slaves are the living instruments of their masters, as axes, saws, hoes, and plows would be if they could move of their own accord, like the tripods and kettles which Vulcan made and which went into battle of their own accord.[38] The master lays down his commands and supplies what is needed, nor could the servant do anything apart from his master, and yet nobody says the servant does nothing at all when he follows the orders of his lord. So this analogy does not fit the taking away of free choice, but rebukes the pride of a wicked ruler who attributed his deeds not to God but to his own might and wisdom. Nor is it any harder to resolve what Origen quotes from Ezek. 36⟨:26⟩: "And I will take out of your flesh the

---

[38] The marvelous implements fashioned by Hephaistos are mentioned in the *Iliad* (xviii. 369 ff.): "He was making a set of twenty three-legged tables to stand round the walls of his well-built hall. He had fitted golden wheels to all their legs so that they could run by themselves to a meeting of the gods and amaze the company by running home again" (E. V. Rieu's translation). Aristotle's teaching about slaves is found in *Politics* I.ii.4–6, where he quotes the passage from the *Iliad* here referred to. This feeling about slaves is characteristic of the Greek and even more of the Roman world.

heart of stone and give you a heart of flesh." A teacher might use the same metaphor when correcting some mistakes by his pupil: "I will take away your barbarian tongue and insert in you a Roman one." Nevertheless, he requires industry in the pupil, even though apart from his teacher the pupil cannot acquire a new language. What is "a heart of stone"? An incorrigible heart, obstinate in wickedness. What is "a heart of flesh"? A teachable heart which responds to the divine grace. Those who support free choice nonetheless admit that a soul which is obstinate in evil cannot be softened into true repentance without the help of heavenly grace. He who makes you teachable demands nonetheless your endeavor toward learning. David prays in Ps. 51(:10): "Create in me a clean heart, O God," and Paul says: "If anyone purifies himself" ⟨II Tim. 2:21⟩; Ezekiel says ⟨Ezek. 18:31⟩: "And get yourselves a new heart and a new spirit"; on the other hand, David says: "Uphold me with a willing spirit" ⟨Ps. 51:12⟩; David prays: "Blot out all my iniquities" ⟨Ps. 51:9⟩; against this, John: "And everyone who thus hopes in him purifies himself as he is pure" ⟨I John 3:3⟩; David prays: "Deliver me from bloodguiltiness, O God" ⟨Ps. 51:14⟩; the prophet cries: "Loose the bonds from your neck, O captive daughter of Zion" ⟨Isa. 52:2⟩. And Paul: "Let us then cast off the works of darkness" ⟨Rom. 13:12⟩; and so Peter: "So put away all malice and all guile and insincerity and envy and all slander" ⟨I Peter 2:1⟩; Paul to the Philippians ⟨Phil. 2:12⟩: "Work out your own salvation with fear and trembling," and the same, earlier, to the Corinthians ⟨I Cor. 12:6⟩: "But it is the same God who works all things in all men." There are hundreds more passages of this kind in Holy Scripture. If man does nothing, why say, "Work out"? If man does something, why say, "God works all things in all men"? If you wish to twist the one passage to support a special interpretation, man does nothing. On the other hand, if you wish to turn the other to your cause, man does it all. If man does nothing, there is no room for merits; where there is no room for merits, there is no room for punishments or rewards. If man does all, there is no room for grace, which Paul urges so many times. The Holy Spirit does not fight against himself, whose inspiration produced the canonical Scriptures. Both sides embrace and acknowledge the inviolable majesty of Scripture, but an interpretation must be found which will unravel this knot. Those who suppress free choice interpret it thus: "Stretch out your hand to whatever you will" ⟨Ecclus. 15:16⟩, that is, "Grace will stretch out your hand to what it wills." "Get yourselves a new heart" ⟨Ezek. 18:31⟩, that is, the grace of God will make in you a new heart. "Everyone who has this hope sanctifies himself therein" ⟨I John 3:3⟩, that is, grace sanctifies him. "Let us then cast off the works of darkness" ⟨Rom. 13:12⟩, that is, let grace cast them off. Very often we meet this refrain in Holy Scripture: "He worked righteousness, he committed iniquity," and wherever they occur, we shall expound them as "God did it and worked righteousness and iniquity in him." Now, if I bring forward the interpretation of the orthodox Fathers or even of Councils, the objection is raised at once, "Ah! But they were only men!" But in face of such a forced and twisted interpretation, may I not be allowed to ask, "And Luther, is he not also a man?"

Certainly the victory goes to them, if it is allowable for them to interpret Scripture in terms to suit themselves, while it is not permitted to us to follow the interpretation of the Fathers, or to bring forward our own view. And this Scripture is too clear to need any interpreter: "Stretch out your hand to whatever you wish," that is, "Grace will stretch out your hand to what it wills," which interpretation of the most approved doctors will be a fantasy, not to say, as some have not refrained from saying, "a prompting of Satan."

And so these passages, which seem to be in conflict with one another, are easily brought into harmony if we join the striving of our will with the assistance of divine grace. In the figure of the potter and of the ax, they urge us sharply to take the words in their literal meaning, because it fits their cause, but here they impudently go back on the words of the divine Scriptures and they interpret them no more truly than if somebody said, "Peter writes" and, if another interpreted it, that Peter himself did not write but somebody else wrote it in his house.

PART III. EXAMINATION OF LUTHER'S ARGUMENTS IN HIS *Assertio*

Genesis 6:3: *The Meaning of "Flesh" and "Spirit"*

Now, let us examine how strong are the arguments that Martin Luther adduces to undermine free choice. For he quotes Gen. 6⟨:3⟩: "My spirit shall not abide in man forever, for he is flesh." In this passage Scripture does not interpret "flesh" simply to mean wicked desire, as Paul takes it on occasion when he commands the works of the flesh to be mortified, but to mean the weakness of our nature which is prone to sin, just as he calls the Corinthians carnal because they were not yet capable of more solid teaching, but only babes in Christ. And Jerome in his *Hebrew Ques-*

tions [39] says that the Hebrews had a different text from that which we read, namely, "My spirit will not judge these men forever, for they are flesh," words which do not speak of the severity of God, but of his clemency. For "flesh" is what he calls our created weakness which is prone to evil; "spirit," on the other hand, he calls wrath. Thus he denies that he wishes to save them for eternal punishment, but he wishes in his mercy to inflict punishment on them here below. And yet this saying does not apply to the whole human race, but only to the men of that day, completely corrupt through infamous vices. And so he says, "In these men." Nor did it apply entirely to the men of that age, for Noah is praised as a righteous man pleasing to God. In the same way can be explained the quotation from the same work, ch. 8⟨:21⟩: "For the thought and imagination of man's heart are prone to evil from his youth," and ch. 6⟨:5⟩: "Every imagination of his heart was intent on only evil continually." Yet this proneness to evil which is in most men does not take away free choice altogether, even though evil is not fully to be overcome without the aid of divine grace. For if no part of repentance depends on the will, but all things are done by God through a certain necessity, why is man there given room for repentance? "But his days shall be a hundred and twenty years" ⟨Gen. 6:3⟩. For Jerome in his *Hebrew Questions* would refer this passage not to the space of human life, but to the time of the Flood—and says that the delay was granted so that, if they would, they might repent. If they refused, then they would deserve the divine vengeance, since they had despised the clemency of the Lord. Moreover, the passage he adduces from Isa. 40⟨:2⟩: "She has received from the Lord's hand double for all her sins" Jerome interprets in terms of the divine vengeance, not of grace given in return for our evil deeds. For although Paul says: "Where sin increased, grace abounded all the more" ⟨Rom. 5:20⟩, it does not necessarily follow that before that "grace which makes acceptable" a man may not, with the help of God, prepare himself by morally good work for the divine favor, as we read of Cornelius, the centurion, who was not yet baptized and had not been inspired by the Holy Spirit: "Your prayers and your alms have ascended as a memorial before God" ⟨Acts 10:4⟩. If all works are evil which are done before the receipt of the highest grace, are we to say then that evil works bring us into the favor of God?

Now, as to Luther's quotation from the same chapter of Isaiah: "All flesh is grass, and all its glory is like the flower of the grass. The grass withers and the flower fades, because the Spirit of the

[39] *Liber Hebraicarum quaestionum in Genesim* (*MPL* 23. 948).

Lord blows upon it . . . but the word of our God will stand forever" ⟨Isa. 40:6-8⟩. It seems to me very forced to apply this to the
subject of grace and free choice. Jerome takes "spirit" in this place
to mean the divine wrath, "flesh" for the natural weakness of
mankind which avails nought against God, and "flower" for the
glory which is born from the happiness of corporeal things. The
Jews gloried in the Temple, in circumcision, in sacrificial victims;
the Greeks gloried in their wisdom. Now in the gospel the wrath
of God is revealed from heaven, and all that glory is withered. Yet
not all human desire is flesh, but there is that part of man which
is called his soul, and that which is called his spirit, with which we
strive after virtue, which part of the soul is called the reason (or
hēgemonikon, that is, the "governing part") , unless there was not
among the philosophers a single man who strove for virtue, who
taught that we should sooner die a thousand deaths than commit
evil, even though we knew that nobody would ever know of it, and
that God would pardon it. That does not mean that corrupt reason does not often judge falsely. "Ye know not," said the Lord "of
what spirit ye are." In their error they sought vengeance, as fire
descended from heaven at the prayer of Elijah, and burned captains of fifty with their men and followers. And there is also in
good men a human spirit from the Spirit of God, as Paul declares
in Rom. 8⟨:16⟩: "It is the Spirit himself bearing witness with our
spirit that we are children of God." So that if anybody should wish
to argue that the most excellent part of human nature is none other
than flesh, that is, wicked desire, I would readily yield—if he
proves his assertion by the testimony of Holy Scripture! "That
which is born of the flesh is flesh, and that which is born of the
Spirit is spirit" ⟨John 3:6⟩. Moreover, John teaches that those who
believe the gospel are born of God and become sons of God, yes
even Gods. And Paul distinguishes the carnal man, who knows
not the things of God, from the spiritual man who judges all
things. Elsewhere he calls him a new creature in Christ. If the
whole man, even reborn in faith, is none other than flesh, where
is the spirit which is born of the Spirit? Where is the son of God?
Where is the new creature? I wish to be instructed on these points.
Meanwhile, I shall make full use of the authority [40] of the Fathers
who say that there are certain seeds of virtue implanted in the
minds of men by which they in some way see and seek after virtue,
but mingled with grosser affections which incite them to other

[40] *"Abutor"*: Luther (p. 277, and n. 84) plays on the double sense of the
word, and in effect accuses Erasmus of "abusing" the authority of the Fathers.

things. It is this flexible will which is called free choice and, although on account of the propensity to sin which remains in us, our will is perhaps more prone to evil than to good, yet no one is actually forced to do evil except with his own consent.

Again, his quotation from Jer. 10⟨:23⟩: "I know, O Lord, that the way of man is not in himself; that it is not in any man to walk and direct his steps." But this text refers rather to the outcome of joyous and sorrowful experiences than to the power of free choice. For it frequently happens that when men most fear to encounter evil, they are most caught up in it. Nor is freedom of choice taken away on that account, either from those who suffer, because they had not foreseen coming evil, or from those who inflict it, because they do not afflict their enemies in the same mind in which God works these things through them, that is, for their chastisement. Even if you so twist it as to make it apply to free choice, nobody denies that apart from the grace of God, none can hold a straight course in life. We pray every day: "O Lord God, make my way straight in thy sight ⟨Ps. 5:9⟩. Nevertheless, we too meanwhile exert ourselves as best we are able. We pray: "Incline my heart to thy testimonies" ⟨Ps. 119:36⟩. One who seeks help does not cease from trying. Again, Prov. 16⟨:1⟩: "It is for man to make ready the heart, but the government of the tongue is from the Lord." And this refers to the outcome of events which can befall or not befall altogether apart from the loss of eternal salvation. And how is a man to prepare his heart, since Luther says that all things happen by necessity? And in the same passage it says: "Commit your work to the Lord, and your plans will be established" ⟨Prov. 16:3⟩. You hear "your work," "your plans," neither of which things can be said if God works in us both good and evil. "The beginning of a good life is pity and truth." There are a host of other passages which are on the side of those who support free choice. As to his quotation from the same chapter, v. 4: "The Lord has made everything for its purpose, even the wicked for the day of trouble"; but God did not create any nature evil in itself, and yet he so directs by his ineffable wisdom that he even makes evil to turn to our good and his glory; for he did not create Lucifer evil but he kept him for eternal torments who had fallen away of his own free choice and, through Lucifer's malice, he disciplines the godly and punishes the wicked. Nor is that more plausible which he alleges from Prov. 21⟨:1⟩: "The king's heart is a stream of water in the hand of the Lord; he shall turn it wherever he will." He who turns does not immediately coerce the mind; and yet nobody denies, as I said, that God can bring pressure to bear on human planning, can strike down what man willed, and implement in him a new will, and He can even take away man's understanding. That does not mean that free choice does not as a general rule remain ours, so that if Solomon's opinion here is as Luther interprets it, why does he speak particularly of the heart of a king, when all hearts are in the hands of the Lord? This text rather agrees with what we read in Job 34⟨:30⟩: "Who makes the hypocrite to reign, on account of the sins of the people" and, similarly, in Isa. 3⟨:4⟩: "And I will make boys their princes, and effeminates shall rule over them." When God is propitious to his people, and inclines the heart of a king to good things, He does not apply necessity to his will. On the other hand, He is said to incline to evil, when he is offended with the sins of his people, and does not turn back the mind of a foolish prince prone to robbery, war, and tyranny but permits him to be driven along madly, that through his wickedness He may punish his people. Yet if it sometimes happened that God impelled a ruler to wickedness on account of his deserts, there is no need to make this a particular instead of a general rule. Of this sort of testimony which Luther adduces from the book of Proverbs, an immense number of instances could be cited, but they would make for quantity rather than victory. These are the arguments which the rhetoricians like to throw into a debate. They are mostly of a kind which, given a certain interpretation, can be made to support free choice or argue against it.

That which Luther reckons to be his weapon of Achilles [41] and a decisive argument is what Christ says in John 15⟨:5⟩: "Apart from me you can do nothing." And yet to my mind this can be answered in several ways. First, in common parlance, that man is said to do nothing who does not achieve the end for which he strives, although one who strives has often made some progress. In this sense it is very true that without Christ we can do nothing, for he is speaking there of the fruit of the gospel, which does not come except to those who abide in the Vine, that is, Christ Jesus. With such a figure Paul says: "So neither he who plants nor he who waters is anything, but only God who gives the growth" ⟨I Cor. 3:7⟩. That which is of least moment, and in itself useless, he calls "nothing." likewise so in I Cor. 13⟨:2⟩: "If I have not love, I am nothing," and again, v. 3: "I gain nothing." Again, in Rom. 4⟨:17⟩: "He calls into existence the things that do not exist." Again, from Hos. 1⟨:9⟩, the Lord addresses as "not my people" a people despised and rejected. There is a similar figure of speech in

[41] This phrase may refer either to the arrow that killed Achilles or more probably to his invincibility and prowess.

The Psalms: "But I am a worm, and no man" ⟨Ps. 22:6⟩. Other-wise, if you press this word "nothing," then it would not be pos-sible to sin without Christ, for by Christ here I think is meant his grace, unless they fly to that long-exploded idea that sin is nothing. And this is in some sense true, since we can neither live nor move nor have our being without Christ. But they themselves admit that, apart from grace, free choice avails only unto sin, and Luther has placed this at the head of his *Assertion*. To this is relevant also the word of John the Baptist: "A man cannot receive anything unless it is given him from heaven" ⟨John 3:27⟩. But from this it does not follow that there is no strength or use in free choice. The fact that fire warms comes from heaven. The fact that we naturally seek what is profitable and avoid what is harmful, that too is from heaven; that the will after the Fall is impelled to better things, this too is from heaven; that with tears, alms, prayers, we attain the grace which makes us pleasing to God, that too is from heaven.

The Will Is Not Powerless Though It Cannot Attain Its End Without Grace

Nor in the meanwhile does our will achieve nothing, although it does not attain the things that it seeks without the help of grace. But since our own efforts are so puny, the whole is ascribed to God, just as a sailor who has brought his ship safely into port out of a heavy storm does not say: "I saved the ship" but "God saved it." And yet his skill and his labor were not entirely useless. Similarly, the peasant who brings a rich harvest from the fields into his barn does not say: "I have got a fine harvest this year for myself," but "God bestowed it." And yet who would say that the farmer did nothing to provide the harvest? So we say in common speech, "God gave you lovely children," though there was a part played by the father in begetting! And "God gave me back my health," when the doctor did a great deal. Just as we say, "The king conquered his enemies," when yet it was his captains and soldiers who did the work. Nothing happens without rain from heaven, and yet the good earth bears fruit, for bad soil brings forth no good fruit. But since human labor does nothing except when divine favor is also present, the whole is ascribed to the divine beneficence. "Unless the Lord builds the house, those who build it labor in vain. Unless the Lord watches over the city, the watchman stays awake in vain" ⟨Ps. 127:1⟩. Yet meanwhile the care of the workman does not cease from building, nor the vigilance of the watchman from keeping guard. Now, "for it is not you who speak, but the Spirit of your

Father speaking through you" ⟨Matt. 10:20⟩ at first sight seems to take away free choice, but really it takes away from us the anxiety of forethought, because we are about to speak in Christ's cause. Otherwise, all preachers would sin who prepare themselves by study for divine service. It is not to be expected by all that they should receive the same gift as the unlettered disciples who received at the same time the Holy Spirit and the gift of tongues. And if at any time the Spirit inspired them, yet in speaking, their will was conformed to the breath of the Spirit, and acted together with the directing Spirit. And this plainly is a case of free choice, unless we are to suppose that God spoke through the mouths of the apostles, just as he spoke to Balaam through an ass's mouth. More important is the passage in John 6⟨:44⟩: "No one can come to me unless the Father who sent me draws him." The word "draws" sounds as though it implied necessity and excluded freedom of choice. But in truth this drawing is not an act of violence, but it makes you will what yet you may refuse, just as if we show a boy an apple and he runs for it, and as we show a sheep a green willow twig and he follows it, so God knocks at our soul with his grace, and we willingly embrace it. In this way is also to be interpreted in the same Gospel, ch. 14⟨:6⟩: "No one comes to the Father, but by me." As the Father glorifies the Son, the Son the Father, so the Father draws to the Son, the Son to the Father. But we are so drawn that we then run willingly. Thus you read in The Song of Songs: "Draw me after you, let us make haste," etc.

Out of Paul's letters some passages can be collected which appear to destroy entirely the power of free choice. Of such a kind is II Cor. 3⟨:5⟩: "Not that we are sufficient of ourselves to claim anything as coming from us; our sufficiency is from God." Yet here we can defend free choice in two ways. For first, some of the orthodox Fathers distinguish three stages of human action: the first is thought, the second will, the third accomplishment. In the first and the third they give no place for the working of free choice; our soul is impelled by grace alone to think good thoughts, and by grace alone is moved to perform what it has thought. Yet in the second phase, that is, in consenting, grace and the human will act together, but in such a way that grace is the principal cause, and the secondary cause our will. Since, however, the sum of the matter is attributed to him who brings the whole to performance, man cannot achieve anything by his own good works, and even the fact that he can consent and cooperate with divine grace is itself the work of God. Again, this preposition *ex* means the origin and source, and therefore Paul specifically says "from us" as meaning "out of us," *"aph heautōn hōs ex heauton,"* that is, *"ex nobis ipsis."* This could be said even by the man who admitted that man really can achieve something by his own natural powers, since man has not these powers from himself. For who denies that all good proceeds from God, as from a fountain? And this, too, Paul frequently teaches, in order to take away from us our arrogance and self-confidence, as he says elsewhere, "What have you that you did not receive? If, then, you received it, why do you boast as if it were not a gift?" You note "boast," which he represses with this saying. The servant who gave account to his master of the gains accruing to his money would have heard the same sentiment if he had claimed for himself the praise for such well-placed investments: "What have you that you did not receive?" And yet, because of his diligent endeavors, he is praised by the Lord. James sings the same song in ch. 1⟨:17⟩: "Every good endowment and every perfect gift is from above." So Paul, Eph. 1⟨:11⟩: "Who accomplishes all things according to the counsel of his will." And the upshot of it is that we should not arrogate anything to ourselves but attribute all things we have received to the divine grace, which called us when we were turned away, which purified us by faith, which gave us this gift, that our will might be *synergos* ("fellow-worker") with grace, although grace is itself sufficient for all things and has no need of the assistance of any human will.

Man's Cooperation with God

But as to the phrase in Phil. 2⟨:13⟩: "For God is at work in us, both to will and to work for his good pleasure," this does not exclude free choice, for when Paul says, "for his good pleasure," if you refer it to man, as Ambrose interprets it, you understand by it that a good will cooperates with the action of grace. And there immediately precedes the sentence: "Work out your own salvation with fear and trembling," from which you understand that God works in us and that our will and our carefulness rest on God. And lest any should reject this interpretation, there precedes, as we have seen, this passage "Work out your own salvation" (*ergazesthe*), which more accurately means *"operari"* than the word *energein*, which is reserved for God (*"ho energōn"*), for *energei* properly refers to that which acts and impels. But since *ergazesthai* and *energein* have the same force, this passage certainly teaches that both man and God work. But what does man achieve in addition, if our will is to God as a vase to a potter? "For it is not you who speak, but the Spirit of your Father speaking through you" ⟨Matt.

10:20⟩—this was said to the apostles. And yet Peter says in Acts 4⟨:8⟩: "Then Peter, filled with the Holy Spirit, said to them . . ." How can these contraries agree—you shall not speak, but the Spirit; and Peter spoke, full of the Spirit—unless the Spirit so speaks in the apostles that they themselves speak under the influence of the Spirit? And yet it is true that they do not speak; not that they do nothing, but that they themselves are not the prime authors of the words. So we read concerning Stephen: "But they could not withstand the wisdom and the Spirit with which he spoke" ⟨Acts 6:10⟩, and yet he himself addressed the Council. So Paul: "It is no longer I who live, but Christ who lives in me" ⟨Gal. 2:20⟩, and yet he says that the just man lives by faith. How, then, does the living not live? Because he makes his life acceptable to the Spirit of God. And in I Cor. 15⟨:10⟩: "Though it was not I, but the grace of God which is with me"; if Paul did nothing, why did he previously say that he had done something? "I worked harder than any of them" ⟨v. 10⟩. If what he said was true, why does he here correct it as though he disavowed it? But the correction did not mean to convey that he had done nothing, but that he should not seem to ascribe to his own powers that which he did with the help of the grace of God. So that the correction excluded the suspicion of insolence, not collaboration in the work. God in fact does not wish man to ascribe anything to himself, even if there were something which he had some right so to ascribe. When you have done all that which you have been enjoined to do, say, "We are unworthy servants; we have done that which it was our duty to do." But has not he who keeps all the commandments of God done something remarkable (I do not know that such a one can be found)? And yet if such there are, they have their orders; they are to say: "We are unworthy servants" ⟨Luke 17:10⟩. It is not denied that they have done what they have done, but they are taught to avoid a dangerous arrogance. Man speaks in one way, God in another. Man says, "I am a man; I am a servant and a useless servant." What does God say? "Well done, good servant" ⟨Luke 19:17⟩ and, "No longer do I call you servants . . . but I have called you friends" ⟨John 15:15⟩. Instead of calling them servants, he calls them brothers. And those who call themselves unworthy servants, he calls his sons, and those who now proclaim themselves to be useless servants hear from the Lord: "Come, O blessed of my Father" ⟨Matt. 25:34⟩ and hear commemorated the good deeds that they did not know they had performed.

I consider the best key toward the understanding of Holy Scripture is to consider what theme is examined in that passage; when that is determined, it will be useful to gather together what in parables and similitudes is relevant to our purpose. In the parable of the steward who on the eve of his dismissal changes fraudulently the debts owed by the debtors to his master, how many details are there which are not essential to the meaning of the parable! There is simply this to be drawn from it—that each should study in earnest to bestow generously for the help of his neighbors those things which God has given him, before death shall take him away. So it is in the parable, which recently we have just touched on, Luke 17⟨:7–9⟩: "Will any one of you, who has a servant plowing or keeping sheep, say to him when he has come in from the field, 'Come at once and sit down at table'? Will he not rather say to him: 'Prepare supper for me, and gird yourself and serve me, till I eat and drink; and afterward you shall eat and drink'? Does he thank the servant because he did what was commanded?" I think not. The sum of this parable is that those who simply fulfill the Lord's command should strenuously perform their tasks, yet take no credit to themselves on this account. Besides, the Lord himself contradicts this parable when he himself takes the part of a servant and treats his disciples as though they were guests of honor. And he gives thanks when he says: "Well done, good servant," and: "Come, O blessed." And so he did not go on to say: "And when you have done all, the Lord will not reckon you worthy of any grace, and he will reckon you unworthy servants," but he says: "You are to call yourselves unworthy servants," so Paul, who labored more abundantly than they, calls himself the least of the apostles and unworthy of the name of an apostle. Similarly, in Matt. 10⟨:29⟩: "Are not two sparrows sold for a penny? And not one of them falls to the ground without your Father."

First, you must pay attention to what God is doing here, for he does not wish to teach a kind of Diomedean necessity,[42] as they say, but he puts forward this example, that he may rid the disciples of the fear of men, that they should know themselves to be in God's care and that they cannot be harmed by men without his permission, and that he would not give that permission were it not expedient for them and for the gospel. And Paul says in another place, I Cor. 9⟨:9⟩: "Doth God care for oxen?" It seems that there is here, as in the following passage in the Gospel, a hyperbole: "But even the hairs of your head are all numbered" ⟨Matt. 10:30⟩. So many hairs fall to the ground every day, and shall these be accounted for? What is this hyperbole intended to convey then?

[42] For this allusion, see Appendix. In fact, the phrase merely means "necessity" and is illustrated by a picturesque story.

Surely that which follows: "Fear not"! Just as therefore these figures of speech take away the fear of men, and confirm confidence toward God, without whose providence nothing at all happens, so those figures we have adduced above are not intended to take away free choice, but to deter us from presumption, which is hateful to God. It is safer to ascribe the whole to God, for he is kind, and he not only renders to us what is ours, but what is his he commands to be ours also. How is the prodigal son said to have wasted his substance if there was no portion in his own hand? What he had he received from his father. We, too, confess all our natural powers to be gifts given us by God. He had his portion even then when it was in his father's hand, and he had it more safely.

What, then, does it mean that he demanded his portion and went away from his father? Plainly it means to arrogate the gifts of nature to ourselves, and instead of turning them to fulfill the commands of God, to employ them to satisfy the lusts of the flesh. What is hunger? It is the affliction whereby God arouses the mind of a sinner, to make him know and hate himself, and to be smitten with a longing for the Father whom he has left. What is meant by the son talking to himself and meditating confession and return? It is the will of man turning himself toward the impulse of grace, which is, as we said, called prevenient grace. What is meant by the father going to meet his son? It is the grace of God which bears onward our will that we may perform what we will. This interpretation, were it my own, would surely be more probable than that of those who, to prove that the will of man achieves nothing, interpret "Stretch out your hand to whatever you wish" as meaning "Grace stretches out your hand to whatever it wishes"; but since this opinion is handed down from the orthodox Fathers, I do not see why it should be despised. The same applies to the two mites, that is, all her substance, which the widow brings and puts in the treasury.

What Merit Is There Without Free Choice?

I ask what merit can a man arrogate to himself if whatever, as a man, he is able to achieve by his natural intelligence and free choice, all this he owes to the one from whom he receives these powers? And yet God himself imputes this to our merit, that we do not turn our soul away from his grace, and that we apply our natural powers to simple obedience. And this surely goes to show that it is not wrong to say that man does something and yet attributes the sum of all that he does to God as its author, from whom it has come about that he was able to ally his own effort with the grace of God. So Paul says: "But by the grace of God I am what I am" ⟨I Cor. 15:10⟩. He recognizes the author of his being, but when you hear him say: "And his grace toward me was not in vain," you recognize the human will relying on the divine assistance. He means the same when he says: "Though it was not I, but the grace of God which is with me" (the Greek reads, "ē syn emoi"). And that Hebrew preacher of wisdom wishes that the divine wisdom may stand by him to be with him and work with him. It assists as adviser and helper just as an architect helps his assistant, tells him what is to be done, shows him the why and wherefore, puts him right wherever he has begun to go wrong, and comes to his aid where he fails in anything; the work is ascribed to the architect without whose help nothing could be done, and yet nobody would say that the assistant and pupil has done nothing. What the architect is to his pupil, grace is to our will. Thus Paul in Rom. 8⟨:26⟩: "Likewise, the Spirit helps us in our weakness." Nobody calls him weak who can do nothing at all, but rather him whose powers are insufficient to perform what is attempted; nor is he said to be a helper who does everything by himself. The whole Scripture speaks of help, resource, assistance, succour. But who is said to give help except to one who is himself in action? The potter does not help the clay to become a pot, nor the craftsman help an ax to make a stool. Thus to those who maintain that man can do nothing without the help of the grace of God, and conclude that therefore no works of men are good—to these we shall oppose a thesis to me much more probable, that there is nothing that man cannot do with the help of the grace of God, and that therefore all the works of man can be good. Hence, all the passages in the Divine Scriptures which speak of help serve also to establish free choice, and they are innumerable. I shall already have won the day if the issue is settled by the number of testimonies.

EPILOGUE

A Reasonable Approach to the Problem

So far we have brought together those passages in the Holy Scriptures which establish free choice and those on the other side which seem to take it wholly away. Since, however, the Holy Spirit, who is their author, cannot be in conflict with himself, we are forced willy-nilly to seek some moderation of our opinion. Moreover, since different men have assumed different opinions from the same Scripture, each must have looked at it from his own point of view, and in the light of the end he is pursuing. Those who remembered how great is the apathy of mankind in seeking after godliness, and how great an evil it is to despair of salvation; these, while seeking to cure these evils, have fallen unawares into others and attributed too much to free choice. On the other hand, those who ponder how destructive it is of true godliness to trust in one's own powers and merits and how intolerable is the arrogance of some who boast their own works and sell them by measure and weight, just as oil and soap is sold; in their great diligence to avoid this evil, these either so diminish free choice that it avails nothing whatever toward a good work, or even cut its throat entirely by bringing in the absolute necessity of all things. No doubt it seems to them most desirable for the simple obedience of a Christian mind that the whole man should depend on the divine will, place all his hope and confidence in God's promises, recognize how miserable he is of himself, and love God's immense mercy, which he freely bestows on us, and submit himself wholly to God's will, whether he wills to save or destroy: to arrogate to himself no praise for good deeds, but to ascribe all the glory to God's grace, considering man to be nothing else than a living instrument of the divine Spirit, who himself purified and consecrated him with his free goodness, and who, in accordance with his inscrutable wisdom, fashions him and molds him.[43] Here there is nothing that a man can arrogate to his own strength and yet, with sure confidence, he may hope for the reward of eternal life from God, not because he has merited it with his good deeds, but because it seemed in accordance with God's goodness to promise it to those who trust in him. It is man's part to pray without ceasing that God will impart and increase in us his Spirit, giving thanks if anything is done well by us, that we may marvel at his power in all things, everywhere wondering at his wisdom, everywhere loving such goodness. This way of viewing the matter seems to me also compellingly plausible, for it agrees with Holy Scripture, and answers to the confession of those who, once for all dead to the world, are buried together with Christ in baptism, that the flesh having been mortified, they afterward may live and act in the Spirit of Jesus, in whose body they have been implanted by faith. Undoubtedly a godly sentiment and worthy of favor, for it takes away from us all arrogance, and transfers to Christ all the glory and confidence, which takes away from us the fear of men and demons and, though we distrust our own strength, yet makes us

[43] The idea in *"moderatur ac temperat"* is one of restraint and discipline.

EPILOGUE 87

nonetheless strong and of good courage in the Lord. This view we praise to the point of extravagance.

For when I hear that the merit of man is so utterly worthless that all things, even the works of godly men, are sins, when I hear that our will does nothing more than clay in the hand of a potter, when I hear all that we do or will referred to absolute necessity, my mind encounters many a stumbling block. First, why does one so often read that godly men, full of good works, have wrought righteousness and walked in the presence of God, turning neither to the right nor to the left, if the deeds of even the most godly men are sin, and sin of such character that, did the mercy of God not intervene, it would have plunged into hell even him for whom Christ died? How is it that we hear so much about reward if there is no such thing as merit? With what impudence is the obedience of those who obey the divine commands praised, and the disobedience of those who do not obey condemned? Why is there so frequent a mention of judgment in Holy Scriptures if there is no weighing of merits? Or are we compelled to be present at the Judgment Seat if nothing has happened through our own will, but all things have been done in us by sheer necessity? There is the further objection: What is the point of so many admonitions, so many precepts, so many threats, so many exhortations, so many expostulations, if of ourselves we do nothing, but God in accordance with his immutable will does everything in us, both to will and to perform the same? He wishes us to pray without ceasing, to watch, to fight, to contend for the prize of eternal life. Why does he wish anything to be unceasingly prayed for which he has already decreed either to give or not to give, and cannot change his decrees, since he is immutable? Why does he command us to seek with so many labors what he has decided freely to bestow? We are afflicted, we are cast out, we are reviled, we are tortured, we are killed, and thus the grace of God in us strives, conquers, and triumphs. The martyr suffers these torments and yet there is no merit given him, nay, rather, he may be said to sin in exposing his body to torments in hope of eternal life. But why has the most merciful God so willed to work in the martyrs? For a man would seem cruel, if he had decided to give something as a free gift to a friend, not to give it unless that friend were tortured to the point of despair.

But when we come to so dark a depth of the divine counsel, perhaps we shall be ordered to adore that which it is not right to pursue. The human mind will say: "He is God, he can do what he wills, and since his nature is altogether the best, everything

that he wills must also be for the best." This, too, can be said
plausibly enough, that God crowns his gifts in us, and orders his
benefit to be our reward and what he has worked in us that he
wills by his free goodness to be imputed to those who trust in him
as though it were a debt to them, wherewith they may attain
eternal life. But I know not how they are to appear consistent who
so exaggerate the mercy of God to the godly that as regards others
they almost make him cruel. Pious ears can admit the benevolence
of one who imputes his own good to us; but it is difficult to explain how it can be a mark of his justice (for I will not speak of
mercy) to hand over others to eternal torments in whom he has
not deigned to work good works, when they themselves are incapable of doing good, since they have no free choice or, if they
have, it can do nothing but sin. If a certain king should give a
huge reward to somebody who did nothing in a war while those
who behaved bravely got nothing more than their usual pay, perhaps he could reply to the murmuring soldiers: "What wrong do
you suffer if it pleases me to be freely generous to this man?" But
who could seem just and clement if he crowned with highest
honors a general for his good conduct, a general whom he had
sent to war abundantly provided with what he needed, with ma-
chines, with men, with money, while he put another to death for
failure after having sent him to battle with no equipment at all?
Would not the dying man have a right to say to the king: "Why do
you punish in me what was done through your fault? If you had
fitted me out like him, I would have won too." Again, if a master
were to free a slave who had merited nothing, he might have reason perhaps to say to the other servants who murmured against
this, "You are no worse off if I am kinder to this one; you have
your due." But anyone would deem a master cruel and unjust who
flogged his slave to death because his body was too short or his
nose too long or because of some other inelegance in his form.
Would not the slave rightly cry out to his master under the blows,
"Why am I punished for what I cannot help?" and he would say
this with still more justice if it were in his lord's power to alter
the bodily blemish of his slave, as it is in the power of God to
change our will, or if the lord had himself given the slave this de-
formity which had offended, as for example by cutting off his nose
or making his face hideous with scars. In this same way God, in the
view of some, works even evil in us. Again, as concerns the precepts, if a lord were constantly to order a slave who was bound
by the feet in a treadmill, "Go there, do that, run, come back,"
with frightful threats if he disobeyed and did not meanwhile re-
lease him, and even made ready the lash if he disobeyed, would not

the slave rightly call the master either mad or cruel who beat a man to death for not doing what he was unable to do?

Further, when these people so immensely exaggerate faith and love in God, our ears are not offended, for we judge that the fact that the life of Christians is everywhere so corrupted by sins proceeds from no other cause than that our faith is so cold and sleepy, since it makes our belief in God a matter of words, and floats upon our lips, according to Paul: "For man believes with his heart and so is justified" (Rom. 10:10). I will not specially argue with those who refer all things to faith as the fountain and head of all, even though to me faith seems to be born from charity and charity in turn from faith: certainly charity nourishes faith just as oil feeds the light in a lantern; the more strongly we love him the more freely do we trust him. Nor are there lacking some who think of faith as the beginning of salvation rather than the sum, but these questions are not here in dispute.

A Mediating View, and a Parable of Grace and Free Choice

But this, meanwhile, is to be avoided, that while we are wholly absorbed in extolling faith, we overthrow free choice, for if this is done away with I do not see any way in which the problem of the righteousness and the mercy of God is to be explained. Since the Early Fathers could not extricate themselves from these difficulties, some of them were driven to posit two Gods: one of the Old Testament, whom they represented as just, but not as good; another of the New Testament who was good but not just—whose wicked opinion Tertullian sufficiently exploded. Manichaeus, as we have said, dreamed of two natures in man, one which could not avoid sin, and another which could not avoid doing good. Pelagius, while he feared for the justice of God, ascribed too much to free choice, and those are not so far distant from him who ascribe such power to the human will that by their own natural strength they can merit, through good works, that supreme grace by which we are justified. These seem to me, through showing man a good hope of salvation, to have wished to incite him to more endeavor, just as Cornelius by his prayers and alms deserved to be taught by Peter, and the eunuch by Philip, and as the blessed Augustine when he avidly sought Christ in the letters of Paul deserved to find him. Here we can placate those who cannot bear that man can achieve any good work which he does not owe to God, when we say that it is nevertheless true that the whole work is due to God, without whom we do nothing; that the contribution of free choice is extremely small, and that this itself is part of the divine gift, that we can turn our souls to those things pertaining to salvation, or work together (*synergein*) with grace.

After his battle with Pelagius, Augustine became less just toward free choice than he had been before. Luther, on the other hand, who had previously allowed something to free choice, is now carried so far in the heat of his defense as to destroy it entirely. But I believe it was Lycurgus [44] who was rebuked by the Greeks because, in his hatred of drunkenness, he gave the order for the vines to be cut down, when he should rather, by giving access to the fountains, have excluded drunkenness without destroying the use of wine.

For in my opinion free choice could have been so established as to avoid that confidence in our merits and the other dangers which Luther avoids, without counting those which we have mentioned already, and without losing those benefits that Luther admires. That is to my mind the advantage of the view of those who attribute entirely to grace the first impulse which stirs the soul, yet in the performance allow something to human choice which has not withdrawn itself from the grace of God. For since there are three stages in all things—, beginning, progress, and end—they attribute the first and last to grace, and only in progress say that free choice achieves anything, yet in such wise that in each individual action two causes come together, the grace of God and the will of man: in such a way, however, that grace is the principal cause and the will secondary, which can do nothing apart from the principal cause, since the principal is sufficient in itself. Just as fire burns by its native force, and yet the principal cause is God who acts through the fire, and this cause would of itself be sufficient, without which the fire could do nothing if he withdrew from it.

On this more accommodating view, it is implied that a man owes all his salvation to divine grace, since the power of free choice is exceedingly trivial [45] in this regard and this very thing which it can do is a work of the grace of God who first created free choice and then freed it and healed it. And so we can appease, if they are capable of being appeased, those who cannot bear that man should own anything good which he does not owe to God. He owes Him this indeed but otherwise and under another name, just as an inheritance which legally comes to children is not called a benevolence because this is a common right of all men; but if something is given beyond the bounds of common law, it is called a benevo-

---

[44] There is no reference to this in Plutarch's life of Lycurgus, and the authority Erasmus had in mind is uncertain.
[45] "*Perpusillum*"; see Luther, p. 291.

lence, and yet the children's debt to their parents is called inheritance.

Let us try to express our meaning in a parable. A human eye that is quite sound sees nothing in the dark, a blind one sees nothing in the light; thus the will though free can do nothing if grace withdraws from it, and yet when the light is infused, he who has sound eyes can shut off the sight of the object so as not to see, can avert his eyes, so that he ceases to see what he previously saw. When anyone has eyes that once were blinded through some defect, but can now see, he owes even more gratitude. For first he owes it to his Creator, then to the physician. Just as before sin our eye was sound, so now it is vitiated by sin; what can a man who sees boast for himself? And yet he has some merit to claim if prudently he shuts or averts his eyes. Take another illustration: A father lifts up a child who has fallen and has not yet strength to walk, however much it tries, and shows it an apple which lies over against it; the child longs to run, but on account of the weakness of its limbs it would have fallen had not its father held its hand and steadied its footsteps, so that led by its father it obtains the apple which the father willingly puts in its hand as a reward for running. The child could not have stood up if the father had not lifted it, could not have seen the apple had the father not shown it, could not advance unless the father had all the time assisted its feeble steps, could not grasp the apple had the father not put it into his hand. What, then, can the infant claim for itself? And yet it does something. But it has nothing to glory about in its own powers, for it owes its very self to its father. Let us apply this analogy to our relation with God. What, then, does the child do here? It relies with all its powers on the one who lifts it, and it accommodates as best it can its feeble steps to him who leads. No doubt the father could have drawn the child against its will, and the child could have resisted by refusing the outstretched apple; the father could have given the apple without the child's having to run to get it, but he preferred to give it in this way, as this was better for the child. I will readily allow that less is due to our industry in following after eternal life than to the boy who runs to his father's hand.

The Extravagances of Those Who Totally Deny Free Choice

But although we see so little attributed to free choice, yet to some even this seems to be too much. For they would have grace alone to be working in us and our mind in all things to be only passive as an instrument of the divine Spirit, so that good can in no way be said to be ours save insofar as the divine benevolence freely imputes it to us; for grace does not work in us *through,* so much as *in,* free choice, in the same way as a potter works in the clay and not through the clay. But where, then, is there any room for mention of the crown and of the reward? God, they say, crowns his own gifts in us and orders his benefit to be our reward, and what he has wrought in us, he deigns to impute to us making us a partner in his Heavenly Kingdom. This I do not see, how they maintain a free choice which is quite inactive. For if they were to say that it is acted upon by grace in such a way as to cooperate with it, that would be an easier explanation; just as according to the scientists our body receives from the soul its first motion, nor can it move without the soul, and yet not only does it move itself, but it also moves other things and, as a partner in the work, is called to share in glory. But if God works in us as the potter in clay, what can be imputed to us, for good or ill? The soul of Jesus Christ we do not wish to call in question here, though that also was an instrument of the Holy Spirit. For if the infirmity of the flesh means that human merit is diminished, yet he also feared death and wished not for his own will to be done, but his Father's; and yet these people admit that he is the fountain of all merits, who yet take away from the rest of the saints all the merit of good work. Moreover, those who deny free choice entirely, but say that all things happen by absolute necessity, aver that God works in all men not only good but even evil works. Whence it would seem to follow that just as man can by no reason be said to be the author of good works, so he can in no way be said to be the author of evil works. Although this view seems plainly to ascribe cruelty and injustice to God, a sentiment offensive to pious ears (for he would not be God if there were found in him any blemish or imperfection), yet its champions can make this plea in support of their unconvincing case: "He is God. His work must necessarily be of supreme excellence and beauty; so if you look at the order of the universe, even things evil in themselves are good seen as a whole, and show forth the glory of God, nor is it for any creature to pass judgment on the counsel of God but to submit himself entirely to it; and so, if God chooses to condemn this or that man, he ought not to complain, but embrace whatever is His good pleasure, being fully persuaded that all things are done by Him for the best, nor could they be done in any other way than the best. Otherwise, who could endure a man who said to God, 'Why did you not make me an angel?' Could not God fairly reply, 'Impudent one, if I had made you a frog, what would you have to complain about?' And if a frog were to complain to God, 'Why did you not make me a peacock bright with many-colored plumage?' would he not rightly reply: 'Ungrateful wretch, I could have made you a mushroom or an onion. Now you can leap, drink, and sing.' Again, if a snake or a basilisk said, 'Why did you make me an animal shunned by men as deadly to all creatures, rather than a sheep?' What would God reply? Perhaps he would say: 'So it seemed good to me and in fitness with the beauty and order of the universe. There is no more injustice in it in your case than for flies and mosquitoes and other insects, each one of which I have so fashioned as a marvel to behold. The spider is not less admirable and beautiful because it is different from the elephant, nay, there is more to wonder at in the spider than in the elephant. Is it not enough for you to be an animal perfect in your species? Poison was not given to you to kill, but that you may defend with this weapon yourself and your offspring, just as the ox has horns, and lions their claws, the wolf his teeth, and the horse his hooves. Each kind of animal has his usefulness: the horse bears burdens, the ox plows, the ass and dog assist labor, the sheep brings to man the boon of food and clothing, and you provide material for remedies.' "

But let us cease from arguing from these creatures which lack reason. Our disputation was about man, whom God made in his image and likeness and for whose sake he created all things. When indeed we see some born with the most comely bodies, with outstanding qualities, as though they were born to virtue; again, others with monstrous bodies, others liable to horrible diseases, others with minds so stupid that they are but little removed from inanimate brutes and some even more brutish than the beasts, and others with minds so prone to crime that they seem almost borne onward by fate, and others openly mad and demoniac; in what ways shall we explain here the problem of the justice and mercy of God? Or shall we say with Paul: "O the depth of the riches and wisdom and knowledge of God!" (Rom. 11:33), for this I think to be better than with wicked boldness to judge the divine counsels, which are beyond the investigation of man. But it would be far more difficult to explain why God in some crowns his own benefits with immortal glory, and in others punishes his own wrongdoings with eternal punishment. To defend this paradox there is need for many more paradoxes if the line of battle is to be assured against the other side. They immeasurably exaggerate original sin, by which they would have even the most excellent powers of human nature to be so corrupt that they can do nothing of themselves except to be ignorant of God and to hate him. And they aver that, even though justified by faith, a man cannot of himself do anything but sin. And that very proneness toward sin which is left in us by the sin of our first parents, they will have it to be sin and indeed invincible sin, so that there is no precept of God which even a man justified by faith can fulfill; but so many commandments of God have no other end than to magnify the grace of God, which bestows salvation upon men without consideration of merit.

Meanwhile, these people seem to me in one place to restrict the divine mercy that in another they may widen it, as though one should provide for one's guests a very slender lunch so that the dinner may seem more sumptuous, in a way imitating those artists who, when they want to give the illusion of light in one part of their picture, darken with shadows the parts next to it. They begin, therefore, by making God almost cruel, since on account of another's sin he thus rages against the whole human race, especially when they have repented of their sins and have grievously expiated them all their days. But when they say that even those who are justified by faith do nothing but sin, nay, that in loving and trusting God we earn God's hatred, do they not here make extremely niggardly the grace of God, who so justifies man by faith that he still does nothing but sin? Furthermore, when God burdens man with so many commandments that serve for no other purpose than to make him hate God more and be more terribly damned, do not they make him worse than the tyrant Dionysius of Sicily [46] who deliberately made many laws that he suspected the majority would not keep in the absence of restraint, and at first took no notice, and then when he saw that everybody was breaking them, he began to summon them to punishment, in this way bringing everyone into his power? And yet his laws were of such a kind that they could easily be kept if anyone wished.

I will not now examine the reasons why they say that all the commandments of God are impossible to us, for that was not my intention; I simply wished to show by the way that these men, by their excess of zeal in enlarging in one place the role of grace in the plan of salvation, obscure it in other places. And I fail to see

---

[46] This presumably refers to Dionysius I, tyrant of Sicily from 405 to 367 B.C. Our chief authority for his life is Diodorus Siculus, in his *Historical Library*, Books xiii to xv. In xiii.91–96, Diodorus lists many similarly repressive measures taken by Dionysius but does not allude to that here mentioned.

how these points of view can be consistent. Having cut the throat of free choice, they teach that a man is now led by the Spirit of Christ, whose nature will not suffer any association with sin. And yet these same people assert that even when he has received grace, a man does nothing but sin. Luther seems to delight in this kind of extravagant statement, for he seeks to put down the extravagances of others in the words of the proverb by cutting a poor knot with a blunt chopper.[47] This boldness on the part of some goes as far as hyperbole, for they sell not only their own merits, but those of all the saints. And what works are these? Singing, the murmuring of psalms, the eating of fish, fasting, clothes, titles. This nail Luther has driven out with another when he says that all the merits of the saints are nothing but that all the deeds of men, however holy, have been sins, bringing eternal damnation, unless the mercy of God came to the rescue.

The Dire Results of Exaggerated Views

One party has made a considerable profit out of confessions and satisfactions, with which they marvelously encumbered the consciences of men, and likewise out of purgatory, concerning which they have asserted certain paradoxes. This fault the other side corrected by saying that confession is an invention of Satan; the most moderate of them say that confession is not compulsory and there is no need of satisfaction for sins, since Christ has paid the penalty for all sins; and finally that there is no purgatory. The one side go so far as to profess that the commands of petty priors are obligatory on pain of hellfire, nor do they hesitate to promise eternal life to him who shall obey. The opposite party meet this extravagance by saying that all the decrees of popes, councils, bishops, are heretical and anti-Christian. Thus one party has enlarged the power of the pontiff beyond all bounds (*"panu hyperbolikōs"*), the other speaks openly of him in terms that I would not dare repeat. Again, one party says that the vows of monks and priests are perpetually binding on pain of hellfire, the other says that such vows are thoroughly wicked, that they are not to be undertaken, and if undertaken are not to be kept.

It is from the conflict of such exaggerated views that have been born the thunders and lightnings which now shake the world. And if each side continues to defend bitterly its own exaggerations, I can see such a fight coming as was that between Achilles and Hector whom, since they were both equally ruthless, only

[47] Another proverb expounded by Erasmus in the *Adagia*. See Appendix.

death could divide. It is commonly said that the only way to make a crooked stick straight is to bend it in the opposite direction: [48] that may be right for the correction of morals, but whether it is tolerable in the matter of doctrine I do not know. In exhorting or dissuading, I see that there *is* sometimes a place for hyperbole; thus to give confidence to a timid man you may say: "Fear nothing, it is God who will speak and act all things in you." And to rebuke the insolence of a wicked man it may be useful, perhaps, to say that a man is nothing but sin: and against those who wish their dogmas to be made equal with Scripture you may usefully say: "Man is nothing but a liar." But where axioms are put forward in the disputing of truth, I do not consider paradoxes of this kind should be used, for they are almost riddles, and in these matters it is moderation which pleases me at any rate. Pelagius has no doubt attributed too much to free choice, and Scotus quite enough, but Luther first mutilated it by cutting off its right arm; then not content with this he thoroughly cut the throat of free choice and despatched it. I prefer the view of those who do attribute much to free choice, but most to grace.

Nor was it necessary, in avoiding the Scylla of arrogance, that you should be wrecked on the Charybdis of despair or indolence. Nor in mending a dislocated limb need you twist another, but rather put it back into place; nor is it necessary so to fight with an enemy in front that incautiously you receive a wound in the back. The result of this moderation will be the achievement of some good work, albeit imperfect, from which no man can arrogate anything to himself: there will be some merit, but such that the sum *is* owed to God. There is an abundance in human life of weakness, vices, crimes, so that if any man wishes to look at himself he can easily put down his conceit, although we do not assert that man however justified can do nothing but sin, especially since Christ calls him reborn, and Paul, a new creature. Why, you will say, grant anything to free choice? In order to have something to impute justly to the wicked who have voluntarily come short of the grace of God, in order that the calumny of cruelty and injustice may be excluded from God, that despair may be kept away from us, that complacency may be excluded also, and that we may be incited to endeavor. For these reasons, almost everyone admits free choice, but as inefficacious apart from the perpetual grace of God, lest we arrogate aught to ourselves. One may object, to what does free choice avail if it accomplishes nothing? I reply, to what does the whole man avail if God so works in him as a potter with clay and just as he could act on a pebble?

[48] Another proverb from the *Adagia*. See Appendix.

As to Which Side Is Right, Let the Reader Be Judge

And so, if it is now sufficiently demonstrated that this matter is such that it is not conducive to godliness to search into it deeply, particularly before the unlearned; if we have shown that our opinion is supported by more and plainer testimonies of Scripture than the other; if it is agreed that Holy Scripture is in very many places obscured by figures of speech, or even that in some places it seems at first sight to be self-contradictory; and if, by reason of this, we are forced willy-nilly to forsake the literal sense of the words and seek their meaning modified by interpretation; finally, if it has been shown how inconvenient, not to say absurd, are the consequences if free choice is entirely taken away; if it has been clearly shown that, in accepting this conclusion, nothing is destroyed of what Luther has written in pious and Christian vein of the unbounded love of God, of rejecting all confidence in merits, of works and of our own powers, and of putting our whole confidence in God and his promises: now, then, I would ask that the reader will also consider whether it is reasonable to condemn the opinion of so many doctors of the Church, which the consensus of so many centuries and peoples has approved, and to accept in their stead certain paradoxes on account of which the Christian world is now in an uproar.

If these latter are sound, I naïvely confess the dimness of my own mind, because I do not follow them. Certainly I do not knowingly resist the truth, and with all my heart I favor true evangelical liberty and detest whatever is opposed to the gospel. Nor do I act here the part of a judge, as I have said, but of a disputant, and yet I can truly affirm that in this dispute I have kept the oath, which formerly in capital causes was demanded from sworn judges. Although I am getting on in years, I am not, and shall never be, ashamed or annoyed to learn from any young man if he teaches me more evident truths with evangelical courtesy. Here I know I shall hear somebody say: "Let Erasmus learn Christ and bid farewell to human prudence. These things nobody can understand unless he has the Spirit of God." If I do yet understand what Christ is, I have indeed so far been wandering wide of the mark. However, I would willingly learn the Spirit that animated so many doctors and Christian peoples, for it is demonstrable that the people have understood the teaching of their bishops for thirteen hundred years and yet have not understood this.

> I have completed my discourse; now let others pass judgment.

LUTHER

De Servo Arbitrio

On the Bondage of the Will

by

Martin Luther

THE TEXT

INTRODUCTION ⟨*WA* 18, 600–602⟩

TO THE VENERABLE MASTER ERASMUS OF ROTTERDAM,
MARTIN LUTHER SENDS GRACE AND PEACE IN CHRIST.

*Luther Explains His Delay in Replying and Admits
Erasmus' Superior Talent*

THAT I HAVE TAKEN SO LONG TO REPLY TO YOUR *Diatribe Concerning Free Choice,* venerable Erasmus, has been contrary to everyone's expectation and to my own custom; for hitherto I have seemed not only willing to accept, but eager to seek out, opportunities of this kind for writing. There will perhaps be some surprise at this new and unwonted forbearance—or fear!—in Luther, who has not been roused even by all the speeches and letters his adversaries have flung about, congratulating Erasmus on his victory and chanting in triumph, "Ho, ho! Has that Maccabee, that most obstinate Assertor,[1] at last met his match, and dares not open his mouth against him?" Yet not only do I not blame them, but of myself I yield you a palm such as I have never yielded to anyone before; for I confess not only that you are far

---

[1] The Maccabees were the intrepid leaders of the Jewish revolt against the tyranny of Antiochus Epiphanes (ca. 166 B.C.). "Assertor" refers to Luther's *Assertio* or "Assertion of All the Articles Condemned by the Latest Bull of Leo X" (1521); see above, p. 13 n. 1.

superior to me in powers of eloquence and native genius (which we all must admit, all the more as I am an uncultivated fellow who has always moved in uncultivated circles), but that you have quite damped my spirit and eagerness, and left me exhausted before I could strike a blow.

There are two reasons for this: first, your cleverness in treating the subject with such remarkable and consistent moderation as to make it impossible for me to be angry with you; and secondly, the luck or chance or fate by which you say nothing on this important subject that has not been said before. Indeed, you say so much less, and attribute so much more to free choice than the Sophists [2] have hitherto done (a point on which I shall have more to say later) that it really seemed superfluous to answer the arguments you use. They have been refuted already so often by me,[3] and beaten down and completely pulverized in Philip Melanchthon's *Commonplaces* [4]—an unanswerable little book which in my judgment deserves not only to be immortalized but even canonized. Compared with it, your book struck me as so cheap and paltry that I felt profoundly sorry for you, defiling as you were your very elegant and ingenious style with such trash, and quite disgusted at the utterly unworthy matter that was being conveyed in such rich ornaments of eloquence, like refuse or ordure being carried in gold and silver vases.

You seem to have felt this yourself, from the reluctance with which you undertook this piece of writing. No doubt your conscience warned you that, no matter what powers of eloquence you brought to the task, you would be unable so to gloss it over as to prevent me from stripping away the seductive charm of your words and discovering the dregs beneath, since although I am unskilled in speech, I am not unskilled in knowledge, by the grace of God. For I venture thus with Paul ⟨II Cor. 11:6⟩ to claim knowledge for myself that I confidently deny to you, though I grant you eloquence and native genius such as I willingly and very properly disclaim for myself.

---

[2] The Scholastic theologians.

[3] E.g., in the *Lectures on Romans* (1516), the *Quaestio de viribus et voluntate hominis* and the *Disputatio contra scholasticam theologiam* (1517; *WA* 1, 145 ff.), the *Disputatio Heidelbergae habita*, Th. 13–15 (1518; *WA* 1, 353 ff.), the *Lectures on the Psalms* (1519–1521; *WA* 5, 172 ff., 622 ff.), and the *Assertio omnium articulorum* and *Grund und Ursach* (1521; *WA* 7, 142 ff., 446 ff.).

[4] The *Loci communes rerum theologicarum*, first edition, 1519. Melanchthon was an intimate friend and colleague of Luther, and the *Loci* may be regarded as the first systematic statement of Luther's reforming theology.

What I thought, then, was this. If th
imbibed so little of our teaching or taker
strongly supported by Scripture though
moved by these trivial and worthless th
guments of Erasmus, then they do not c
to their rescue with an answer. Nothin
that would be sufficient for such peop
recourse to thousands of books a tho
might just as well plow the seashore a
try to fill a cask full of holes with water. Those ...
the Spirit who holds sway in our books have had a sufficient ...
from us already, and they can easily dispose of your performances;
but as for those who read without the Spirit, it is no wonder if
they are shaken like a reed by every wind.[5] Why, God himself
could not say enough for such people, even if all his creatures
were turned into tongues.[6] Hence I might well have decided to
leave them alone, upset as they were by your book, along with
those who are delighted with it and declare you the victor.

It was, then, neither pressure of work, nor the difficulty of the
task, nor your great eloquence, nor any fear of you, but sheer disgust, anger, and contempt, or—to put it plainly—my considered
judgment on your *Diatribe* that damped my eagerness to answer
you. I need hardly mention here the good care you take, as you
always do, to be everywhere evasive and equivocal; you fancy yourself steering more cautiously than Ulysses between Scylla and
Charybdis as you seek to assert nothing while appearing to assert
something. How, I ask you, is it possible to have any discussion
or reach any understanding with such people, unless one is clever
enough to catch Proteus?[7] What I can do in this matter, and what
you have gained by it, I will show you later, with Christ's help.

There have, then, to be special reasons for my answering you
at this point. Faithful brethren in Christ are urging me to do so,
and point out that everyone expects it, since the authority of
Erasmus is not to be despised, and the truth of Christian doctrine
is being imperiled in the hearts of many. Moreover, it has at
length come home to me that my silence has not been entirely
honorable, and that I have been deluded by my mundane prudence[8]—or knavery—into insufficient awareness of my duty,

---

[5] Cf. Matt. 11:7.   [6] Cf. Luke 19:40.

[7] A figure of Greek mythology, supposed to have the power of changing himself into different shapes so as to avoid capture. Cf. Ovid, *Metamorphoses*
viii.730 f.; Erasmus, *Adagia* XLIII.

[8] Literally, "the prudence or knavery of my flesh" ("*carnis meae*").

I am under obligation both to the wise and to the fool-
om. 1:14), especially when I am called to it by the entreaties
o many brethren. For although the subject before us demands
ore than an external teacher, and besides him who plants and
him who waters outwardly ⟨I Cor. 3:7⟩, it requires also the Spirit
of God to give the growth and to be a living teacher of living
things inwardly (a thought that has been much in my mind) , yet
since the Spirit is free, and blows not where we will but where he
wills ⟨John 3:8⟩, we ought to have observed that rule of Paul, "Be
urgent in season and out of season" ⟨II Tim. 4:2⟩, for we do not
know at what hour the Lord is coming ⟨Matt. 24:42⟩. There may
be, I grant, some who have not yet sensed the Spirit who informs
my writings, and who have been bowled over by that *Diatribe* of
yours; perhaps their hour has not yet come.

And who knows but that God may even deign to visit you, excellent Erasmus, through such a wretched and frail little vessel
of his as myself, so that in a happy hour—and for this I earnestly
beseech the Father of mercies through Christ our Lord—I may
come to you by means of this book, and win [9] a very dear brother.
For although you think and write wrongly about free choice, yet
I owe you no small thanks, for you have made me far more sure
of my own position by letting me see the case for free choice put
forward with all the energy of so distinguished and powerful a
mind, but with no other effect than to make things worse than
before. That is plain evidence that free choice is a pure fiction;
for, like the woman in the Gospel ⟨Mark 5:25 f.⟩, the more it is
treated by the doctors, the worse it gets. I shall therefore abundantly pay my debt of thanks to you, if through me you become
better informed, as I through you have been more strongly confirmed. But both of these things are gifts of the Spirit, not our own
achievement. Therefore, we must pray to God that he may open
my mouth and your heart, and the hearts of all men, and that he
may himself be present in our midst as the master who informs
both our speaking and hearing.

But from you, my dear Erasmus, let me obtain this request, that
just as I bear with your ignorance in these matters, so you in turn
will bear with my lack of eloquence. God does not give all his
gifts to one man, and "we cannot all do all things"; [10] or, as Paul
says: "There are varieties of gifts, but the same Spirit" ⟨I Cor.
12:4⟩. It remains, therefore, for us to render mutual service with
our gifts, so that each with his own gift bears the burden and need
of the other. Thus we shall fulfill the law of Christ ⟨Gal. 6:2⟩.

[9] *"Lucrifaciam"*; cf. Matt. 18:15; I Cor. 9:19 ff.
[10] *"Non omnia possumus omnes"* (Vergil, *Eclogue* VIII.63) .

PART I. REVIEW OF ERASMUS' PREFACE

Christianity Involves Assertions; Christians Are No Skeptics
⟨WA 603–605⟩

I want to begin by referring to some passages in your Preface, in which you rather disparage our case and puff up your own. I note, first, that just as in other books you censure me for obstinate assertiveness, so in this book you say that you are so far from delighting in assertions that you would readily take refuge in the opinion of the Skeptics wherever this is allowed by the inviolable authority of the Holy Scriptures and the decrees of the Church, to which you always willingly submit your personal feelings, whether you grasp what it prescribes or not. This is the frame of mind that pleases you. ⟨E., p. 37.⟩

I take it (as it is only fair to do) that you say these things in a kindly and peace-loving spirit. But if anyone else were to say them, I should probably go for him in my usual manner; and I ought not to allow even you, excellent though your intentions are, to be led astray by this idea. For it is not the mark of a Christian mind to take no delight in assertions; on the contrary, a man must delight in assertions or he will be no Christian. And by assertion —in order that we may not be misled by words—I mean a constant adhering, affirming, confessing, maintaining, and an invincible persevering; nor, I think, does the word mean anything else either as used by the Latins or by us in our time.

I am speaking, moreover, about the assertion of those things which have been divinely transmitted to us in the sacred writings. Elsewhere we have no need either of Erasmus or any other instructor to teach us that in matters which are doubtful or useless and unnecessary, assertions, disputings, and wranglings are not only foolish but impious, and Paul condemns them in more than one place. Nor are you, I think, speaking of such things in this place—unless, in the manner of some foolish orator, you have chosen to announce one topic and discuss another, like the man with the turbot,[1] or else, with the craziness of some ungodly

---

[1] "Ut ille ad Rhombum": The allusion is obscure, as there are two meanings of the word rhombus. One is "magician's wheel," and examples of this meaning are found in Ovid, Amores, i.8.7, and Propertius, Elegiae ii.28. 35, but it is difficult to see the relevance of either of these passages to Luther's meaning here. Much more probable is an allusion to the other meaning of rhombus, "turbot." In the fourth satire of Juvenal a huge turbot is caught and taken to the emperor Domitian, who holds a solemn council to decide what to do with it. Among the characters is an evil informer named Catullus, who is blind and who sycophantically praises the

writer, you are contending that the article about free choice is doubtful or unnecessary.

Let Skeptics and Academics [2] keep well away from us Christians, but let there be among us "assertors" twice as unyielding as the Stoics themselves. How often, I ask you, does the apostle Paul demand that *plērophoria* (as he terms it [3]) —that most sure and unyielding assertion of conscience? In Rom. 10⟨:10⟩ he calls it "confession," saying, "with the mouth confession is made unto salvation." And Christ says: "Everyone who confesses me before men, I also will confess before my Father" ⟨Matt. 10:32⟩. Peter bids us give a reason for the hope that is in us ⟨I Peter 3:15⟩. What need is there to dwell on this?

Nothing is better known or more common among Christians than assertion. Take away assertions and you take away Christianity. Why, the Holy Spirit is given them from heaven, that a Christian may glorify Christ and confess him even unto death— unless it is not asserting when one dies for one's confession and assertion. Moreover, the Spirit goes to such lengths in asserting, that he takes the initiative and accuses the world of sin ⟨John 16:8⟩, as if he would provoke a fight; and Paul commands Timothy to "exhort" and "be urgent out of season" ⟨II Tim. 4:2⟩. But what a droll exhorter he would be, who himself neither firmly believed nor consistently asserted the thing he was exhorting about! Why, I would send him to Anticyra! [4]

But it is I who am the biggest fool, for wasting words and time on something that is clearer than daylight. What Christian would agree that assertions are to be despised? That would be nothing but a denial of all religion and piety, or an assertion that neither religion, nor piety, nor any dogma is of the slightest importance. Why, then, do you too assert, "I take no delight in assertions," and

---

turbot, groping in one direction while the turbot lies in the other:
*Nemo magis rhombum stupuit; nam plurima dixit/in laevum
conversus, at illi dextra iacebat/belua.*
                                        (Juvenal, *Satires* iv.119–121.)
Here at least we have the idea of a man making a speech off the point, praising something while looking in a different direction, so that Luther's condemnation of Erasmus for taking up one thing and treating another does seem from one aspect like Juvenal's satirical picture of the blind Catullus.

[2] Adherents of the philosophic school of Plato (the Academy), some of whose later followers adopted a skeptical attitude.

[3] Cf. Col. 2:2; I Thess. 1:5; Heb. 6:11; 10:22.

[4] The modern Aspraspitia; a town in Phocis, on the bay of Anticyra, in the Corinthian Gulf; formerly famous for its black hellebore, an herb regarded as a cure for insanity. Cf. Horace, *Satires* ii.3.166; *Ars poetica* 300.

that you prefer this frame of mind to its opposite?

However, you will wish it to be understood that you have said nothing here about confessing Christ and his dogmas. I am rightly reminded of that, and as a favor to you I will waive my right and my custom,[5] and not judge of your heart, but will leave that for another time or to other people. Meanwhile, I advise you to correct your tongue and your pen and to refrain in future from using such expressions, for however upright and honest your heart may be, your speech (which they say is the index of the heart) is not so. For if you think that free choice is a subject we need know nothing about, and one that has nothing to do with Christ, then your language is correct, but your thought is impious. If, on the other hand, you think it is a necessary subject, then your language is impious, though your thought is correct. And in that case, there was no room for such a mass of complaints about useless assertions and wranglings, for what have these to do with the question at issue?

But what will you say about this statement of yours, in which you do not refer to the subject of free choice alone, but to all religious dogmas in general, when you say that if it were allowed by the inviolable authority of the divine writings and the decrees of the Church, you would take refuge in the opinion of the Skeptics, so far are you from delighting in assertions? ⟨E., p. 37.⟩ What a Proteus [6] is in these words "inviolable authority" and "decrees of the Church"! You pose as having a great reverence for the Scriptures and the Church, and yet make it plain that you wish you were at liberty to be a Skeptic. What Christian would talk like that?

If you are speaking about useless and indifferent dogmas, what are you saying that is new? Who would not wish for the liberty to adopt a skeptical attitude here? Indeed, what Christian does not in fact freely make use of this liberty, and condemn those who are committed and bound to any particular opinion? Unless you take Christians in general (as your words almost suggest) to be the kind of people who hold useless dogmas over which they stupidly wrangle and wage battles of assertions. If on the other hand you are speaking of dogmas that are vital, what more ungodly assertion could anyone make than that he wished for the liberty of asserting nothing in such cases?

This is how a Christian will rather speak: So far am I from delighting in the opinion of the Skeptics that, whenever the infirmity

[5] "*Meo iuri et mori cedo.*" Luther's Latin is a *constructio ad sensum.*
[6] See above, p. 103 n. 7.

of the flesh will permit, I will not only consistently adhere to and assert the sacred writings, everywhere and in all parts of them, but I will also wish to be as certain as possible in things that are not vital and that lie outside of Scripture. For what is more miserable than uncertainty?

What, furthermore, are we to say of the comment you add: "To which I everywhere willingly submit my personal feelings, whether I grasp what it prescribes or not"? What are you saying, Erasmus? Is it not enough to have submitted your personal feelings to the Scriptures? Do you submit them to the decrees of the Church as well? What can she decree that is not decreed in the Scriptures? Then what becomes of the liberty and power to judge those who make the decrees, as Paul teaches in I Cor. 14⟨:29⟩: "Let the others judge"? Does it displease you that anyone should sit in judgment on the decrees of the Church, although Paul enjoins it? What new religion, what new humility is this, that you would deprive us by your own example of the power of judging the decrees—of *men,* and subject us in uncritical submission—to *men?* Where does the Scripture of God impose this on us?

Then again, what Christian would so throw the injunctions of Scripture and the Church to the winds, as to say, "Whether I grasp them or not"? Do you submit yourself without caring at all whether you grasp them? Anathema be the Christian who is not certain and does not grasp what is prescribed for him! How can he believe what he does not grasp? For by "grasp" you must mean here to "apprehend with certainty" and not to "doubt like a Skeptic"; for otherwise, what is there in any creature that any man could "grasp" if "grasp" meant perfect knowledge and insight? In that case, there would be no possibility that anyone should at the same time grasp some things and not others; for if he had grasped one thing, he would have grasped all—in God, I mean, since whoever does not "grasp" God never "grasps" any part of his creation.[7]

In short, what you say here seems to mean that it does not matter to you what anyone believes anywhere, so long as the peace of the world is undisturbed, and that in case of danger to life, reputation, property, and goodwill, it is permissible to act like the fellow who said, "Say they yea, yea say I; say they nay, nay say I,"[8]

---

[7] To "grasp" God is as curious an expression in English as *"assequi Deum"* in Latin. Luther means that the whole range of our knowledge of creation is conditional on our knowledge of God; his argument demands the word *assequi* in the last clause which qualifies the whole paragraph, where *assequi* is used throughout. It is, of course, the word Erasmus has used.

[8] Cf. Terence, *Eunuchus* II.ii.21.

and to regard Christian dogmas as no better than philosophical and human opinions, about which it is quite stupid to wrangle, contend, and assert, since nothing comes of that but strife and the disturbance of outward peace. Things that are above us, you would say, are no concern of ours. So, with a view to ending our conflicts, you come forward as a mediator, calling a halt to both sides, and trying to persuade us that we are flourishing our swords about things that are stupid and useless.

That, I say, is what your words seem to mean; and I think you understand, my dear Erasmus, what I am driving at. But as I have said, let the words pass. Meanwhile, I absolve your heart so long as you display it no further. See that you fear the Spirit of God, who tries the minds and hearts ⟨Ps. 7:9; Jer. 11:20⟩, and is not deceived by cleverly devised phrases. For I have said all this so that you may henceforward cease from charging me with obstinacy and willfulness in this matter. By such tactics you only succeed in showing that you foster in your heart a Lucian,[9] or some other pig from Epicurus'[10] sty who, having no belief in God himself, secretly ridicules all who have a belief and confess it. Permit us to be assertors, to be devoted to assertions and delight in them, while you stick to your Skeptics and Academics till Christ calls you too. The Holy Spirit is no Skeptic, and it is not doubts or mere opinions that he has written on our hearts, but assertions more sure and certain than life itself and all experience.

The Clarity of Scripture ⟨WA 606–609⟩

I come now to the second passage, which is of a piece with this. Where you distinguish between Christian dogmas, pretending that there are some which it is necessary to know, and some which it is not, you say that some are secret and some plain to see. ⟨E., p. 38.⟩ You thus either play games with other men's words or else you are trying your hand at a rhetorical sally of your own. You adduce, however, in support of your view, Paul's saying in Rom. 11⟨:33⟩: "O the depth of the riches and wisdom and knowledge of God," and also that of Isa. 40⟨:13⟩: "Who has directed the Spirit of the

---

[9] Lucian of Samosata (ca. A.D. 125–180), a Greek satirist. Erasmus had published an edition of his *Dialogues*.

[10] Epicurus (341–270 B.C.), Greek philosopher; taught that pleasure is the highest good (hedonism). The "pig from Epicurus' sty" is quoted from Horace, *Epistles* i.4.16, where the poet uses the phrase as a humorous description of himself. (Pleasure is not intended in its grosser sense by Epicurus. He means rather "happiness" resulting from the relinquishment of desires, fears, and ambitions. Of course many Greeks and very many Romans corrupted his doctrine to suit their own gross tastes.)

Lord, or what counselor has instructed him?"

It was easy for you to say these things, since you either knew you were not writing to Luther, but for the general public, or you did not reflect that it was Luther you were writing against, whom I hope you allow nonetheless to have some acquaintance with Holy Writ and some judgment in respect of it. If you do not allow this, then I shall force you to it. The distinction I make—in order that I, too, may display a little rhetoric or dialectic—is this: God and the Scripture of God are two things, no less than the Creator and the creature are two things.

That in God there are many things hidden, of which we are ignorant, no one doubts—as the Lord himself says concerning the Last Day: "Of that day no one knows but the Father" ⟨Mark 13:32⟩, and in Acts 1⟨:7⟩: "It is not for you to know times and seasons"; and again: "I know whom I have chosen" ⟨John 13:18⟩, and Paul says: "The Lord knows those who are his" ⟨II Tim. 2:19⟩, and so forth. But that in Scripture there are some things abstruse, and everything is not plain—this is an idea put about by the ungodly Sophists, with whose lips you also speak here, Erasmus; but they have never produced, nor can they produce, a single article to prove this mad notion of theirs. Yet with such a phantasmagoria [11] Satan has frightened men away from reading the Sacred Writ, and has made Holy Scripture contemptible, in order to enable the plagues he has bred from philosophy to prevail in the Church.

I admit, of course, that there are many texts in the Scriptures that are obscure and abstruse, not because of the majesty of their subject matter, but because of our ignorance of their vocabulary and grammar; but these texts in no way hinder a knowledge of all the subject matter of Scripture. For what still sublimer thing can remain hidden in the Scriptures, now that the seals have been broken, the stone rolled from the door of the sepulcher ⟨Matt. 27:66; 28:2⟩, and the supreme mystery brought to light, namely, that Christ the Son of God has been made man, that God is three and one, that Christ has suffered for us and is to reign eternally? Are not these things known and sung even in the highways and byways? Take Christ out of the Scriptures, and what will you find left in them?

The subject matter of the Scriptures, therefore, is all quite accessible, even though some texts are still obscure owing to our ignorance of their terms. Truly it is stupid and impious, when we know that the subject matter of Scripture has all been placed in the

11 *"Talibus autem larvis."*

clearest light, to call it obscure on account of a few obscure words. If the words are obscure in one place, yet they are plain in another; and it is one and the same theme, published quite openly to the whole world, which in the Scriptures is sometimes expressed in plain words, and sometimes lies as yet hidden in obscure words. Now, when the thing signified is in the light, it does not matter if this or that sign of it is in darkness, since many other signs of the same thing are meanwhile in the light. Who will say that a public fountain is not in the light because those who are in a narrow side street do not see it, whereas all who are in the marketplace do see it?

Your reference to the Corycian cave,[12] therefore, is irrelevant; that is not how things are in the Scriptures. Matters of the highest majesty and the profoundest mysteries are no longer hidden away, but have been brought out and are openly displayed before the very doors. For Christ has opened our minds so that we may understand the Scriptures ⟨Luke 24:45⟩, and the gospel is preached to the whole creation ⟨Mark 16:15⟩; "Their voice has gone out to all the earth" ⟨Rom. 10:18⟩, and "Whatever was written was written for our instruction" ⟨Rom. 15:4⟩; also: "All Scripture inspired by God is profitable for teaching" ⟨II Tim. 3:16⟩. See, then, whether you and all the Sophists can produce any single mystery that is still abstruse in the Scriptures.

It is true that for many people much remains abstruse; but this is not due to the obscurity of Scripture, but to the blindness or indolence of those who will not take the trouble to look at the very clearest truth. It is as Paul says of the Jews in II. Cor. ⟨3:15⟩: "A veil lies over their minds"; and again: "If our gospel is veiled, it is veiled only to those who are perishing, whose minds the god of this world has blinded" ⟨II Cor. 4:3 f.⟩. With similar temerity a man might veil his own eyes or go out of the light into the darkness and hide himself, and then blame the sun and the day for being obscure. Let miserable men, therefore, stop imputing with blasphemous perversity the darkness and obscurity of their own hearts to the wholly clear Scriptures of God.

Now, when you quote Paul's saying: "Unsearchable are his judgments" ⟨Rom. 11:33⟩, you appear to make the pronoun *eius* refer to Scripture; but Paul does not say that the judgments of Scripture are unsearchable, but the judgments of God. Similarly, Isa. 40⟨:13⟩ does not say, "Who has known the mind of the Scripture," but "the mind of the Lord"; [13] and although Paul asserts

---

[12] See note on the passage in Erasmus ⟨E., p. 38⟩.
[13] Isa. 40:13 is here quoted as in Rom. 11:34 and I Cor. 2:16.

that the mind of the Lord *is* known to Christians, he is referring of course to "the gifts bestowed on us," as he says in the same passage, I Cor. 2⟨:12⟩. So you see how inattentively you have looked at these passages of Scripture, and how aptly you have quoted them—just as aptly as in almost all your quotations on behalf of free choice.

Similarly, the examples you go on to give, though not without a suspicion of sarcasm, are quite wide of the mark—things such as the distinction of the Persons ⟨of the Trinity⟩, the conjunction of the divine and human natures ⟨in Christ⟩, and the unforgivable sin; in all these cases, you say, there is ambiguity that has never been cleared up. ⟨E., p. 39.⟩ If you have in mind the questions debated by the Sophists in connection with these subjects, what has Scripture in its entire innocence of such things done to you that you should make the abuse of it by scoundrelly men a reproach to its purity? Scripture simply confesses the trinity of God and the humanity of Christ and the unforgivable sin, and there is nothing here of obscurity or ambiguity. But *how* these things can be, Scripture does not say (as you imagine) , nor is it necessary to know. It is their own dreams that the Sophists are busy with here, so you should accuse and condemn them, and acquit the Scriptures. If, on the other hand, what you have in mind is the fact itself, again you should not accuse the Scriptures, but the Arians, and those for whom the gospel is so veiled that, through the working of their god Satan, they do not see the very clearest testimonies concerning the trinity of the Godhead and the humanity of Christ.

To put it briefly, there are two kinds of clarity in Scripture,[14] just as there are also two kinds of obscurity: one external and pertaining to the ministry of the Word, the other located in the understanding of the heart. If you speak of the internal clarity, no man perceives one iota of what is in the Scriptures unless he has the Spirit of God. All men have a darkened heart, so that even if they can recite everything in Scripture, and know how to quote it, yet they apprehend and truly understand nothing of it. They neither believe in God, nor that they themselves are creatures of God, nor anything else, as Ps. 13⟨14:1⟩ says: "The fool has said in his heart, 'There is no god.' " For the Spirit is required for the understanding of Scripture, both as a whole and in any part of it. If, on the other hand, you speak of the external clarity, nothing at all is left obscure or ambiguous, but everything there is in the Scriptures has been brought out by the Word into the most definite light, and published to all the world.

[14] Cf. below, pp. 158 ff.

It Is Vital to Know the Truth About Free Choice
⟨WA 609–614⟩

But what is still more intolerable is that you count this subject of free choice among the things that are useless and unnecessary, and replace it for us with a list of the things you consider sufficient for the Christian religion. ⟨E., pp. 39 f.⟩ It is such a list as any Jew or Gentile totally ignorant of Christ could certainly draw up with ease, for you make not the slightest mention of Christ, as if you think that Christian godliness can exist without Christ so long as God is worshiped with all one's powers as being by nature most merciful. What am I to say here, Erasmus? You reek of nothing but Lucian,[15] and you breathe out on me the vast drunken folly of Epicurus.[16] If you consider this subject unnecessary for Christians, then please quit the field; you and I have nothing in common, for I consider it vital.

If it is irreverent, if it is inquisitive, if it is superfluous, as you say ⟨E., p. 39⟩, to know whether God foreknows anything contingently; whether our will accomplishes anything in things pertaining to eternal salvation, or simply suffers the action of grace; whether it is of mere necessity that we do, or rather suffer, whatever we do of good or ill; then what, I ask you, is there that it is reverent or serious or useful to know? This is no use at all, Erasmus; you go much too far.[17] It is difficult to attribute this to your ignorance, for you are no longer young, and you have lived among Christians and have long studied Holy Writ, so that you leave no room for us to excuse you or to think well of you. And yet the papists pardon and put up with these enormities of yours simply because you are writing against Luther; otherwise, if Luther were out of the way and you wrote such things, they would get their teeth into you and tear you to shreds.

Let Plato be a friend and Socrates a friend, but truth must be honored above all.[18] For suppose you had no great understanding

---

[15] See above, p. 109 n. 9.

[16] See above, p. 109 n. 10.

[17] "Das ist zu viel"—Luther drops into German here (for the first and only time in the book), no doubt owing to the intensity of his feelings on the subject.

[18] Aristotle, Eth. N. i.4.1096ᵃ16. This is an allusion to the introduction to Aristotle's Nicomachean Ethics i.6.1096ᵃ16, where Aristotle refers to the Platonic theory of ideas, with which he disagrees, and says that although Plato is his friend and master, "it is necessary, in order to preserve truth, that we should sacrifice private feelings, especially as we are philosophers; for both being dear to us, it is our sacred duty to prefer truth." Plato himself says (Republic 595 D) that "a man is not to be honored above truth."

of the Scriptures or of Christian piety, surely even an enemy of Christians ought to have known what Christians regard as necessary and useful, and what they do not. But when you who are a theologian and a teacher of Christians set out to describe the nature of Christianity for them, so far from showing even your usual skeptical hesitation about what is useful and necessary for them, you actually fall into precisely the opposite error. For contrary to your natural bent, and with an assertion unprecedented for you, you declare that those things are not necessary; whereas, unless they are necessary and known with certainty, then neither God, nor Christ, nor gospel, nor faith, nor anything is left, not even of Judaism, much less of Christianity. By the immortal God, Erasmus, what a "window" ⟨E., p. 41⟩ or rather, what a wide arena you open for one to act and speak against you! How could you write anything good or true about free choice when by saying things of this kind you confess such an ignorance of Scripture and piety? But I will draw in my sails, and not deal with you here in my own words (as I may perhaps later) , but in yours.

Christianity as you describe it ⟨E., p. 39⟩ includes this among other things: that we should strive with all our might, have recourse to the remedy of penitence, and entreat by all means the mercy of the Lord, without which no human will or endeavor is effective; also, that no one should despair of the pardon of a God who is by nature most merciful. These words of yours, devoid of Christ, devoid of the Spirit, are colder than ice itself, so that they even tarnish the beauty of your eloquence. Perhaps they were dragged out of you, poor fellow, by fear of the pontiffs and tyrants, lest you should seem to be altogether an atheist! They do, however, assert that there are powers in us, that there is a striving with all our powers, that there is a mercy of God, that there are means of entreating mercy, that God is by nature just, by nature most merciful, etc. If, then, anyone does not know what those powers are, what they can achieve, what they can passively receive, what their striving means, and what their efficacy or lack of it may be, what is he to do? What would *you* tell him to do?

It is, you say, irreverent, inquisitive, and superfluous to want to know whether our will does anything in matters pertaining to eternal salvation or whether it is simply passive under the action of grace. Yet now you contradict this by saying that Christian godliness means striving with all one's powers, and that without the mercy of God the will is not effective. Here you plainly assert that the will does something in matters pertaining to eternal salvation, when you represent it as striving, though you make it passive when you say it is ineffective apart from mercy. You do not, however, state precisely how this activity and passivity are to be understood, for you take good care to keep us in ignorance of what God's mercy and our will *can* achieve, even while you are telling us what they actually do. Thus that prudence of yours makes you veer about, determined not to commit yourself to either side, but to pass safely between Scylla and Charybdis; with the result that, finding yourself battered and buffeted by the waves in the midst of the sea, you assert everything you deny and deny everything you assert.

Let me show you by a few analogies what your theology is like. Suppose that a man who wants to compose a good poem or speech should not consider what sort of talent he has, or ask himself what he is and is not capable of, and what the subject he has chosen requires—plainly ignoring that precept of Horace about "what the shoulders can stand, and what they will refuse to bear" [19]—but instead should just rush headlong to work, thinking: "The effort must be made to get it done; it is inquisitive and superfluous to ask whether such learning, such eloquence, such force of intellect as it requires is forthcoming." Or suppose someone who wants to get a good crop from his land should not be inquisitive and take superfluous care to examine the soil, as Vergil inquisitively and vainly teaches in his *Georgics*,[20] but should rush blindly on, thinking of nothing but the work, plowing the seashore and sowing the seed in whatever turns up, whether sand or mud. Or suppose someone who is going to war and wants a glorious victory, or who has any other public duty to fulfill, should not be so inquisitive as to give careful thought to what it is in his power to do—whether he has sufficient funds, whether his troops are fit, whether there is any scope for action—but should completely disregard the historian's remark that "before you act, careful thought is needed, and when you have thought, prompt action," [21] and rush in with his eyes and ears shut, simply shouting, "War, war!" and press on with the job. What, I ask you, Erasmus, would be your verdict on such poets, farmers, generals, and heads of state? I will add the Gospel saying about one who desires to build a tower, and does not first sit down and count the cost, and whether he has enough to complete it.[22] What is Christ's verdict on him?

But this is just what you are doing. You prescribe our actions,

[19] *Ars poetica* 39 f.
[20] *Georgics* i.50 ff. The adverbs are a sarcastic application of Erasmus' mode of thinking to Vergil.
[21] Sallust, *De conjuratione Catilinae* I.   [22] Luke 14:28.

but forbid us first to examine and measure our powers, or to find out what we can and cannot do, as if that were inquisitive and superfluous and irreverent. Hence, while with your excessive prudence you abhor recklessness and make a show of sober judgment, you arrive at the point of actually teaching the utmost recklessness. For whereas the Sophists are indeed reckless and mad in pursuing their inquisitive inquiries, yet their sin is less serious than yours, who make madness and recklessness the positive point of your teaching. And to make the madness all the greater, you try to persuade us that this recklessness is the most beautiful Christian piety, sobriety, godly seriousness, and salvation; and unless we do as you say, you assert that we are irreverent, inquisitive, and vain—you who are such an enemy of assertions! A fine job you make of avoiding Scylla while you are steering clear of Charybdis!

But it is confidence in your own wits that has driven you to this, for you believe you can so impose on everyone's intelligence by your eloquence that no one will notice what you cherish in your heart and what your purpose is with these slippery writings of yours. But God is not mocked (Gal. 6:7), and it is not safe to run up against him. Furthermore, if the matter at issue were composing poems, preparing crops, conducting wars or other public undertakings, or building houses, and you had taught us such recklessness, then although it would be intolerable in so eminent a man, you would nevertheless have been deserving of some indulgence, at least among Christians, who set no store on temporal affairs. But when you tell Christians themselves to become reckless workers, and order them not to be inquisitive about what they can and cannot do in the matter of obtaining eternal salvation, this is beyond question the truly unforgivable sin. For as long as they are ignorant of what and how much they can do, they will not know what they should do; and being ignorant of what they should do, they cannot repent if they do wrong; and impenitence is the unforgivable sin. This is what your moderate Skeptical Theology leads us to.

Therefore, it is not irreverent, inquisitive, or superfluous, but essentially salutary and necessary for a Christian, to find out whether the will does anything or nothing in matters pertaining to eternal salvation. Indeed, as you should know, this is the cardinal issue between us, the point on which everything in this controversy turns. For what we are doing is to inquire what free choice can do, what it has done to it,[23] and what is its relation to the grace of God. If we do not know these things, we shall know

23 *"Quid patiatur."*

nothing at all of things Christian, and shall be worse than any heathen. Let anyone who does not feel this confess that he is no Christian, while anyone who disparages or scorns it should know that he is the greatest enemy of Christians. For if I am ignorant of what, how far, and how much I can and may do in relation to God, it will be equally uncertain and unknown to me, what, how far, and how much God can and may do in me, although it is God who works everything in everyone ⟨I Cor. 12:6⟩. But when the works and power of God are unknown, I do not know God himself, and when God is unknown, I cannot worship, praise, thank, and serve God, since I do not know how much I ought to attribute to myself and how much to God. It therefore behooves us to be very certain about the distinction between God's power and our own, God's work and our own, if we want to live a godly life.

So you see that this problem is one half [24] of the whole sum of things Christian, since on it both knowledge of oneself and the knowledge and glory of God quite vitally depend. That is why we cannot permit you, my dear Erasmus, to call such knowledge irreverent, inquisitive, and vain. We owe much to you, but godliness claims our all. Why, you yourself are aware that all the good in us is to be ascribed to God, and you assert this in your description of Christianity. ⟨E., p. 39.⟩ But in asserting this, you are surely asserting also that the mercy of God alone does everything, and that our will does nothing, but rather is passive; otherwise, all is not ascribed to God. Yet a little later you say that it is not religious, pious, and salutary to assert or to know this. But it is a mind at variance with itself, uncertain and inexpert in matters of religion, that is compelled to talk like that.

God's Foreknowledge; Contingence and Necessity ⟨WA 614–620⟩

The other half [25] of the Christian *summa* is concerned with knowing whether God foreknows anything contingently, and whether we do everything of necessity. And this, too, you find irreverent, inquisitive, and vain, just as all ungodly men do, or rather, as the demons and the damned find it hateful and detestable. You are well advised to steer clear of such questions if you can, but you are a pretty poor rhetorician and theologian when you presume to discuss and expound free choice without the two subjects just mentioned. I will act as a whetstone and, although no rhetorician myself, will teach a distinguished rhetorician his business.

[24] *"Altera pars."*   [25] *"Alteram partem."*

Suppose Quintilian,[26] proposing to write about oratory, were to say: "In my judgment, that stupid and superfluous stuff about choice of subject, arrangement of material, style, memorization, delivery, ought to be omitted; suffice it to know that oratory is the art of speaking well"—would you not ridicule such an exponent of the art? Yet you act no differently yourself. You propose to write about free choice, and you begin by rejecting and throwing away the whole substance and all the elements of the subject on which you are going to write. For you cannot possibly know what free choice is unless you know what the human will can do, and what God does, and whether he foreknows necessarily.

Do not even your rhetoricians teach you that when you are going to speak on any subject, you ought to say first whether it exists, then what it is, what its parts are, what things are contrary to it, akin to it, similar to it, etc.? But you deprive free choice (poor thing!) of all these advantages, and lay down no question concerning it, unless perhaps the first, namely, whether it exists; and you do this with arguments (as we shall see) of such a kind that, apart from the elegance of the language, I have never seen a feebler book on free choice. The very Sophists provide at least a better discussion on this subject, for while they have no idea of style, yet when they tackle free choice they do define all the questions connected with it—whether it exists, what it is, what it does, how it is related, etc.—though even they do not succeed in doing what they set out to do. In this book, therefore, I shall press you and all the Sophists hard until you define for me the strength and effectiveness of free choice; and I shall press you (with Christ's aid) so hard that I hope I shall make you repent of ever having published your *Diatribe*.

Here, then, is something fundamentally necessary and salutary for a Christian, to know that God foreknows nothing contingently, but that he foresees and purposes and does all things by his immutable, eternal, and infallible will. Here is a thunderbolt by which free choice is completely prostrated and shattered, so that those who want free choice asserted must either deny or explain away this thunderbolt, or get rid of it by some other means. However, before I establish this point by my own argument and the authority of Scripture, I will first deal with it in your words.

Was it not you, my dear Erasmus, who asserted a little earlier that God is by nature just, by nature most merciful? ⟨E., p. 39.⟩ If this is true, does it not follow that he is immutably just and merciful—that as his nature never changes, so neither does his

---

[26] Roman rhetorician (ca. A.D. 35–95), author of the *Institutio oratoria*, which Luther knew and valued highly.

justice or mercy? But what is said of his justice and mercy must also be said of his knowledge, wisdom, goodness, will, and other divine attributes. If, then, the assertion of these things concerning God is, as you state, religious, pious, and salutary, what has come over you that you now contradict yourself by asserting that it is irreverent, inquisitive, and vain to say that God foreknows necessarily? You declare that the will of God is to be understood as immutable, yet you forbid us to know that his foreknowledge is immutable. Do you, then, believe that he foreknows without willing or wills without knowing? If his foreknowledge is an attribute of his will, then his will is eternal and unchanging, because that is its nature; if his will is an attribute of his foreknowledge, then his foreknowledge is eternal and unchanging, because that is its nature.

From this it follows irrefutably that everything we do, everything that happens, even if it seems to us to happen mutably and contingently,[27] happens in fact nonetheless necessarily[28] and immutably, if you have regard to the will of God. For the will of God is effectual and cannot be hindered, since it is the power of the divine nature itself; moreover it is wise, so that it cannot be deceived. Now, if his will is not hindered, there is nothing to prevent the work itself from being done, in the place, time, manner, and measure that he himself both foresees and wills. If the will of God were such that, when the work was completed, the work remained but the will ceased—like the will of men, which ceases to will when the house they want is built, just as it also comes to an end in death—then it could be truly said that things happen contingently and mutably. But here the opposite happens; the work comes to an end and the will remains, so remote is it from possibility that the work itself, during its production and completed existence, should exist or persist contingently. To happen contingently, however—in order that we may not misuse terms—means in Latin, not that the work itself is contingent, but that it is done by a contingent and mutable will, such as there is not in God. Moreover, a work can only be called contingent when *from our point of view* it is done contingently and, as it were, by chance and without our expecting it, because our will or hand seizes on it as something presented to us by chance, when we have thought or willed nothing about it previously.

[29] ⟨I could wish indeed that another and a better word had been

---

[27] I.e., in such a way that it could have been otherwise.
[28] I.e., in such a way that it could not have been otherwise.
[29] This bracketed paragraph did not appear in the 1525 and 1526 editions of the *De servo arbitrio*, but was included in the Jena edition and in Justus

introduced into our discussion than this usual one, "necessity," which is not rightly applied either to the divine or the human will. It has too harsh and incongruous a meaning for this purpose, for it suggests a kind of compulsion, and the very opposite of willingness, although the subject under discussion implies no such thing. For neither the divine nor the human will does what it does, whether good or evil, under any compulsion, but from sheer pleasure or desire, as with true freedom; and yet the will of God is immutable and infallible, and it governs our mutable will, as Boethius sings: "Remaining fixed, Thou makest all things move"; and our will, especially when it is evil, cannot of itself do good. The reader's intelligence must therefore supply what the word "necessity" does not express, by understanding it to mean what you might call the immutability of the will of God and the impotence of our evil will, or what some have called the necessity of immutability, though this is not very good either grammatically or theologically.)

The Sophists have labored for years over this point, but in the end they have been beaten and forced to admit that everything happens necessarily, though by the necessity of consequence (as they say) and not by the necessity of the consequent. They have thus eluded the full force of this question, or indeed it might rather be said they have deluded themselves. For how meaningless this is I shall have no difficulty in showing. What they call the necessity of consequence means broadly this: If God wills anything, it is necessary for that thing to come to pass, but it is not necessary that the thing which comes to pass should exist; for God alone exists necessarily, and it is possible for everything else not to exist if God so wills. So they say that an action of God is necessary if he wills it, but that the thing done is not itself necessary. But what do they achieve by this playing with words? This, of course, that the thing done is not necessary, in the sense that it has not a necessary existence. But this is no different from saying that the thing done is not God himself. Nevertheless, it remains a fact that everything that comes into being does so necessarily, if the action of God is necessary, or if there is a necessity of consequence, however true it is that, when it has been brought into being, it does not exist necessarily, that is to say, it is not God and has not a necessary existence. For if I myself am brought into existence

---

Jonas' German translation. The Latin text is given as a footnote in *WA* 18, 616. The importance of its contents sufficiently explains its inclusion here. Whether or not it came from Luther's hand we cannot tell, but it undoubtedly expresses his view.

necessarily, it is of little concern to me that my being or becoming is mutable; for my contingent and mutable self, though not the necessary being that God is, is nonetheless brought into existence.

Hence their amusing idea, that everything happens by necessity of consequence but not by necessity of the consequent, amounts to no more than this: all things are indeed brought about necessarily, but when they have thus been brought about, they are not God himself. But what need was there to tell us this? As if there were any fear of our asserting that created things are God, or that they have a divine and necessary nature! Hence the proposition stands, and remains invincible, that all things happen by necessity. Nor is there here any obscurity or ambiguity. It says in Isaiah: "My counsel shall stand and my will shall be done" (ch. 46:10). What schoolboy does not know the meaning of these terms "counsel," "will," "shall be done," "shall stand"?

But why are these things abstruse to us Christians, so that it is irreverent and inquisitive and vain to discuss and come to know them, when heathen poets and even the common people speak of them quite freely? How often does Vergil (for one) remind us of Fate! "By changeless law stand all things fixed"; [30] "Each man's day stands fixed"; [31] "If the Fates call thee"; [32] "If thou canst break the harsh bonds of Fate." [33] That poet has no other aim than to show that in the destruction of Troy and the rise of the Roman Empire, Fate counts for more than all the endeavors of men, and therefore it imposes a necessity on both things and men. Moreover, he makes even their immortal gods subject to Fate, to which even Jupiter himself and Juno must necessarily yield. Hence the current conception of the three Parcae, immutable, implacable, irrevocable. The wise men of those days were well aware of what fact and experience prove, namely, that no man's plans have ever been straightforwardly realized, but for everyone things have turned out differently from what he thought they would. Vergil's Hector says, "Could Troy have stood by human arm, then it had stood by mine." [34] Hence the very common saying on everyone's lips, "God's will be done"; and "God willing, we will do it," or "Such was the will of God." "So it pleased those above"; "Such was your will," says Vergil. From this we can see that the knowledge of God's predestination and foreknowledge remained with the common people no less than the awareness of his existence

---

[30] Manilius, *Astronomica* iv.14, *"certa stant omnia lege";* not, as Luther and previous editors supposed, from Vergil.
[31] *Aeneid* x.467.   [32] *Ibid.,* vi.146.   [33] *Ibid.,* vi.882.
[34] *Ibid.,* ii.291.

itself. But those who wished to appear wise went so far astray in their reasonings that their hearts were darkened and they became fools (Rom. 1⟨:21 f.⟩), and denied or explained away the things that the poets and common people, and even their own conscience, regarded as entirely familiar, certain, and true.

I go farther and say, not only how true these things are—as will be shown more fully below from the Scriptures—but also how religious, devout, and necessary a thing it is to know them. For if these things are not known, there can be neither faith nor any worship of God. For that would indeed be ignorance of God, and where there is such ignorance there cannot be salvation, as we know. For if you doubt or disdain to know that God foreknows all things, not contingently, but necessarily and immutably, how can you believe his promises and place a sure trust and reliance on them? For when he promises anything, you ought to be certain that he knows and is able and willing to perform what he promises; otherwise, you will regard him as neither truthful nor faithful, and that is impiety and a denial of the Most High God. But how will you be certain and sure unless you know that he knows and wills and will do what he promises, certainly, infallibly, immutably, and necessarily? And we ought not only to be certain that God wills and will act necessarily and immutably, but also to glory in this fact; as Paul says in Rom. 3⟨:4⟩: "Let God be true though every man be false," and again ⟨in ch. 9:6⟩: "Not as though the word of God had failed," and elsewhere: "But God's firm foundation stands, bearing this seal: 'The Lord knows those who are his' " ⟨II Tim. 2:19⟩. And in Titus 1⟨:2⟩ he says: "Which God, who never lies, promised ages ago," and in Heb. 11⟨:6⟩: "Whoever would draw near to God must believe that he exists and that he rewards those who hope in him."

Therefore, Christian faith is entirely extinguished, the promises of God and the whole gospel are completely destroyed, if we teach and believe that it is not for us to know the necessary foreknowledge of God and the necessity of the things that are to come to pass. For this is the one supreme consolation of Christians in all adversities, to know that God does not lie, but does all things immutably, and that his will can neither be resisted nor changed nor hindered.

See now, my dear Erasmus, what that most moderate and peace-loving theology of yours leads to! You warn us off, and forbid us to try to understand the foreknowledge of God and the necessity laid on things and men, advising us to leave such things alone, and to shun and condemn them. And by this ill-advised labor of yours you teach us both to cultivate ignorance of God (which comes of its own accord, and indeed is inborn in us), and to despise faith, let go the promises of God, and treat all the consolations of the Spirit and certitudes of conscience as of no account. Such advice Epicurus himself would scarcely give! Then, not content with this, you call anyone who seeks knowledge of such things irreverent, inquisitive, and vain, but one who despises them, religious, devout, and sober. What else do you imply by these words than that Christians are inquisitive, vain, and irreverent, and that Christianity is a matter of no moment at all, but vain, foolish, and really quite impious? So it happens again that while you wish above all to preserve us from temerity, you are carried away, as foolish people often are, and do the very opposite, teaching nothing but the greatest temerities, impieties, and perditions. Do you not see that in this part your book is so impious, blasphemous, and sacrilegious that it is without an equal anywhere?

I am not, as I said above, speaking of your heart, nor do I think you so abandoned that at heart you desire either to teach these things or to see them taught and practiced. But I am trying to show you what frightful things a man is bound to babble if he undertakes to support a bad cause, and what it means to run counter to divine truth and divine Scripture when we put on an act to please others and play a part that is foreign to us against our conscience. It is no game or joke to give instruction in Holy Writ and godliness, for it is very easy to fall here in the way that James describes: "Whoever fails in one point has become guilty of all" ⟨James 2:10⟩. For thus it comes about that when we think we mean to trifle only a little, and do not treat Holy Writ with sufficient reverence, we are soon involved in impieties and immersed in blasphemies, just as has happened to you here, Erasmus—may the Lord forgive you and have mercy on you.

That the Sophists have produced such swarms of questions on these subjects, and have mixed up a lot of other useless things with them, many of which you specify, we know and admit as you do, and we have attacked them more sharply and more fully than you have. But you are imprudent and rash when you mix up, confuse, and assimilate the purity of sacred realities [35] with the profane and stupid questions of ungodly men. "They have defiled the gold and changed its good color," as Jeremiah says ⟨Lam. 4:1⟩, but the gold must not forthwith be treated like rubbish and thrown away, as you are doing. The gold must be rescued from these men, and the pure Scripture separated from their dregs and filth, as I

[35] *"Sacrarum rerum."*

have always sought to do, in order that the divine writings may be kept in one place, and their trifles in another. And it ought not to disturb us that nothing has come of these questions, "except that with the loss of harmony we love one another the less, while seeking to be wiser than we need" ⟨E., p. 40⟩. For us the question is not what the Sophists have gained by their questions, but how we may become good Christians; and you ought not to blame it on Christian doctrine that the ungodly behave badly, since that has nothing to do with the case, and you could have spoken of it in another place and spared your paper here.

Should Divine Truth Be Kept from Common Ears? ⟨WA 620–630⟩

In the third section you proceed to turn us into modest and peace-loving Epicureans, with a different sort of advice, though no sounder than the two already mentioned. That is to say, you tell us that some things are of such a kind that even if they were true and might be known, it would not be proper to prostitute them before common ears. ⟨E., p. 40.⟩

Here again you confuse and mix everything up in your usual way, putting the sacred on a level with the profane and making no distinction between them at all, so that once again you have fallen into contempt and abuse of Scripture and of God. I said above that things which are either contained in or proved by Holy Writ are not only plain, but also salutary, and can therefore safely be published, learned, and known, as indeed they ought to be. Hence your saying that they ought not to be prostituted before common ears is false if you are speaking of the things that are in Scripture; and if you are speaking of other things, what you say does not interest us and is out of place, so that you are wasting your time and paper on it. Besides, you know that there is no subject on which I agree with the Sophists, so that you might well have spared me and not cast their misdoings in my teeth. For it was against me that you were to speak in that book of yours. I know where the Sophists go wrong without needing you to tell me, and they have had plenty of criticism from me. I should like this said once for all, and repeated every time you mix me up with the Sophists and make my case look as crazy as theirs, for you are being quite unfair, as you very well know.

Now, let us see the reasons for your advice. Even if it were true that "God, according to his own nature, is no less present in the hole of a beetle" or even in a sewer than in heaven (though you are too reverent to say this yourself, and blame the Sophists for blathering [36] so), yet you think it would be unreasonable [37] to discuss such a subject before the common herd ⟨E., p. 40⟩.

First, let them blather who will; we are not here discussing what men do, but what is right and lawful, not how we live, but how we ought to live. Which of us always lives and acts rightly? But law and precept are not condemned on that account, but they rather condemn us. Yet you go looking for irrelevancies like these, and rake a pile of them together from all sides, because this one point about the foreknowledge of God upsets you; and since you have no real argument with which to overcome it, you spend the time trying to tire out your reader with a lot of empty talk. But we will let that pass, and get back to the subject. What, then, is the point of your contention that certain matters ought not to be discussed publicly? Do you count the subject of free choice among them? In that case, all I said above about the necessity of understanding free choice will round on you again. Moreover, why did you not follow your own advice and leave your *Diatribe* unwritten? If it is right for you to discuss free choice, why do you denounce such discussion? If it is wrong, why do you do it? On the other hand, if you do not count free choice among the prohibited subjects, you are again evading the real issue, dealing like a wordy rhetorician with topics that are irrelevant and out of place.

Even so, you are wrong in the use you make of this example, and in condemning as unprofitable the public discussion of the proposition that God is in the hole or the sewer. Your thoughts about God are all too human. There are, I admit, some shallow preachers who, from no motives of religion or piety, but perhaps from a desire for popularity or a thirst for some novelty or a distaste for silence, prate and trifle in the shallowest way. But these please neither God nor men, even if they assert that God is in the heaven of heavens. But where there are serious and godly preachers who teach in modest, pure, and sound words, they speak on such a subject in public without risk, and indeed with great profit. Ought we not all to teach that the Son of God was in the womb of the Virgin and came forth from her belly? But how does a human belly differ from any other unclean place? Anyone could describe it in foul and shameless terms, but we rightly condemn those who do, seeing that there are plenty of pure words with which to speak of that necessary theme even with decency and grace. Again, the body of Christ himself was human as ours is, and what is fouler than that? Are we therefore not to say that God

[36] *"Ita garrire"* (Erasmus' word).
[37] *"Irrationabiliter."* Erasmus says *"inutiliter."*

dwelt in it bodily, as Paul has said ⟨Col. 2:9⟩? What is fouler than death? What more horrifying than hell? Yet the prophet glories that God is present with him in death and hell ⟨Ps. 139:8⟩.

Therefore, a godly mind is not shocked to hear that God is present in death or hell, both of which are more horrible and foul than either a hole or a sewer. Indeed, since Scripture testifies that God is everywhere and fills all things ⟨Jer. 23:24⟩, a godly mind not only says that He is in those places, but must needs learn and know that he is there. Or are we to suppose that if I am captured by a tyrant and thrown into a prison or a sewer—as has happened to many saints—I am not to be allowed to call upon God there or to believe that he is present with me, but must wait until I come into some finely furnished church?

If you teach us to talk such nonsense about God, and are so set against the locating of his essence,[38] you will end by not even allowing him to remain for us in heaven; for the heaven of heavens cannot contain him, nor is it worthy of him ⟨I Kings 8:27⟩. But as I have said, it is your habit to stab at us in this hateful way in order to disparage our case and make it odious, because you see that for you it is insuperable and invincible.

As for your second example, I admit that the idea that there are three Gods is a scandal if it is taught; but it is neither true, nor does Scripture teach it. The Sophists speak in this way with their newfound dialectic, but what has that to do with us?

In the remaining example, regarding confession and satisfaction, it is wonderful to see with what felicitous prudence you put your case. Everywhere you walk so delicately,[39] as is your habit, in order to avoid giving the impression either that you do not wholeheartedly condemn our views or that you are not opposed to the tyranny of the popes, for that would be by no means safe for you. So you bid adieu meanwhile to God and to conscience—for how does it concern Erasmus what God wills in these matters and what is good for the conscience?—and launch an attack on mere externals,[40] charging the common people with abusing the preaching of free confession and satisfaction[41] and turning it into carnal liberty to suit their own evil inclination, whereas by the necessity of confessing (you say) they were at all events restrained.

---

[38] "Locis essentiae eius offenderis."

[39] "Super aristas graderis": "You walk over the ears of the corn"; a proverbial expression. Cf. the German auf Eiern gehen, "to walk on eggs."

[40] "In larvam externam."

[41] I.e., the preaching that confession and satisfaction are not obligatory, but free.

What outstandingly brilliant reasoning! Is that the way to teach theology? To bind souls by laws and, as Ezekiel says ⟨Ezek. 13:18 f.⟩, to slay them when they are not bound by God? By this token you set up for us again the whole tyranny of papal laws, as being useful and salutary because by them too the wickedness of the common people is restrained. But instead of attacking this passage in the way it deserves, let me put the point briefly. A good theologian teaches as follows: the common people are to be restrained by the external power of the sword when they behave wickedly, as Paul teaches in Rom. 13⟨:4⟩; but their consciences are not to be ensnared with false laws, so that they are burdened with sins where God has not willed that there should be sins. For consciences are bound only by a commandment of God, so that the interfering tyranny of the popes, which falsely terrifies and kills souls inwardly and vainly wearies the body outwardly, has simply no place in our midst. For although it makes confession and other outward burdens compulsory, the mind is not kept in order by these means, but is rather provoked into hatred of God and men; and it is in vain that the body is tortured to death with outward observances, for this makes mere hypocrites, so that legal tyrants of this kind are nothing else but ravening wolves, thieves, and robbers of souls ⟨Matt. 7:15; John 10:8⟩. Yet it is these that you, good spiritual counselor that you are, commend to us again. You set before us the cruellest of soul destroyers, and want us to let them fill the world with hypocrites who blaspheme and dishonor God in their hearts, as long as outwardly they are kept in some degree of order, as if there were not another means of keeping them in order, which makes no hypocrites and is applied without any ruination of consciences, as I have said.

Here you produce analogies, of which you seek to give the impression that you have an abundant store and make very apt use. You say, for instance, that there are diseases which are less evil to bear than their removal, such as leprosy, etc. You also bring in the example of Paul, who distinguished between things lawful and things expedient ⟨I Cor. 6:12; 10:23⟩. It is lawful, you say, to speak the truth, but it is not expedient to do so to everybody at every time in every way. What a fluent orator you are! Yet you understand nothing of what you are saying. In a word, you treat this subject as if it were simply an affair between you and me about the recovery of a sum of money, or some other quite trivial matter, the loss of which (as being of much less value than your precious external peace) ought not to trouble anyone enough to prevent him from giving way, and doing or suffering as the occasion requires, so as to make it unnecessary for the world to be thrown into such an uproar. You thus plainly show that outward peace and quietness [42] are to you far more important than faith, conscience, salvation, the Word of God, the glory of Christ, and God himself.

Let me tell you, therefore—and I beg you to let this sink deep into your mind—that what I am after in this dispute is to me something serious, necessary, and indeed eternal, something of such a kind and such importance that it ought to be asserted and defended to the death, even if the whole world had not only to be thrown into strife and confusion, but actually to return to total chaos and be reduced to nothingness. If you do not understand this or are not concerned about it, then mind your own affairs and let those understand and be concerned about it on whom God has laid the charge.

For even I, by the grace of God, am not such a fool or so mad as to have been willing to maintain and defend this cause for so long, with so much zeal and constancy (which you call obstinacy), amid so many dangers to life, so much hatred, so many treacheries, in short, amid the fury of men and demons, simply for the sake of money (which I neither possess nor desire), or popularity (which I could not obtain if I wished, in a world so incensed against me), or physical safety (of which I cannot for a moment be certain). Do you think that you alone have a heart that is moved by these tumults? Even we are not made of stone, or born of the Marpesian rocks; [43] but when nothing else can be done, we prefer to be battered by temporal tumult, rejoicing in the grace of God, for the sake of the Word of God, which must be asserted with an invincible and incorruptible mind, rather than to be shattered by eternal tumult under the wrath of God, with intolerable torment. May Christ grant, as I hope and pray, that your mind may not come to that, although your words certainly sound as if you thought, like Epicurus, that the Word of God and a future life were fables; for you seek with your magisterial advice to persuade us that, as a favor to pontiffs and princes or for the sake of peace, we ought if occasion arises, to give way and set aside the most sure Word of God. But if we do that, we set aside God, faith, salvation, and everything Christian. How much better is the admonition of Christ, that we should rather spurn the whole world ⟨Matt. 16:26⟩!

You say things like these, however, because you do not read or

---

[42] *"Pacem . . . et tranquillitatem carnis."*

[43] Cf. Vergil, *Aeneid* vi.471. Mt. Marpesus on the island of Paros was famed for its marble quarries. Vergil uses this simile of Dido's stony indifference to Aeneas in the underworld.

do not observe that it is the most unvarying fate of the Word of God to have the world in a state of tumult because of it. This is plainly asserted by Christ, when he says: "I have not come to bring peace, but a sword" ⟨Matt. 10:34⟩, and in Luke: "I came to cast fire upon the earth" ⟨ch. 12:49⟩. And Paul in I ⟨II⟩ Cor. 6⟨:5⟩ says: "In tumults," etc. And the prophet in the Second Psalm abundantly testifies the same, asserting that the nations are in tumult, the peoples murmur, kings rise up, princes conspire, against the Lord and against his Christ; as if he would say, numbers, rank, wealth, power, wisdom, righteousness, and whatever is exalted in the world, opposes itself to the Word of God. Look into The Acts of the Apostles and see what happens in the world on account of Paul's word alone, to say nothing of the other apostles. See how he alone sets both Gentiles and Jews by the ears, or as his enemies themselves say in the same place, he turns the world upside down ⟨Acts 17:6; cf. 24:5⟩. Under Elijah the Kingdom of Israel was troubled, as Ahab complains ⟨I Kings 18:17⟩. And what tumult there was under the other prophets! They are all killed or stoned, while Israel is taken captive to Assyria and Judah to Babylon! Was this peace? The world and its god cannot and will not endure the Word of the true God, and the true God neither will nor can keep silence; so when these two Gods are at war with one another, what can there be but tumult in the whole world?

To wish to stop these tumults, therefore, is nothing else but to wish to suppress and prohibit the Word of God. For the Word of God comes, whenever it comes, to change and renew the world. Even the heathen writers testify that changes of things cannot take place without commotion and tumult, nor indeed without bloodshed. But it is the mark of a Christian to expect and endure these things with presence of mind, as Christ says: "When you hear of wars and rumors of wars, see that you are not alarmed; for this must take place, but the end is not yet" ⟨Matt. 24:6⟩. For myself, if I did not see these tumults I should say that the Word of God was not in the world; but now, when I do see them, I heartily rejoice and have no fear, because I am quite certain that the kingdom of the pope, with all his followers, is going to collapse; for it is against this in particular that the Word of God, now at large in the world, is directed.

I am aware, of course, that you, my dear Erasmus, complain in many books about these tumults and the loss of peace and concord, and with the best of intentions (as I verily believe) you try hard to find a remedy for them. But this gouty foot laughs at your doctoring hands; for here in truth you are, as you say, rowing against the stream, or rather, you are putting out a fire with straw. Stop your complaining, stop your doctoring; this tumult has arisen and is directed from above, and it will not cease till it makes all the adversaries of the Word like the mud on the streets. But it is sad to have to remind a theologian like you of these things, as if you were a pupil instead of one who ought to be teaching others.

It is here, therefore, that your aphorism (which is neat enough, though your use of it is inapposite) really belongs—I mean your aphorism about diseases that are less evil to bear than their removal. You should say that the diseases which are less evil to bear are these tumults, commotions, disturbances, seditions, sects, discords, wars, and anything else of this sort, by which the whole world is shaken and shattered on account of the Word of God. These things, I say, because they are temporal, are less evil to bear than the inveterate wickedness through which souls will inevitably be lost if they are not changed by the Word of God; and if that Word were taken away, then eternal good, God, Christ, the Spirit, would go with it. But surely it is preferable to lose the world rather than God the creator of the world, who is able to create innumerable worlds again, and who is better than infinite worlds! For what comparison is there between things temporal and things eternal? This leprosy of temporal evils ought therefore to be borne, rather than that all souls should be slaughtered and eternally damned while the world is kept in peace and preserved from these tumults by their blood and perdition, seeing that the whole world cannot pay the price of redemption for a single soul.

You have some elegant and unusual analogies and aphorisms, but when you are dealing with sacred matters your application of them is puerile and indeed perverse, for you creep on the ground and never have a thought that rises above human comprehension. For the operations of God are not childish or bourgeois [44] or human, but divine and exceeding human grasp. But you do not seem to see that these tumults and divisions are marching through the world by the counsel and operation of God, and you are afraid lest the heavens should fall. But I, by the grace of God, see this clearly, because I see other greater troubles in time to come, by comparison with which these present seem no more than the whisper of a breeze or the murmur of a gentle stream.

But the dogma concerning the freedom of confession and satisfaction you either deny or do not know to be the Word of God. That is another question. We, however, know and are sure that it is God's Word by which Christian freedom is asserted, so that we

44 *"Ciuilia."*

may not allow ourselves to be trapped and brought into bondage by human traditions and laws. This we have abundantly taught elsewhere; and if you wish to go into the question, we are prepared to state our case or debate it with you as well. There are not a few books of ours available on this subject.[45]

But at the same time, you will say, the laws of the pontiffs ought in charity to be borne with and observed equally with divine laws, if by any chance it is possible in this way to maintain both eternal salvation through the Word of God and also the peace of the world. I have said above that that is not possible. The prince of this world does not allow the pope and his own pontiffs to have their laws observed freely, but his purpose is to capture and bind consciences. This the true God cannot tolerate, and so the Word of God and the traditions of men are irreconcilably opposed to one another, precisely as God himself and Satan are mutually opposed, each destroying the works and subverting the dogmas of the other like two kings laying waste each other's kingdoms. "He who is not with me," says Christ, "is against me" (Matt. 12:30).

As to your fear that many who are inclined to wickedness will abuse this freedom, this should be reckoned as one of the said tumults, part of that temporal leprosy which has to be endured and that evil which has to be borne. Such people should not be considered so important that in order to prevent their abusing it the Word of God must be taken away. If all cannot be saved, yet some are saved, and it is for their sake that the Word of God comes. These love the more fervently and are the more inviolably in concord. For what evil did ungodly men not do even before, when there was no Word? Or rather, what good did they do? Was not the world always inundated with war, fraud, violence, discord, and every kind of crime? Does not Micah liken the best of the men of his day to a thorn hedge (Micah 7:4)? And what do you think he would call the rest? But now the coming of the gospel begins to be blamed for the fact that the world is wicked, whereas the truth is that the good light of the gospel reveals how bad the world was when it lived in its own darkness without the gospel. In a similar way the uneducated find fault with education because their ignorance is shown up where education flourishes. That is the gratitude we show for the Word of life and salvation.

What apprehension must we not suppose there was among the Jews when the gospel set everyone free from the law of Moses?

[45] E.g., *The Babylonian Captivity* (1520; *WA* 6, 484 ff.); *On Christian Liberty* (1520; *WA* 7, 12 ff.); *On Monastic Vows* (1521; *WA* 8, 564 ff.); *That the Doctrines of Men Are to Be Avoided* (1522; *WA* 10, 2, 61 ff.).

What did not so great a freedom seem likely to permit to evil men? Yet the gospel was not on that account taken away, but the ungodly were allowed to go their own way, while the godly were charged not to use their freedom as an opportunity to indulge the flesh ⟨Gal. 5:13⟩.

Nor is that part of your advice or remedy of any value, where you say it is lawful to speak the truth, but not expedient to do so to everybody at every time in every way; and it is quite inappropriate for you to quote Paul's saying: "All things are lawful for me, but not all things are expedient" ⟨I Cor. 6:12⟩. Paul is not there speaking of doctrine or the teaching of the truth, in the way that you misinterpret him and make him mean what you want. Paul wishes the truth to be spoken everywhere at every time and in every way. He can therefore rejoice even when Christ is preached in pretense and from envy, and he declares plainly and in so many words that he rejoices in whatever way Christ is preached ⟨Phil. 1:15 ff.⟩. Paul is speaking factually and about the use made of the doctrine, that is, about those who boasted of Christian freedom but were seeking their own ends and took no account of the hurt and offense given to the weak. Truth and doctrine must be preached always, openly, and constantly, and never accommodated or concealed; for there is no scandal in it, for it is the scepter of righteousness ⟨Ps. 45:6-7⟩.

Who has empowered you or given you the right to bind Christian doctrine to places, persons, times, or causes when Christ wills it to be proclaimed and to reign throughout the world in entire freedom? "The word of God is not bound," says Paul ⟨II Tim. 2:9⟩; and will Erasmus bind the Word? God has not given us a Word that shows partiality in respect of persons, places, or times; for Christ says: "Go into all the world" ⟨Mark 16:15⟩. He does not say, "Go to one place and not another," as Erasmus does. And he says, "Preach the gospel to every creature" ⟨*ibid.*⟩, not "to some and not to others." In short, you prescribe for us respect of persons, respect of places and customs, and respect of times, in the service of the Word of God, whereas it is one great part of the glory of the Word that (as Paul [46] says) there is no *prosōpolēmpsia* and God is no respecter of persons. You see again how rashly you run counter to the Word of God, as if you much prefer your own ideas and counsels.

If we now asked you to distinguish for us the times, persons, and ways in which the truth ought to be spoken, when would you be

---

[46] Rom. 2:11; Eph. 6:9; Col. 3:25.

ready to do it? The world would reach the limit of time [47] and its own end before you had established any certain rule. Meanwhile, what would become of the ministry of teaching and the souls that should be taught? But how could you be able to give us a rule when you know no means of assessing either persons or times or methods? And even if you most decidedly did, yet you do not know men's hearts. Or does "method," "time," and "person" mean for you that we should teach the truth in such a way as not to offend the pope or annoy the emperor or upset the pontiffs and princes, and not to cause any commotions and tumults in the world, lest many be made to stumble and become worse? What sort of advice this is, you have seen above; but you would rather spin fine though useless phrases than say nothing at all.

How much better it would be for us miserable men to let God, who knows all men's hearts, have the glory of prescribing the manner, persons, and times for speaking the truth! For he knows what should be spoken to each, and when and how. As it is, however, he has enjoined that his gospel, which is necessary for all, should know no limit of place or time, but should be preached to all in every time and place. And I have proved above that the things set forth in the Scriptures are of a kind intended for all, and must necessarily be broadcast and are thoroughly salutary— as even you yourself have stated, with better sense than you show now, in your *Paraclesis*.[48] Those who do not want souls redeemed, like the pope and his crowd—let it be left to them to bind the Word of God and keep men from life and the Kingdom of Heaven, so that they neither enter themselves nor permit others to enter ⟨Matt. 23:13⟩; to whose madness you perniciously pander, Erasmus, by this advice of yours.

The same sort of prudence underlies your next bit of advice, that if some wrong definition had been made in the Councils, it ought not to be proclaimed, lest a handle should be given to scorn the authority of the Fathers. ⟨E., p. 41.⟩ This, of course, was just what the pope wanted you to say; he would rather hear it than the gospel, and he is the worst of ingrates if he does not reward you

---

[47] The words *"ante suum clauso componit tempore finem"* form a hexameter, but the lexicons give us no assistance in identifying it, and it is therefore possible that Luther wrote the words unconscious of their rhythm, although the fact that the following words also form practically a hexameter heightens the probability that they are an imperfectly remembered quotation.

[48] Erasmus' *Paraclesis, or Exhortation to the Study of Christian Philosophy,* was published in 1516.

with a cardinal's hat and the income that goes with it. But in the meantime, Erasmus, what will souls do that are bound and slain by that unjust statute? Is that nothing to you?

You, of course, always hold, or profess to hold, that human statutes can be observed without peril along with the Word of God. If they could, I should not hesitate to join you in the view you express here. So if you do not know it, I tell you again: Human statutes cannot be observed together with the Word of God, because they bind consciences, while the Word sets them free. The two are as mutually incompatible as water and fire, unless the human statutes are kept freely, that is, as not being binding—a thing that the pope will not and cannot allow, unless he wants his kingdom ruined and brought to an end, since it is only maintained by the ensnaring and binding of consciences which the gospel asserts to be free. Therefore the authority of the Fathers is neither here nor there, and statutes wrongly enacted (as are all which are not in accordance with the Word of God) ought to be torn up and thrown away, for Christ ranks higher than the authority of the Fathers. In short, if this view of yours has reference to the Word of God, it is impious; if it refers to other things, your wordy argument in support of it is nothing to us, for we are arguing about the Word of God.

Should the Truth of God's Necessitating Will Be Suppressed? ⟨WA 630–634⟩

In the last part of your Preface ⟨E., p. 41⟩, where you seriously try to dissuade me from my kind of doctrine, you think you have as good as won your point. What, you say, could be more useless than to publish this paradox to the world, that whatever is done by us is not done by free choice, but by sheer necessity? And Augustine's saying, that God works in us good and evil, and rewards his own good works in us and punishes his evil works in us—what is the use of that? You are profuse in giving, or rather demanding, a reason here. What a window to impiety, you say, would the public avowal of this opinion open to mortal men! What evildoer would correct his life? Who would believe he was loved by God? [49] Who would war against his own flesh? I am surprised that in your great vehemence and contentiousness you did not remember the point at issue and say, Where would free choice then remain?

My dear Erasmus, let me too say in turn: If you think these

---

[49] Erasmus does not say this but, "Who will be able to bring himself to love God . . . ?" Cf. below, p. 136.

paradoxes are inventions of men, what are you contending about? Why are you so roused? Against whom are you speaking? Is there anyone in the world today who has more vigorously attacked the dogmas of men than Luther? Therefore, your admonition has nothing to do with me. But if you think these paradoxes are words of God, how can you keep your countenance, where is your shame, where is—I will not say that well-known moderation of Erasmus, but the fear and reverence that are due to the true God, when you say that nothing more useless could be proclaimed than the Word of God? Naturally, your Creator must learn from you his creature what it is useful or useless to preach! That foolish, that thoughtless God did not previously know what ought to be taught until you his master prescribed for him how to be wise and how to give commandments! As though he himself would not have known, if you had not taught him, that the consequences you mention would follow from this paradox! If, therefore, God has willed that such things should be openly spoken of and published abroad without regard to the consequences, who are you to forbid it?

The apostle Paul, in his epistle to the Romans, discusses these same things, not in a corner, but publicly and before all the world, in the freest manner and in even harsher terms, when he says: "Whom he will he hardeneth," and, "God, willing to show his wrath," etc. (Rom. 9:18, 22). What could be harsher (to the carnal nature [50] at any rate) than Christ's saying: "Many are called, but few chosen" (Matt. 22:14), or: "I know whom I have chosen" (John 13:18)? We have it, of course, on your authority that nothing more profitless could be said than things like these, because ungodly men are led by them to fall into desperation, hatred, and blasphemy.

Here, I see, you are of the opinion that the truth and usefulness of Scripture is to be measured and judged by the reactions of men, and the most ungodly men at that, so that only what has proved pleasing or seemed tolerable to them should be deemed true, divine, and salutary, while the opposite should forthwith be deemed useless, false, and pernicious. What are you aiming at with this advice, unless that the words of God should depend on, and stand or fall with, the choice and authority of men? Whereas Scripture says on the contrary that all things stand or fall by the choice and authority of God, and all the earth should keep silence before the Lord (Hab. 2:20). To talk as you do, one must imagine the Living God to be nothing but a kind of shallow and ignorant ranter declaiming from some platform, whose words you

[50] *"Sed carni."*

can if you wish interpret in any direction you like, and accept or reject them according as ungodly men are seen to be moved or affected by them.

Here, my dear Erasmus, you plainly reveal how sincerely you meant your earlier advice that we should reverence the majesty of the divine judgments. There, when we were dealing with the dogmas of Scripture, which there was no need to reverence as things abstruse and hidden, since they are nothing of the kind, you warned us so very solemnly against rushing inquisitively into the Corycian cavern, that we were almost frightened off the reading of Scripture altogether, strongly though Christ and the apostles urge us to read it, as you yourself do elsewhere. But here, where we are concerned not with the dogmas of Scripture and the Corycian cavern only, but in very truth with the awful secrets of the Divine Majesty (namely, why he works in the way we have said), here you smash through bolts and bars and rush in all but blaspheming, as indignant as possible with God because you are not allowed to see the meaning and purpose of such a judgment of his. Why do you not put up a screen of ambiguities and obscurities here also? Why do you not restrain yourself and deter others from prying into things that God has willed to be hidden from us, and has not set forth in the Scriptures? It was here you should have put your finger to your lips in reverence for what lay hidden, and adoring the secret counsels of the Majesty you should have cried with Paul: "O man, who art thou that contendest with God?" (Rom. 9:20).

Who, you say, will take pains to correct his life? (E., p. 41.) I answer: No man will and no man can, for God cares nothing for your correctors without the Spirit, since they are hypocrites. But the elect and the godly will be corrected by the Holy Spirit, while the rest perish uncorrected. Augustine does not say that no man's or all men's good works are crowned, but that some men's are. So there will be some who correct their life.

Who will believe, you say, that he is loved by God? [51] I answer: No man will or can believe this; but the elect will believe while the rest perish in unbelief, indignant and blaspheming as you are here. So some will believe.

As to your saying that a window is opened for impiety by these dogmas, let it be so; such people belong to the above-mentioned leprosy of evil that must be borne. Nevertheless, by these same dogmas there is opened at the same time a door to righteousness, an entrance to heaven and a way to God for the godly and the

[51] Cf. above, p. 134.

elect. But if, as you advise, we left these dogmas alone and concealed this Word of God from men, so that they were deluded by
a false assurance of salvation and no one learned to fear God and
be humbled, so as to come through fear at length to grace and love,
then we might very well have closed your window, but in its
place we should be opening for ourselves and all men floodgates,
or rather great chasms and gulfs, not only to impiety, but to the
depths of hell. In this way we should neither enter heaven ourselves nor allow those who would enter to go in ⟨Matt. 23:13⟩.

What then, you may ask, is the utility or necessity of publishing such things when so many evils appear to proceed from them?
I answer: It would be enough to say that God has willed them to
be published, and we must not ask the reason for the divine will,
but simply adore it, giving God glory that, since he alone is just
and wise, he does no wrong to anyone and can do nothing fool-
ishly or rashly, though it may seem far otherwise to us. With this
answer the godly are content. Still, out of our abundance we will
do a work of supererogation [52] and mention two considerations
which demand that such things should be preached. The first is
the humbling of our pride, and the knowledge of the grace of God;
and the second is the nature of Christian faith itself.

First, God has assuredly promised his grace to the humble ⟨I
Peter 5:5⟩, that is, to those who lament and despair of themselves.
But no man can be thoroughly humbled until he knows that his
salvation is utterly beyond his own powers, devices, endeavors,
will, and works, and depends entirely on the choice, will, and work
of another, namely, of God alone. For as long as he is persuaded
that he himself can do even the least thing toward his salvation,
he retains some self-confidence and does not altogether despair of
himself, and therefore he is not humbled before God, but presumes that there is—or at least hopes or desires that there may be
—some place, time, and work for him, by which he may at length
attain to salvation. But when a man has no doubt that everything
depends on the will of God, then he completely despairs of himself
and chooses nothing for himself, but waits for God to work; then
he has come close to grace, and can be saved.

It is thus for the sake of the elect that these things are published, in order that being humbled and brought back to nothingness by this means they may be saved. The rest resist this hu-
miliation, indeed they condemn this teaching of self-despair, wishing for something, however little, to be left for them to do themselves; so they remain secretly proud and enemies of the grace of

[52] *"Ut ex abundantia supererogemus."*

God. This, I say, is one reason, namely, that the godly, being humbled, may recognize, call upon, and receive the grace of God.

The second reason is that faith has to do with things not seen ⟨Heb. 11:1⟩. Hence in order that there may be room for faith, it is necessary that everything which is believed should be hidden. It cannot, however, be more deeply hidden than under an object, perception, or experience which is contrary to it. Thus when God makes alive he does it by killing, when he justifies he does it by making men guilty, when he exalts to heaven he does it by bringing down to hell, as Scripture says: "The Lord kills and brings to life; he brings down to Sheol and raises up" (I Sam. 2⟨:6⟩). This is not the place to speak at length on this subject, but those who have read my books have had it quite plainly set forth for them.

Thus God hides his eternal goodness and mercy under eternal wrath, his righteousness under iniquity. This is the highest degree of faith, to believe him merciful when he saves so few and damns so many, and to believe him righteous when by his own will he makes us necessarily damnable, so that he seems, according to Erasmus ⟨E., p. 41⟩, to delight in the torments of the wretched and to be worthy of hatred rather than of love. If, then, I could by any means comprehend how this God can be merciful and just who displays so much wrath and iniquity, there would be no need of faith. As it is, since that cannot be comprehended, there is room for the exercise of faith when such things are preached and published, just as when God kills, the faith of life is exercised in death. That is now enough by way of preface.[53]

My way of dealing with people who argue about these paradoxes is better than yours. You advise silence and refusal to be drawn, with the idea of humoring their impiety; but you really achieve nothing by this. For if you either believe or suspect them to be true (since they are paradoxes of no small moment), such is the insatiable desire of mortals to probe into secret matters, especially when we most want them kept secret, that as a result of your publishing this warning everybody will now want to know all the more whether these paradoxes are true. They will have been aroused by your contention to such a degree that no one on our side will ever have provided such an opportunity for publicizing these paradoxes as you have done by this solemn and vehement warning. You would have been much wiser to say nothing at all about the

---

53 "*Haec nunc in praefatione satis.*" The ablative seems to settle the point that Luther means his own prefatory remarks rather than Erasmus' ("So much at the moment for *your* preface"), which would have required "*in praefationem.*"

need to beware of them if you wanted to see your desire fulfilled. The game is up when you do not directly deny that they are true; they cannot be kept dark, but the suspicion of their truth will prompt everybody to investigate them. Either, then, you must deny that they are true or set the example of silence if you want others to keep silence too.

Divine Necessity and the Human Will ⟨WA 634–639⟩

As for the second paradox, that whatever is done by us is done not by free choice but of sheer necessity, let us look briefly at this and not permit it to be labeled most pernicious. What I say here is this: When it has been proved that salvation is beyond our own powers and devices, and depends on the work of God alone (as I hope to prove conclusively below in the main body of this disputation), does it not follow that when God is not present and at work in us everything we do is evil and we necessarily do what is of no avail for salvation? For if it is not we, but only God, who works salvation in us, then before he works we can do nothing of saving significance, whether we wish to or not.

Now, by "necessarily" I do not mean "compulsorily," [54] but by the necessity of immutability (as they say) and not of compulsion.[55] That is to say, when a man is without the Spirit of God he does not do evil against his will,[56] as if he were taken by the scruff of the neck and forced to it, like a thief or robber carried off against his will to punishment, but he does it of his own accord and with a ready will.[57] And this readiness or will to act he cannot by his own powers omit, restrain, or change, but he keeps on willing and being ready; and even if he is compelled by external force to do something different, yet the will within him remains averse and he is resentful at whatever compels or resists it. He would not be resentful, however, if it were changed and he willingly submitted to the compulsion. This is what we call the necessity of immutability: It means that the will cannot change itself and turn in a different direction, but is rather the more provoked into willing by being resisted, as its resentment shows. This would not happen if it were free or had free choice. Ask experience how impossible it is to persuade people who have set their heart on anything. If they yield, they yield to force or to the greater attraction of something else; they never yield freely. On the other hand, if they are not set on anything, they simply let things take their course.

[54] "Coacte."   [55] "Non coactionis."   [56] "Nolens."   [57] "Libenti voluntate."

By contrast, if God works in us, the will is changed, and being gently breathed upon by the Spirit of God, it again wills and acts from pure willingness and inclination and of its own accord, not from compulsion, so that it cannot be turned another way by any opposition, nor be overcome or compelled even by the gates of hell, but it goes on willing and delighting in and loving the good, just as before it willed and delighted in and loved evil. This again is proved by experience, which shows how invincible and steadfast holy men are, who when force is used to compel them to other things are thereby all the more spurred on to will the good, just as fire is fanned into flames rather than extinguished by the wind. So not even here is there any free choice, or freedom to turn oneself in another direction or will something different, so long as the Spirit and grace of God remain in a man.

In short, if we are under the god of this world, away from the work and Spirit of the true God, we are held captive to his will, as Paul says to Timothy ⟨II Tim. 2:26⟩, so that we cannot will anything but what he wills. For he is that strong man armed, who guards his own palace in such a way that those whom he possesses are in peace ⟨Luke 11:21⟩, so as to prevent them from stirring up any thought or feeling against him; otherwise, the kingdom of Satan being divided against itself would not stand ⟨Luke 11:18⟩, whereas Christ affirms that it does stand. And this we do readily and willingly, according to the nature of the will, which would not be a will if it were compelled; for compulsion is rather (so to say) "unwill." [58] But if a Stronger One comes who overcomes him and takes us as His spoil, then through his Spirit we are again slaves and captives—though this is royal freedom—so that we readily will and do what he wills. Thus the human will is placed between the two like a beast of burden.[59] If God rides it, it wills and goes where God wills, as the psalm says: "I am become as a beast ⟨before thee⟩ and I am always with thee" ⟨Ps. 73:22 f.⟩. If Satan rides it, it wills and goes where Satan wills; nor can it choose to run to either of the two riders or to seek him out, but the riders themselves contend for the possession and control of it.

What if I can prove from the words you yourself use in asserting freedom of choice that there is no free choice? What if I convict you of unwittingly denying what you seek so carefully to affirm? Frankly, unless I do so, I swear to regard everything I write against you in the entire book as revoked, and everything your *Diatribe* either asserts or queries against me as confirmed.

You make the power of free choice very slight and of a kind that

58 *"Noluntas."*   59 On this simile, see Introduction, p. 18.

is entirely ineffective apart from the grace of God. Do you not agree? Now I ask you, if the grace of God is absent or separated from it, what can that very slight power do of itself? It is ineffective, you say, and does nothing good. Then it cannot do what God or his grace wills, at any rate if we suppose the grace of God to be separated from it. But what the grace of God does not do is not good. Hence it follows that free choice without the grace of God is not free at all, but immutably the captive and slave of evil, since it cannot of itself turn to the good. If this is granted, I give you leave to make the power of free choice, instead of something very slight, something angelic, indeed if possible something quite divine; yet if you add this mournful rider, that apart from the grace of God it is ineffective, you at once rob it of all its power. What is ineffective power but simply no power at all?

Therefore, to say that free choice exists and has indeed some power, but that it is an ineffective power, is what the Sophists call *oppositum in adjecto* ⟨"a contradiction in terms"⟩. It is as if you said that there is a free choice which is not free, which is as sensible as calling fire cold and earth hot. For fire may have the power of heat, even infernal heat, but if it does not burn or scorch, but is cold and freezes, let no one tell me it is a fire at all, much less a hot one, unless you mean a painted or imaginary fire. But if the power of free choice were said to mean that by which a man is capable of being taken hold of by the Spirit and imbued with the grace of God, as a being created for eternal life or death, no objection could be taken. For this power or aptitude, or as the Sophists say, this disposing quality or passive aptitude, we also admit; and who does not know that it is not found in trees or animals? For heaven, as the saying is, was not made for geese.

It is settled, then, even on your own testimony, that we do everything by necessity, and nothing by free choice, since the power of free choice is nothing and neither does nor can do good in the absence of grace—unless you wish to give "efficacy" a new meaning and understand it as "perfection," as if free choice might very well make a start and will something, though it could not carry it through. But that I do not believe, and will say more about it later. It follows now that free choice is plainly a divine term, and can be properly applied to none but the Divine Majesty alone; for he alone can do and does (as the psalmist says ⟨Ps. 115:3⟩) whatever he pleases in heaven and on earth. If this is attributed to men, it is no more rightly attributed than if divinity itself also were attributed to them, which would be the greatest possible sacrilege. Theologians therefore ought to have avoided this term when they wished to speak of human ability, leaving it to be applied to God alone. They should, moreover, have removed it from the lips and language of men, treating it as a kind of sacred and venerable name for their God. And if they attributed any power at all to men, they should teach that it must be called by another name than free choice, especially as we know and clearly perceive that the common people are miserably deceived and led astray by that term, since they hear and understand it in a very different sense from that which the theologians mean and discuss.

For the expression "free choice" is too imposing, too wide and full, and the people think it signifies—as the force and nature of the term requires—a power that can turn itself freely in either direction, without being under anyone's influence or control. If they knew that it was not so, but that hardly the tiniest spark of power was meant by this term, and a spark completely ineffectual by itself as a captive and slave of the devil, it would be surprising if they did not stone us as mockers and deceivers who say one thing and mean something quite different, or rather who have not yet decided or agreed on what we do mean. For he who speaks sophistically is hateful, as the Wise Man says ⟨Prov. 6:17⟩, particularly if he does this in matters of piety, where eternal salvation is at stake.

Since, then, we have lost the meaning and content of such a vainglorious term, or rather have never possessed it (as the Pelagians wanted us to, who like you were led astray by the term), why do we so stubbornly hold on to an empty term, deceptive and dangerous as it is for the rank and file of believers? It is as sensible as when kings and princes hold on to or claim for themselves and boast about empty titles of kingdoms and countries, when in fact they are practically paupers and anything but the possessors of those kingdoms and countries. That, however, can be tolerated, since they deceive or mislead no one by it, but simply feed themselves on vanity, quite fruitlessly. But in the present case there is a danger to salvation and a thoroughly injurious illusion.

Who would not think it ridiculous, or rather very objectionable, if some untimely innovator in the use of words attempted to introduce, against all common usage, such a manner of speaking as to call a beggar rich, not because he possessed any riches, but because some king might perhaps give him his, especially if this were done in seeming seriousness and not in a figure of speech, such as antiphrasis [60] or irony. In this way, one who was mortally

---

[60] I.e., the use of words in a good sense, contrary to the real meaning, such as Eumenides for Erinyes.

ill could be said to be perfectly well because some other might give him his own health, and a thoroughly illiterate fellow could be called very learned because someone else might perhaps give him learning. That is just how it sounds here: Man has free choice —if, of course, God would hand over his own to him! By this misuse of language, anyone might boast of anything, as for instance, that man is lord of heaven and earth—if God would grant it to him. But that is not the way for theologians to talk, but for stage players and public informers. Our words ought to be precise, pure, and sober, and as Paul says, sound and beyond censure ⟨Titus 2:8⟩.

But if we are unwilling to let this term go altogether—though that would be the safest and most God-fearing thing to do—let us at least teach men to use it honestly, so that free choice is allowed to man only with respect to what is beneath him and not what is above him. That is to say, a man should know that with regard to his faculties and possessions he has the right to use, to do, or to leave undone, according to his own free choice, though even this is controlled by the free choice of God alone, who acts in whatever way he pleases. On the other hand in relation to God, or in matters pertaining to salvation or damnation, a man has no free choice, but is a captive, subject and slave either of the will of God or the will of Satan.

Such are my comments on the main heads of your Preface, which even in themselves cover practically the whole subject—more almost than the main body of the book that follows. Yet all I have said might have been summed up in this short alternative: Your Preface is complaining either about the words of God or the words of men. If it is about the words of men, it has been written wholly in vain and is no concern of ours. If it is about the words of God, it is wholly impious. It would therefore have been more useful to have a statement as to whether they were God's words or men's about which we are disputing. But perhaps this question will be dealt with in the Introduction which follows, and in the Disputation itself.

The points you raise in the epilogue to your Preface, however, do not impress me. ⟨E., p. 42.⟩ You call our dogmas "fables" and "useless," and suggest that we ought rather to follow Paul's example of preaching Christ crucified and speaking wisdom among the perfect ⟨I Cor. 1:23; 2:2, 6 ff.⟩; and you say that Scripture has a language of its own, variously adapted to the state of the hearers, so that you think it must be left to the prudence and charity of the teacher to teach what is expedient for his neighbor. All this is inept and ignorant, for we too teach nothing but Jesus crucified. But Christ crucified brings all these things with him, even including that "wisdom among the perfect"; for there is no other wisdom to be taught among Christians than that which is hidden in a mystery and pertains to the perfect, not to mere children of a Jewish and legal people that glories in works without faith, as Paul shows in I Cor., ch. 2—unless you want the preaching of Christ crucified to mean nothing other than the making of the bare statement, "Christ has been crucified."

As for your saying that "God in Scripture is angry, rages, hates, grieves, has mercy, repents, yet none of these changes takes place in God," here you are looking for a bone to pick,[61] for these things do not make Scripture obscure or in need of adaptation to the various hearers, except that some people like to make difficulties where there are none. These are matters of grammar and the figurative use of words, which even schoolboys understand; but we are concerned with dogmas, not grammatical figures, in this discussion.

PART II. COMMENTS ON ERASMUS' INTRODUCTION

The Evidence of Tradition on Behalf of Free Choice
⟨WA 639–649⟩

In introducing the Disputation, then, you promise to abide by the canonical Scriptures, since Luther holds himself bound by the authority of no other writer. ⟨E., p. 42.⟩ Very well, I accept your promise, although you do not give it because you regard those other writers as useless for your purpose, but in order to spare yourself fruitless labor. For you do not really approve of my audacity, or whatever else this principle of mine should be called. You are not a little impressed by such a numerous body of most learned men, who have found approval in so many centuries, among whom were some most skilled in divine studies, some of most godly life, some of them martyrs, many renowned for miracles, besides more recent theologians and so many universities, councils, bishops and popes. In short, on that side stand erudition, genius, multitude, magnitude, altitude, fortitude, sanctity, miracles—everything one could wish. On my side, however, there is only Wyclif[1] and one

---

61 "Nodus in scirpo quaeritur": "You are looking for a knot in a bulrush," i.e., seeking difficulties where there are none; a proverbial expression.

1 English theologian and Reformer (1324–1384); declared heretical by the Council of Constance, 1415.

other, Laurentius Valla [2] (though Augustine, whom you overlook, is entirely with me), and these carry no weight in comparison with those; so there remains only Luther, a private individual and a mere upstart,[3] with his friends, among whom there is no such erudition or genius, no multitude or magnitude, no sanctity, no miracles—for they could not even cure a lame horse ⟨E., p. 45⟩. They make a parade of Scripture, yet they are as uncertain about it as the other side, and though they boast of the Spirit they give no sign of possessing it; and there are other things "which at great length thou couldst recount." [4] So it is the same with us as the wolf said to the nightingale he had devoured, "You are a voice and nothing more." [5] They talk, you say, and for this alone they want to be believed.

I confess, my dear Erasmus, that you have good reason to be moved by all these things. I myself was so impressed by them for more than ten years that I think no one else has ever been so disturbed by them. I, too, found it incredible that this Troy of ours, which for so long a time and through so many wars had proved invincible, could ever be taken. And I call God to witness on my soul, I should have continued so, I should be just as moved today, but for the pressure of my conscience and the evidence of facts that compel me to a different view. You can well imagine that my heart is not of stone; and even if it were, it could well have melted in the great waves and storms with which it had to struggle and the buffeting it received, when I dared to do what I saw would bring down all the authority of those whom you have listed, like a flood, upon my head.

But this is not the place to tell the story of my life or works, nor have we undertaken these things in order to commend ourselves, but in order to extol the grace of God. The sort of person I am, and the spirit and purpose with which I have been drawn into this affair, I leave to Him who knows that all these things have been effected by his free choice, not mine—though the whole world itself ought to have been long ago aware of this. You clearly put me into a very unpleasant position by this Introduction of yours, since I cannot easily get out of it without singing my own praises and censuring so many of the Fathers. But I will be brief. In erudition, genius, the number of authorities supporting me, and everything else I am, as you rightly judge, inferior. But suppose I ask you what is a manifestation of the Spirit, what miracles are, what

[2] Italian humanist (ca. 1406–1457); famed for his exposure of the forged "Donation of Constantine" and attacks on other spurious documents.
[3] *"Nuper natus."*   [4] Vergil, *Aeneid* iv.333 f.   [5] Proverbial phrase.

sanctity is; to these three questions, so far as I know you from your letters and books, you would seem to be too inexperienced and ignorant to give one syllable of an answer. Or if I should press you to say which man, of all those you boast about, you can certainly show to have been or to be a saint, or to have had the Spirit, or to have performed real miracles, I think you would have to work very hard at it, and all to no purpose. You repeat many things that are commonly said and publicly preached, and you do not realize how much of credibility and authority they lose when summoned to the bar of conscience. It is a true proverb that many pass for saints on earth whose souls are in hell.

But we will grant you, if you wish, that they all were saints, all had the Spirit, all performed miracles—though you do not ask for this. Tell me this: Was it in the name or by the power of free choice, or to confirm the dogma of free choice, that any of them became a saint, received the Spirit, and performed miracles? Far from it, you will say; it was in the name and by the power of Jesus Christ, and in support of the doctrine of Christ, that all these things were done. Why, then, do you adduce their sanctity, their possession of the Spirit, and their miracles in support of the dogma of free choice when these were not given or done for that purpose? Their miracles, their possession of the Spirit, and their sanctity, therefore, speak for us who preach Jesus Christ and not the powers or works of men. Now, how is it surprising if those men, holy, spiritual, and workers of miracles as they were, sometimes under the influence of the flesh spoke and acted according to the flesh, when this happened more than once even to the apostles in the time of Christ himself? For you yourself do not deny, but assert, that free choice is not a matter of the Spirit or of Christ, but a human affair, so that the Spirit, who was promised in order to glorify Christ ⟨John 16:14⟩ could in any case not preach free choice. If, therefore, the Fathers have sometimes preached free choice, they have certainly spoken from carnal motives (since they were but men) and not by the Spirit of God, and much less have they performed miracles in support of free choice. So what you say about the sanctity, Spirit, and miracles of the Fathers is beside the point, since what is proved by them is not free choice but the dogma of Jesus Christ as opposed to the dogma of free choice.

But go on, you who are on the side of free choice, and who assert that a dogma of this kind is true (that is, that it has come from the Spirit of God) ; go on, I say, and manifest the Spirit, perform your miracles, display your sanctity! You who assert, assuredly owe these things to us who deny. From us who deny, the

Spirit, sanctity, and miracles ought not to be demanded, but from you who assert, they ought. For a negative posits nothing, is nothing, and is held to prove nothing, nor is it obliged to be proved; it is the affirmative that ought to be proved. You people affirm the power of free will, which is a human affair, and no one has ever yet seen or heard of a miracle done by God in support of any dogma concerning a human affair, but only in support of one that is divine. And we are commanded not to admit any dogma that is not first proved by divine attestations (Deut. 18⟨:22⟩). Moreover, Scripture calls man "vanity" ⟨Eccl. 1:2; cf. Ps. 39:5; 62:9⟩ and a "lie" ⟨Rom. 3:4⟩, which is nothing else than saying that all things human are vanities and lies. Go on, then, go on, I say, and prove that your dogma concerning a human vanity and lie is true! Where is now your manifestation of the Spirit, where is your sanctity, where are your miracles? I see talent, learning, authority; but God has given those even to the heathen.

We will not, however, compel you to produce great miracles, nor even to cure a lame horse,[6] lest you plead in excuse the carnality of the age; though God is wont to confirm his dogmas by miracles without regard to the carnality of the age, for he is not moved by the merits or demerits of a carnal age, but by sheer mercy, grace, and a love of establishing souls in solid truth for his glory. You are given the option of working a miracle as small as you please. Indeed, to spur your Baal to action I will taunt and challenge you ⟨I Kings 18:27⟩ to create as much as a single frog in the name and by the power of free choice, though the heathen and ungodly magicians in Egypt were able to create a great many ⟨Ex. 8:7⟩. I will not set you the heavy task of creating lice, which they could not produce either ⟨Ex. 8:18⟩. I will say something still easier. Take a single flea or louse—since you tempt and mock our God with this talk about curing a lame horse—and if, after combining all the powers and concentrating all the efforts both of your god and all your supporters, you succeed in killing it in the name and by the power of free choice, you shall be the victors, your case shall be established, and we too will at once come and worship that god of yours, that wonderful killer of the louse. Not that I deny that you could even remove mountains; but it is one thing to say that something has been done by the power of free choice and another to prove it.

And what I have said about miracles, I say also about sanctity. If from such a series of ages, men, and everything else you have mentioned, you can show one work (if only the lifting of a straw

6 See above, p. 145.

from the ground), or one word (if only the syllable "my"), or one thought (if only the faintest sigh), arising from the power of free choice, by which they have applied themselves to grace or merited the Spirit or obtained pardon or done anything alongside God, however slight (I do not say by which they have been sanctified), then again you shall be the victors and we the vanquished—by the power, I say, and in the name of free choice. (For the things that are done in men by the power of divine creation have testimonies of Scripture in abundance.) And you certainly ought to give such a demonstration, unless you want to look ridiculous as teachers by spreading dogmas through the world with such a superior air and such authority about a thing for which you produce no tangible evidence. Otherwise, they will be called dreams and of no consequence whatever, which is by far the most shameful thing that could happen to such great men of so many centuries with all their learning and sanctity and their power to work miracles. In that case we shall prefer the Stoics to you, for although even they described such a wise man as they never saw,[7] yet they did endeavor to express some aspect of him in their lives. You people are not able to express anything at all, not even the shadow of your dogma.

I say the same with regard to the Spirit. If out of all the assertors of free choice you can show a single one who has had the strength of mind or feeling even in such small degree as to be able in the name and by the power of free choice to look beyond a single farthing, to forgo a single crumb, or to bear a single word or gesture of ill will (to say nothing of despising wealth, life, and reputation), then take the palm again, and we will willingly admit defeat. And this you really ought to demonstrate to us, after all your bragging words about the power of free choice, or again you will seem to be wrangling about goat's wool,[8] like the man who watched the play in an empty theater.[9] But I can easily show you,

---

[7] From Zeno onward to Seneca, Epictetus, and Marcus Aurelius, the Stoics portrayed an ideal man who should be unmoved by family affections or by any sort of calamity or misfortune, because he was consciously acting as a soldier under orders or as an actor given his part by the great Dramaturge. This belief tended to make its adherents lose touch with ordinary humanity. (See, e.g., Gilbert Murray, *The Stoic Philosophy* [1915].)

[8] Horace, *Epistles* i.18.15. Cf. A. S. Wilkins, *ad loc.*: "Ready to come to blows on the question whether goat's hair, used for weaving into cloth, is properly to be called wool or not," i.e., wrangling about the merest trifles.

[9] *Ibid.*, ii.2.128–130. Horace depicts for us a man who suffered from the delusion that he was watching tragedies in an empty theater. He was cured at great expense by his friends, and then upbraided them for robbing him of an illusion that gave him great pleasure while it lasted. There is no basis for Wilkins' conjecture that the man was listening to his own plays.

on the contrary, that holy men such as you boast about, whenever they come to pray or plead with God, approach him in utter forgetfulness of their own free choice, despairing of themselves and imploring nothing but pure grace alone, though they have merited something very different. This was often the case with Augustine, and it was so with Bernard when, at the point of death, he said, "I have lost my time, because I have lived like a lost soul." [10] I do not see that any power is claimed here which could apply itself to grace, but every power is accused of having done nothing but turn away from grace. It is true that these same saints sometimes in their disputations spoke differently about free choice, but that is just what I see happening to everybody; they are different when they are intent on words or arguments from what they are when they are concerned with feelings and actions. In the former case they speak differently from what they previously felt, and in the latter they feel differently from what they previously said. But men are to be measured by their feelings rather than their talk, whether they are godly or ungodly.

But we grant you still more. We do not demand miracles, the Spirit, sanctity; we return to the dogma itself. All we ask is that you should at least indicate to us what work or word or thought this power of free choice stirs up, attempts, or performs, in order to apply itself to grace. It is not enough to say, "There is a power, there is a power, there is a definite power of free choice," for what is easier to say than this? Nor is this worthy of those most learned and holy men who have found approval in so many centuries. The child must be named, as the German proverb says. We must have a definition of what that power is, what it does, what it suffers, what happens to it. For example, to put it very crudely, the question is whether this power has a duty, or makes an attempt, to pray, or fast, or labor, or discipline the body, or give alms, or anything else of this kind; for if it is a power, it must do some sort of work. But here you are dumber than Seriphian frogs and fishes.[11] And how could you give a definition, when on your own testimony you are still uncertain about the power itself, disagreeing with each other and inconsistent with yourselves? What is to be done about a definition when the thing defined does not itself remain constant?

But let us suppose that sometime after Plato's enigmatic number of years [12] you reach agreement about the power itself, and its

---

[10] Bernard of Clairvaux, Sermo 20 in *Canticles* (*MPL* 183.867).

[11] Pliny the Elder, *Natural History* viii.83.2. "A frog from Seriphos" was a proverb for a silent person.

[12] *"Post annos Platonis."* Cf. Cicero, *Epistola ad Atticum* vii.13B.5: *"Est*

work is then defined as being to pray or fast or to do some such thing as still perhaps lies hidden in the world of Plato's Ideas. Who can assure us that this is true, that it is pleasing to God, and that we are safe and on the right lines? Especially when you yourselves admit that it is a human affair, which does not have the testimony of the Spirit, since it has been much discussed by the philosophers and was in the world before Christ came and the Spirit was sent down from heaven. So it is very certain that this dogma was not sent down from heaven, but sprang from the earth long before; and therefore a great deal of evidence is needed to confirm it as certain and true.

Granted, then, that we are private individuals and few in number, while you are publicans [13] and there are many of you; we are uneducated, you most learned; we stupid, you most talented; we were born yesterday, you are older than Deucalion; [14] we have never been accepted, you have the approval of so many centuries: in a word, we are sinners, carnal men, and dolts, while you with your sanctity, Spirit, and miracles inspire awe in the very demons. You should at least grant us the right of Turks and Jews, and let us ask the reason for your dogma, as your St. Peter has commanded you ⟨I Peter 3:15⟩. Our request is very modest, for we do not demand that it should be proved by sanctity, the Spirit, or miracles, though on your principles we could do so, since you demand this of others. Indeed, we do not even require you to produce any in-

---

enim numero Platonis obscurius," from a letter of Cicero to Atticus in which he professes himself unable to understand a guarded allusion that Atticus has made to personalities of the day. The phrase had evidently passed into a proverb, and if one refers to the eighth book of Plato's *Republic,* one can see why. At 546C, Plato refers in extremely enigmatic terms to a supposed "nuptial number" governing the period of human gestation, and derives from the phenomenon of premature birth the gradual declension of the human race until a period of $(3 \times 4 \times 5)^4$ years was reached, i.e., 12,960,000 years, which was the duration of a Great Year in the life of the universe. Like Pythagoras, Plato was obsessed by the theory of numbers, and his argument here is that the perfect city did in fact exist long ago and will exist again. Adam calls this "notoriously the most difficult passage in his writings" and collects a vast amount of material on the subject in his edition of the *Republic,* Vol. II, pp. 264–312.

[13] *"Publicani."* The use of this word instead of *publici* contains an obvious reference to the "publicans" (tax collectors) of the New Testament, with the implication perhaps that just as these public figures were often notorious for their exactions, so the supporters of free choice not only enjoy publicity, but deserve notoriety on account of the abuses (such as the traffic in indulgences) which their teaching allows.

[14] Ovid, *Metamorphoses* i.318 ff. Deucalion, son of Prometheus, is the Noah of Greek Mythology, who survived the Flood and became the ancestor of the Hellenes.

stance of a thought, word, or deed in connection with your dogma, but only to explain the thing itself and make clear what you wish us to understand by it, and in what form.

If you will not or cannot give an example of it, at least let us try to do so. Imitate the pope and his crowd, who say, "Do as we say, not as we do." Tell us what work that power requires to be done, and we will set about it and leave you at leisure. Shall we not obtain at least this request from you? The more numerous, ancient, and important you are, and the more you on all counts surpass us, the greater is your disgrace that when we, who in your eyes are of no account whatsoever, wish to learn and practice your dogma, you are unable to prove it to us either by a miracle, such as the killing of a louse, or by any tiny motion [15] of the Spirit, or any tiny work of sanctity. You are unable, in fact, to exemplify it in a single deed or word; what is more—and this is unprecedented— you cannot even give an account of its form or meaning, so that at least we might imitate it. What fine teachers of free choice you are! What are you now but "a voice and nothing more"? [16] Who is it now, Erasmus, that boasts of the Spirit and manifests nothing of it, or who merely talks and waits forthwith to be believed? Is it not those friends of yours, who have been so extolled to the skies? Is it not you, who do not even speak, and yet make such boasts and demands?

We entreat you therefore for Christ's sake, my dear Erasmus, you and your friends, to give us leave at least to be alarmed by the peril to our conscience, and to tremble with fear, or at least to defer our assent to a dogma that you yourself see to be nothing but an empty sound and a mere grinding out of syllables—I mean, "There is a power of free choice, there is a power of free choice"— even if you had achieved your utmost aim and all your points were proved and granted. Moreover, it is still uncertain even among your own party whether this empty term exists or not, since they are at variance with each other and inconsistent with themselves. It is most unfair, or rather it is quite the most wretched thing in the world, that our consciences, which Christ has redeemed with his own blood, should be harassed with the mere phantom of a single petty term, and that of doubtful status. Yet if we refuse to let ourselves be troubled by it, we are charged with unprecedented pride for having despised so many Fathers of so many centuries who have asserted free choice; though the truth is, as you see from what has been said, that they have entirely failed to give any defini- tion of free choice, and the dogma of free choice is set up under

[15] "Affectulo."   [16] See above, p. 31.

the cover of their authority, although they are unable to make clear either its species or its names, and thus delude the world with a lying word.

And here, Erasmus, we recall your own advice given earlier, when you urged that questions of this kind should be left alone and that we should rather preach Christ crucified and the things that suffice for Christian godliness. This has all along been the object of our inquiry and discussion. For what else are we aiming at but that the simplicity and purity of Christian doctrine may prevail, while the things that have been invented and introduced alongside of it by men may be abandoned and disregarded? But you who give such advice to us do not follow it yourself, but rather the opposite: you write diatribes, you exalt the decrees of the popes, you boast of the authority of men, and you make every attempt to sidetrack us into things irrelevant and foreign to the Holy Scriptures, and to involve us in discussion of nonessentials, so that we may corrupt and confound the simplicity and genuineness of Christian godliness with man-made accretions. From this it is easily seen that you were not sincere in giving us that advice and are not serious in anything you write, but are confident that you can lead the world in any direction you like with the empty baubles of your words. Yet in fact you lead it nowhere, since you utter nothing but sheer contradiction always and everywhere, so that whoever called you a veritable Proteus [17] or Vertumnus [18] was perfectly right. As Christ said: "Physician, heal thyself!" (Luke 4:23). " 'Tis disgrace for a teacher when his own fault finds him out." [19]

Until you prove your affirmative, therefore, we stand by our negative; and even under the judgment of that whole choir of saints which you invoke, or rather of the whole world, we dare to say, and we glory in saying, that it is our duty not to admit something which is nothing and the nature of which cannot with certainty be shown. Furthermore, we charge all of you with incredible presumption or insanity when you demand that we admit this thing for no other reason than that it pleases you—who are so many, so great, and so ancient—to assert something which you

---

[17] See above, p. 103 n. 7.

[18] The Etruscan god of the changing year, who could assume any shape he wished; cf. Horace, *Satires* ii.7, 14.

[19] *"Turpe est doctori, quem culpa redarguit ipsum."* Cato, *Disticha moralis*, Lib. I. A collection of edifying moral couplets is attributed to one Cato who lived at the close of the third century A.D. and who was obviously aiming at copybook fame in schools. Luther quotes an aphorism from this collection, possibly a memory of school days.

yourselves confess to be nothing. Is it worthy conduct on the part of Christian teachers to delude the unhappy common people in the matter of piety by treating something that is nothing as if it were of great moment for salvation? Where is now that sharp Greek mind of yours ⟨E., p. 43⟩ which used to invent lies with at least some semblance of charm, but is here uttering falsehoods naked and unadorned? Where is that Latin industry which equaled the Greek, but which now can thus deceive and be deceived by the emptiest of words? But that is what happens to careless or evil-minded readers of books when they treat things that are the result of weakness in the Fathers and the saints as being all of the highest authority, so that the fault lies not with the authors, but with the readers. It is as though someone relying on the sanctity and authority of St. Peter should contend that everything St. Peter ever said was true, even including what he said when in Matt. 16⟨:22⟩ he sought, through his human weakness,[20] to dissuade Christ from suffering, or when he bade Christ depart from him out of the ship ⟨Luke 5:8⟩, and many other instances, for which he was rebuked by Christ himself.

People of this kind are like those irresponsibles who, in order to raise a laugh, say that not everything in the Gospel is true, and seize on that verse in John 8⟨:48⟩ where the Jews say to Christ: "Are we not right in saying that you are a Samaritan and have a demon?"; or this: "He deserves death" ⟨Matt. 26:66⟩; or this: "We found this man perverting our nation, and forbidding us to give tribute to Caesar" ⟨Luke 23:2⟩. The assertors of free choice do the same, though for a different purpose, and not willfully like them, but through blindness and ignorance, when they take out of the Fathers what the latter, led astray by human weakness,[21] have said in favor of free choice, and even oppose it to what the same Fathers in the strength of the Spirit have elsewhere said against free choice; then they proceed to press and force their point so that the better gives way to the worse. It thus comes about that they ascribe authority to the worse expressions because these are in accord with their worldly mind,[22] and deny it to the better because those are contrary to their worldly mind. Why do we not rather choose the better, for there are many such in the Fathers? Let me give an example. What more worldly,[23] nay, more impious, sacrilegious, and blasphemous thing could be said than Jerome's familiar statement that "virginity peoples heaven, marriage the earth," [24] as if

---

[20] *"Ex carnis infirmitate."*
[22] *"Sensum carnis suae."*
[24] *Ad Eustochium, Ep.* XX, c. 19 *(MPL* 22.405) .
[21] *"Infirmitate carnis."*
[23] *"Carnalius."*

it were earth and not heaven that was intended for the patriarchs and apostles and Christian husbands and wives, or as if heaven were meant for heathen vestal virgins without Christ? Yet these and similar things the Sophists collect out of the Fathers, relying on quantity rather than quality to procure authority for them, just like that idiot Faber of Constance,[25] who recently presented that "Pearl" of his, I mean that Augean stable, to the public in order that the pious and learned might have something to disgust and sicken them.

The True Church, Which Does Not Err, Is Hidden from Men's Sight ⟨WA 649–652⟩

This is my answer to your statement that it is incredible that God should have concealed an error in his Church for so many centuries, and should not have revealed to any of his saints what we claim to be the chief doctrine of the gospel. ⟨E., p. 46.⟩ First, we do not say that this error has been tolerated by God in his Church or in any of his saints. For the Church is ruled by the Spirit of God and the saints are led by the Spirit of God (Rom. 8⟨:14⟩). And Christ remains with his Church even to the end of the world ⟨Matt. 28:20⟩; and the Church of God is the pillar and ground of the truth ⟨I Tim. 3:15⟩. These things, I say, we know; for the creed that we all hold affirms, "I believe in the holy catholic church"; so that it is impossible for the Church to err, even in the smallest article. And even if we grant that some of the elect are bound in error all their lives, yet they must necessarily return to the right way before they die, since Christ says in John 10 ⟨:28⟩: "No one shall snatch them out of my hand."

But here is the toil, here is the task,[26] to determine whether those whom you call the Church are the Church, or rather, whether after being in error all their lives they were at last brought back before they died. For it does not immediately follow that if God has permitted all those whom you quote, from as

---

[25] Johann Faber (1478–1541), German theologian, Vicar-general of the Bishop of Constance and later himself Bishop of Vienna; wrote against Luther in 1522 and 1524. From the title of his second book, *Malleus in haeresin Lutheranam,* he became known as "the hammer of the heretics." It is probably this book to which Luther refers here; Faber may himself have regarded it as his "pearl."

[26] This is an allusion to the Sibyl's warning to Aeneas about the perils of visiting the underworld (*Aeneid* vi.126–129): *"Facilis descensus Averno:/ noctes atque dies patet atri ianua Ditis;/sed revocare gradum, superasque evadere ad auras,/hoc opus, hic labor est.*

many centuries as you like and most learned though they were, to be in error, therefore he has permitted his Church to err. Look at Israel, the people of God, where in so long a line of kings over so long a period of time not a single king is listed who did not err. And in the time of the prophet Elijah, everybody and everything in the public life of this people had so far fallen into idolatry that Elijah thought he alone was left ⟨I Kings 18:22⟩; and yet, although kings, princes, priests, prophets, and everything that could be called the People or Church of God was going to perdition, God had kept for himself seven thousand ⟨I Kings 19:18⟩. But who saw them, or knew them to be the People of God? Who, then, even at the present time would venture to deny that, concealed under those outstanding figures—for you mention none but men of public office and distinction—God has preserved for himself a Church among the common people, and has permitted those others to perish as he did in the Kingdom of Israel? For it is characteristic of God to lay low the picked men of Israel and slay their strong ones (Ps. 78⟨:31⟩), but to preserve the dregs and remnant of Israel, as Isaiah says ⟨ch. 10:22⟩.

What happened in Christ's own time, when all the apostles fell away ⟨Matt. 26:31, 56⟩ and he himself was denied and condemned by the whole people, and scarcely more than a Nicodemus, a Joseph, and the thief on the cross were saved? Were these then called the People of God? They were the remnant of the People, but they were not so called, and what was so called was not the People of God. Who knows but that the state of the Church of God throughout the whole course of the world from the beginning has always been such that some have been called the People and the saints of God who were not so, while others, a remnant in their midst, really were the People or the saints, but were never called so, as witness the stories of Cain and Abel, Ishmael and Isaac, Esau and Jacob? Look at the time of the Arians,[27] when scarcely five Catholic bishops were preserved in the whole world, and they were driven from their sees, while the Arians reigned everywhere in the public name and office of the Church; nevertheless, Christ preserved his Church under these heretics, though in such a way that it was far from being recognized and regarded as the Church.

[27] The followers of Arius (d. 336), presbyter of Alexandria, excommunicated in 318 for denying the full divinity of Christ. His teaching, variously modified, won widespread acceptance and had the support of several emperors before the orthodox doctrine, formulated at the Council of Nicaea in 325, finally prevailed.

Under the reign of the pope, show me one bishop discharging his duty, show me one Council that has been concerned with matters of piety rather than robes,[28] rank, revenues, and other profane trifles, which no one who was not insane could attribute to the Holy Spirit. Yet they are nonetheless called the Church, although all of them, at least while they live like this, are reprobates and anything but the Church. Yet even under them Christ has preserved his Church, but not so as to have it called the Church. How many saints do you suppose the minions of the Inquisition [29] alone have burned and murdered during the last few centuries? I mean men like John Hus, in whose time without doubt there lived many holy men in the same spirit.

Why do you not rather express amazement at this, Erasmus, that from the beginning of the world there has always been more outstanding talent, greater learning, and more earnest application among the heathen than among Christians or the People of God? For as Christ himself confesses, the children of this world are wiser than the children of light ⟨Luke 16:8⟩. What Christian can be compared to a Cicero alone (not to mention the Greeks) for talent, learning, or diligence? What, then, are we to say impeded such men, so that none of them was able to attain to grace? For they certainly exercised free choice to the utmost of their powers, and who will dare to say there was none among them who sought after truth with the utmost application? Yet we cannot but assert that none of them found it. Will you here too say it is incredible that all through history God should have left so many great men to themselves and let them strive in vain? Surely, if free choice were anything or could do anything, it must have existed and been able to do something in those men, in some one instance at least. But it has effected nothing, or rather, it always wrought in the contrary direction, so that by this single argument it can be sufficiently proved that free choice is nothing, since no sign of it can be produced from the beginning of the world to the end.

But to return to the point. How is it surprising if God allows all

---

28 *"Pallia."* The pallium is an ecclesiastical vestment bestowed by the pope on metropolitans, primates, and archbishops as a symbol of the jurisdiction delegated to them by the Holy See. It was much coveted, and the payments made to obtain it were an important source of papal revenue.

29 *"Inquisitores haereticae pravitatis,"* "inquisitors of heretical depravity"; a title bestowed by the pope in the early part of the thirteenth century on special agents for the extirpation of heresy. This marked a significant stage in the development of antiheretical legislation which, beginning in the time of Theodosius I, reached its climax of horror in the Spanish Inquisition.

the great ones of the Church to walk in their own ways, when he has thus allowed all the nations to walk in their own ways, as Paul says in Acts ⟨14:16⟩? The Church of God is not as commonplace a thing, my dear Erasmus, as the phrase "the Church of God"; nor are the saints of God met with as universally as the phrase "the saints of God." They are a pearl and precious jewels, which the Spirit does not cast before swine ⟨Matt. 7:6⟩ but keeps hidden, as Scripture says ⟨Matt. 11:25⟩, lest the ungodly should see the glory of God. Otherwise, if they were plainly recognized by all, how could they possibly be as harassed and afflicted in the world as they are? As Paul says: "If they had known, they would not have crucified the Lord of glory" ⟨I Cor. 2:8⟩.

I do not say these things as denying that those whom you mention are the saints or the Church of God, but because if anyone does deny it, it cannot be proved that they are saints, but remains entirely uncertain, so that an argument based on their sanctity is not reliable enough for the confirmation of any dogma. I call them saints and regard them as such; I call them and believe them to be the Church of God; but I do so by the rule of love, not the rule of faith. For love, which always thinks well of everyone, and is not suspicious but believes and assumes the best about its neighbors, calls anyone who is baptized a saint; and no harm is done if it makes a mistake, for it is in the nature of love to be deceived, seeing it is exposed to all the uses and abuses of all men as the general servant of good and bad, faithful and unfaithful, true and false alike. But faith calls no one a saint unless he is declared so by a divine judgment, because it is in the nature of faith not to be deceived. Therefore, although we ought all to be regarded as saints by one another according to the law of love, yet no one ought to be decreed a saint according to the law of faith, so as to make it an article of faith that this or that person is a saint. That is the way in which that enemy of God, the pope, puts himself in the place of God ⟨II Thess. 2:4⟩ and canonizes men of his own party, whom he does not know, as saints.

All I say about these saints of yours, or rather ours, is that since they disagree with one another, those ought rather to have been followed who have spoken best, that is, against free choice and in support of grace, while those ought to have been ignored who, because of the infirmity of the flesh, have borne witness rather to the flesh than the Spirit. Similarly, with regard to those who are not consistent with themselves, the passages should have been selected and held on to where they speak under the influence of the Spirit, and those where they savor of the flesh should have been ignored.

That was the proper thing for a Christian reader to do, as a clean beast that parts the hoof and chews the cud ⟨Lev. 11:3⟩. As it is, by failing to exercise judgment we swallow everything indiscriminately, or what is worse, by a perversion of judgment we throw away the better and accept the worse parts of the same authors. Then we attach to these worse parts the title and authority of their author's sanctity, which has been deserved only because of what is best in them, and on account of the Spirit alone, not because of free choice or the flesh.

Scripture, with Its "Internal" and "External" Clarity, as the Test of Truth ⟨WA 652–661⟩

What, then, are we to do? The Church is hidden, the saints are unknown. What and whom are we to believe? Or, as you very pointedly argue, who gives us certainty? How shall we prove the Spirit? ⟨E., p. 44.⟩ If you look for learning, on both sides there are scholars; if for quality of life, on both sides are sinners; if for Scripture, both sides acknowledge it. But the dispute is not so much about Scripture ⟨E., p. 43.⟩, which may not yet be sufficiently clear, as about the meaning of Scripture; and on both sides are men, of whom neither numbers nor learning nor dignity, much less fewness, ignorance, and humility, have anything to do with the case. The matter therefore remains in doubt and the case is still *sub judice*,[30] so that it looks as if we might be wise to adopt the position of the Skeptics, unless the line you take is best, when you express your uncertainty in such a way as to aver that you are seeking to learn the truth, though in the meantime you incline to the side that asserts free choice, until the truth becomes clear.

To this I reply that there is something in what you say, but not the whole truth. For we shall not prove the spirits by arguments about learning, life, talent, numbers, dignity, ignorance, crudity, rarity, and lowliness. Nor do I approve of those who have recourse to boasting of the Spirit; for I have had this year and am still having, a sharp enough fight with those fanatics who subject the Scriptures to the interpretation of their own spirit.[31] It is on this account also that I have hitherto attacked the pope, in whose kingdom nothing is more commonly stated or more generally accepted

[30] Cf. Horace, *Ars poetica,* 78.
[31] The reference is to the *Schwärmer,* or "Enthusiasts," as Luther called them, whom he had first encountered in the spring of 1522, and had more recently attacked in his book *Against the Heavenly Prophets* (1525), for which see *WA* 18, 62 ff.

than the idea that the Scriptures are obscure and ambiguous, so that the spirit to interpret them must be sought from the Apostolic See of Rome. Nothing more pernicious could be said than this, for it has led ungodly men to set themselves above the Scriptures and to fabricate whatever they pleased, until the Scriptures have been completely trampled down and we have been believing and teaching nothing but the dreams of madmen. In a word, that saying is no human invention, but a virus sent into the world by the incredible malice of the prince of all demons himself.

What we say is this: the spirits are to be tested or proved by two sorts of judgment. One is internal, whereby through the Holy Spirit or a special gift of God, anyone who is enlightened concerning [32] himself and his own salvation, judges and discerns with the greatest certainty the dogmas and opinions of all men. Of this it is said in I Cor. 1⟨2:15⟩: "The spiritual man judges all things, but himself is judged by no one." This belongs to faith and is necessary for every individual Christian. We have called it above [33] "the internal clarity of Holy Scripture." Perhaps this was what those had in mind who gave you the reply that everything must be decided by the judgment of the Spirit. ⟨E., p. 45.⟩ But this judgment helps no one else, and with it we are not here concerned, for no one, I think, doubts its reality.

There is therefore another, an external judgment, whereby with the greatest certainty we judge the spirits and dogmas of all men, not only for ourselves, but also for others and for their salvation. This judgment belongs to the public ministry of the Word and to the outward office, and is chiefly the concern of leaders and preachers of the Word. We make use of it when we seek to strengthen those who are weak in faith and confute opponents. This is what we earlier called "the external clarity of Holy Scripture." Thus we say that all spirits are to be tested in the presence of the Church at the bar of Scripture. For it ought above all to be settled and established among Christians that the Holy Scriptures are a spiritual light far brighter than the sun itself, especially in things that are necessary to salvation.[34] But because we have for so long been persuaded of the opposite by that pestilential saying of the Sophists that the Scriptures are obscure and ambiguous, we are obliged to begin by proving even that first principle of ours by which everything else has to be proved—a procedure that among the philosophers would be regarded as absurd and impossible.

[32] *"Pro"*; literally, "on behalf of."   [33] Cf. p. 112.
[34] *"Ad salutem vel necessitatem."* See Introduction, p. 30.

First, then, Moses says in Deut. 17⟨:8 ff.⟩ that if any difficult case arises, they are to go to the place which God has chosen for his name, and consult the priests there, who must judge it according to the law of the Lord. "According to the law of the Lord," he says.[35] But how can they judge unless the law of the Lord is externally quite clear,[36] so as to give satisfaction to those concerned? Otherwise, it would have been enough to say that they must judge "according to their own spirit." In all government of peoples, however, it is the rule that all matters of dispute should be settled by means of laws. But how could they be settled if the laws were not entirely certain and like shining lights among the people? For if laws are ambiguous and uncertain, not only would no disputes be decided, but neither would there be any certain norms of conduct; for laws are made in order that conduct may be regulated according to a certain pattern, and questions of dispute thus settled. That which is the standard and measure of other things, therefore, as the law is, ought to be the clearest and most certain of all. And if this light and certainty in laws is necessary, and is granted freely to the whole world by the bounty of God, in profane societies which have to do with temporal things, how is it conceivable that he should not give his Christians, his elect, laws and rules of much greater light and certainty by which they might direct themselves and settle all their disputes, seeing that he wishes temporal things to be despised by those who are his? For if God so clothes the grass of the field, which today is, and tomorrow is cast into the oven, how much more us ⟨Matt. 6:30⟩? But let us go on and overwhelm that pestilent saying of the Sophists with the Scriptures. Psalm 18⟨19:9⟩ says: "The commandment of the Lord is lightsome,[37] or pure, enlightening the eyes"; and surely what enlightens the eyes is not obscure or ambiguous. Psalm 118 ⟨119:130⟩ says: "The unfolding [38] of thy words gives light; it imparts understanding to the simple." Here the words of God are represented as a kind of door, or an opening, which is plain for all to see and even illuminates the simple. Isaiah 8⟨:20⟩ sends all questions "to the law and the testimony," and threatens that unless we do so the light of dawn will be denied us. In Zech., ch. 2,[39] it is commanded to seek the law from the mouth of the priest, as being the messenger of the Lord of Hosts; and what a fine messenger or ambassador of

---

[35] *Deut.* 17:11 (Vulg.).

[36] I.e., by contrast with the internal clarity mentioned earlier, which meant the illumination of the Spirit in the individual soul.

[37] "*Lucidum,*" rendered as "lightsome" in the Douay Version (Ps. 18:9).

[38] "*Ostium,*" "door."   [39] The correct reference is Mal. 2:7.

the Lord he would be if his message were both ambiguous to himself and obscure to the people, so that neither he knew what he was saying nor they what they were hearing! And what in the whole Old Testament, especially in Ps. 118⟨119⟩, is more often said in praise of the Scripture than that it is a most certain and evident light? The psalmist celebrates its clarity thus: "A lamp to my feet and a light to my path" ⟨Ps. 119:105⟩. He does not say, "A lamp to my feet is thy Spirit alone," though he speaks of the work of the Spirit too: "Thy good Spirit shall lead me on the level ground" [40] ⟨Ps. 143:10⟩. In this way it is called both a "way" and a "path," no doubt because of its entire certainty.

Let us turn to the New Testament. Paul says in Rom. 1⟨:2⟩ that the gospel was promised through the prophets in the Holy Scriptures, and in ch. 3⟨:21⟩ that the righteousness of faith is witnessed to by the Law and the Prophets. Now, what sort of witness is it if it is obscure? But in all his epistles Paul represents the gospel as a word of light, a gospel of glory,[41] and he does this explicitly and at length in II Cor., chs. 3 and 4, where he argues magnificently about the glory [42] of both Moses and Christ. Peter, too, says in II Peter 1⟨:19⟩: "We have the very sure word of prophecy, to which you will do well to pay attention as to a lamp shining in a dark place." Here Peter makes the Word of God a shining lamp and all else darkness; and do we want to make obscurity and darkness of the Word? Christ so often calls himself the light of the world ⟨John 8:12; 9:5; etc.⟩ and John the Baptist a burning and shining lamp ⟨John 5:35⟩, not because of the holiness of their lives, but without doubt because of the Word. So in Thessalonians,[43] Paul calls them shining lights in the world because he says: "You hold fast the word of life" ⟨Phil. 2:16⟩; for life without the Word is uncertain and obscure.

And what are the apostles doing when they prove their own preachings by the Scriptures? Are they trying to obscure for us their own darkness with yet greater darkness? Or to prove something well known by something known less well? What is Christ doing in John 5⟨:39⟩, where he tells the Jews to search the Scriptures because they bear witness to him? Is he trying to put them in doubt about faith in him? What are those people in Acts 17⟨:11⟩

---

[40] "In terra recta." Vulgate reads "in terram rectam," which Douay translates "into the right land." RSV has "on a level path."

[41] "Euangelion claritatis."

[42] "De claritate." The commoner word in the Vulgate of II Cor., chs. 3 and 4, is gloria; claritas occurs only in ch. 3:18 and 4:6, where the English versions have "glory."

[43] Philippians is obviously meant.

doing, who after hearing Paul were reading the Scriptures day and night to see if these things were so? Do not all these things prove that the apostles, like Christ himself, point us to the Scriptures as the very clearest witnesses to what they themselves say? What right have we, then, to make them obscure? I ask you, are these words of Scripture obscure or ambiguous: "God created heaven and earth"; "the Word became flesh"; and all those affirmations which the whole world has taken as articles of faith? And where have they been taken from? Isn't it from the Scriptures?

And what is it that preachers do, to this very day? Do they interpret and expound the Scriptures? Yet if the Scripture they expound is uncertain, who can assure us that their exposition is certain? Another new exposition? And who will expound the exposition? At this rate we shall go on forever. In short, if Scripture is obscure or ambiguous, what point was there in God's giving it to us? Are we not obscure and ambiguous enough without having our obscurity, ambiguity, and darkness augmented for us from heaven? What, then, will become of that word of the apostle: "All Scripture inspired by God is profitable for teaching, for reproof, for correction" ⟨II Tim. 3:16⟩? Nay, Paul, it is not profitable at all, but the things you attribute to Scripture must be sought from the Fathers who have been approved for hundreds of years, and from the Roman See! So the statement must be revoked which you make in writing to Titus, that a bishop must be able to give instruction in sound doctrine and also to confute those who contradict it, and silence empty talkers and deceivers ⟨Titus 1:9 ff.⟩. How can he, when you leave the Scriptures obscure to him, giving him, as it were, arms of tow and slender reeds for a sword? Then Christ, too, will have to recant, for he makes us a false promise when he says: "I will give you a mouth and wisdom, which none of your adversaries will be able to withstand" ⟨Luke 21:15⟩. How will they not withstand when we oppose them with obscure and uncertain weapons? And why do you yourself, Erasmus, set out the nature of Christianity for us if the Scriptures are obscure to you?

But I fancy I have long since grown wearisome, even to dullards, by spending so much time and trouble on a matter that is so very clear. But that impudent and blasphemous saying that the Scriptures are obscure had to be overwhelmed in this way so that even you, my dear Erasmus, might realize what you are saying when you deny that Scripture is crystal clear. For you are bound to admit at the same time that all your saints whom you quote are much less crystal clear. For who is there to make us sure of their light if you make the Scriptures obscure? So those who deny that the

Scriptures are quite clear and plain leave us nothing but darkness.

But here you will say, "All this is nothing to me; I do not say that the Scriptures are obscure in all parts (for who would be so crazy?), but only in this and similar parts." I reply: neither do I say these things in opposition to you only, but in opposition to all who think as you do; moreover, in opposition to you I say with respect to the whole Scripture, I will not have any part of it called obscure. What we have cited from Peter holds good here, that the Word of God is for us "a lamp shining in a dark place" (II Peter 1:19). But if part of this lamp does not shine, it will be a part of the dark place rather than of the lamp itself. Christ has not so enlightened us as deliberately to leave some part of his Word obscure while commanding us to give heed to it, for he commands us in vain to give heed if it does not give light.

Consequently, if the dogma of free choice is obscure or ambiguous, it does not belong to Christians or the Scriptures, and it should be abandoned and reckoned among those fables which Paul condemns Christians for wrangling about.[44] If, however, it does belong to Christians and the Scriptures, it ought to be clear, open, and evident, exactly like all the other clear and evident articles of faith. For all the articles of faith held by Christians ought to be such that they are not only most certain to Christians themselves, but also fortified against the attacks of others by such manifest and clear Scriptures that they shut all men's mouths and prevent their saying anything against them; as Christ says in his promise to us: "I will give you a mouth and wisdom, which none of your adversaries will be able to withstand" (Luke 21:15). If, therefore, our mouth is so weak at this point that our adversaries can withstand it, his saying that no adversary can withstand our mouth is false. Either, therefore, we shall have no adversaries while maintaining the dogma of free choice (which will be the case if free choice does not belong to us), or if it does belong to us, we shall have adversaries, it is true, but they will not be able to withstand us.

But this inability of the adversaries to withstand (since the point arises here) does not mean that they are compelled to abandon their own position, or are persuaded either to confess or keep silence. For who can compel men against their will to believe, to confess their error, or to be silent? "What is more loquacious than vanity?" as Augustine says.[45] But what is meant is that their mouth is so far stopped that they have nothing to say in reply and, although they say a great deal, yet in the judgment of common sense

[44] Cf. I Tim. 4:7; II Tim. 2:14; Titus 3:9.   [45] De civitate Dei V.xxvi.2.

they say nothing. This is best shown by examples.

When Christ in Matt. 22⟨:23 ff.⟩ put the Sadducees to silence by quoting Scripture and proving the resurrection of the dead from the words of Moses in Ex. 3⟨:6⟩: "I am the God of Abraham," etc.; "He is not the God of the dead, but of the living," here they could not resist or say anything in reply. But did they therefore give up their own opinion? And how often did he confute the Pharisees by the plainest Scriptures and arguments, so that the people clearly saw them convicted, and even they themselves perceived it? Nevertheless, they continued to be his adversaries. Stephen in Acts 7⟨6:10⟩ spoke, according to Luke, in such a way that they could not withstand the wisdom and the Spirit with which he spoke. But what did they do? Did they give way? On the contrary, being ashamed to be beaten, and not being able to withstand, they went mad, and shutting their ears and eyes they set up false witnesses against him (Acts 8⟨6:11-14⟩).

See how this man stands before the Council and confutes his adversaries! After enumerating the benefits which God had bestowed on that people from the beginning, and proving that God had never ordered a temple to be built for him (for this was the question at issue and the substance of the charge against him), he at length concedes that a temple was in fact built under Solomon, but then he qualifies it in this way: "Yet the Most High does not dwell in houses made with hands," and in proof of this he quotes Isa. 66⟨:1⟩: "What house is this that you build for me?" Tell me, what could they say here against so plain a Scripture? Yet they were quite unmoved and remained set in their own opinion; which leads him to attack them directly, in the words: "Uncircumcised in heart and ears, you always withstand the Holy Spirit," etc. ⟨Acts 7:51⟩. He says they withstand, although they were unable to withstand.

Let us come to our own times. When John Hus argues as follows against the pope on the basis of Matt. 16⟨:18⟩: "The gates of hell do not prevail against my church" (is there any ambiguity or obscurity here?), "but against the pope and his followers the gates of hell do prevail, for they are notorious the world over for their open impiety and wickednesses" (is this also obscure?), "therefore the pope and his followers are not the church of which Christ speaks"—what could they say in reply to this, or how could they withstand the mouth that Christ had given him? Yet they did withstand, and they persisted until they burned him, so far were they from altering their opinion. Nor does Christ overlook this when he says, "Your adversaries will not be able to withstand." They are adversaries, he says; therefore, they will withstand, for otherwise they would not be adversaries but friends; and yet they will not be able to withstand. What else does this mean but that in withstanding they will not be able to withstand?

If, accordingly, we are able so to confute free choice that our adversaries cannot withstand, even if they persist in their own opinion and withstand in spite of their conscience, we shall have done enough. For I have had enough experience to know that no one wants to be beaten and, as Quintilian [46] says, there is no one who would not rather seem to know than to learn, though it is a sort of proverb on everyone's lips nowadays (from use, or rather abuse, more than from conviction) : "I wish to learn, I'm ready to be taught, and when shown a better way, to follow it; I'm only human, and I may be wrong." The fact is that under this mask, this fair show of humility, they find it possible quite confidently to say: "I'm not satisfied, I don't see it, he does violence to the Scriptures, he's an obstinate assertor"; because, of course, they are sure that no one will suspect such very humble souls of stubbornly resisting and even vigorously attacking recognized truth. So it is made to seem that their refusal to alter their opinion ought not to be set down to their own perverseness, but to the obscurity and ambiguity of the arguments.

That is just what the Greek philosophers did too; for lest any of them should seem to give way to another, even if he was plainly proved wrong, they began to deny first principles, as Aristotle records. Meanwhile, we blandly persuade ourselves and others that there are many good men in the world who would willingly embrace the truth if there were anyone to teach it clearly, and that it is not to be supposed that so many learned men for so many centuries have been in error or ignorance. As if we did not know that the world is the kingdom of Satan, where besides the blindness we are born with from our carnal nature, we are under the dominion of the most mischievous spirits, so that we are hardened in that very blindness and imprisoned in a darkness no longer human but demonic. If, then, Scripture is crystal clear, you say, why have men of outstanding talent in so many centuries been blind in this regard? ⟨E., p. 44.⟩ I reply that they have been thus blind for the praise and glory of free choice, in order that this highly extolled power, by which man is able to apply himself to the things that pertain to eternal salvation—that is to say, a power that neither sees sights nor hears sounds, much less understands or seeks after them—might be shown to be what it is. For here the text applies

[46] In the Preface to his *Institutio oratoria*.

that Christ and the Evangelists so often quote from Isaiah: "You shall indeed hear but never understand, and you shall see but never perceive" ⟨Isa. 6:9-10; Matt. 13:14; etc.⟩. What else does this mean but that free choice or the human heart is so held down by the power of Satan that unless it is miraculously raised up by the Spirit of God it cannot of itself either see or hear things that strike the eyes and ears themselves so plainly as to be palpable?

Such is the misery and blindness of the human race! For thus even the Evangelists themselves, as they wonder how it could be that the Jews were not won by the works and words of Christ, which were plainly unanswerable and undeniable, find the answer in this passage of Scripture, namely, that man left to himself sees but does not perceive and hears but does not understand. What could be more unnatural? "The light," he says, "shines in the darkness, and the darkness does not comprehend it" ⟨John 1:5⟩. Who would believe this? Who ever heard anything like it? That the light shines in the darkness, and yet the darkness remains darkness and is not illuminated?

It is therefore not astonishing that in divine things men of outstanding talent through so many centuries have been blind. In human things it would be astonishing. In divine things the wonder is rather if there are one or two who are not blind, but it is no wonder if all without exception are blind. For what is the whole human race without the Spirit but (as I have said) the kingdom of the devil, a confused chaos of darkness ⟨Gen. 1:2⟩? That is why Paul calls the demons "the rulers of this darkness" ⟨Eph. 6:12⟩, and says in I Cor. ⟨2:8⟩: "None of the princes of this world knew the wisdom of God." What do you suppose he thinks of the rest, when he asserts that the princes of the world are the slaves of darkness? For by princes he means the first and highest persons in the world, whom you call men of outstanding talent? Why were all the Arians [47] blind? Were there not among them men of outstanding talent? Why is Christ "foolishness to Gentiles" ⟨I Cor. 1:23⟩? Are there not among the Gentiles men of outstanding talent? Why is he a "stumbling block to Jews"? Have there not been among the Jews men of outstanding talent? "God knows the thoughts of the wise," says Paul, "that they are vain" ⟨I Cor. 3:20⟩. He chose not to say "of men," as the text itself does ⟨Ps. 94:11⟩, but points to the first and foremost among men, so that from these we may form a judgment about the rest.

But more about these things later perhaps. It may suffice for a beginning to have laid it down that the Scriptures are perfectly

[47] See above, p. 155 n. 27.

clear, and that by them such a defense of our position may be made that our adversaries will not be able to gainsay it. What cannot be defended in this way is no concern of ours and is no business of Christians. But if there are any who do not perceive this clarity, and are blind or blunder in this sunlight, then they only show—if they are ungodly—how great is the majesty and power of Satan over the sons of men, to make them neither hear nor take in the very clearest words of God. It is as if someone was deceived by a conjuring trick and imagined the sun to be a piece of dead coal or a stone to be gold. If they are godly, they may be reckoned among those of the elect who are led into error at times [48] in order that the power of God may be demonstrated in us, without which we can neither see nor do anything at all.

For it is not due to the weakness of the human mind (as you make out) ⟨E., p. 41⟩ that the words of God are not understood, but, on the contrary, nothing is more fitted for understanding the words of God than such weakness; for it was for the sake of the weak and to the weak that Christ both came and sends his word. It is due to the malice of Satan, who sits enthroned in our weakness, resisting the Word of God. If Satan were not at work, the whole world of men would be converted by a single word of God once heard, and there would be no need of more.

Why do I go on? Why do we not end the case with this Introduction, and pronounce sentence on you from your own words, according to that saying of Christ: "By your words you will be justified, and by your words you will be condemned" ⟨Matt. 12:37⟩? For you say that Scripture is not crystal clear on this point, and then you suspend judgment and discuss both sides of the question, asking what can be said for it and what against; and you do nothing else in the whole of this book, which for that reason you have chosen to call a Diatribe rather than an Apophasis [49] or anything else, because you write with the intention of collating everything and affirming nothing.

If, then, Scripture is not crystal clear, how is it that those of whom you boast are not only blind at this point, but rash and foolish enough to define and assert free choice on the basis of Scripture, as though it were quite positive and plain? I mean your numerous body of most learned men who have found approval in so many centuries down to our day, most of whom have godliness of life as well as a wonderful skill in divine studies to commend

[48] "*Aliquando*." An alternative reading is *aliquanto,* "a little."
[49] Diatribe = "Collation" or "Discourse"; Apophasis = "Declaration."

them, and some gave testimony with their blood to the doctrine of Christ that they had defended with their writings. ⟨E., p. 42.⟩ If you say this sincerely, it is a settled point with you that free choice has assertors endowed with a wonderful skill in Holy Writ, and that such men even bore witness to it with their blood. If that is true, they must have regarded Scripture as crystal clear; otherwise, what meaning would there be in that wonderful skill they had in Holy Writ? Besides, what levity and temerity of mind it would argue to shed their blood for something uncertain and obscure! That is not the act of martyrs of Christ, but of demons!

Now, you also should "consider whether more weight ought not to be ascribed to the previous judgments of so many learned men, so many orthodox, so many saints, so many martyrs, so many theologians old and new, so many universities, councils, bishops, and popes," who have found the Scriptures crystal clear and have confirmed this both by their writings and their blood, or to your own "private judgment" alone when you deny that the Scriptures are crystal clear, and when perhaps you have never shed a single tear or uttered one sigh on behalf of the doctrine of Christ ⟨E., p. 43⟩. If you think those men were right, why do you not imitate them? If you do not think so, why do you rant and brag with such a spate of words, as if you wanted to overwhelm me with a sort of tempest and deluge of oratory—which nevertheless falls with the greater force on your own head, while my ark rides aloft in safety? For you attribute to all these great men the greatest folly and temerity when you describe them as so highly skilled in Scripture and as having asserted it by their pen, their life and their death, although you maintain that it is obscure and ambiguous. This is nothing else but to make them most inexpert in knowledge and most foolish in assertion. I should not have paid them such a compliment in my private contempt of them as you do in your public commendation of them.

I have you here, therefore, on the horns of a dilemma, as they say. For one or the other of these two things must be false: either your saying that those men were admirable for their skill in Holy Writ, their life, and their martyrdom or your saying that Scripture is not crystal clear. But since you are drawn rather to believing that the Scriptures are not crystal clear (for that is what you are driving at throughout your book), we can only conclude that you have described those men as experts in Scripture and martyrs for Christ either in fun or in flattery and in no way seriously, merely in order to throw dust into the eyes of the uneducated public and make difficulties for Luther by loading his cause with odium and contempt by means of empty words. I, however, say that neither statement is true, but both are false. I hold, first, that the Scriptures are entirely clear; secondly, that those men, insofar as they assert free choice, are most inexpert in Holy Writ; and thirdly, that they made this assertion neither by their life nor their death, but only with their pen—and that while their wits were wandering.

I therefore conclude this little debate as follows. By means of Scripture, regarded as obscure, nothing definite has ever yet been settled or can be settled concerning free choice, on your own testimony. Moreover, by the lives of all men from the beginning of the world, nothing has been demonstrated in favor of free choice, as has been said above. Therefore, to teach something which is neither prescribed by a single word inside the Scriptures nor demonstrated by a single fact outside them is no part of Christian doctrine, but belongs to the *True History* of Lucian,[50] except that Lucian, by making sport with ludicrous subjects in deliberate jest, neither deceives nor harms anyone, whereas these friends of ours with their insane treatment of a serious subject, and one that concerns eternal salvation, lead innumerable souls to perdition.

In this way I also might have put an end to this whole question about free choice, seeing that even the testimony of my adversaries favors my position and conflicts with theirs, and there can be no stronger proof than the personal confession and testimony of a defendant against himself. But since Paul bids us silence empty talkers ⟨Titus 1:10 f.⟩, let us go into the details of the case and deal with the subject in the order in which the *Diatribe* proceeds, first confuting the arguments adduced in favor of free choice, then defending arguments of our own that have been attacked, and lastly contending against free choice on behalf of the grace of God.

PART III. REFUTATION OF ARGUMENTS IN SUPPORT OF FREE CHOICE

Erasmus' Definition of Free Choice ⟨WA 661–667⟩

Now first we will begin quite properly with the definition you give of free choice, where you say: "By free choice in this place we mean a power of the human will by which a man can

---

[50] For Lucian, see above, p. 109 n. 9. The *True History* is a novel of fantastic adventure, about which the writer warns the reader at the start: "I write of things which . . . are not and never could have been, and therefore my reader should by no means believe them" (*V.H.* i.4).

apply himself to the things which lead to eternal salvation, or turn away from them" ⟨E., p. 47⟩. It is very prudent of you to give only a bare definition and not to explain (as others usually do) any part of it—perhaps because you were afraid you might be shipwrecked on more than one point. I am thus compelled to look at your definition in detail. The thing defined, if it is examined closely, is certainly itself wider than the definition, which is of a kind that the Sophists would call "vicious," a term they apply whenever a definition does not exhaust the thing defined. For we have shown above that free choice properly belongs to no one but God alone. You might perhaps rightly attribute some measure of choice to man, but to attribute free choice to him in relation to divine things is too much; for the term "free choice," in the judgment of everyone's ears, means (strictly speaking) that which can do and does, in relation to God, whatever it pleases, uninhibited by any law or any sovereign authority. For you would not call a slave free, who acts under the sovereign authority of his master; and still less rightly can we call a man or angel free, when they live under the absolute sovereignty of God (not to mention sin and death) in such a way that they cannot subsist for a moment by their own strength.

Here, therefore, at the very outset, there is a conflict between the definition of the name and the definition of the object, because the term signifies one thing and the object is understood as another. It would be more correct to speak of "vertible choice" or "mutable choice," in the way in which Augustine and the Sophists after him limit the glory and range of the word "free" by introducing the disparaging notion of what they call the vertibility of free choice. In such a way it would be fitting for us to speak, to avoid deceiving the hearts of men with inflated and high-sounding but empty words; just as Augustine also thinks we ought to make it a definite rule to speak only in sober and strictly appropriate words. For in teaching, simplicity and appropriateness of speech is required, not bombast and persuasive rhetorical images. But in order not to appear to delight in quarreling about words, let us for the moment accept this misuse of terms, serious and dangerous though it is, and allow free choice to be the same as vertible choice. Let us also grant Erasmus his point when he makes free choice a power of the human will, as if angels did not have free choice, since in his book he has undertaken to deal only with the free choice of men; otherwise, in this respect too the definition would be narrower than the thing defined.

Let us come to those parts of the definition on which the whole matter hinges. Some of them are plain enough, but others shun the light as though guiltily aware that they have everything to fear; yet nothing ought to be more plainly and unhesitatingly expressed than a definition, since to define obscurely is the same as giving no definition at all. The plain parts are these: "a power of the human will," "by which a man is able," and "to eternal salvation"; but the following are like blindfold gladiators: [1] "to apply," "to the things which lead," and "to turn away." How are we going to divine what this applying and turning away means? And what are the "things which lead to eternal salvation"? What is all this about? I am dealing, I see, with a real Scotus [2] or Heraclitus,[3] and am to be worn out by the double labor involved. For first I have to go groping nervously about amid pitfalls and darkness (which is a venturesome and risky thing to do) in quest of my adversary, and unless I find him I shall be tilting at ghosts and beating the air in the dark. Then if I do manage to drag him into the light, I shall have to come to grips with him on equal terms when I am already wearied with looking for him.

I take it, then, that what is meant by "a power of the human will" is a capacity or faculty or ability or aptitude for willing, unwilling, selecting, neglecting, approving, rejecting, and whatever other actions of the will there are. Now, what it means for that same power to "apply itself" and to "turn away" I do not see, unless it is precisely this willing and unwilling, selecting, neglecting, approving, rejecting, or in other words, precisely the action of the will. So that we must imagine this power to be something between the will itself and its action, as the means by which the will itself produces the action of willing and unwilling, and by which the action of willing and unwilling is itself produced. Anything else it is impossible either to imagine or conceive here. If I am mistaken, let the author be blamed who has given the definition, not I who am trying to understand it; for as the lawyers rightly say, if a man speaks obscurely when he could speak more clearly, his words are to be interpreted against himself. And here

---

[1] *"Andabatae";* a kind of gladiators who wore helmets without openings for the eyes, so that they struck about blindly and with no certain aim. The word occurs once in the letters of Cicero and twice polemically in Jerome, from whom Luther probably takes it.

[2] John Duns Scotus (ca. 1265–1308), British philosopher and theologian of the Franciscan Order; taught in Oxford, Paris, and Cologne; known as *Doctor Subtilis,* "the subtle doctor."

[3] Greek philosopher (ca. 540–475 B.C.), born at Ephesus. His lonely life, the obscurity of his sayings, and his contempt for mankind earned him the name of *skoteinos,* "the dark one."

for the moment I want to forget my Modernist friends [4] with their subtleties, since there is need of plain, blunt speaking for the sake of teaching and understanding.

Now, the things which lead to eternal salvation I take to be the words and works of God, which are presented to the human will so that it may apply itself to them or turn away from them. By the words of God, moreover, I mean both the law and the gospel, the law requiring works and the gospel faith. For there is nothing else that leads either to the grace of God or to eternal salvation except the word and work of God, since grace or the Spirit is life itself, to which we are led by God's word and work.

This life or eternal salvation, however, is something that passes human comprehension, as Paul quotes from Isaiah ⟨64:4⟩ in I Cor. 2⟨:9⟩: "What no eye has seen, nor ear heard, nor the heart of man conceived, what God has prepared for those who love him." It is also included among the chief articles of our faith, where we say ⟨in the creed⟩: "And the life everlasting." And what free choice is worth in relation to this article, Paul shows in I Cor. 2⟨:10⟩, where he says: "God has revealed it to us through his Spirit." This means that unless the Spirit had revealed it, no man's heart would have any knowledge or notion of it, much less be able to apply itself to it or seek after it. Take a look at experience. What have the most distinguished minds among the heathen thought about the future life and the resurrection? Is it not the case that the more distinguished they have been, the more absurd the idea of a future life and resurrection has seemed to them to be?

Were they not talented philosophers and Greeks who when Paul taught these things at Athens called him a babbler and a preacher of foreign divinities ⟨Acts 17:18⟩? Porcius Festus in Acts 24 ⟨26:24⟩ called Paul mad on account of his preaching of eternal life. What does Pliny yap about these things in his seventh book? [5] What does Lucian,[6] great wit that he is? Were those men unintelligent? Why, the majority even today, the more intelligent and learned they are the more they ridicule this article as a fable, and that publicly. For privately there is simply no one, unless he is thoroughly imbued with the Holy Spirit, who knows, believes, or desires eternal salvation, even though they never stop talking and writing about it. And I wish that both you and I were free from that same leaven,

---

[4] "Modernos meos"; the followers of the via moderna of late Scholastic thought, in which Luther himself had been trained.

[5] Pliny the Elder (ca. 23–79) in his Natural History vii.55 declares his disbelief in immortality.

[6] See above, p. 109 n. 9.

my dear Erasmus, so rare is a believing mind in respect of this article. Have I got the sense of this definition?

On the authority of Erasmus, then, free choice is a power of the will that is able of itself to will and unwill the word and work of God, by which it is led to those things which exceed both its grasp and its perception. But if it can will and unwill, it can also love and hate, and if it can love and hate, it can also in some small degree do the works of the law and believe the gospel. For if you can will or unwill anything, you must to some extent be able to perform something by that will, even if someone else prevents your completing it. Now, in that case, since the works of God which lead to salvation include death, the cross, and all the evils of the world, the human will must be able to will both death and its own perdition. Indeed, it can will everything when it can will the word and work of God; for how can there be anything anywhere that is below, above, within, or without the word and work of God, except God himself? But what is left here to grace and the Holy Spirit? This plainly means attributing divinity to free choice, since to will the law and the gospel, to unwill sin and to will death, belongs to divine power alone, as Paul says in more than one place.

Clearly then, no one since the Pelagians [7] has written more correctly about free choice than Erasmus! For we have said above that free choice is a divine term and signifies a divine power, although no one has yet attributed this power to free choice except the Pelagians; for the Sophists, whatever they may think, certainly speak very differently. Erasmus, however, far outdoes even the Pelagians, for they attribute this divinity to the whole of free choice, but Erasmus only to half of it. They reckon with two parts of free choice—the power of discerning and the power of selecting —one of which they attach to reason, the other to the will, as the Sophists also do. But Erasmus neglects the power of discerning and extols only the power of selecting. So it is a crippled and only half-free choice that he deifies. What do you think he would have done if he had set about describing the whole of free choice?

But not content with this, he outdoes the philosophers too. For with them it is not yet finally settled whether anything can set itself in motion, and on this point the Platonists and Peripatetics [8] disagree throughout the entire range of philosophy. But as Eras-

[7] See above, pp. 11 f.

[8] The followers of Aristotle (384–322 B.C.), so called either from Aristotle's habit of walking about as he taught (*peripatein*) or from the covered walk (*peripatos*) where he instructed his followers in the Lyceum.

mus sees it, free choice not only moves itself by its own power, but also applies itself to things which are eternal, that is, incomprehensible to itself. Here is truly a novel and unprecedented definer of free choice, who leaves Pelagians, Sophists, and everyone else far behind! Nor is that enough for him; for he does not spare even himself, but is more at cross-purposes with himself than with all the rest. For he had previously said that the human will was completely incapacitated without grace [9] (unless he said this in jest), but here where he is giving a serious definition, he says that the human will possesses this power by which it is capable of applying itself to the things which belong to eternal salvation, that is, to things which are incomparably beyond that power. So in this part Erasmus even surpasses himself as well.

Do you see, my dear Erasmus, that with this definition you put yourself on record (unwittingly, I presume) as understanding nothing at all of these things, or as writing about them quite thoughtlessly and contemptuously, unaware of what you are saying or affirming? And as I said above, you say less and attribute more to free choice than all the others, in that you describe only part and not the whole of free choice and yet attribute everything to it. Far more tolerable is the teaching of the Sophists, or at least of their father, Peter Lombard,[10] when they say that free choice is the capacity for discerning and then also choosing the good if grace is present, but evil if grace is absent.[11] Lombard clearly thinks with Augustine that free choice by its own power alone can do nothing but fall and is capable only of sinning; [12] which is why Augustine, in his second book against Julian, calls it an enslaved rather than a free choice.[13]

You, however, make free choice equally potent in both directions, in that it is able by its own power, without grace, both to

---

[9] Erasmus said (p. 49) the power of the will was "not completely (*prorsus*) extinguished" but it was "unable to perform the good (*inefficacem ad honesta*)." For Luther this means it was "completely incapacitated (*prorsus inefficacem*)" as regards salvation.

[10] Famous medieval theologian (ca. 1100–ca. 1160), author of *Sententiarum libri quattuor,* mainly a collection of opinions of the Fathers, which became the standard theological textbook of the Middle Ages, and from which the author came to be known as the "Master of the Sentences."

[11] In *Sent.* II, *dist.* 25, 5, Lombard states that the will (*arbitrium*) is free in that "it is able without coercion (*coactione*) or necessity to seek after or choose what it has discerned by reason."

[12] Augustine, *De spiritu et litera* iii.5 (*MPL* 44.203) : "For free choice is not capable of anything but sinning if the way of truth is not known."

[13] *Contra Iulianum* II.viii.23 (*MPL* 44.689) : "For here you want man to be perfected, and would that it were by the gift of God and not by the free, or rather enslaved, choice of his own will."

apply itself to the good and to turn away from the good. You do not realize how much you attribute to it by this pronoun "itself"— its very own self! [14]—when you say it can "apply itself"; for this means that you completely exclude the Holy Spirit with all his power, as superfluous and unnecessary. Your definition is therefore to be condemned even by the standards of the Sophists, who if only they were not so enraged by blind envy of me, would be rampaging instead against your book. As it is, since it is Luther you are attacking, everything you say is holy and catholic, even if you contradict both yourself and them, so great is the endurance of saintly men.[15]

I do not say this because I approve the view of the Sophists regarding free choice, but because I consider it more tolerable than that of Erasmus, since they come nearer the truth. For although they do not say, as I do, that free choice is nothing, yet when they (and particularly the Master of the Sentences) say that it can do nothing without grace, they take sides against Erasmus; indeed, they seem to take sides against themselves too, and to be racked with dissension merely about a word, as if they were fonder of controversy than of truth, as might be expected of Sophists. For suppose one of the least objectionable Sophists were brought to me, with whom I could discuss these things privately in intimate conversation and ask for his free and candid judgment in some such way as this: If anyone told you that a thing was free which could operate by its own power only in one direction (the bad one), while in the other (the good one) it could of course operate, though not by its own power, but only by the help of another— would you be able to keep a straight face, my friend?

By that sort of method I can easily make out that a stone or a log of wood has free choice because it can move both upward and downward, though by its own power only downward, and upward only by the help of another. And as I said above, we shall end with a topsy-turvy use of language and vocabulary by which we say, "No man is all men," and, "Nothing is everything," making one term refer to the thing itself, and the other to another that may have an incidental or accidental connection with it. That is how after excessive disputing they come in the end to make free choice free "accidentally," as something that can on occasion be set free by means of some other thing. The question, however, is what free choice is in itself and as regards its substance; and if that question is to be answered, nothing remains of free choice but the empty

[14] "*SE vel SEIPSAM.*"
[15] Probably a sarcastic allusion to Rev. 12:10; 14:12.

name, whether they like it or not. The Sophists are at fault in this too, that they attribute to free choice the power of distinguishing between good and evil. They also depreciate regeneration and renewal in the Holy Spirit ⟨Titus 3:5⟩, and make it a purely external reinforcement that never identifies itself with the will, a point on which I shall say more later. But that is enough about your definition. Now, let us look at the arguments which are to inflate this empty little word.

The first ⟨E., p. 47⟩ is that from Ecclus. 15⟨:14-17⟩: "God made man from the beginning, and left him in the hand of his own counsel. He added his commandments and precepts. If thou wilt observe [16] the commandments and keep [17] acceptable fidelity forever, they shall preserve thee. He hath set water and fire before thee; stretch forth thine hand for which thou wilt. Before man is life and death, good and evil; that which he shall choose shall be given him." [18] Although I could rightly reject this book, for the time being I accept it so as not to waste time by getting involved in a dispute about the books received in the Hebrew canon. For you poke more than a little sarcastic fun at this when you compare Proverbs and The Song of Solomon (which with a sneering innuendo you call the "Love Song") with the two books of Esdras, Judith, the story of Susanna and the Dragon, and Esther (which despite their inclusion of it in the canon deserves more than all the rest in my judgment to be regarded as noncanonical).

But let me reply briefly in your own words and say that Scripture is in this passage obscure and ambiguous, and therefore it proves nothing with certainty. We, however, as maintaining the negative, insist that you must produce a passage which shows convincingly in unambiguous terms what free choice is and what it can do. Perhaps you will manage to do this by the Greek calends,[19] though in order to avoid this necessity you waste a lot of good words, walking so very warily [20] and quoting so many opinions on free choice that you almost turn Pelagius into an Evangelical. Moreover, you invent a fourfold grace to enable you to attribute some sort of faith and charity even to the philosophers; and with it a threefold law, of nature, works, and faith, which is indeed a new fable, to enable you to assert that the precepts of the philosophers agree

[16] *"Conservare"* (Douay: "keep").
[17] *"Servare"* (Vulg.: *"facere"*; Douay: "perform").
[18] Luther quotes the Vulgate; so also Erasmus.
[19] A day that will never come. The Greeks had no calends to their months as the Latins had.
[20] *"Super aristas incaedis."* See above, p. 126 n. 39.

very markedly with the precepts of the gospel. Again, you take that saying of Ps. 4⟨:6⟩, "The light of thy countenance, O Lord, is impressed upon us," [21] which refers to the knowledge of the very countenance of God, that is, to faith, and apply it to blinded reason. ⟨E., p. 49.⟩

Now, let any Christian put all these things together, and he will be bound to suspect that you are mocking and deriding the dogmas and religion of Christians. For I find it very difficult to put such things down to ignorance in one who has reviewed everything of ours [22] and so diligently stored them up in his memory. I will not, however, pursue this question at the moment, but will be content to have pointed it out until a more suitable opportunity occurs. But I beg of you, my dear Erasmus, not to go on teasing us in this way, like one of those who say, "Who can see us?" [23] It is not safe in so important a matter to be continually playing tricks with words [24] on all and sundry. But let us return to the point.

Three Views of Grace and Free Choice—or Three Statements of One View? ⟨WA 667–671⟩

Out of one opinion on free choice you make three. ⟨E., pp. 51 ff.⟩ You regard as hard, though probable enough, the opinion of those who deny that man can will the good without peculiar grace. They deny that he can begin, progress, or reach his goal, etc.; and this you approve because it leaves man to study and strive, but does not leave him with anything to ascribe to his own powers. Harder, you think, is the opinion of those who contend that free choice is of no avail save to sin, that grace alone accomplishes good in us, etc. But hardest is the view of those who say that free choice is a mere empty name, that it is God who works both good and evil in us, and that all things which happen come about by sheer necessity. It is against these last positions that you profess to be writing.

Do you really know what you are saying, my dear Erasmus? You express here three opinions as if they belonged to three different schools, not realizing that they are the same thing variously stated, in different words at different times, by us who remain the same persons and exponents of one school only; but let us draw your

---

[21] The Vulgate.
[22] I.e., the writings of Luther and his friends.
[23] Ref. to Ps. 64:5? Or to some game?
[24] Literally, "playing with vertumnuses of words." For Vertumnus, see above, p. 152 n. 18.

attention to this and point out the carelessness or stupidity of your judgment.

I ask you, how does the definition of free choice given by you earlier square with this first and probable enough opinion? For you said there that free choice is a power of the human will by which a man can apply himself to the good; but here you say, and approve of its being said, that man without grace cannot will good. The definition asserts what the illustration of it denies, and there is found in your free choice both a Yes and a No, so that you at once both approve and condemn us, and condemn and approve also yourself, in one and the same dogma and article. Or do you think it is not good to apply oneself to the things which pertain to eternal salvation? That is what your definition attributes to free choice; and yet there is no need of grace if there were so much good in free choice that it could apply itself to the good. Hence the free choice you define is a different thing from the free choice you defend; so now Erasmus, in contrast to the rest of us, has two free choices, and those entirely at variance with each other.

But let us put aside that free choice which the definition has invented, and look at the contrary one which the "opinion" itself implies. You grant that man cannot will good without special grace—for we are not now discussing what the grace of God can do, but what man can do without grace. You grant, then, that free choice cannot will good. This means nothing else but that it cannot apply itself to the things which pertain to eternal salvation, as your definition cheerfully stated it could. Indeed, you say a little before, that the human will since the Fall [25] is so depraved that having lost its liberty, it is obliged to serve sin and cannot bring itself back to any better issue.[26] And unless I am mistaken, you make out that the Pelagians were of this opinion. I think Proteus [27] has now no way of escape here; he is caught and held fast by the plain statement that the will, having lost its liberty, is perforce held fast in bondage to sin. What an exquisitely free choice, which has lost its liberty and is called by Erasmus himself a slave of sin! When Luther said this, nothing more absurd had ever been heard, nothing more mischievous than this paradox could be published, so that even diatribes must be written against him!

But perhaps no one will take my word for it that these things are said by Erasmus; so let this passage of the *Diatribe* be read, and it will be a surprise. Not that I am greatly surprised. For when a man does not take this subject seriously and feels no personal in-

---

[25] *"Post peccatum,"* "after sin."   [26] *"Se revocare ad meliorem frugem."*
[27] See above, p. 103 n. 7.

terest in it, never has his heart in it and finds it wearisome, chilling, or nauseating, how can he help saying absurd, inept, and contradictory things all the time, since he conducts the case like one drunk or asleep, belching out between his snores, "Yes, No," as different voices fall on his ears? That is why the rhetoricians require feeling in an advocate; and all the more does theology require such feeling as will make a man vigilant, penetrating, intent, astute, and determined.

If, therefore, free choice apart from grace, having lost its liberty, is forced to serve sin and cannot will good, I should like to know what that desire and that endeavor are, which the first and probable opinion leaves to a man? It cannot be a good desire and good endeavor, because he cannot will good, as the opinion states and as has been agreed. There remains, therefore, an evil desire and evil endeavor, which having lost its liberty, is forced to serve sin. But what is meant, pray, by saying that this opinion leaves man with desire and endeavor, but does not leave him anything to ascribe to his own powers? Who can conceive this? If desire and endeavor are left to the powers of free choice, why should they not be ascribed to those powers? If they are not ascribed to them, how are they left to them? Are the desire and endeavor that go before grace also left to the grace itself that comes after, and not to free choice, so that they are at the same time both left and not left to the same free choice? If these are not paradoxes, or rather monstrosities, then what are monstrosities?

But perhaps Diatribe is dreaming that there is a mean between the two—between being able to will good and not being able to will good—which is willing in the absolute sense, without reference either to good or evil, so that by a certain logical subtlety we may thus steer clear of the rocks and say that there is in man's will a kind of willing which, while it cannot indeed turn toward the good without grace, yet even without grace does not forthwith will only evil, but is a willing pure and simple,[28] which by grace can be turned upward to the good, by sin downward to evil. But then what becomes of the statement that having lost its liberty, it is forced to serve sin? Where are the desire and endeavor that are left to it? Where is the power of applying itself to the things which pertain to eternal salvation? For the power of applying itself to salvation cannot be a merely abstract willing, unless salvation itself is to be called nothing. Nor, again, can desire and endeavor be a merely abstract willing, since desire must strive and endeavor in some direction—toward the good, for instance—and cannot either be a

[28] *"Purum et merum velle."*

movement toward nothingness or a mere inactivity. In short, no matter where Diatribe turns, she cannot escape from contradictions and inconsistencies, so that she herself is more of a prisoner than the free choice which she is defending. For in setting choice free she so entangles herself that she is held fast along with free choice in indissoluble bonds.

It is, moreover, a mere dialectical fiction that there is in man a neutral [29] and unqualified [30] willing, nor can those who assert it prove it. It is the result of ignoring facts and paying too much attention to words, as if a thing were always in reality just as it is represented in words. There are innumerable examples of this in the Sophists. The truth of the matter is rather as Christ says: "He who is not with me is against me" ⟨Luke 11:23⟩. He does not say: "He who is not with me is not against me either, but neutral." [31] For if God is in us, Satan is absent, and only a good will is present; if God is absent, Satan is present, and only an evil will is in us. Neither God nor Satan permits sheer unqualified willing [32] in us, but as you have rightly said, having lost our liberty, we are forced to serve sin, that is, we will sin and evil, speak sin and evil, do sin and evil. See how the invincible and all-powerful truth has cornered witless Diatribe and turned her wisdom into folly, so that while meaning to speak against us, she is compelled to speak for us and against herself. This is exactly what befalls free choice with its "good deeds": in the very act of going against evil it does the worst possible damage to good; the Diatribe in speech is just like free choice in action. Indeed, the whole Diatribe is itself nothing else but an egregious performance of free choice, condemning by defending and defending by condemning, and so being doubly stupid while wishing to be thought wise.

The first opinion, then, when compared with itself, is such as to deny that man can will anything good, and yet to maintain that a desire is left to him which nevertheless is not his own. Now, let us compare it with the other two. The second is that harder one which holds that free choice avails for nothing but sinning. This is Augustine's view, which he expresses in many places, but particularly in his book *On the Spirit and the Letter,* in the fourth or fifth chapter, if I am not mistaken, where he uses those very words.[33] The third and hardest opinion is that of Wyclif and Luther, that free choice is an empty name and all that we do comes about by sheer necessity. It is with these two views that Diatribe quarrels.

---

[29] *"Medium."*   [30] *"Purum."*   [31] *"In medio."*   [32] *"Merum et purum velle."*
[33] *De spiritu et litera* iii.5 (*MPL* 44.203).

Here I admit that perhaps I am not Latin or German enough to have been able to put the fact of the matter plainly into words; but God is my witness that I meant to say nothing else, and to have nothing else understood, by the words of the last two opinions than what is stated in the first opinion. I neither think that Augustine meant anything else, nor do I find any other meaning in his words than what the first opinion says, so that the three opinions cited by Diatribe are to me nothing but that one single opinion of my own. For when it has been conceded and agreed that free choice, having lost its liberty, is perforce in bondage to sin and cannot will anything good, I can make no other sense of these words than that free choice is an empty phrase, of which the reality has been lost. Lost liberty, according to my grammar, is no liberty at all, and to give the name of liberty to something that has no liberty, is to employ an empty phrase. If I am wrong here, let anyone put me right who can; if these things are obscure and ambiguous, let anyone who is able shed light on them and settle what they mean. I for my part cannot call lost health, health; and if I ascribed it to a sick person, I do not think I should have ascribed anything but an empty name.

But let us have done with verbal monstrosities. For who can bear this abuse of language by which we both say that man has free choice and at the same time assert that having lost his liberty he is perforce in bondage to sin and can will nothing good? These things are contrary to common sense and completely destroy the common use of language. It is Diatribe that ought rather to be accused, who drowsily dribbles out her own words and pays no attention to what others say. I mean, she does not consider what it means and how much it involves to say, "Man has lost his liberty, is forced to serve sin, and cannot will anything good" ⟨E., pp. 48 f.⟩. If she were awake and observant, she would plainly see that the meaning of the three opinions, which she makes diverse and conflicting, is one and the same. For when a man has lost his liberty and is forced to serve sin and cannot will good, what can be more truly inferred about him than that he sins, or wills evil, necessarily? Even the Sophists would draw this conclusion by means of their syllogisms. So Diatribe is really most unfortunate in taking up the cudgels against the last two opinions while approving the first, which is the same as they are; for once again, in her usual way, she condemns herself and proves our point in one and the same article.

Ecclesiasticus 15:14-17. The Foolishness of Reason
⟨WA 671–676⟩

Now let us turn to the passage from Ecclesiasticus and compare with it, too, that first "probable" opinion. The opinion says that free choice cannot will good, but the passage from Ecclesiasticus is cited to prove that free choice is something and can do something. The opinion that is to be confirmed by Ecclesiasticus, therefore, states one thing and Ecclesiasticus is cited in confirmation of another. It is as if someone set out to prove that Christ was the Messiah, and cited a passage which proved that Pilate was governor of Syria, or something else equally wide of the mark.[34] That is just how free choice is proved here, not to mention what I pointed out above, that nothing is clearly and definitely said or proved as to what free choice is or can do. But it is worthwhile to examine this whole passage.

First it says, "God made man from the beginning." Here it speaks of the creation of man, and says nothing as yet either about free choice or about precepts. Then follows: "And left him in the hand of his own counsel." What have we here? Is free choice set up here? But not even here is there any mention of precepts, for which free choice is required, nor do we read anything on this subject in the account of the creation of man. If anything is meant, therefore, by "the hand of his own counsel," it is rather as we read in Gen. chs. 1 and 2, that man was appointed lord of things, so as to exercise dominion over them freely, as Moses says: "Let us make man, and let them have dominion over the fish of the sea" ⟨Gen. 1:26⟩. Nor can anything else be proved from those words. For in that state, man was able to deal with things according to his own choice, in that they were subject to him; and this is called man's counsel, as distinct from God's counsel. But then, after saying that man was thus made and left in the hand of his own counsel, it goes on: "He added his commandments and precepts." What did he add them to? Surely the counsel and choice of man, and over and above the establishing of man's dominion over the rest of the creatures. And by these precepts he took away from man the dominion over one part of the creatures (for instance, over the tree of the knowledge of good and evil) and willed rather that he should not be free.

Then, however, when the precepts have been added, he comes

---

[34] "*Quod disdiapason conveniat.*" *Disdiapason* = "double octave," a term from the Greek musical vocabulary, used metaphorically to express the widest possible divergence.

to man's choice in relation to God and the things of God: "If thou wilt observe the commandments, they shall preserve thee," etc. It is therefore at this point, "If thou wilt," that the question of free choice arises. We thus learn from Ecclesiasticus that man is divided between two kingdoms, in one of which he is directed by his own choice and counsel, apart from any precepts and commandments of God, namely, in his dealings with the lower creatures.[35] Here he reigns and is lord, as having been left in the hand of his own counsel. Not that God so leaves him as not to cooperate with him in everything, but he has granted him the free use of things according to his own choice, and has not restricted him by any laws or injunctions. By way of comparison one might say that the gospel has left us in the hand of our own counsel, to have dominion over things and use them as we wish; but Moses and the pope have not left us to that counsel, but have coerced us with laws and have subjected us rather to their own choice.

In the other Kingdom, however, man is not left in the hand of his own counsel, but is directed and led by the choice and counsel of God, so that just as in his own kingdom he is directed by his own counsel, without regard to the precepts of another, so in the Kingdom of God he is directed by the precepts of another without regard to his own choice. And this is what Ecclesiasticus means by: "He added his precepts and commandments. If thou wilt," etc.

If, then, these things are sufficiently clear, we have gained our point that this passage of Ecclesiasticus is evidence, not for, but against free choice, since by it man is subjected to the precepts and choice of God, and withdrawn from his own choice. If they are not sufficiently clear, at least we have made the point that this passage cannot be evidence in favor of free choice, since it can be understood in a different sense from theirs, namely in ours, which has just been stated, and which is not absurd but entirely sound and in harmony with the whole tenor of Scripture, whereas theirs is at variance with Scripture as a whole and is derived from this one passage alone, in contradiction to it. We stand, therefore, quite confidently by the good sense that the negative of free choice makes here, until they confirm their strained and forced affirmative.

When, therefore, Ecclesiasticus says: "If thou wilt observe the commandments and keep acceptable fidelity forever, they shall preserve thee," I do not see how free choice is proved by these words. For the verb is in the subjunctive mood ("If thou wilt"), which asserts nothing. As the logicians say, a conditional asserts

35 *"In rebus sese inferioribus."*

nothing indicatively: for example, "If the devil is God, it is right to worship him; if an ass flies, an ass has wings; if free choice exists, grace is nothing." Ecclesiasticus, however, should have spoken as follows, if he had wished to assert free choice: "Man can keep the commandments of God," or: "Man has the power to keep the commandments."

But here Diatribe will retort that by saying, "If thou wilt keep," Ecclesiasticus indicates that there is in man a will capable of keeping and not keeping commandments; otherwise, what point is there in saying to one who has no will, "If thou wilt"? Would it not be ridiculous to say to a blind person, "If you will look, you will find a treasure," or to a deaf person, "If you will listen, I will tell you a good story"? This would simply be laughing at their misfortune. I reply: These are the arguments of human Reason, which has a habit of producing such bits of wisdom. We now have to argue, therefore, not with Ecclesiasticus, but with human Reason about an inference; for Reason interprets the Scriptures of God by her own inferences and syllogisms, and turns them in any direction she pleases. We will do this gladly and with confidence, knowing that she talks nothing but follies and absurdities, especially when she starts displaying her wisdom on sacred subjects.

To begin with, if I ask how it is proved that the presence of a free will in man is signified or implied every time it is said, "If thou wilt, if thou shalt do, if thou shalt hear," Reason will say, "Because the nature of words and the use of language among men seem to require it." She thus measures divine things and words by the usage and concerns of men; and what can be more perverse than this, seeing that the former are heavenly and the latter earthly? So the stupid thing betrays herself, showing how she has nothing but human thoughts about God. But what if I prove that the nature of words and the use of language even among men is not always such as to make a laughingstock of those who are impotent whenever they are told: "If thou wilt, if thou shalt do, if thou shalt hear"? How often do parents have a game with their children by telling them to come to them, or to do this or that, simply for the sake of showing them how unable they are, and compelling them to call for the help of the parents' hand! How often does a good doctor order a self-confident patient to do or stop doing things that are either impossible or painful to him, so as to bring him through his own experience to an awareness of his illness or weakness, to which he could not lead him by any other means? And what is more frequent than words of insult and provocation when we want to show either friends or enemies what they can and cannot do?

I mention these things merely in order to show Reason how foolish she is in tacking her inferences onto the Scriptures, and how blind she is not to see that they are not aways applicable even with regard to human speech and action, for if she sees a thing happen once or twice, she immediately jumps to the conclusion that it happens quite generally and with regard to all the words of God and men, making a universal out of a particular in the usual manner of her wisdom.

If now God deals with us as a father with his children, so as to show our ignorant selves our helplessness, or like a good doctor makes our disease known to us, or tramples on us as enemies of his who proudly resist his counsel, and in laws which he issues (the most effective method of all) says: "Do, hear, keep," or, "If thou shalt hear, if thou wilt, if thou shalt do," will the correct conclusion to be drawn from this be: "Therefore we can act freely, or else God is mocking us"? Why does it not rather follow: "Therefore, God is putting us to the test so as to lead us by means of the law to a knowledge of our impotence if we are his friends or truly and deservedly to trample on and mock us if we are his proud enemies"? That is the reason why God gives laws, as Paul teaches ⟨Rom. 3:20⟩. For human nature is so blind that it does not know its own powers, or rather diseases, and so proud as to imagine that it knows and can do everything; and for this pride and blindness God has no readier remedy than the propounding of his law, a subject on which we shall have more to say in the proper place. Let it suffice here to have glanced at it for the confutation of that conclusion of foolish, mundane [36] wisdom: " 'If thou wilt': therefore thou canst will freely."

Diatribe dreams that man is sound and whole, as within his own province he is, so far as human observation goes; and hence she pertly argues that by the words "If thou wilt, if thou shalt do, if thou shalt hear" man is mocked unless his choice is free. Scripture, however, lays it down that man is corrupt and captive, and what is more, that he displays a proud contempt and ignorance of his corruption and captivity. So by those words it prods him and seeks to arouse him and make him recognize from undeniable experience how incapable he is of any of those things.

But let me address myself to Diatribe herself. If you really think, Madam Reason, that those inferences hold good ("If thou

[36] *"Carnalis."*

wilt": therefore thou canst act freely), why do you not imitate
them yourself? For according to that probable opinion of yours,
you say that free choice cannot will anything good. By what sort
of inference can this be produced simultaneously out of that passage ("If thou wilt keep") from which you say it follows that man
is able to will and not will freely? Can sweet and bitter flow from
the same fountain ⟨James 3:11⟩? Are you not yourself mocking
man even more here, when you say that he can "keep" things
which he can neither will nor wish? Therefore, even you do not
seriously think it a fair inference ("If thou wilt": therefore thou
canst act freely), though you contend for it so strongly, or else you
are not serious when you call that opinion probable which maintains that man cannot will good. Reason is so captivated by her
inferences and the words of her own wisdom that she does not
know what she is saying or what she is talking about, though it is
most fitting that free choice should be defended by such arguments as mutually devour and make an end of each other, just as
the Midianites destroyed themselves by mutual slaughter when
they fought against Gideon and the People of God ⟨Judg. 7:22⟩.

But let me remonstrate more fully with this wisdom of Diatribe's. Ecclesiasticus does not say, "If thou shalt have the desire or
endeavor to keep, which is not to be ascribed to your own powers,"
as you make out, but what it says is this: "If thou wilt keep the
commandments, they shall preserve thee." If we now wish to draw
conclusions in the manner of your wisdom, we shall infer: "Therefore man can keep the commandments," and by doing so we shall
not leave only a tiny spark of desire or some little bit of endeavor
in man, but we shall credit him with the whole fullness and abundance of power to keep the commandments. Otherwise, Ecclesiasticus would be mocking the misery of man by commanding him to
"keep" when he knew him unable to keep; and it would not be
enough simply to grant him endeavor and desire, since not even
so would he avoid the suspicion of mockery, unless he indicated
that there was in him the power to keep.

But let us suppose this desire and endeavor of free choice to be
something. What shall we say to those—I mean the Pelagians—
who on the basis of this passage used to deny grace altogether and
attribute everything to free choice? Clearly, the Pelagians will
have won the day if Diatribe's inference is allowed to stand, for
the words of Ecclesiasticus speak of keeping, not of endeavoring
or desiring. But if you refuse to grant the Pelagians the inference
about keeping, they in turn will much more properly refuse to
grant you the inference about endeavoring; and if you take away

the whole of free choice from them, they also will take from you the little particle of it which you say remains, so that you cannot claim for the particle what you have denied to the whole. Whatever, therefore, you say against the Pelagians when they attribute a whole free choice to man on the basis of this passage, we shall say the same with much more force against that little spark of desire which constitutes your free choice. And the Pelagians will agree with us to this extent, that if their opinion cannot be proved from this passage, much less can any other be proved from it; for if the case is to be argued by means of inferences, Ecclesiasticus is on the side of the Pelagians most strongly of all, inasmuch as he speaks about total keeping: "If thou wilt keep the commandments." Indeed, he speaks about faith as well: "If thou wilt keep acceptable faith," so that by the same inference it ought to be in our power to keep faith also, although that is a rare and peculiar gift of God, as Paul says ⟨Eph. 2:8⟩.

In short, when so many opinions are mustered in support of free choice, and none of them but claims this passage of Ecclesiasticus in its own support, and yet they are divergent and contrary, this can only mean that they hold Ecclesiasticus to be contradictory, as expressing opposite views in the selfsame set of words. Consequently, they can prove nothing from him, though if that inference is admitted, he makes for the Pelagians alone, against all the rest. Therefore, he makes also against Diatribe, who is hoist with her own petard here.

We, however, hold as we said from the start that this passage of Ecclesiasticus favors absolutely none of those who assert free choice, but is opposed to them all. For that inference, "If thou wilt": therefore thou canst, is inadmissible, and instead it must be understood that by this and similar expressions man is warned of his impotence, which in his ignorance and pride, without these divine warnings, he would neither acknowledge nor be aware of.

Now, here we are speaking not only of the first man, but of any and every man, though it is of little importance whether you understand it of the first man or of other men, for although the first man was not impotent when he had the assistance of grace, yet by means of this precept God shows him plainly enough how impotent he would be in the absence of grace. But if that man, even when the Spirit was present, was not able with a new will to will a good newly proposed to him (that is, obedience), because the Spirit did not add it to him, what should we be able to do without the Spirit in respect of a good that we have lost? It is thus shown in that first man, as a frightening example and for the breaking down of our pride, what our free choice can do when it is left to itself and not continually and increasingly actuated and augmented by the Spirit of God. If that man could do nothing toward increasing his share of the Spirit, whose firstfruits he possessed, but fell away from the firstfruits of the Spirit, how should we in our fallen state be able to do anything toward recovering the firstfruits of the Spirit that have been taken away, especially when Satan now reigns in us in full force, who prostrated that man by temptation alone, when he was not yet reigning in him?

No stronger argument could be brought against free choice than the discussion of this passage of Ecclesiasticus in connection with the fall of Adam; but this is not the place for it, and perhaps the subject will crop up elsewhere. Meanwhile, it is enough to have shown that Ecclesiasticus says precisely nothing in support of free choice in this passage, although its advocates regard it as their principal text, and that this and similar passages—"If thou wilt, if thou shalt hear, if thou shalt do"—show not what men can do but what they ought to do.

Other Old Testament Passages, and the Imperative and Indicative Moods ⟨WA 676–680⟩

Another passage is quoted by our Diatribe, from Gen. 4⟨:7⟩, where the Lord says to Cain: "The desire of sin shall be under thee, and thou shalt have dominion over it." [37] It is shown here, says Diatribe, that the motions of the mind toward evil can be overcome, and that they do not carry with them the necessity of sinning. ⟨E., p. 54.⟩ This statement, that the motions of the mind toward evil can be overcome, is ambiguous; but the whole tenor of the sentence, the inference and the facts themselves, compel us to take it as meaning that it is the business of free choice to overcome its own motions toward evil, and that these motions do not carry with them the necessity of sinning. Once again, what is omitted here as not attributed to free choice? What need is there of the Spirit or of Christ or of God if free choice can overcome the motions of the mind toward evil? Where, again, is the probable opinion which says that free choice cannot even will good? Yet here the victory over evil is attributed to that which neither wills nor wishes anything good! It is really too, too thoughtless of our Diatribe.

Here is the truth of the matter in a nutshell. As I have said, by

---

[37] The literal rendering of the Vulgate text (quoted identically by Erasmus and Luther) is necessary here for the sake of Luther's subsequent argument.

such sayings man is shown what he ought to do, not what he can do. Cain therefore is being told that he ought to master sin and keep its appetite under his control; but this he neither did nor could do, as he was already held down under the alien yoke of Satan. For it is well known that the Hebrews frequently use the future indicative for the imperative, as in Ex. 20⟨:3, 13 f.⟩: "Thou shalt have none other gods"; "Thou shalt not kill"; "Thou shalt not commit adultery"; and countless similar instances. Otherwise, if they were taken indicatively (as they are expressed), they would be promises of God, and since God cannot lie, the result would be that no man would sin, and then there would be no need of them as precepts. Hence our translator would have rendered this passage more correctly thus: "Let its appetite be subject to thee, and do thou master it," just as he should also have said regarding the woman: "Be thou subject to thy husband, and let him have dominion over thee" ⟨Gen. 3:16⟩. That it was not spoken indicatively to Cain is proved by the fact that it would then have been a divine promise; but it was not a promise, because the very reverse happened and was done by Cain.

The third passage is from Moses: "I have set before your face the way of life and of death. Choose what is good," etc. ⟨Deut. 30:15, 19⟩. What, says Diatribe, could be put more plainly? God leaves man freedom to choose. I reply: What is more plain than that you are blind here? How, pray, does he leave freedom to choose? By saying, "Choose"? Do they then choose as soon as Moses says, "Choose"? Then once more the Spirit is not necessary. And seeing you so often repeat and hammer away at the same things, it will be permissible for me too to go over the same things again and again. If there is freedom of choice, why has the "probable opinion" said that free choice cannot will good? Can it choose without willing or against its will? But let us listen to your simile. It would be ridiculous, you say, to say to a man standing at a crossroad, "You see these two roads; take which you like," when only one was open to him.

This is just what I said before about the arguments of human [38] Reason, that she thinks man is mocked by an impossible precept, whereas we say that he is warned and aroused by it to see his own impotence. Truly, therefore, we are at a crossroad, but only one way is open; or rather, no way is open, but by means of the law it is shown how impossible one of them is, namely, the way to the good, unless God gives the Spirit, and how broad and easy the other is if God allows us to take it. It would not be ridiculous,

[38] *"Rationis carnalis."*

therefore, but a matter of due seriousness, to say to a man stand-ing at a crossroad, "Take which way you like," if he was either in-clined to imagine himself strong when he was weak, or was con-tending that neither road was closed.

The words of the law are spoken, therefore, not to affirm the power of the will, but to enlighten blind reason and make it see that its own light is no light and that the virtue of the will is no virtue. "Through the law," says Paul, "comes knowledge of sin" (Rom. 3:20); he does not say the "abolition" or "avoidance" of sin. The whole meaning and purpose of the law is simply to fur-nish knowledge, and that of nothing but sin; it is not to reveal or confer any power. For this knowledge is not power, nor does it confer power, but it instructs and shows that there is no power there, and how great a weakness there is. For what else can the knowledge of sin be but the awareness of our own weakness and wickedness? For he does not say, "Through the law comes knowl-edge of virtue or the good," but all that the law does, according to Paul, is to make sin known.

That is the passage from which I drew my reply that by the words of the law man is warned and instructed as to what he ought to do, not what he is able to do; their purpose is that he may know his sin, not that he may believe himself to have any power. Accordingly, my dear Erasmus, as often as you quote the words of the law against me, I shall quote Paul's statement against you, that through the law comes knowledge of sin, not virtue in the will. Heap up, therefore, all the imperative verbs (from the major concordances, if you like) into one chaotic mass, and pro-vided they are not words of promise, but of demand and the law, I shall say at once that what is signified by them is aways what men ought to do and not what they do or can do. This is some-thing that even grammarians and street urchins know, that by verbs of the imperative mood nothing else is signified but what ought to be done. What is done, or can be done, must be ex-pressed by indicative verbs.

How is it, then, that you theologians drivel like people in their second childhood, so that as soon as you get hold of an imperative verb you take it as implying the indicative, as if once a thing is commanded it must forthwith necessarily be done or be possible to do? For how often there are slips between the cup and the lip, so that what you have commanded, and what indeed was possible enough, nevertheless does not happen; so far apart are imperative and indicative verbs, even in ordinary and quite straightforward matters. Yet you, in dealing with things farther apart than heaven and earth, and similarly unattainable, suddenly make indicatives for us out of imperatives, and will have it that things are kept, done, chosen, and fulfilled, or are going to be so, by our own powers, as soon as ever you hear the word of command, "Do, keep, choose"!

In the fourth place, you quote from Deut., chs. 3 and 30, many similar verbs of choosing, turning away, keeping, such as, "If thou shalt keep, if thou shalt be drawn away, if thou shalt choose," etc. It would, you say, be inappropriate to use these expressions if the will of man were not free toward the good. I reply that it is also quite inappropriate when you, my dear Diatribe, infer freedom of choice from those expressions, for you were going to prove only an endeavor and desire of free choice, yet you cite no passage that proves such endeavor, but instead passages which, if your inference were valid, would attribute everything to free choice.

Let us therefore distinguish here again between the words quoted from Scripture and the inference tacked on to them by Diatribe. The words quoted are imperatives, and only say what ought to be done; for Moses does not say, "Thou hast the strength or power to choose," but, "Choose, keep, do!" He issues commandments about doing, but does not describe man's ability to do. The inference tacked on by that dilettante Diatribe, however, concludes: Therefore man is able to do such things, otherwise they would be commanded in vain. The answer to this is: Madam Diatribe, your reasoning is bad and you do not prove your conclusion, but in your blindness and carelessness you only imagine that this follows and is proved. The commandments are not, however, either inappropriate or purposeless, but are given in order that blind, self-confident man may through them come to know his own diseased state of impotence if he attempts to do what is commanded. So again your simile is worthless, when you say ⟨E., p. 55⟩: "Otherwise, it would be as if one were to say to a man so bound that he could only raise his hand to the left, 'See, you have the best wine at your right hand, you have poison on your left— choose which you will.' "

I have an idea that you are mightily pleased with those similes of yours, but you fail to see that if they hold good, they prove a good deal more than you set out to prove; in fact, they prove what you deny and want condemned, namely, that free choice can do everything. For throughout the discussion you forget that you have said that free choice can do nothing without grace, and you prove instead that free choice can do everything without grace. For the upshot of your inferences and similes is this, that either

free choice can do by itself the things which are said and commanded, or else those things are commanded to no purpose, ri-
diculously and irrelevantly. But these are the old songs of the Pelagians, which even the Sophists have exploded and you yourself
have condemned. Meanwhile, however, you show by this forgetfulness and bad memory of yours how completely you lack either understanding of the subject or interest in it. For what could be
more disgraceful in a rhetorician than to be perpetually discussing
and proving things irrelevant to the point at issue, or rather, to be
continually declaiming against both his own cause and himself?

I therefore say again, the words of Scripture quoted by you are
imperative, and they neither prove nor determine anything with
regard to human ability, but prescribe things to be done and left
undone; while your inferences (or additions) and similes, if they
prove anything, prove this—that free choice can do everything
without grace. This proposition, however, is one that you have not
undertaken to prove, but have rather denied, so that proofs of this
sort are nothing but the strongest disproofs. For if I argue—to see
if I can rouse Diatribe from her lethargy—that when Moses says,
"Choose life and keep the commandment," then unless man were
able to choose life and keep the commandment, it would be ridiculous for Moses to tell him to do it, have I proved by this argument that free choice can do nothing good or that it possesses
an endeavor apart from its own powers? On the contrary, I have
proved by a pretty conclusive argument that either man can
choose life and keep the commandment, as he is bidden to do, or
Moses is a ridiculous legislator. But who would dare to call Moses
a ridiculous legislator? It follows, then, that man can do what is
commanded. This is the way Diatribe continually argues, contrary to her own intention and her promise not to maintain any
such position but to demonstrate a certain conative power in free
choice. Of this, however, she makes little mention in the whole
series of her arguments, and so far is she from proving it that she
rather proves the opposite, so that it is rather she herself who persistently speaks and argues absurdly.

Now as to its being absurd, on the lines of the simile you have
introduced, that a man with his right arm tied should be told to
put out his hand on the right when he can do so only on the left;
surely it is not ridiculous even for a man with both arms tied, if he
proudly maintains or ignorantly presumes that he can do what he
pleases on either side of him, to be told to put out a hand on
both sides, not in order to make fun of him in his captivity, but
to show the falsity of his claim to possess freedom and power, or

to bring home to him his ignorance of his own captivity and misery. Diatribe persists in representing man to us as one who can either do what is commanded or at least knows that he cannot. But such a man nowhere exists; and if there were such a man, then truly it would either be ridiculous to give him impossible commandments, or the Spirit of Christ would be in vain.[39]

Scripture, however, represents man as one who is not only bound, wretched, captive, sick, and dead, but in addition to his other miseries is afflicted, through the agency of Satan his prince, with this misery of blindness, so that he believes himself to be free, happy, unfettered, able, well, and alive. For Satan knows that if men were aware of their misery, he would not be able to retain a single one of them in his kingdom, because God could not but at once pity and succour them in their acknowledged and crying wretchedness, seeing he is so highly extolled throughout Scripture as being near to the contrite in heart ⟨Ps. 34:18⟩, as Christ too declares himself according to Isa., ch. 61, to have been sent to preach the gospel to the poor and to bind up the brokenhearted ⟨Luke 4:18⟩. Accordingly, it is Satan's work to prevent men from recognizing their plight and to keep them presuming that they can do everything they are told. But the work of Moses or a lawgiver is the opposite of this, namely, to make man's plight plain to him by means of the law and thus to break and confound him by self-knowledge, so as to prepare him for grace and send him to Christ that he may be saved. They are therefore not absurd but emphatically serious and necessary things that are done by the law.

Those who now understand these things have no difficulty in understanding at the same time that Diatribe achieves absolutely nothing by her whole series of arguments, seeing she does nothing but collect imperative verbs out of the Scriptures, without any understanding of what they mean or why they are said. Then by adding her own inferences and human analogies [40] she mixes such a potent brew [41] that she asserts and proves more than she had intended, and actually argues against herself. There should therefore be no need to run through the details any further, for they are all dealt with when one is dealt with, since they all depend on the same argument. Nevertheless, in order that she may be

[39] If he can do what is commanded, he does not need the Spirit; if he knows he cannot, he does not need the commandments to enlighten him.
[40] "Similitudinibus carnalibus."
[41] "Tam robustam offam miscet." Offa = "bite," "morsel," especially a little ball or pellet made of flour; hence "bait," as in Vergil, Aeneid vi.420, or "shapeless mass" or "abortion," as in Juvenal, Satires ii.33; Persius, Satires v.4.

overwhelmed with the profusion with which she wanted to overwhelm me, I will proceed to review a few more.

Isaiah 1⟨:19 f.⟩ reads: "If you are willing and obedient, you
shall eat the good of the land," where it would have been more
appropriate, in Diatribe's judgment, to say, "If I am willing"; "if
I refuse," if there is no freedom of will. The answer is sufficiently
evident from what has been said above. Moreover, what appropriateness would there be here in saying, "If I am willing, you
shall eat the good of the land"? Does Diatribe in her excessive
wisdom think that the good of the land can be eaten if God is not
willing, or that it is an extraordinary and novel idea that we receive good things only if God is willing? Similarly, there is Isa.
21⟨:12⟩: "If you will inquire, inquire; turn and come." [42] What is
the point, asks Diatribe, of exhorting those who are in no way under their own control, as if one were to say to a person bound in
chains, "Bestir yourself there!"? I ask, on the other hand, what is
the point of quoting texts that prove nothing by themselves, and
then adding an inference which is a distortion of their meaning
and makes them attribute everything to free choice, when all that
should have been proved was some sort of endeavor, and that not
attributable to free choice?

The same may be said regarding Isa. 45⟨:20, 22⟩: "Assemble
yourselves and come. . . . Turn [43] to me and be saved," and ch.
52⟨:1 ff.⟩: "Awake, awake, shake yourself from the dust; loose the
bonds from your neck." Then there is Jer. 15⟨:19⟩: "If you return,
I will restore you,[44] and if you will separate what is precious from
what is worthless, you shall be as my mouth." Still more clearly
Zechariah shows the endeavor of free choice and the grace that is
ready to respond to the endeavor, when he says: "Return to me,
says the Lord of Hosts, and I will return to you, says the Lord." [45]

Erasmus' Failure to Distinguish Between Law and Gospel
⟨WA 680–684⟩

In these passages our Diatribe makes no distinction whatever
between expressions of the law and of the gospel; for she is so
blind and ignorant that she does not know what law and gospel
are. For out of the whole of Isaiah, apart from that one verse, "If
you are willing," she quotes not a single word of the law, all the
rest being Gospel passages, in which the brokenhearted and af-

---

42 *"Convertimini et venite."*   43 *"Convertimini."*
44 *"Si converteris, convertam te."*
45 *"Convertimini . . . et convertar."* (Zech. 1:3.)

flicted are called to take comfort from a word of proffered grace. But Diatribe turns them into words of law. Now, I ask you, what good will anyone do in a matter of theology or Holy Writ, who has not yet got as far as knowing what the law and what the gospel is, or if he knows, disdains to observe the distinction between them? Such a person is bound to confound everything—heaven and hell, life and death—and he will take no pains to know anything at all about Christ. On this subject I will admonish dear Diatribe more fully below.

Look at those words from Jeremiah and Zechariah: "If you return, I will restore you" and "Return to me, and I will return to you." Does it follow from "Return" that you are therefore able to return? Does it follow from "Love the Lord your God with all your heart" that you will therefore be able to love him with all your heart? What, then, do arguments of this kind prove, unless that free choice does not need the grace of God but can do everything in its own strength? How much more correctly, therefore, are the words taken as they stand? "If you shall return,[46] I also will restore you," that is, if you leave off sinning, I also will leave off punishing you, and if after returning [47] you live a good life, I also will do good to you by turning away [48] your captivity and all your ills. But it does not follow from this that man returns [49] by his own power, nor do the words themselves say so, but they say simply: "If you return," by which man is told what he ought to do; and once he knew this and saw that he could not do it, he would seek the means to enable him to do it, if Diatribe's leviathan (that is, her added comment and inference) did not intervene to say: "But it would be meaningless to say, 'Return,' if a man could not return by his own power." What sort of notion that is, and what it implies, has already been sufficiently stated.

Only a man in a stupor or a daze of some sort could suppose that the power of free choice is established by words such as "Return" and "If you return" without noticing that on the same principle it would also be established by the saying, "Thou shalt love the Lord thy God with all thy heart," since the meaning of the one who commands and demands is the same in both cases. The love of God is certainly no less required than our conversion and the keeping of all the commandments, since the love of God is our true conversion. Yet no one tries to prove free choice from the commandment of love, though everyone argues for it from sayings such as "If thou art willing"; "If thou wilt hear"; "Return!" If, then, it does not follow from that saying ("Love the Lord thy God

[46] "Si conversus fueris."   [47] "Si conversus."   [48] "Vertens."   [49] "Convertatur."

with all thy heart") that free choice is anything or can do anything, it certainly does not follow from sayings such as "If thou art willing"; "If thou art obedient"; "Return!" which either demand less or demand it less imperiously than: "Love God!"; "Love the Lord!"

Whatever, therefore, can be said against the use of the expression "Love God!" as an argument for free choice, the same can be said against the use of all other verbs of command or demand as arguments for free choice. And what can be said is that by the command to love we are shown the essential shape of the law and what we ought to do, but not the power of the will or what we are able to do, but rather what we are not able to do; and the same is shown by all other expressions of demand. For it is well known that even the Schoolmen, with the exception of the Scotists [50] and the Moderns,[51] affirm that man cannot love God with all his heart; and in that case, neither can he fulfill any of the other commandments, since all of them depend on this one, as Christ testifies (Matt. 22:40). So the fact remains, even on the testimony of the Scholastic doctors, that the words of the law are no evidence for the power of free choice, but show what we ought to do and cannot do.

But our Diatribe, still more ineptly, not only infers the indicative from Zechariah's imperative "Return to me," but even claims to prove the endeavor of free choice and a grace prepared to respond to it. Here at long last she remembers her "endeavor," and by a new kind of grammar "to return" signifies the same for her as "to endeavor," so that the meaning is "Return to me," i.e., "I will endeavor to return to you." She thus ends by attributing endeavor even to God—perhaps intending to prepare grace for him, too, as an endeavorer. For if "to return" signifies "to endeavor" in one place, why not in all? Again, she says that Jer. 15⟨:19⟩: "If you separate what is precious from what is worthless," proves not simply endeavor but freedom to choose, though she had previously taught us that this was lost and had turned into a necessity of serving sin. You see, then, that Diatribe truly possesses a free choice in her handling of the Scriptures, so that words of one and the same type are for her obliged to prove endeavor in one place and freedom in another, exactly as she pleases.

But to put vanities aside, the word "return" [52] has two uses in the Scriptures, one legal, the other evangelical. In its legal use it is an expression of exacting and imperious command, which re-

[50] See above, p. 171 n. 2.   [51] See above, p. 172 n. 4.
[52] "Verbum convertendi."

quires not merely an endeavor but a change of the whole life. Jeremiah frequently makes this use of it, as when he says: "Return every one of you from his evil way" ⟨Jer. 18:11; 25:5; 35:15⟩ and "Return to the Lord" ⟨ch. 4:1⟩; for there it quite plainly involves obedience to the demands of all the precepts. In its evangelical use it is an expression of divine comfort and promise, by which nothing is demanded from us, but the grace of God is offered to us, as, for instance, in Ps. 15⟨14:7⟩: "When the Lord turns [53] the captivity of Zion," and Ps. 22: "Return, O my soul, to your rest." [54] Zechariah, therefore, has given us the briefest possible epitome of both kinds of preaching, both of law and of grace; for it is nothing but law, law at its peak, when he says, "Return to me," and it is grace when he says, "I will return to you." So to the extent that free choice is proved by the expression "Love the Lord!" or by any other particular expression of the law, to that extent it is proved by this summary expression of the law, "Return!" It is therefore the mark of a discerning reader of Scripture to notice what are words of law and what of grace, so as not to have them all jumbled up as the filthy Sophists and this yawning Diatribe do.

See now how the Diatribe treats that famous verse of Ezek., ch. 18: "As I live, says the Lord, I desire not the death of a sinner, but rather that he should turn [55] and live." [56] ⟨E., p. 56.⟩ First, Diatribe says: "In every case the words 'turns away . . . has done . . . has performed . . .' are repeated again and again, in the matter of doing good or evil, and where are those who deny that man can do anything?" Notice, please, the remarkable consequence. She was going to prove endeavor and desire on the part of free choice, and she proves a complete act, everything fully carried out by free choice. Where now, I ask you,[57] are those who insist on grace and the Holy Spirit? For this is the subtle kind of way she argues: "Ezekiel says, 'If a wicked man turns away from all his sins and does what is lawful and right, he shall live' ⟨Ezek. 18:21⟩; therefore, the wicked man forthwith does so and is able to do so." Ezekiel intimates what ought to be done, and Diatribe takes it that this is being and has been done, again trying to teach

---

[53] *"Converterit."*

[54] Luther refers here to Ps. 22 (Vulg.) = Ps. 23 (English versions), where v. 3 reads: *"Animam meam convertit,"* "He restoreth my soul." See, however, Ps. 116:7.

[55] *"Convertatur."*

[56] Erasmus quoted from Ezek. 18:21, 24, 32, and 33:11. Luther sums it all up with Ezek 33:11.

[57] *"Ubi sunt,"* i.e., "Where are they"—as a result of that argument? Answer: Nowhere! Out of the picture!

us by a new sort of grammar that to owe is the same as to have, to be required as to be provided, to demand as to pay.

Then she takes ⟨E., p. 56⟩ that word of sweetest gospel, "I desire not the death of a sinner," etc., and gives this twist to it: "Does the good Lord deplore the death of his people which he himself works in them? If he does not will our death and if we nonetheless perish, it is to be imputed to our own will. But what can you impute to a man who can do nothing either good or ill?" This is just the song Pelagius sang, when he attributed not merely desire or endeavor, but the complete power of fulfilling and doing everything, to free choice. For it is this power that these inferences prove if they prove anything, as we have said, so that they conflict just as violently and even more so with Diatribe herself, who denies that free choice has this power, and claims for it only an endeavor, as they conflict with us who deny free choice altogether. But not to dwell on her ignorance, we will confine ourselves to the point at issue.

It is an evangelical word and the sweetest comfort in every way for miserable sinners, where Ezekiel ⟨Ezek. 18:23, 32⟩ says: "I desire not the death of a sinner, but rather that he may turn and live," like Ps. 28⟨30:5⟩: "For his anger is but for a moment, and his favor is for a lifetime." [58] Then there is Ps. 68⟨109:21⟩: "How sweet is thy mercy, O Lord" [59] and "For I am merciful" ⟨Jer. 3:12⟩, and also Christ's saying in Matt. 11⟨:28⟩: "Come unto me, all you who labor, and I will give you rest," and that in Ex. 20⟨:6⟩: "I show mercy to many thousands, to those who love me." What, indeed, does almost more than half of Holy Scripture contain but sheer promises of grace, in which mercy, life, peace, and salvation are offered by God to men? And what else do words of promise have to say but this: "I desire not the death of a sinner"? Is it not the same thing to say, "I am merciful," as to say, "I am not angry, I do not want to punish, I do not want you to die, I want to pardon, I want to spare"? And if these divine promises were not there to raise up consciences afflicted with the sense of sin and terrified with the fear of death and judgment, what place would there be for pardon or hope? What sinner would not despair? But just as free choice is not proved by other words of mercy or promise or

---

[58] Luther presumably meant Ps. 29:6 (Vulg.), though he corrects its rendering of the Hebrew.

[59] Luther here mixes up Ps. 68:17 (Vulg.), which reads: "*Quoniam benigna est misericordia tua,*" and Ps. 108:21 (Vulg.): "*Quia suavis est misericordia tua.*" He gives the former reference and the latter text, with the substitution of *quam* for *quia.*

comfort, so neither is it proved by this one: "I desire not the death of a sinner," etc.

But our Diatribe, again making no distinction between words of law and of promise, takes this verse of Ezekiel as an expression of the law, and expounds it thus: "I desire not the death of a sinner," that is, "I do not want him to sin mortally or become a sinner liable to death, but rather that he may turn [60] from his sin, if he has committed any, and so may live." For if she did not expound it so, it would not serve her purpose at all. But this means completely throwing overboard the loveliest thing in Ezekiel, "I desire not death." If that is how in our blindness we wish to read and understand the Scriptures, what wonder is it if they are obscure and ambiguous? For he does not say, "I desire not the sin of a man," but, "I desire not the death of a sinner," plainly showing that he is speaking of the penalty of sin, which the sinner experiences for his sin, namely, the fear of death. And he lifts up and comforts the sinner from his affliction and despair, so as not to quench the smoking flax and break the bruised reed ⟨Isa. 42:3⟩, but to give hope of pardon and salvation, so that he may rather be converted (by turning [61] to salvation from the penalty of death) and live, that is, be at peace and happy with an untroubled conscience.

For this also must be observed, that just as the voice of the law is not raised except over those who do not feel or acknowledge their sin, as Paul says in Rom. 3⟨:20⟩: "Through the law comes knowledge of sin," so the word of grace does not come except to those who feel their sin and are troubled and tempted to despair. Thus in all expressions of the law you see that sin is revealed, inasmuch as we are shown what we ought to do, just as you see in all the words of promise, on the other hand, that the evil is indicated under which sinners, or those who are to be lifted up, are laboring. Here, for instance, "I desire not the death of a sinner" explicitly names death and the sinner, that is, the evil that is felt as well as the person who feels it. But in the words "Love God with all your heart," we are shown the good we ought to do, not the evil we feel, in order that we may recognize how unable we are to do that good.

Hence nothing could have been more inappropriately quoted in support of free choice than this passage of Ezekiel, which actually stands in the strongest opposition to free choice. For here we are shown what free choice is like, and what it can do about sin when sin is recognized, or about its own conversion to God; that is to

[60] *"Convertatur."*   [61] *"Conversione."*

say, nothing but fall into a worse state and add despair and impenitence to its sins, if God did not quickly come to its aid and call it back and raise it up by a word of promise. For God's solicitude in promising grace to recall and restore the sinner is a sufficiently strong and reliable argument that free choice by itself cannot but go from bad to worse and (as Scripture says) fall down into hell, unless you credit God with such levity as to pour out words in profusion for the mere pleasure of talking, and not because they are in any way necessary for our salvation. So you can see that not only all the words of the law stand against free choice, but also all the words of promise utterly refute it; which means that Scripture in its entirety stands opposed to it.

God Preached, God Hidden; God's Will Revealed, God's Will Secret (WA 684–688)

This word, therefore, "I desire not the death of a sinner," has as you see no other object than the preaching and offering of divine mercy throughout the world, a mercy that only the afflicted and those tormented by the fear of death receive with joy and gratitude, because in them the law has already fulfilled its office and brought the knowledge of sin. Those, however, who have not yet experienced the office of the law, and neither recognize sin nor feel death, have no use for the mercy promised by that word. But why some are touched by the law and others are not, so that the former accept and the latter despise the offered grace, is another question and one not dealt with by Ezekiel in this passage. For he is here speaking of the preached and offered mercy of God, not of that hidden and awful will of God whereby he ordains by his own counsel which and what sort of persons he wills to be recipients and partakers of his preached and offered mercy. This will is not to be inquired into, but reverently adored, as by far the most awe-inspiring secret of the Divine Majesty, reserved for himself alone and forbidden to us much more religiously than any number of Corycian caverns.[62]

When now Diatribe pertly asks (E., p. 56), "Does the good Lord deplore the death of his people, which he himself works in them?" —for this really does seem absurd—we reply, as we have already said, that we have to argue in one way about God or the will of God as preached, revealed, offered, and worshiped, and in another way about God as he is not preached, not revealed, not offered, not worshiped. To the extent, therefore, that God hides himself and

[62] See above, p. 38 n. 10.

wills to be unknown to us, it is no business of ours. For here the saying truly applies, "Things above us are no business of ours." And lest anyone should think this is a distinction of my own, I am following Paul, who writes to the Thessalonians concerning Antichrist that he will exalt himself above every God that is preached and worshiped ⟨II Thess. 2:4⟩. This plainly shows that someone can be exalted above God as he is preached and worshiped, that is, above the word and rite through which God is known to us and has dealings with us; but above God as he is not worshiped and not preached, but as he is in his own nature and majesty, nothing can be exalted, but all things are under his mighty hand.

God must therefore be left to himself in his own majesty, for in this regard we have nothing to do with him, nor has he willed that we should have anything to do with him. But we have something to do with him insofar as he is clothed and set forth in his Word, through which he offers himself to us and which is the beauty and glory with which the psalmist celebrates him as being clothed.[63] In this regard we say, the good God does not deplore the death of his people which he works in them, but he deplores the death which he finds in his people and desires to remove from them. For it is this that God as he is preached is concerned with, namely, that sin and death should be taken away and we should be saved. For "he sent his word and healed them" ⟨Ps. 107:20⟩. But God hidden in his majesty neither deplores nor takes away death, but works life, death, and all in all. For there he has not bound himself by his word, but has kept himself free over all things.

Diatribe, however, deceives herself in her ignorance by not making any distinction between God preached and God hidden, that is, between the word of God and God himself. God does many things that he does not disclose to us in his word; he also wills many things which he does not disclose himself as willing in his word. Thus he does not will the death of a sinner, according to his word; but he wills it according to that inscrutable will of his. It is our business, however, to pay attention to the word and leave that inscrutable will alone, for we must be guided by the word and not by that inscrutable will. After all, who can direct himself by a will completely inscrutable and unknowable? It is enough to know simply that there is a certain inscrutable will in God, and as to what, why, and how far it wills, that is something we have no right whatever to inquire into, hanker after, care about, or meddle with, but only to fear and adore.

[63] Cf. Ps. 93:1; 104:1, 3.

It is therefore right to say, "If God does not desire our death, the fact that we perish must be imputed to our own will." It is right, I mean, if you speak of God as preached; for he wills all men to be saved ⟨I Tim. 2:4⟩, seeing he comes with the word of salvation to all, and the fault is in the will that does not admit him, as he says in Matt. 23⟨:37⟩: "How often would I have gathered your children, and you would not!" But why that majesty of his does not remove or change this defect of our will in all men, since it is not in man's power to do so, or why he imputes this defect to man, when man cannot help having it, we have no right to inquire; and though you may do a lot of inquiring, you will never find out. It is as Paul says in Rom. 11⟨9:20⟩: "Who are you, to answer back to God?" Let these remarks suffice for that passage of Ezekiel, and let us go on to the rest.

Diatribe next argues that all the exhortations in the Scriptures must be quite pointless, as must also the promises, threats, expostulations, reproaches, entreaties, blessings and curses, and all the swarms of precepts, if it is not in anyone's power to keep what is commanded ⟨E., p. 57⟩. Diatribe is always forgetting the question at issue and doing something other than she set out to do, not realizing how it all militates more strongly against herself than against us. For on the basis of all these passages, by the force of the inference that she suggests from the words quoted, she proves a freedom and ability to keep everything, though what she wanted to prove was such a free choice as can will nothing good without grace, and a certain endeavor not ascribable to its own powers. I do not find that such an endeavor is proved by any of the passages quoted, but only that a demand is made regarding what ought to be done. This had already been said too often, were not such repetition necessary because Diatribe so often blunders on the same string,[64] putting off her readers with a useless flow of words.

Almost the last passage she quotes from the Old Testament is that of Moses in Deut. 30⟨:11 ff.⟩: "This commandment which I command you this day is not above you, neither is it far off. It is not in heaven, that you should say, 'Who can go up for us to heaven, and bring it to us, that we may hear it and do it?' . . . But the word is very near you; it is in your mouth and in your heart, so that you can do it." Diatribe contends ⟨E., p. 57⟩ that by this passage it is declared not only that what is commanded is implanted in us, but also that it is like going downhill, i.e., is easy[65]

---

[64] Cf. Horace, *Ars poetica* 355 f.: "*Citharoedus/Ridetur, chorda qui semper oberret eadam,*" "The harpist is laughed at who always blunders on the same string."

[65] "*In proclivi esse, hoc est, facile.*"

or at least not difficult. We are grateful for such erudition! If, then, Moses so distinctly announces that there is in us not only a faculty, but also a facility for keeping all the commandments, why are we sweating so much? Why did we not promptly produce this passage and assert free choice on a free field? [66] What need is there now of Christ or of the Spirit? We have found a passage that shuts everyone's mouth, and not only distinctly asserts freedom of choice, but also distinctly teaches that the keeping of the commandments is easy. How foolish it was of Christ to purchase for us at the price of his shed blood the Spirit we did not need, in order that we might be given a facility in keeping the commandments, when we already have one by nature!

Nay, even Diatribe herself must recant her own words, in which she said that free choice could do nothing good without grace. Let her now say instead that free choice possesses such virtue that it not only wills good, but also finds it an easy task to keep the greatest and indeed all the commandments. Look, if you please, at what comes of having a mind out of sympathy with the subject, how it cannot help betraying itself! Is there still any need to confute Diatribe? Who could confute her more thoroughly than she confutes herself? She must be that beast they talk of which eats itself! [67] How true it is that a liar ought to have a good memory! [68]

We have spoken of this passage in our commentary on Deuteronomy,[69] so here we shall be brief; and we shall discuss it without reference to Paul, who has a powerful treatment of it in Rom. 10(:6 ff.). You can see that nothing whatever is stated or even suggested by any syllable here about the ease or difficulty, power or impotence, of free choice or of man in the matter of keeping or not keeping the commandments, except insofar as those who entangle the Scriptures in the net of their own inferences and fancies make them obscure and ambiguous for themselves so as to be able to make of them what they please. If you cannot use your eyes, at least use your ears or feel your way with your hands! Moses says it is "not above you, neither is it far off. It is not in heaven . . . Neither is it beyond the sea." What is "above you"?

[66] The phrase would naturally mean "on a free, that is, open, plain," i.e., in an open contest with complete freedom of maneuver.

[67] The "beast that eats itself" is an obscure reference. The fourth-century writer Julius Capitolinus refers to the serpent as *"anguis . . . se a cauda medium comedit"* (*Antoninus Pius* 9.4), and Augustine in *Contra Iulianum* of A.D. 421 also refers to the *"bestiam, quae se ipsam comesset"* (*Contra Iulianum* III.xxi.47). This latter reference is very probably in Luther's mind, and the story may have originated from the snake's habit of casting off its slough, which gives Vergil a memorable simile in *Aeneid* ii.469–475.

[68] A quotation from Quintilian, *Institutio oratoria* iv.2.91.

[69] *WA* 30, 3, 334, 8.

What is "far off"? What is "in heaven"? What is "beyond the sea"? Will they make even grammar and the commonest words obscure for us, till we are able to say nothing certain, just to gain their point that the Scriptures are obscure?

According to my grammar, it is not the quality or quantity of human powers but the distance of places that is signified by these terms. What is meant by "above you" is not a certain strength of will, but a place that is above us. Similarly, "far off," "beyond the sea," and "in heaven" say nothing about any power in man, but denote a place at a distance from us, upward, on the right, on the left, backward, or forward. I may be laughed at for making such an obvious point and treating such great men to an elementary explanation, as if they were little boys learning their alphabet and I were teaching them to put syllables together. But what am I to do when in so bright a light I see them looking for darkness and earnestly wishing to be blind as they reckon up for us such a succession of centuries, so many geniuses, so many saints, so many martyrs, so many doctors, and with such great authority produce and flaunt this passage of Moses, without ever condescending to examine the syllables of which it consists or to control their own flights of fancy so far as to give a moment's consideration to the passage they are shouting about? Let Diatribe now go on and tell us how it is possible for a single private individual to see what so many public figures, the leading lights of so many centuries, have not seen! For certainly this passage, as even a child could judge, proves them to have been not seldom blind.

What, then, does Moses mean by these very plain and open words, except that he himself has fulfilled his office as a faithful lawgiver excellently? For he has removed every obstacle to their knowing and keeping clearly before them all the commandments, and left them no room for the excuse that they were unaware of or did not possess the commandments, or had to seek them from elsewhere. Hence if they do not keep them, the fault will lie neither with the law nor with the lawgiver, but with themselves; for since the law is there, and the lawgiver has taught it, there remains no excuse on the grounds of ignorance, but only a charge of negligence and disobedience. It is not necessary, he says, to fetch laws from heaven or from places overseas or a long way off, nor can you pretend that you have not heard of them or do not possess them, for you have them close at hand. You have heard them by God's command through my lips,[70] you have understood them in your heart and have received them as a subject of constant reading

[70] *"Me authore."*

and oral exposition by the Levites in your midst, as this very word and book of mine bear witness. All that remains is for you to do them. I ask you, what is here attributed to free choice, except the requisite observance of the laws given to it? For any excuse of ignorance or absence of laws is taken away.

These are just about all the texts which Diatribe quotes from the Old Testament in support of free choice, and when these are dismissed nothing remains that is not equally dismissed, whether she quotes any more or intends to quote more. For she can quote nothing but subjunctive or optative expressions, which signify, not what we do or can do (as we have so often told Diatribe in answer to her repeated assertions), but what we ought to do and what is demanded of us, in order that we may be made aware of our impotence and brought to the knowledge of sin. Otherwise, if by the addition of inferences and similes invented by human reason these texts prove anything, they prove this, that free choice consists not simply of some little bit of endeavor or desire, but of a full and free ability and power to do everything without the grace of God, without the Holy Spirit. Hence nothing is farther from being proved by all that long, repetitive, and emphatic disputation than what had to be proved, namely, that "probable opinion" whereby free choice is defined as being so impotent that it can will nothing good without grace, but is forced to serve sin, though it possesses an endeavor that must not be ascribed to its own powers, and so consists in a quite obvious contradiction.

New Testament Passages: Matthew 23:37—Man Must Not Pry Into the Secret Will of God (WA 688–690)

We come now to the New Testament, where again a host of imperative verbs is mustered in support of that miserable bondage of free choice, and the aid of carnal Reason with her inferences and similes is called in, just as in a picture or a dream you might see the king of the flies with his lances of straw and shields of hay arrayed against a real and regular army of seasoned human troops. That is how the human dreams of Diatribe go to war with the battalions of divine words.

First, there steps forward as a sort of Achilles [71] of the flies that saying from Matt. 23⟨:37⟩: "O Jerusalem, Jerusalem, how often would I have gathered your children together, and you would not!" If all is determined by necessity, she says, could not Jerusalem rightly reply to the Lord: "Why do you torment yourself

[71] See above, p. 78 n. 41.

with vain tears? If you did not wish us to listen to the prophets, why did you send them? Why impute to us what has been done by your will and our necessity?" That is what Diatribe says (E., p. 59). And here is our reply. Let us grant for the moment that this inference and proof of hers is right and good; what in fact is proved by it? The probable opinion which says that free choice cannot will the good? It instead proves that the will is free, sound, and capable of doing everything the prophets have said. But that is not what Diatribe set out to prove.

Indeed, let Diatribe herself reply to the following questions. If free choice cannot will good, why is it imputed to it that it has not given heed to the prophets, to whom as teachers of good things it could not give heed by its own powers? Why does Christ weep vain tears, as if they could have willed what he certainly knows they cannot will? Let Diatribe, I say, acquit Christ of insanity in order to maintain that probable opinion of hers, and our opinion will soon be quit of that Achilles of the flies. This passage from Matthew, therefore, either proves total free choice or it militates just as strongly against Diatribe herself and strikes her down with her own weapon.

We say, as we have said before, that the secret will of the Divine Majesty is not a matter for debate, and the human temerity which with continual perversity is always neglecting necessary things in its eagerness to probe this one, must be called off and restrained from busying itself with the investigation of these secrets of God's majesty, which it is impossible to penetrate because he dwells in light inaccessible, as Paul testifies (I Tim. 6:16). Let it occupy itself instead with God incarnate, or as Paul puts it, with Jesus crucified, in whom are all the treasures of wisdom and knowledge, though in a hidden manner (Col. 2:3); for through him it is furnished abundantly with what it ought to know and ought not to know. It is God incarnate, moreover, who is speaking here: "I would . . . you would not"—God incarnate, I say, who has been sent into the world for the very purpose of willing, speaking, doing, suffering, and offering to all men everything necessary for salvation. Yet he offends very many, who being either abandoned or hardened by that secret will of the Divine Majesty do not receive him as he wills, speaks, does, suffers, and offers, as John says: "The light shines in the darkness, and the darkness does not comprehend it" (John 1:5); and again: "He came to his own home, and his own people received him not" (John 1:11). It is likewise the part of this incarnate God to weep, wail, and groan over the perdition of the ungodly, when the will of the Divine Majesty purposely abandons and reprobates some to perish. And it is not for us to ask why he does so, but to stand in awe of God who both can do and wills to do such things.

No one, I think, will wish to deny that this will concerning which it is said: " How often would I . . ." was disclosed to the Jews before God became incarnate, inasmuch as they are accused of having killed the prophets before Christ, and so of having resisted his will. For it is well known among Christians that everything done by the prophets was done in the name of the Christ who was to come, concerning whom it had been promised that he should be God incarnate. Hence whatever has been offered to men from the beginning of the world through the ministers of the word is rightly called the will of Christ.

Here, however, Reason in her saucy, sarcastic way will say: This is a splendidly devised way out, if every time we are hard pressed by the arguments, we have recourse to that awful will of the Divine Majesty, and can reduce our opponent to silence whenever he becomes troublesome; it is just the same as when the astrologers with their epicycles dodge all questions about the motion of the heavens as a whole.[72] Our answer is that this is not our invention, but a principle firmly based on the Divine Scriptures. Thus Paul says in Rom. 11⟨9:19 ff.⟩: "Why, then, does God find fault? Who can resist his will? O man, who are you to contend with God? Has the potter no right . . . ?" and the rest; and before him, Isa. 58⟨:2⟩: "Yet they seek me daily, and desire [73] to know my ways, as if they were a nation that did righteousness . . . ; they ask of me righteous judgments, they desire to draw near to God." I think it is sufficiently shown by these words that it is not permissible for men to pry into the will of the Divine Majesty.

Our present subject, however, is of a kind which most of all tempts perverse human beings to pry into that awful will, so that it is most of all in place here to exhort them to silence and reverence. In other cases we do not do this, where matters are under discussion for which a reason can be given, and for which we have been commanded to give a reason. But if anyone persists in investigating the reason for that will, refusing to pay heed to our warning, we let him go on and fight with God like the Giants,[74]

[72] *Epicycle* = a small circle having its center on the circumference of a greater one. Ancient astronomy used this idea to explain the movements of the moon and planets.
[73] *"Volunt."* ASV and RSV say "delight"; Douay, "desire . . . are willing."
[74] The mythical sons of Earth and Tartarus, who stormed the heavens but were blasted by Jove's thunderbolt and buried under Mt. Etna. See Ovid, *Metamorphoses* i.

while we wait to see what triumphs he will bring back, certain that
he will do no harm to our cause and no good to his own. For the
fact will remain unchanged, that either he will prove free choice
capable of doing everything or the Scriptures he cites will militate
against himself. In either case he lies prostrate and vanquished
while we stand up as victors.

Precepts and Rewards in the New Testament:
The Question of Merit ⟨WA 690–696⟩

The second text is from Matt. 19⟨:17⟩: "If you would enter into
life, keep the commandments." With what effrontery would it be
said, "If you will . . ." to one whose will is not free? So asks Diatribe. ⟨E., p. 59.⟩ To which we reply: So the will is free, is it, according to this word of Christ? But you were wanting to prove
that free choice cannot will anything good, but necessarily serves
sin, in the absence of grace. With what face, then, do you now
make it wholly free?

The same may be said with regard to the words: "If you would
be perfect" ⟨Matt. 19:21⟩; "If any man would come after me";
"Whoever would save his life" ⟨Luke 9:23 f.⟩; "If you love me";
"If you abide" ⟨John 14:15; 15:7⟩. In short, let all the conjunctive
"ifs" and the imperative verbs be collected up, as I have said, so
that we may assist Diatribe at least by the quantity of words at her
disposal. "All these precepts," she says, "are pointless if nothing is
attributed to the human will . . . How inapposite the conjunction 'if' when all was necessity!"

We reply: If they are pointless, that is your fault; you make
them pointless, and indeed senseless, by asserting on the one hand
that nothing is to be attributed to the human will, since you make
free choice unable to will any good, and then on the other hand
making it able to will all good—unless with you the same words
blow hot and cold at the same time, inasmuch as they assert and
deny everything at once. I am astonished that an author should
have taken such pleasure in repeating the same things so often,
and continually forgetting his own stated purpose—unless perhaps
having no real confidence in his case he wanted to gain his point
by the mere size of his book or to wear out his opponent with the
toil and tedium of reading it. By what sort of logic,[75] I ask you,
does it follow that the will and the ability must be present as soon
as it is said, "If you will, if any man will, if you are willing"? Do

---

[75] *"Qua consequentia."*

we not very often use such expressions to signify instead impotence and impossibility? For instance: "If you wish to equal Vergil in singing, my dear Maevius, you must sing other songs!"; [76] "If you, Scotus,[77] want to surpass Cicero, you will have to replace your sophistries with consummate eloquence"; "If you wish to be compared with David, you must write psalms like his." Here it is obvious that the things mentioned are impossible as far as our own powers are concerned, though they could all be done by divine power. That is how it is in the Scriptures too; there also expressions like these are used in order to show what can be done in us by the power of God, and what we cannot do ourselves.

Of course, if such expressions were used about things that were absolutely impossible, since not even God would ever do them, then they would rightly be said to be either pointless or ridiculous, since they would be used to no purpose. As it is, however, they are used not only in order to show the impotence of free choice, by means of which none of them is done, but also to intimate that someday all such things will be done, though by a power not our own but God's—if we are to admit at all that such expressions contain some indication of things possible and intended to be done. They might be interpreted like this: "If someday you have the will to keep the commandments (which you will have, however, not from yourself, but from God, who will give it to whom he will), then they will preserve you." Or to speak more frankly, these expressions, and particularly the subjunctive clauses, seem to be put as they are because of our ignorance of the predestination of God, which they imply, as if what they meant to say was this: "If you will; if you are willing," that is, "If you are such in the sight of God that he deigns to give you this will to keep the commandments, you will be saved." By this turn of phrase [78] we are given to understand both things, namely, that we can do nothing of ourselves, and that whatever we do, God works it in us.

That is what I should say to those who refused to be satisfied with the statement that only our impotence is shown by those words, and sought to maintain that some kind of strength and ability to do the things that are commanded is also proved. It would then be true, both that we can do nothing of the things commanded, and that at the same time we can do them all; the former being attributable to our own powers, the latter to the grace of God.

[76] Maevius was a third-rate poet contemporary with Horace and Vergil. See Horace, *Epodes* X.2, and Vergil, *Eclogues* III.90.
[77] See above, p. 171 n. 2. [78] "*Quo tropo.*"

The third consideration that moves Diatribe is this: "Where there is such frequent mention of good and bad works, where there is mention of reward," she says, "I do not see how the text can be interpreted of mere necessity. There is nothing meritorious about nature or necessity" ⟨E., pp. 59f.⟩. The only thing clear to *me* is this: that whereas the "probable opinion" asserts mere necessity when it says that free choice can will nothing good, yet here it attributes even merit to it. Free choice has made such progress during the growth of Diatribe's book and disputation, that now it not only possesses an endeavor and desire of its own (though by powers not its own), nay rather, it not only wills and does good, but it even merits eternal life, because Christ says in Matt. 5⟨:12⟩: "Rejoice and be glad, for your reward is great in heaven." "Your" means "free choice's"—that is how Diatribe understands this text, so that Christ and the Spirit count for nothing. For what need of them will there be if we possess good works and merits by means of free choice?

I say these things to help us to see that it is not uncommon for men of outstanding intellect to be habitually blind in a matter which is plain even to a dull and uninstructed mind, and to show how weak an argument drawn from human authority is in divine affairs, where divine authority alone has weight.

There are two questions to be discussed here, the first regarding the precepts of the New Testament, the second regarding merit. We will deal with each of them quite briefly, as we have spoken of them more fully elsewhere. The New Testament properly consists of promises and exhortations, just as the Old Testament properly consists of laws and threats. For in the New Testament the gospel is preached, which is nothing else but a message [79] in which the Spirit and grace are offered with a view to the remission of sins, which has been obtained for us by Christ crucified; and all this freely,[80] and by the sole mercy of God the Father, whereby favor is shown to us, unworthy as we are and deserving of damnation rather than anything else. Then follow exhortations, in order to stir up those who are already justified and have obtained mercy, so that they may be active in the fruits of the freely given righteousness of the Spirit, and may exercise love by good works and bravely bear the cross and all other tribulations of the world. This is the sum of the whole New Testament.

How little Diatribe understands of this matter is very clearly shown by the fact that she has no idea of making any distinction

---

[79] *"Sermo."*   [80] *"Gratis."*

between the Old and the New Testament, for she sees almost nothing in either except laws and precepts, by which men are to be trained in good manners. What the new birth is, however, or renewal, regeneration, and the whole work of the Spirit, of this she sees nothing at all, and I am amazed and astounded that a man can be so utterly ignorant of Holy Writ who has worked so long and hard at it.

That saying, then, "Rejoice and be glad, for your reward is great in heaven" (Matt. 5:12) squares as well with free choice as light agrees with darkness. For Christ is there exhorting, not free choice, but the apostles, who were not only above free choice as being in a state of grace and righteous, but were also appointed to the ministry of the word, which is the highest point of grace, so that they were bearing the tribulations of the world. We, however, are discussing free choice precisely as it is without grace, and arguing that by laws and threatenings, or the Old Testament, it is brought to knowledge of itself, so that it may run to the promises set forth in the New Testament.

As to merit or the offer of a reward, what else is this but a kind of promise? But it does not prove that we can do anything, since no more is expressed by it than that if anyone does this or that, he shall have a reward. Our question, however, is not on what terms the reward is given, or what the reward is to be, but whether we are able to do the kind of things for which a reward is given. For that was what was to be proved. Is it not ridiculous to draw the conclusion that because the prize is exhibited to all on the racecourse, therefore they can all run and obtain it (I Cor. 9:24)? If Caesar conquers the Turks, he will be master of Syria; *ergo* Caesar can and does conquer the Turks. If free choice masters sin, it will be holy to the Lord; *ergo* free choice is holy to the Lord. But let us have no more of such very crude and obviously absurd notions—though it is very fitting that free choice should be proved by such delightful arguments.

Instead, we will discuss the proposition that necessity has neither merit nor reward. This is true if we are speaking of a necessity of compulsion,[81] but if we are speaking of the necessity of immutability, it is false. For who would give a reward or ascribe merit to an involuntary worker? But for those who voluntarily do good or evil, even though they cannot alter their will by their own powers, reward or punishment follows naturally and necessarily, as it is written: "Thou wilt render to every man ac-

---

[81] *"Necessitate coactionis."*

cording to his works" ⟨Rom. 2:6⟩. It follows naturally: If you are submerged in water, you will drown; if you swim out, you will be saved.

To put it briefly, merit or reward is a matter either of worthiness or of consequence. If you consider worthiness, there is no merit and no reward. For if free choice cannot will good when left to itself, but wills good through grace alone (for we are discussing free choice apart from grace, and asking about the power that is proper to each), who does not see that the good will, the merit, and the reward all come from grace alone? And here again Diatribe disagrees with herself when she tries to prove the freedom of the will on the basis of merit, and thus she comes under the same condemnation as I do, because she is just as much opposed to herself as I am in saying that there is merit, there is reward, there is freedom, when she has already asserted that free choice wills nothing good, and has undertaken to prove as much.

If you consider consequence, there is nothing either good or evil that does not have its reward. Error arises from the fact that where merits and rewards are concerned, we engage in useless speculations and questionings about worthiness, which does not exist, when we ought to be arguing about consequence only. For hell and the judgment of God await the ungodly by a necessary consequence, even though they themselves neither desire nor think of such a reward for their sins, but rather detest it exceedingly and, as Peter says, execrate it.[82] Similarly, a kingdom awaits the godly, even though they themselves neither seek it nor think of it, for it has been prepared for them by the Father, not only before they themselves existed, but even before the foundation of the world ⟨Matt. 25:34⟩.

What is more, if they did good works for the sake of obtaining the Kingdom, they would never obtain it, but would rather belong among the ungodly who with an evil and mercenary eye [83] "seek their own" [84] in God. But the children of God do good with a will that is disinterested,[85] not seeking any reward, but only the glory and will of God, and being ready to do good even if—an impossible supposition—there were neither a kingdom nor a hell.

---

[82] Possibly a reference to II Peter 2:12: *"In his quae ignorant blasphemantes,"* "reviling in matters of which they are ignorant" (with "execrate" suggested by the *"execrabile iudicium,"* the "reviling judgment," of the preceding verse?).

[83] Matt. 6:23; John 10:12.

[84] *"Ea quae sua sunt, quaerunt etiam in Deo,"* "look after their own interests, even in their relations with God"; cf. Phil. 2:21; I Cor. 13:5.

[85] *"Gratuita voluntate."*

These things are, I think, sufficiently established by that one saying of Christ's which I have just quoted from Matt. 25⟨:34⟩: "Come, O blessed of my Father, inherit the Kingdom prepared for you from the foundation of the world." How can they merit that which is already theirs and is prepared for them before they are born? We could more truly say that the Kingdom of God merits us as its possessors rather, and thus place merit where they place reward and reward where they place merit. For the Kingdom is not being prepared, but has been prepared, while the sons of the Kingdom are being prepared, not preparing the Kingdom; that is to say, the Kingdom merits the sons, not the sons the Kingdom. So also hell merits and prepares its children rather than they it, for Christ says: "Depart, you cursed, into the eternal fire prepared for the devil and his angels" ⟨Matt. 25:41⟩.

What, then, is the point of the texts that promise the Kingdom and threaten hell? What is the meaning of the word "reward" which occurs so frequently in the Scriptures? "Your work," it says, "shall be rewarded" ⟨II Chron. 15:7⟩; "I am your exceeding great reward" ⟨Gen. 15:1⟩; also, "Who renders to every man according to his works" ⟨Rom. 2:6 f.⟩; and Paul in Rom. 2⟨:7⟩ says: "To those who seek it by patience in good works, ⟨he will give⟩ eternal life"; and there are many similar passages. The answer is that by all these passages nothing is proved but a consequence of reward, and by no means a worthiness of merit. For it is clear that those who do good things do them in no servile and mercenary spirit for the sake of gaining eternal life, yet they are seeking eternal life in the sense that they are on the road by which they will arrive at and find eternal life. Hence "to seek" means to strive earnestly and endeavor with prompt diligence toward that which is the regular result of a good life.

Now, the fact that these things will come about, and will follow on a good or bad life, is declared in the Scriptures in order that men may be instructed, moved, awakened, terrified. For as "through the law comes knowledge of sin" ⟨Rom. 3:20⟩ and a warning of our impotence, and yet from this it cannot be inferred that we are able of ourselves to do anything, so by means of these promises and threats we are warned and taught the consequences of sin and our own impotence which the law has revealed, and yet nothing of worthiness is thereby attributed to our merit. Accordingly, just as the words of the law are for the purpose of instruction and illumination, to teach us what we ought to do and show us that we cannot do it, so the words about reward, signifying what is to be, are for the purpose of exhortation and commination, whereby the godly are awakened, comforted, and raised up to go forward, persevere, and conquer in doing good and enduring evil, lest they should grow weary or lose heart. It is like Paul exhorting his Corinthians and saying: "Be courageous, knowing that in the Lord your labor is not in vain ⟨I Cor. 15:58; 16:13⟩; and similarly, God upholds Abraham by saying: "I am your exceeding great reward" ⟨Gen. 15:1⟩. It is just the same as when you try to cheer someone up by telling him that his works are undoubtedly pleasing to God, which is a kind of consolation that Scripture quite frequently uses. And it is no small comfort to know that one is pleasing to God, even if there were nothing else to follow from it, though that is impossible.

Everything that is said about hope and expectation has to do with this fact, that the things which we hope for will certainly take place, although the godly do not hope merely because of these things, or seek them for their own sake. Similarly, by words of commination and future judgment the ungodly are terrified and cast down, so that they may cease and abstain from evil and not be puffed up, or grow complacent and insolent in their sins.

But here Reason may turn up her nose and say: "Why should God will these things to be done by means of words, when nothing is accomplished by such words, and the will is unable to turn itself in either direction? Why does he not do what he does without speaking a word, seeing he is able to do everything without a word, and the will of itself neither gains in strength nor effectiveness from hearing the word, if the inward movement of the Spirit is lacking, nor would it lose any strength or effectiveness through not hearing the word if the Spirit were present, since everything depends on the power and operation of the Holy Spirit?" We shall reply: It has thus pleased God to impart the Spirit, not without the Word, but through the Word, so as to have us as cooperators with him ⟨I Cor. 3:9⟩ when we sound forth outwardly what he himself alone breathes inwardly wherever he wills,[86] thus doing things that he could of course do without the Word, but does not will so to do. And who are we that we should inquire into the cause of the divine will ⟨cf. Rom. 9:20⟩? It is enough to know that God so wills, and it is becoming for us to reverence, love, and adore his will, putting a restraint on the rashness of Reason. Similarly, he could nourish us without bread, and in fact has provided a means of nourishing us without bread, as Matt. 4⟨:4⟩ says: Man is not nourished by bread alone, but by the

---

[86] Cf. John 3:8: *"Spiritus ubi vult spirat,"* "The wind blows where it wills." or "The Spirit breathes where he wills."

Word of God, though it has pleased God by means of bread and together with bread brought to us from without, to nourish us with the Word inwardly.

It is settled, then, that merit is not proved from reward, at any rate in the Scriptures; and also that free choice is not proved from merit, particularly the kind of free choice that Diatribe undertook to prove, which cannot of itself will anything good. For even if you allow that there is such a thing as merit, and bring in also the well-worn analogies and inferences of Reason, to the effect that the commandment is given in vain, the reward is promised in vain, the threats are held out in vain, unless the choice is free, I maintain that if anything is proved by these arguments, it is that free choice can do everything by itself alone. For if it cannot do everything by itself, then Reason's inference still holds good, that the commandment is given in vain, the promise made in vain, the threat held out in vain. In this way Diatribe keeps on arguing against herself all the time she is arguing against us. In fact it is God alone who by his Spirit works in us both merit and reward, though he discloses and proclaims them both to the whole world by his external Word, in order that his power and glory and our impotence and ignominy may be proclaimed even among the ungodly and unbelieving and ignorant, although only the godly perceive this in their heart and hold on to it in faith, while the rest despise it.

Erasmus' Arguments Undermine His Own Case ⟨WA 696–699⟩

Now, it would be much too tiresome to repeat every single imperative verb that Diatribe enumerates from the New Testament, always tacking on her own inferences and speciously arguing that the things said are ineffectual, pointless, ridiculous, empty nothings if the will is not free. For we have long since pointed out with quite nauseating frequency how nothing is achieved by such statements, and that if anything is proved, complete freedom of choice is proved with it; which is a complete subversion of Diatribe, since she undertook to prove such a free choice as can do nothing good and is in bondage to sin, yet she in fact proves one that can do everything, constantly ignoring and forgetting herself. It is mere caviling, therefore, when she says, for instance: " 'You will know them by their fruits,' says the Lord. What he means by fruits are works, and he calls them ours. But they are not ours if they all happen by necessity" ⟨E., p. 60⟩. I ask you, cannot things rightly be said to be ours which we have admittedly not made ourselves but have received from others? Why, then, should not the works be called ours that God has given us through the Spirit? Are we not to call Christ ours because we have not made him but only received him? Again, if we are the makers of things that are called ours, then we must ourselves have made our eyes, we must have made our hands, we must have made our feet, unless eyes, hands, and feet are not to be called ours! But what have we that we have not received, as Paul says ⟨I Cor. 4:7⟩? Are we to say, therefore, that those things are either not ours or they have been made by us ourselves? Suppose, then, that they are called our fruits because we have produced them: what place is there for grace and the Spirit? For he does not say: "By their fruits, which in some small degree are their own, you shall know them." On the contrary, all this is ridiculous, superfluous, ineffectual, pointless, indeed stupid and odious caviling, by which the sacred words of God are polluted and profaned.

So, too, that saying of Christ on the cross is trifled with: "Father, forgive them; for they know not what they do" ⟨Luke 23:34⟩. Here, where one might have expected a statement establishing free choice, she again has recourse to inferences. "How much more justly," she says, "should he have excused them, since their will was not free, nor could they do otherwise" even if they wanted to! ⟨E., p. 60.⟩ Yet not even by this inference is that sort of free choice proved that can will nothing good, which is what we are concerned with, but the sort that can do everything, which nobody is arguing about and everyone denies except the Pelagians.

Now, when Christ expressly says that they know not what they do, is he not at the same time testifying that they cannot will good? For how can you will what you do not know? If you're not wise to it, you can't rise to it,[87] surely. What could tell more heavily against free choice than that it is so utterly worthless that it not only fails to will good, but it is not even aware how much evil it does and what good is? Is there any obscurity in a single word here: "They know not what they do"? What is there left in the Scriptures that may not, according to Diatribe, affirm free choice, when for her this entirely clear and entirely contrary saying of Christ affirms it? Someone may just as easily say that free choice is affirmed also by the words: "The earth was without form and void" ⟨Gen. 1:2⟩, or: "God rested on the seventh day" ⟨Gen. 2:2⟩, and the like. But to dare to handle the divine words in this way argues a mind signally contemptuous of both God and man, and

[87] *"Ignoti nulla cupido,"* "Of what is unknown there is no desire"; Ovid, *Ars amatoria* III.397; a proverbial expression.

deserving of no consideration whatever.

Then there is John 1⟨:12⟩: "He gave them power to become children of God," which she takes like this: "How can power to become children of God be given if there is no freedom in our will?" This passage, too, is a cudgel for free choice, as almost the whole of John's Gospel is, yet it is cited in support of it. Let us please look at it! John is not speaking of any work of man, either great or small, but of the very renewal and transformation of the old man, who is a child of the devil, into the new man who is a child of God. This man is simply passive (as they say) and does nothing, but becomes something, without remainder. It is "becoming" that John is speaking of: "To become children of God," he says, by a power divinely bestowed on us, not by a power of free choice inherent in us. Yet our Diatribe deduces from this that free choice has such power that it makes us children of God; otherwise she is prepared to aver that John's statement is ridiculous and meaningless. But who has ever so far exalted free choice as to attribute to it the power to make children of God, especially such a free choice as cannot will good, which is the sort that Diatribe postulated? However, let this pass, together with the rest of the inferences so frequently repeated, by which, if anything at all is proved, it is just what Diatribe denies, namely, that free choice can do everything.

What John means is this. By the coming of Christ into the world through the gospel, whereby grace is offered and not work demanded, the opportunity is provided for all men, truly a glorious opportunity, of becoming children of God if they are willing to believe. But this willing, this believing in his name, is not only something that free choice never knew or thought of before, but still less something it can do by its own strength. For how could Reason imagine faith in Jesus the Son of God and of Man to be necessary, when even today she neither comprehends nor is able to believe, even if the whole creation cried it aloud, that any person exists who is at once God and Man; for she is instead offended by such talk, as Paul says in I Cor. 1⟨:23⟩, so far is she from being either willing or able to believe it.

John, therefore, is preaching the riches of the Kingdom of God which are offered to the world through the gospel, and not the virtues of free choice; and at the same time he indicates how few there are who accept them. This is due, of course, to the antipathy of free choice, which has no power while Satan rules over it but to spurn grace and the Spirit that fulfills the law, so splendidly effective are its endeavor and desire as regards the fulfilling of the law. We will, however, explain more fully later what a thunderbolt this passage of John is against free choice. Yet I am not a little disturbed that passages so plainly and strongly opposed to free choice should be cited in support of it by Diatribe, who is so obtuse that she sees no difference at all between words of promise and words of law. For after basing free choice most inappropriately on words of law, she proceeds most absurdly of all to buttress it with words of promise. But this absurdity is easily explained if we consider what an unsympathetic and contemptuous mind Diatribe brings to the discussion. It does not matter to her whether grace stands or falls, whether free choice is laid low or enthroned, so long as she with her empty words renders service to tyrants by bringing our cause into disrepute.

After this we come to Paul, the most stubborn foe of free choice, and even he is made to establish free choice by what he says in Rom. 2⟨:4⟩: "Or do you despise the riches of his kindness and forbearance and patience? Do you not know that his kindness is meant to lead you to repentance?" "How," says Diatribe ⟨E., p. 61⟩, "can contempt of the commandment be brought against anyone when the will is not free? Or how does God invite to penitence if he is the author of impenitence? Or how is condemnation just, when the judge himself enforces wrongdoing?" I reply: Let Diatribe attend to these questions; what have they to do with us? For she herself has given it as her probable opinion that free choice cannot will good, and that it is necessarily and perforce in bondage to sin. How, then, can contempt of the commandment be imputed to it if it cannot will good and there is in it no freedom, but a necessary bondage to sin? How can God invite to repentance when he himself makes repentance impossible inasmuch as he deserts or does not confer grace upon man, who left to himself cannot will good? How can the condemnation be just when the Judge by withdrawing his aid compels the ungodly to remain in evildoing, since by his own power the ungodly can do nothing else? All these questions recoil on the head of Diatribe, or else, as I have said, if they prove anything they prove that free choice can do everything, although this is denied by Diatribe herself and by everybody else.

These inferences of reason worry Diatribe all through her quotations of Scripture, because it does seem ridiculous and pointless to inveigh and demand in such vehement terms when there is no one who can perform. But the apostle's aim, of course, is to lead the ungodly and the proud by means of those threatenings to knowledge of themselves and their own impotence, so as to humble them by the knowledge of sin and thus prepare them for grace.

But what need is there to recount one by one all the texts that are quoted from Paul, when she does nothing but collect imperative or subjunctive verbs, or the kind of expressions with which Paul exhorts Christians to produce the fruits of faith? Diatribe, however, with her appended inferences, conceives the power of free choice to be of such a quality and quantity that it is able without grace to do all that Paul in his exhortations prescribes. Christians, however, are not led by free choice but by the Spirit of God, according to Rom. 8⟨:14⟩; and to be led is not to take the initiative [88] but to be impelled,[89] as a saw or an ax is wielded [90] by a carpenter. And here, lest anyone should doubt whether Luther ever said anything so absurd, Diatribe quotes my own words, which I frankly acknowledge. For I take the view that Wyclif's article (that "all things happen by necessity") was wrongly condemned by the Council, or rather the conspiracy and sedition, of Constance. What is more, Diatribe herself defends the same position along with me when she asserts that free choice by its own powers can will nothing good but is necessarily in bondage to sin, although in the process of proving this she establishes the direct opposite.

Part IV. Defense of Arguments Against Free Choice

Let the above suffice in answer to the first part of Diatribe, in which she has endeavored to establish free choice. Let us now look at the later part, in which our arguments—i.e, those whereby free choice is abolished—are confuted. Here you will see what man-made smoke can do against the thunder and lightnings of God!

First ⟨E., pp. 47 ff.⟩, after marshaling innumerable passages of Scripture like a very formidable army in support of free choice (in order to inspire courage in the confessors and martyrs and all the saints of both sexes on the side of free choice, and fear and trembling in all those who deny and sin against free choice), she pretends there is only a contemptible little rabble against free choice, and actually allows only two passages, which are more conspicuous than the rest, to stand on this side, she being intent, of course, only on slaughtering them, and that without much trouble. One of these is Ex. 9⟨:12⟩: "The Lord hardened the heart of Pharaoh," and the other, Mal. 1⟨:2 f.⟩: "Jacob I loved, but Esau I hated." Paul explains both of them at some length in the epistle to the Romans ⟨9:11-21⟩, but in Diatribe's judgment it is surprising that he should

[88] *"Agere."*   [89] *"Rapi."*   [90] *"Agitur."*

have engaged in such a distasteful and unprofitable discussion. Indeed, if the Holy Spirit did not know a little about rhetoric, there was a risk of his being shattered by such an artfully managed show of contempt, so that despairing altogether of the cause he would yield the palm to free choice before the bugle blew.[1] But later on I as a mere reservist [2] will with those two passages let our forces also be seen, although where the fortune of battle is such that one can put ten thousand to flight there is no need of any forces. For if any one text defeats free choice, its numberless forces will profit it nothing.

Erasmus' Use of Tropes in Interpreting Scripture ⟨WA 700–702⟩

Here, then, Diatribe has discovered a new method of eluding the plainest texts by choosing to find a trope [3] in the simplest and clearest words. For just as previously, when she was pleading for free choice, she eluded all the imperative and subjunctive expressions of the law by tacking on inferences and similes, so now, when she is going to plead against us, she twists all the words of divine promise and affirmation in any way she pleases, by discovering a trope in them, so that on both hands she may be an uncatchable Proteus! Indeed, she demands in a very haughty way that this should be allowed her by us, since we ourselves when we are hard pressed are in the habit of escaping by discovering tropes. For instance, with regard to the text: "Stretch out your hand to whatever you will" ⟨Ecclus. 15:16⟩, we say this means "Grace will stretch out your hand to what it wills"; and with regard to: "Get yourselves a new heart" ⟨Ezek. 18:31⟩, we say, "That is, grace will make you a new heart"; and so forth. It seems most unfair, therefore, if it is permissible for Luther to impose such a forced and twisted interpretation that it should not be even more permissible to follow the interpretations of the most highly approved doctors. ⟨E., pp. 73 f.⟩

You see, therefore, that the controversy here is not about the text itself, nor is it any longer about inferences and similes, but about tropes and interpretations. When, then, are we ever going to have a text pure and simple, without tropes and inferences, for

---

[1] *"Ante tubam"* — the signal for the battle or other contest to begin.

[2] *"Succenturiatus."* The word first occurs in Terence, *Phormio* I.iv.55, where it denotes a reserve called in to fill up the ranks. There is an element of mock modesty in Luther's use of it here—he pretends to be coming to the aid of the Holy Spirit.

[3] *"Tropum"* — a figure of speech or figurative meaning. (A technical term in Scholastic exegesis.)

free choice and against free choice? Has Scripture nowhere any such texts? And is the issue of free choice to be forever in doubt, because it is not settled by any certain text, but is argued back and forth with inferences and tropes put forward by men at cross-purposes with one another, like a reed shaken by the wind?

Let us rather take the view that neither an inference nor a trope is admissible in any passage of Scripture, unless it is forced on us by the evident nature of the context [4] and the absurdity of the literal sense [5] as conflicting with one or another of the articles of faith. Instead, we must everywhere stick to the simple, pure, and natural sense of the words that accords with the rules of grammar and the normal use of language as God has created it in man. For if everybody is allowed to discover inferences and tropes in the Scriptures just as he pleases, what will Scripture as a whole be but a reed shaken by the wind or a sort of Vertumnus? [6] Then indeed there will be nothing certain either asserted or proved in connection with any article of faith which you will not be able to quibble away with some trope or other. We ought rather to shun as the deadliest poison every trope that Scripture itself does not force upon us.

Look what happened to that master of tropes, Origen,[7] in his exposition of the Scriptures! What fitting objects of attack he provides for the calumnies of Porphyry,[8] so that even Jerome[9] thinks that the defenders of Origen have an impossible task. What happened to the Arians[10] in that trope by which they made Christ into a merely nominal God?[11] What has happened in our own time to these new prophets regarding the words of Christ, "This is my body," where one finds a trope in the pronoun "this," another in the verb "is," another in the noun "body"?

What I have observed is this, that all heresies and errors in connection with the Scriptures have arisen, not from the simplicity

---

[4] *"Circumstantia verborum evidens."*   [5] *"Absurditas rei manifestae."*

[6] See above, p. 152 n. 18.

[7] Of Alexandria (ca. 185–ca. 254), the most distinguished and influential theologian of the Early Church before Augustine. In his interpretation of Scripture he developed the allegorical method, postulating a threefold sense—literal, moral, and spiritual.

[8] Greek scholar, historian, and philosopher (233–ca. 304), a disciple of the Neoplatonist Plotinus and a violent opponent of Christianity; wrote a work *Against the Christians* in fifteen books.

[9] A native of Dalmatia (ca. 340–420); scholar, ascetic, and canonized saint, translator of the Vulgate version of the Bible; in early life a great admirer of Origen, later a strong critic of his admirers; see his *Ep.* XLVIII.13; LXX.3, and his Preface to The Book of Daniel.

[10] See above, p. 155 n. 27.   [11] *"Deum nuncupativum."*

of the words, as is almost universally stated, but from neglect of the simplicity of the words, and from tropes or inferences hatched out of men's own heads. For example, I have never, so far as I recall, put such a forced interpretation on the words "Stretch out your hand to whatever you will" (Ecclus. 15:16) as to say, "Grace will stretch out your hand to what it wills"; nor have I said that "Get yourselves a new heart" (Ezek. 18:31) means "Grace will make you a new heart," and so forth, although Diatribe misrepresents me in this way in a published work, no doubt because she is so stuffed and fuddled with tropes and inferences that she does not realize what she is saying about anyone or anything. What I have said is this, that by the words "Stretch out your hand," etc., when they are taken simply as they stand, without any tropes and inferences, all that is signified is that a stretching out of the hand is required of us, and this indicates what we ought to do, in accordance with the nature of the imperative verb as the grammarians and ordinary speech employ it. But Diatribe, neglecting this simple use of the verb, and dragging in tropes and inferences, interprets as follows: "Stretch out your hand," that is to say, "You can by your own power stretch out your hand"; "Get yourselves a new heart," that is, "You can make a new heart"; "Believe in Christ," that is, "You can believe." So that for her it is all the same whether a thing is said imperatively or indicatively; otherwise she is prepared to regard Scripture as ridiculous and meaningless. And these interpretations, intolerable as they are to any grammarian, must not be called forced and farfetched when used by theologians, but they are the work of the most highly approved doctors who have been received for so many centuries!

But it is easy for Diatribe to admit and follow tropes in this passage, since it does not matter to her whether what is said is certain or uncertain. Indeed, she aims at making everything uncertain, for her advice is that dogmas concerning free choice should be left alone rather than investigated. It was therefore enough for her to get rid in any way she could of sayings by which she feels herself hard pressed. We, however, for whom a serious issue is at stake, and who are in search of the most certain truth for the establishing of consciences, must act very differently. For us, I say, it is not enough to say that there may be a trope here, but the question is whether there ought to be and must be a trope here. For if you do not show that a trope is of necessity involved, you have accomplished precisely nothing.

Exodus 4:21—The Hardening of Pharaoh's Heart ⟨WA 702–709⟩

Here stands the Word of God: "I will harden Pharaoh's heart" ⟨Ex. 4:21⟩. If you say this should or can be taken to mean, "I will permit it to be hardened," I agree that I hear men can so take it, that this trope is widely used in popular speech, as for instance: "I spoiled you, because I did not immediately correct you when you did wrong." But this is not the place for that kind of proof. The question is not whether that trope is in use, nor yet whether it is possible for anyone to make use of it in this passage of Paul,[12] but the question is whether it is safe to use it and certain that it is rightly used in this passage, and whether Paul intended it to be so used. What is in question is not the use another person, the reader, may make of it, but the use the writer, Paul himself, makes of it.

What would you do with a conscience that questioned you like this: "Look, the Divine Author says, 'I will harden Pharaoh's heart,' and the meaning of the verb 'to harden' is plain and well known; but a human reader tells me that 'to harden' in this passage means 'to give an occasion of hardening,' inasmuch as the sinner is not immediately corrected. By what authority, for what reason, with what necessity is the natural meaning of the word thus twisted for me? What if the reader and interpreter should be wrong? What proof is there that this twisting of the word ought to take place in this passage? It is dangerous, and indeed impious, to twist the word of God without necessity and without authority." Will you proceed to help this troubled little soul by saying: "Origen thought so" or "Give up prying into such things, because they are curious and superfluous"? She will reply: "This warning ought to have been given to Moses and Paul before they wrote, and for that matter to God himself. What is the point of their worrying us with curious and superfluous sayings?"

This miserable refuge of tropes is thus of no help to Diatribe. Our Proteus [13] must be held fast here until she makes us quite certain that there is a trope in this passage, either by the clearest Scripture proofs or by unmistakable miracles. To the fact that she thinks so, even though it is backed by the toilsome researches of all the centuries, we attach no importance whatever, but continue to insist that there can be no trope here, and that what God says must be taken quite simply at its face value. For it is not for us to decide to make and remake the words of God just as we please; otherwise, what remains in the entire Scripture that would not fit

---

[12] Rom. 9:17 f. Cf. above, p. 219. [13] See above, p. 103 n. 7.

in with Anaxagoras' philosophy,[14] so that anything might be made of anything? I might say, for instance, "God created heaven and earth, i.e., he set them in order, but did not make them out of nothing" or "He created heaven and earth, i.e., angels and demons, or the righteous and the ungodly." Who, I ask you, will not in that case become a theologian the moment the book is opened?

Let it be fixed and settled, then, that since Diatribe cannot prove that there is a trope inherent in these texts of ours, which she is trying to water down, she is bound to concede to us that the words must be taken as they stand, even though she might prove that the same trope is extremely common elsewhere, both in all parts of Scripture and in everyone's ordinary speech. On this principle, all the arguments of ours which Diatribe has sought to confute are defended at once, and her confutation is discovered to have absolutely no effect, no power, no reality.

When, therefore ⟨E., p. 65⟩, she interprets that saying of Moses, "I will harden Pharaoh's heart," as meaning "My forbearance in tolerating a sinner brings some, it is true, to repentance,[15] but it will make Pharaoh more obstinate in wrongdoing," this is prettily said, but there is no proof that it ought to be said; and we are not content with mere statement, but want proof. Similarly, Paul's saying, "He has mercy on whom he wills, and he hardens whom he wills," ⟨Rom. 9:18⟩, she plausibly interprets as "God hardens when he does not at once punish the sinner, and has mercy as soon as he invites repentance by means of afflictions." But what proof is there of this interpretation? Then there is Isaiah's saying: "Thou hast made us err from thy ways, thou hast hardened our heart, so that we fear thee not" ⟨Isa. 63:17⟩. Granted that Jerome, following Origen, interprets it thus: "He is said to seduce when he does not at once recall from error," but who can assure us that Jerome and Origen interpret it correctly? In any case, we have an agreement that we are willing to fight each other, not by appealing to the authority of any doctor, but by that of Scripture alone.

Who are these Origens and Jeromes, then, that Diatribe, forgetting our compact, throws at us? For hardly any of the ecclesiastic writers have handled the Divine Scriptures more ineptly and absurdly than Origen and Jerome. To put it in a word, this license of interpretation comes to this, that by a new and unprecedented

---

[14] Greek philosopher, born ca. 500 B.C. at Clazomenae in Asia Minor; taught that matter is compounded of infinitely numerous qualitatively different atoms; is said to have held that there must be blackness in snow because it turns dark when it melts.

[15] Cf. Rom. 2:4.

use of grammar everything is jumbled up, so that when God says "I will harden Pharaoh's heart," you change the person and take it to mean "Pharaoh hardens himself through my forbearance." "God hardens our hearts" means that we harden ourselves when God delays our punishment. "Thou, Lord, hast made us err" means "We have made ourselves err because thou hast not punished us." So God's being merciful no longer means that he gives grace or shows compassion, remits sin, justifies, or delivers from evil, but on the contrary, it means that he inflicts evil and punishes!

With these tropes you will end up by saying that God had mercy on the children of Israel when he deported them to Assyria and Babylon, for there he punished sinners, there he invited repentance. On the other hand, when he brought them back and liberated them, he did not have mercy on them but hardened them; that is, by his forbearance and compassion he gave occasion for them to be hardened. In this way, his sending of Christ as Savior into the world will not be said to be an act of mercy on God's part, but an act of hardening, because by this mercy he has given men occasion to harden themselves. On the other hand, by destroying Jerusalem and dispersing the Jews even down to the present day, he is having mercy on them, because he is punishing them for their sins and inviting them to repent. When he takes the saints up to heaven on the Day of Judgment, this will not be an act of mercy, but of hardening, inasmuch as it will provide an opportunity for them to abuse his goodness. But when he thrusts the ungodly down into hell, he will be having mercy on them, because he is punishing sinners. I ask you, who ever heard of such acts of divine mercy and wrath as these?

It is, of course, true that good men are made better both by the forbearance and the severity of God; yet when we speak of good and bad men together, these tropes will turn the mercy of God into wrath and his wrath into mercy by a thoroughly perverse use of language, calling it wrath when God confers benefits, and mercy when he imposes afflictions. But if God is to be said to harden when he confers benefits and exercises tolerance, and to have mercy when he afflicts and punishes, how can he be said to have hardened Pharaoh any more than the Children of Israel or even the whole world? Does he not tolerate the wicked? Does he not send rain on the good and the evil ⟨Matt. 5:45⟩? Why is he said to have had mercy on the Children of Israel rather than on Pharaoh? Did he not afflict the Children of Israel in Egypt and the wilderness? Granted that some abuse while others rightly use the goodness and the wrath of God; your definition nevertheless equates hardening with showing indulgence to the wicked through forbearance and kindness, whereas showing mercy is the same as not indulging but visiting and punishing. As far as God is concerned, therefore, he does nothing but harden by continual goodness and nothing but show mercy by continual punishment.

Truly this is by far your best effort: God is said to harden when he indulges sinners with his forbearance, but to have mercy when he visits and afflicts them, inviting them to repentance by severity. What, I ask you, did God leave undone in the way of afflicting and punishing Pharaoh and calling him to repentance? Are there not ten plagues recorded? If your definition holds good, that having mercy means punishing and calling the sinner without delay, God certainly had mercy on Pharaoh. Why, then, does God not say, "I will have mercy on Pharaoh" instead of "I will harden Pharaoh's heart"? For in the very act of showing mercy to him, which as you put it means afflicting and punishing him, he says, "I will harden him," which as you put it means, "I will do good to him and bear with him." What more monstrous could be heard? What has now become of your tropes, your Origen, your Jerome? What of your most highly approved doctors whom a solitary individual like Luther is rash enough to contradict? But it is the foolishness of the flesh that compels you to speak like this, for it treats the words of God as a game, not believing them to be meant seriously.

The actual text of Moses, therefore, proves unquestionably that those tropes are worthless fictions in this passage, and that something far other and greater, above and beyond beneficence or affliction and punishment, is signified by the words "I will harden Pharaoh's heart," for we cannot deny that both of those methods were tried in Pharaoh's case with the utmost care and concern. For what wrath and chastisement could have been more prompt than when he was smitten with so many signs and plagues that even Moses himself testifies that there never were any to equal them? [16] Why, Pharaoh himself is moved by them more than once, and seems to be coming to his senses, though he is not moved deeply or with abiding results. What forebearance and beneficence, furthermore, could be more generous than when God so readily takes away the plagues and so often remits his sin, so often restores blessings and so often removes calamities? Yet neither is of any avail, and he still says, "I will harden Pharaoh's heart." You see, therefore, even if your ideas of hardening and mercy (that is, your

[16] Ex. 9:18, 24; 10:6, 14; 11:6.

glosses and tropes) are admitted to the fullest extent, as supported by custom and precedent, and such as one can see in the case of Pharaoh, there is still a hardening, and the hardening of which Moses speaks must be of a different sort from that of which you dream.

But since we are fighting with storytellers and bogeymen, let us raise a bogey ourselves and imagine (what is quite impossible) that the trope of which Diatribe dreams is really valid in this place, so that we may see how she avoids being compelled to affirm that everything happens by the will of God alone and as far as we are concerned by necessity, and how she acquits God of being himself the author and culpable cause of our hardening. If it is true that God can be said to harden us when he bears with us in his long-suffering instead of at once punishing us, then both the following points still hold good. First, man is nonetheless necessarily in bondage to sin; because once it is granted that free choice cannot will anything good (as Diatribe has assumed), it is in no way made better by the forbearance of a long-suffering God, but necessarily worse, unless by the mercy of God the Spirit is added to it; so that everything still happens by necessity as far as we are concerned. Secondly, God appears to be just as cruel in bearing with us through his long-suffering as he is supposed to be when we preach that he hardens men through the action of that inscrutable will of his. For since he sees that free choice cannot will good, and that it is made worse by the forbearance of one who is long-suffering, this very lenience makes him seem extremely cruel, and as if he enjoyed our evil plight; for he could remedy it if he would, and need not tolerate it unless he so willed; indeed, unless he so wished he could not tolerate it. Who is there to compel him if he is unwilling?

So long, then, as that will remains without which nothing happens, and it is granted that free choice can will nothing good, all that is said to excuse God and accuse free choice is said to no purpose. For free choice keeps on saying: "I cannot, and God will not, so what am I to do? Suppose he does show mercy by afflicting me; I gain nothing by that, but must necessarily become worse, unless he gives the Spirit. But this he does not give, though he could if he would; therefore it is certain that he wills not to give."

Nor are the similes that are adduced at all relevant, where it is said: "Just as by the action of the same sun, mud hardens and wax melts, and by the action of the same rain cultivated land brings forth fruit and uncultivated land thorns, so by the same forbearance of God some are made more obstinate while others are converted" ⟨E., p. 65⟩. For we do not divide free choice into two different types, one of them like mud, the other like wax, or one like cultivated, the other like uncultivated, land; but we speak of the one type that is equally impotent in all men and is nothing but mud, nothing but uncultivated land, seeing that it cannot will good. Therefore, just as the mud always gets harder and the uncultivated land thornier, so free choice always gets worse both under the hardening forbearance of the sun and the softening downpour of rain.

If, then, free choice can be defined in only one way and is marked by the same impotence in all men, no reason can be given why it attains to grace in one instance and not in another if nothing else is preached but the forbearance of a long-suffering God and the chastisement of a merciful God. For it has been settled that free choice in all men alike has the same limitations: it can will nothing good. In that case God will elect no one, nor is there any room left for election, but only the freedom of choice that accepts or rejects forbearance and wrath. But if God is robbed of the power and wisdom to elect, what will he be but the false idol, chance, at whose nod everything happens at random?[17] And in the end it will come to this, that men are saved and damned without God's knowledge, since he has not determined by his certain election who are to be saved and who damned, but after offering to all men generally the forbearance that tolerates and hardens, then the mercy that corrects and punishes, he has left it to them to decide whether they want to be saved or damned; and in the meantime he has himself, perhaps, gone off to the banquet of the Ethiopians, as Homer says.[18]

It is just such a God that Aristotle, too, depicts for us, that is to say, one who drowses and lets all and sundry use and abuse his kindness and severity.[19] Nor can Reason judge otherwise of God than Diatribe does here. For just as she herself snores away and despises divine realities, so she judges also about God, as if he snored away and exercised no wisdom, will, or present power in electing, discerning, and inspiring, but had handed over to men the busy and burdensome task of accepting or rejecting his forbearance and wrath. That is what we come to when we seek to

[17] "*Temere.*"
[18] *Odyssey* i.22 f.; *Iliad* i.423 ff. The Ethiopians were "the uttermost of men," living at "the end of the world." Luther is here caricaturing the remoteness of Erasmus' idea of God.
[19] *Metaphysics* xii.7 describes God as enjoying undisturbed blessedness in the contemplation of his own being.

measure God by human reason and make excuses for him, not reverencing the secrets of his majesty but insisting on prying into them. The result is that we are overwhelmed with his glory, and instead of a single excuse for him, we pour out a thousand blasphemies, quite forgetting ourselves for the time and gibbering like lunatics against both God and ourselves in the same breath, though we aspire to speak with great wisdom on behalf of both God and ourselves.

Here you see what Diatribe's trope and gloss make of God, and also how consistent she is with herself when, after first making free choice by a single definition equal and alike in all men, she now in the course of the discussion forgets her own definition and makes one sort cultivated and another uncultivated. She has different sorts of free choices corresponding to the diversity of works and manners and men, one sort that does good and one that does not; and all this by its own powers before grace, though she had previously stated in her definition that by these powers free choice could will nothing good. Thus it comes about that when we do not let God's will alone have the will and power to harden and to show mercy and to do everything, we attribute to free choice itself the ability to do everything without grace, despite our having denied that it can do anything good without grace. The simile of the sun and the rain is therefore quite beside the point here, and it would be more correctly used by a Christian if he let the sun and rain represent the gospel (as in Ps. 18⟨19:4⟩ and the epistle to the Hebrews, ch. 10⟨6:7⟩), and the cultivated land the elect, the uncultivated the reprobate; for the former are edified and made better by the Word, while the latter are offended and made worse. Otherwise, free choice by itself is in all men the kingdom of Satan.

Now let us look also at the reasons for the inventing of this trope in this passage. "It seems absurd," Diatribe says, "that God, who is not only just but good also, should be said to have hardened a man's heart, so that by means of the man's misdeeds He might display his own power." ⟨E., p. 65.⟩ Hence she has recourse to Origen, who admits "that an occasion of hardening was given by God, but he would throw back the blame on Pharaoh." Origen has noted, moreover, that the Lord said, "For this purpose have I raised you up"; he does not say, "For this I made you." "Otherwise, Pharaoh would not have been wicked if God had made him like that: 'Who saw everything that he had made, and behold, it was very good' ⟨Gen. 1:31⟩." That is what Diatribe says.

Absurdity, then, is one of the principal reasons for not taking the words of Moses and Paul literally. But what article of faith does this absurdity sin against? Or who is offended by it? Human Reason is offended, who although she is blind, deaf, stupid, impious, and sacrilegious with regard to all the words and works of God, is brought in at this point as a judge of the words and works of God. On the same line of argument, you will deny all the articles of faith because it is quite the most absurd thing of all, and as Paul says, foolishness to Gentiles and a stumbling block to Jews ⟨I Cor. 1:23⟩, that God should be a man, the son of a virgin, crucified, and seated at the right hand of the Father. It is absurd, I say, to believe such things. Let us therefore invent some tropes with the Arians to prevent Christ from being literally God. Let us invent tropes with the Manichees [20] to prevent his being truly man, and make him a phantom that slipped down through the virgin like a ray of light through a piece of glass, and was crucified. That will be a fine way for us to handle the Scriptures!

But tropes are no use, and there is no avoiding the absurdity. For it remains absurd (as Reason judges) that a God who is just and good should demand of free choice impossible things; that although free choice cannot will good but is in bondage to sin, he should hold this against it; and that when he does not impart the Spirit, he acts no more mildly or mercifully than if he hardened or permitted to be hardened. These things, Reason will repeat, are not the marks of a good and merciful God. They are too far beyond her comprehension, and she cannot bring herself to believe that God is good if he acts in this way, but setting aside faith, she wishes to feel and see and understand how he is good and not cruel. She would, of course, understand if it were said of God that he hardens no one, damns no one, but has mercy on all, saves all, so that with hell abolished and the fear of death removed, there would be no future punishment to be dreaded. That is why she blusters and argues so in the attempt to exonerate God and defend his justice and goodness.

But faith and the Spirit judge differently, for they believe that God is good even if he should send all men to perdition. And what is gained by wearing ourselves out with those reasonings in order to throw the blame for hardening on free choice? Let all the free choice in the world do all it can with all its might, yet it will never produce any evidence of its ability either to avoid hardening if God does not give the Spirit, or to merit mercy if it is left to its own devices. For what difference does it make whether it is

---

[20] Followers of Mani or Manes (early third century A.D.), who taught an uncompromising dualism and identified matter with evil, so that they could not admit, among other things, a real incarnation of God.

hardened or deserves to be hardened, when hardening is necessarily there so long as that impotence is there by which, on Diatribe's own testimony, it cannot will good? Since, therefore, the absurdity is not removed by these tropes, or if it is removed, greater absurdities are introduced and everything is attributed to free choice, let us have done with the useless and misleading tropes and stick to the pure and simple word of God.

The second reason is that the things which God has made are "very good," and that God did not say, "I made you for this purpose," but, "I have raised you up for this purpose." First, we point out that the former was said before the fall of man, when the things that God had made were "very good." But it soon follows, in the third chapter, how man became evil when he was deserted by God and left to himself. From this man, thus corrupted, all are born ungodly, including Pharaoh, as Paul says: "We were by nature children of wrath like the rest" ⟨Eph. 2:3⟩. God therefore did create Pharaoh ungodly, that is, out of an ungodly and corrupt seed, as it says in The Proverbs of Solomon: "The Lord has made everything for its purpose, even the ungodly for the day of trouble" ⟨Prov. 16:4⟩. Hence it does not follow that because God has created the ungodly man, therefore the latter is not ungodly. How can he help being ungodly when he comes from an ungodly seed? As Ps. 50⟨51:5⟩ says: "I was conceived in sin," and Job: "Who can bring a clean thing out of an unclean?" ⟨Job 14:4⟩. For although God does not make sin, yet he does not cease to fashion and multiply the nature that has been vitiated by sin through the withdrawal of the Spirit, as a wood-carver might make statues out of rotten wood. Thus as is human nature, so are men made, God creating and fashioning them out of such a nature.

The second thing to be said is that if you wish the words "they were very good" to be understood of the works of God after the Fall, you will observe that they are spoken, not of us, but of God. For it does not say, "Man saw the things which God had made, and they were very good." Many things as seen by God are very good, which as seen by us are very bad. Thus afflictions, calamities, errors, hell, and indeed all the best works of God are in the world's eyes very bad and damnable. What is better than Christ and the gospel? Yet what is more execrated by the world? Consequently, how things can be good in God's sight which are evil to us only God knows, and those who see with God's eyes, that is, who have the Spirit. But there is no need to argue such a subtle point as that just yet. The preceding answer is enough for the present.

How God's Omnipotence Can Be Said to Work Evil ⟨WA 709–714⟩

It may perhaps be asked how God can be said to work evils in us, such as hardening, giving men up to their lusts ⟨Rom. 1:24⟩, leading them astray, and so forth. We ought, of course, to be content with the words of God, and believe quite simply what they say, since the works of God are entirely beyond description. Yet in order to humor Reason, which is to say human stupidity, I am willing to be a silly stupid and see whether with a bit of babbling we can in any way move her.

To begin with, even Reason and Diatribe admit that God works all in all ⟨I Cor. 12:6⟩ and that without him nothing is effected or effective; for he is omnipotent, and this belongs to his omnipotence, as Paul says to the Ephesians.[21] Now, Satan and man, having fallen from God and been deserted by God, cannot will good, that is, things which please God or which God wills; but instead they are continually turned in the direction of their own desires, so that they are unable not to seek the things of self.[22] This will and nature of theirs, therefore, which is thus averse from God, is not something nonexistent.[23] For Satan and ungodly man are not nonexistent[23] or possessed of no nature or will, although their nature is corrupt and averse from God. That remnant of nature, therefore, as we call it, in the ungodly man and Satan, as being the creature and work of God, is no less subject to divine omnipotence and activity than all other creatures and works of God.

Since, then, God moves and actuates all in all, he necessarily moves and acts also in Satan and ungodly man. But he acts in them as they are and as he finds them; that is to say, since they are averse and evil, and caught up in the movement of this divine omnipotence, they do nothing but averse and evil things. It is like a horseman riding a horse that is lame in one or two of its feet; his riding corresponds to the condition of the horse, that is to say, the horse goes badly. But what is the horseman to do? If he rides such a horse alongside horses that are not lame, this will go badly while they go well, and it cannot be otherwise unless the horse is cured. Here you see that when God works in and through evil men, evil things are done, and yet God cannot act evilly although he does evil through evil men, because one who is himself good cannot act evilly; yet he uses evil instruments that cannot escape the sway and motion of his omnipotence.

It is the fault, therefore, of the instruments, which God does not allow to be idle, that evil things are done, with God himself setting

---

[21] Cf. Eph. 1:11, 19.   [22] *"Quarere quae sua sunt."*   [23] *"Nihil."*

them in motion. It is just as if a carpenter were cutting badly with a chipped and jagged ax. Hence it comes about that the ungodly man cannot but continually err and sin, because he is caught up in the movement of divine power and not allowed to be idle, but wills, desires, and acts according to the kind of person he himself is.

All this is settled and certain if we believe that God is omnipotent and also that the ungodly is a creature of God, although as one averse from God and left to himself without the Spirit of God, he cannot will or do good. The omnipotence of God makes it impossible for the ungodly to evade the motion and action of God. for he is necessarily subject to it and obeys it. But his corruption or aversion from God makes it impossible for him to be moved and carried along with good effect. God cannot lay aside his omnipotence on account of man's aversion, and ungodly man cannot alter his aversion. It thus comes about that man perpetually and necessarily sins and errs until he is put right by the Spirit of God.

Now in all this, Satan still reigns in peace; under this movement of divine omnipotence he keeps his court undisturbed ⟨Luke 11:21⟩. Next, however, follows the business of hardening, which can be illustrated thus: The ungodly, as we have said, is like Satan his prince in being wholly intent on himself and his own affairs; he does not seek after God or care about the things that are God's, but he seeks his own wealth, his own glories, works, wisdom, power, and in short his own kingdom, and these he wishes to enjoy in peace. But if anyone resists him or attempts to encroach upon any of these things, then by the same aversion from God that leads him to seek them, he is moved to indignation and rage against his adversary, and is as incapable of not being angry as of not desiring and seeking; and he is as incapable of not desiring as of not existing, for he is a creature of God, though a vitiated one.

This is the well-known fury [24] of the world against the gospel of God. For by means of the gospel that Stronger One comes who is to overcome the peaceful keeper of the court, and he condemns those desires for glory, wealth, wisdom, and righteousness of one's own, and everything in which he trusts. This provocation of the ungodly, when God says or does to them the opposite of what they wish, is itself their hardening or worsening. For not only are they in themselves averse through the very corruption of their nature, but they become all the more averse and are made much worse when their aversion is resisted or thwarted. So it was when God proposed to wrest ungodly Pharaoh's tyranny from him; He pro-

[24] "*Hic est ille furor*"—the first half of a hexameter, possibly a reminiscence from some epic poet.

voked him and increased the hardness and stubbornness of his heart by thrusting at him through the word of Moses, who threatened to take away his kingdom and withdraw the people from his tyranny, without giving him the Spirit inwardly but permitting his ungodly corrupt nature under the rule of Satan to catch fire, flare up, rage, and run riot with a kind of contemptuous self-confidence.

Let no one suppose, therefore, when God is said to harden or to work evil in us (for to harden is to make evil), that he does so by creating evil in us from scratch. You must not imagine him like an evil-minded innkeeper, full of wickedness himself, who pours or blends poison into an innocent vessel, which itself does nothing but receive or suffer the malignity of the blender. That is the way people seem to imagine that man in himself is good, or at least not evil, and that he suffers an evil work at God's hands, when they hear it said by us that God works in us good things and bad, and that we are subject by sheer passive necessity to God's working; for they do not sufficiently consider how unrestingly active God is in all his creatures, allowing none of them to take a holiday. But anyone who wishes to have any understanding of such matters should think as follows. God works evil in us, i.e., by means of us, not through any fault [25] of his, but owing to our faultiness,[26] since we are by nature evil and he is good; but as he carries us along by his own activity in accordance with the nature of his omnipotence, good as he is himself he cannot help but do evil with an evil instrument, though he makes good use of this evil in accordance with his wisdom for his own glory and our salvation.

In this way he finds the will of Satan evil, not because he creates it so, but because it has become evil through God's deserting it and Satan's sinning; and taking hold of it in the course of his working he moves it in whatever direction he pleases. Yet that will does not cease to be evil even under this movement of God. It was thus that David said of Shimei in II Samuel ⟨16:11⟩: "Let him alone, and let him curse; for the Lord has bidden him to curse David." How could God command him to curse, which is such a harmful and evil thing to do? There was nowhere any outward precept to that effect. David therefore has in mind the fact that Almighty God had only to speak and it was done ⟨Ps. 33:9⟩; that is to say, God does everything by his eternal word. Hence the divine action and omnipotence impels the will of Shimei, which like all his members is already evil and has already been inflamed against David, and when David opportunely appears on the scene as de-

[25] "Culpa."   [26] "Vitio."

serving of such a cursing, the good God himself gives commandment for it through his evil and blasphemous instrument; that is,
he speaks the word and gets this cursing done by the impulsion, as
we must understand, of his own action.

It is thus that he hardens Pharaoh, when he presents to his ungodly and evil will a word and work which that will hates—owing
of course to its inborn defect [27] and natural corruption. And since
God does not change it inwardly by his Spirit, but keeps on pre-
senting and obtruding his words and works from without, while
Pharaoh keeps his eye on his own strength, wealth, and power, in
which by the same natural defect he puts his trust, the result is
that Pharaoh is puffed up and exalted by his own imagined great-
ness on the one hand, and moved to proud contempt on the other
by the lowliness of Moses and the abject form in which the word
of God comes, and is thus hardened and then more and more
provoked and exasperated the more Moses presses and threatens
him. Now, this evil will of his would not be set in motion or hardened if left to itself, but when the omnipotent Mover [28] drives it
along with inevitable motion like the rest of the creatures, it must
of necessity will something. Then, as soon as he presents to it
from without something that naturally provokes and offends it,
it becomes as impossible for Pharaoh to avoid being hardened as
it is for him to avoid either the action of divine omnipotence or
the aversion or badness of his own will. The hardening of Pharaoh
by God, therefore, takes place as follows: God confronts his badness outwardly with an object that he naturally hates, without
ceasing inwardly to move by omnipotent motion the evil will
which he finds there; and Pharaoh in accordance with the badness
of his will cannot help hating what is opposed to him and trusting
in his own strength, until he becomes so obstinate that he neither
hears nor understands, but is possessed by Satan and carried away
like a raving madman.

If we have carried conviction on this point, we have won our
case, and having exploded the tropes and glosses of men, we can
take the words of God literally, with no necessity to make excuses
for God or to accuse him of injustice. For when he says, "I will
harden Pharaoh's heart," he is speaking literally, as if he said, "I
will act so that Pharaoh's heart may be hardened" or "so that
through my working and doing it may be hardened." How this is
brought about we have heard, to this effect: "Inwardly, I will move
his evil will by my general motion so that he may proceed according to his own bent and in his own course of willing, nor will I

[27] "*Vitio.*"   [28] Latin, "*actor.*"

cease to move it, nor can I do otherwise than move it; but outwardly I will confront him with a word and work with which that
evil bent of his will clash, since he cannot do other than will evilly
when I move him, evil as he is, by virtue of my omnipotence."
Thus God was quite certain, and announced with the utmost certainty, that Pharaoh was to be hardened, because he was quite
certain that Pharaoh's will could neither resist the motion of his
omnipotence nor lay aside its own badness nor welcome the introduction of its adversary, Moses, and instead, with his will remaining evil, Pharaoh must necessarily become worse, harder and
prouder so long as in pursuing his own course and following his
own bent he encountered anything that he did not like, and that
he despised through confidence in his own power. Here, then, you
see it confirmed even by this very text, that free choice can do
nothing but evil, when God, who is not misled by ignorance and
does not lie through wickedness, so confidently promises the hardening of Pharaoh, obviously because he is certain that an evil will
can only will evil, and when confronted with a good that is contrary to it, can only become worse.

It therefore remains for someone to ask why God does not cease
from the very motion of omnipotence by which the will of the ungodly is moved to go on being evil and becoming worse. The answer is that this is wanting God to cease to be God on account of
the ungodly if you want his power and activity to cease, which implies that he should cease to be good lest they become worse. But
why does he not at the same time change the evil wills that he
moves? This belongs to the secrets of his majesty, where his judgments are incomprehensible ⟨Rom. 11:33⟩. It is not our business
to ask this question, but to adore these mysteries. And if flesh and
blood is offended here and murmurs ⟨cf. John 6:61⟩, by all means
let it murmur; but it will achieve nothing; God will not change
on that account. And if the ungodly are scandalized and depart
in great numbers ⟨John 6:66 f.⟩, yet the elect will remain. The
same must be said to those who ask why he permitted Adam to
fall, and why he creates us all infected with the same sin, when
he could either have preserved him or created us from another
stock or from a seed which he had first purged. He is God, and
for his will there is no cause or reason that can be laid down as a
rule or measure for it, since there is nothing equal or superior to
it, but it is itself the rule of all things. For if there were any rule
or standard for it, either as cause or reason, it could no longer be
the will of God. For it is not because he is or was obliged so to
will that what he wills is right, but on the contrary, because he

himself so wills, therefore what happens must be right. Cause and reason can be assigned for a creature's will, but not for the will of the Creator, unless you set up over him another creator.

By now I think that Diatribe the trope maker is sufficiently confuted with her trope; yet let us come to the text itself to see how it agrees with her and her trope. It is the habit of all those who elude arguments by means of tropes to show a brave contempt for the text itself and devote all their energy to picking out some particular word and torturing it by means of tropes, crucifying it on the cross of their own opinion without any regard either for the wider context, or the words that follow and precede, or the intention or motive of the author. So in this passage Diatribe takes no notice at all of what Moses is after or the point of what he is saying, but snatches out of the text that little phrase "I will harden" (which she finds offensive) and makes of it just what she pleases, with never a thought of how it is going to be put back again and fitted in to square with the body of the text. And that is the reason why Scripture, in the opinion of the most highly approved and most learned men of so many centuries, is not entirely clear; and no wonder, for the sun itself could not shine if it had such tricks played on it.

I have shown above that Pharaoh cannot rightly be said to have been hardened through being tolerated by the forbearance of God and not at once punished, since he was visited by so many plagues. But leaving that aside, what need was there for God to promise so often, just when the signs were taking place, that he would harden Pharaoh's heart when already before the signs and before this hardening, Pharaoh was the sort of man who (while he was tolerated by divine forbearance and not at once punished) had brought so many evils on the children of Israel, puffed up as he was by success and wealth, if to harden means to be tolerated by divine forbearance and not at once punished? You see, then, that this trope of yours is completely wide of the mark in this passage, since it applies generally to all men who sin when they are tolerated by the forbearance of God. For at that rate we should be saying that all men are hardened, since there is no one who does not sin, and yet no man could sin unless he were tolerated by divine forbearance. This hardening of Pharaoh, therefore, is something other and more than that general tolerance of divine forbearance.

What Moses is doing, however, is not so much to proclaim the wickedness of Pharaoh as the truth and mercy of God, his aim being that the children of Israel should not distrust the promises of God when he promised that he would set them free. This being a very big undertaking, he forewarns them of its difficulty so that they may not waver in faith, since they know that all these things have been foretold and must be thus carried out under the direction of the Giver of the promises himself. It is as if he said, "I really am liberating you, though you will have difficulty in believing it because of the way Pharaoh will resist and delay the matter; but have faith nonetheless, for all this delaying of his will be brought about through my working, so that I may perform all the more and greater miracles in order to confirm you in faith and demonstrate my power, so that thereafter you may have the greater confidence in me as regards everything else." This is what Christ also does when he promises the Kingdom to his disciples at the Last Supper (Matt. 26:29 ff.; Luke 22:29 ff.); he foretells a great many difficulties, his own death and their tribulations, in order that when it had all happened they might thenceforward have much more faith.[29]

Nor does Moses set forth this meaning obscurely to us when he says: "But Pharaoh will not let you go, so that many signs may be done in Egypt" (Ex. 3:19 ff.), and again: "For this very purpose have I raised you up, that I may show my power in you and that my power may be declared throughout all the earth" (Ex. 9:16). You see here that Pharaoh is hardened precisely in order that he may resist God and delay the redemption, so that occasion may be given for many signs and for a declaration of the power of God, so that he may be proclaimed and believed throughout all the earth. What else does this mean but that all these things are done for the confirmation of faith and the consolation of the weak, so that they may thereafter willingly believe in God as true, faithful, mighty, and merciful? It is as if he were talking most soothingly to little children: "Don't be frightened at Pharaoh's hardness, for even that itself is my work and I have it in hand, I who am setting you free; I shall only use it to do many signs and declare my majesty to help your faith."

Hence comes that saying which Moses repeats after nearly every plague: "And the heart of Pharaoh was hardened, so that he did not let the people go, as the Lord had spoken" (Ex. 9:35). What is the point of "as the Lord had spoken" except that the Lord might be seen to be truthful who had foretold that Pharaoh was to be hardened? If there had been any flexibility or freedom of choice in Pharaoh, which could have turned either way, God would not have been able so certainly to predict his hardening.

[29] Cf. John 13:19; 14:29; 16:4.

Since, however, the Giver of the promise is one who can neither be mistaken nor tell a lie, it was necessarily and most certainly bound to come about that Pharaoh should be hardened; which would not be the case unless the hardening were entirely beyond the capacity of man and within the power of God alone. It is just as we said above, namely, that God was certain that he was not going to suspend the general operation of his omnipotence in Pharaoh's case or on Pharaoh's account, since he cannot indeed suspend it. Moreover he was equally certain that the will of Pharaoh, being naturally evil and averse from God, could not consent to a word and work of God that was contrary to it. Consequently, as the impulse to will was preserved inwardly in Pharaoh by means of the omnipotence of God, and its encounter with a contrary word and work was effected from without, nothing else could be the result but umbrage and hardening of heart in Pharaoh. For if God had suspended the action of his omnipotence in Pharaoh at the moment when he confronted him with Moses' contrary word, and if Pharaoh's will could be imagined to have acted alone and by its own power, then there would perhaps have been room for discussion as to which way it could have turned. As things are, however, because he is driven and carried along in his willing, though without any violence being done to his will, since it is not unwillingly compelled but is carried along by the natural operation of God to will naturally, in accordance with its character (which, however, is evil)—therefore it cannot help but fall foul of the word and be hardened. So we see that this passage is strongly opposed to free choice, for the reason that God, who gives the promise, cannot lie, and if he does not lie, Pharaoh cannot help but be hardened.

How God's Foreknowledge Imposes Necessity ⟨WA 714–720⟩

But let us look also at Paul, who takes up this passage from Moses in Rom. 9⟨:15-18⟩. How miserably Diatribe is tormented here; to avoid losing free choice she twists herself into all sorts of shapes. At one moment she says that there is a necessity of consequence but not of the consequent; at another that there is an ordained will, or will signified, which can be resisted, and a will purposed, which cannot be resisted.[30] At another the passages

---

[30] *"Ordinatam seu voluntatem signi, cui resisti potest, Voluntatem placiti, cui resisti non potest."* This is Luther's paraphrase of Erasmus' *"Quicquid Deus vult, ex iustis causis vult, licet nobis aliquoties incognitis. Huic voluntati nemo potest resistere, sed ordinatae voluntati, sive, ut Scholae vocant,*

quoted from Paul are not opposed to free choice, for they are not speaking of man's salvation. At another the foreknowledge of God presupposes necessity, while at yet another it does not. At another grace preveniently moves the will to will, accompanies it on its way, and gives it a happy issue. At another the First Cause does everything, and at yet another it acts through secondary causes while remaining itself at rest. In these and similar bits of juggling with words, her only aim is to gain time by distracting our attention for a while from the main issue to something else. She credits us with being as stupid and senseless or as little concerned about the subject as she is herself. Or else, just as little children in fear or at play will put their hands over their eyes and then imagine that nobody sees them because they see nobody, so in all sorts of ways Diatribe, who cannot bear the rays, or rather lightning flashes, of the clearest possible words, pretends that she does not see the real truth of the matter, hoping to persuade us also to cover our eyes so that even we ourselves may not see.

But these are all signs of a mind under conviction and rashly struggling against invincible truth. That figment about the necessity of consequence and of the consequent has been refuted above.[31] Diatribe may pretend and pretend again, quibble and quibble again, as much as she likes, but if God foreknew that Judas would be a traitor, Judas necessarily became a traitor, and it was not in the power of Judas or any creature to do differently or to change his will, though he did what he did willingly and not under compulsion, but that act of will was a work of God, which he set in motion by his omnipotence, like everything else. For it is an irrefutable and self-evident proposition that God does not lie and is not deceived. There are no obscure or ambiguous words here, even if all the most learned men of all the centuries are so blind as to think and speak otherwise. And however much you boggle at it, your own and everyone else's conscience is convinced and compelled to say that if God is not deceived in what he foreknows, then the thing foreknown must of necessity take place; otherwise, who could believe his promises, who would fear his threats, if what he promises or threatens does not follow necessarily? Or how can he promise or threaten if his foreknowledge is fallible or can be hindered by our mutability? Clearly this very great light of certain truth stops everyone's mouth, puts an end to

---

voluntati signi, nimium saepe resistitur." The antithesis is between God's will publicly signified (viz., in the Bible) which men *can* flout, and God's hidden purpose, which no one can flout—because it is unknown to them. On this cf. also Introduction, p. 20.

[31] See above, p. 120.

all questions, ensures the victory over all evasive subtleties.

We know, of course, that the foreknowledge of men is fallible. We know that an eclipse does not occur because it is foreknown, but is foreknown because it is going to occur. But what concern have we with that sort of foreknowledge? We are arguing about the foreknowledge of God; and unless you allow this to carry with it the necessary occurrence of the thing foreknown, you take away faith and the fear of God, make havoc of all the divine promises and threatenings, and thus deny his very divinity. But even Diatribe herself, after a long struggle in which she has tried every possible way out, is at length compelled by the force of truth to admit our view when she says: "The question of the will and the determination of God is more difficult. For God to will and foreknow are the same thing. And this is what Paul means by 'Who can resist his will if he has mercy on whom he wills and hardens whom he wills?' Truly if there were a king who carried into effect whatever he willed, and nobody could resist him, he could be said to do whatever he willed. Thus the will of God, since it is the principal cause of all things that take place, seems to impose necessity on our will." ⟨E., pp. 66 f.⟩ So says she; and we can at last thank God for some sound sense in Diatribe.

What, then, has now become of free choice? But again this eel wriggles suddenly away by saying: "Paul, however, does not solve this question, but rebukes the questioner, 'O man, who are you to answer back to God?' " ⟨Rom. 9:20⟩. What a beautiful evasion! Is this the way to treat Holy Writ, pontificating like this on one's own authority, out of one's own head, with no Scripture proofs and no miracles, and in fact corrupting the very clearest words of God? Does not Paul solve this question? What then does he do? "He rebukes the questioner," she says. Is not that rebuke the most unqualified explanation? For what was the point of that question about the will of God? Was it not whether it imposes a necessity on our will? But Paul replies that that is precisely the case: "He has mercy," he says, "upon whom he wills, and whom he wills he hardens. It depends not upon man's willing or running, but upon God's mercy" ⟨Rom. 9:16⟩. And not content with this explanation, he proceeds to introduce people who bring objections against it in favor of free choice (prating that there are then no merits and we are damned through no fault of our own, and so forth), in order to put a stop to the murmurings and indignation by saying: "You will say to me then, 'Why does he still find fault? Who can resist his will?' " Do you see the character he puts on? [32] When they hear that the will of God implies [33] necessity for us, they murmur blas-

[32] *"Prosopopeian";* literally, "personification."   [33] *"Inducit."*

phemously and say: "Why does he still find fault?" That is to say, why does God insist, urge, demand, complain, as he does? Why does he accuse, why does he blame, as if we men could do what he demands if we would? He has no just cause for this faultfinding; let him rather accuse his own will, let him find the fault there, let him put the pressure on there. For who can resist his will? Who can obtain mercy when he does not will it? Who can melt if he wills to harden? It is not in our power to change, much less to resist, his will, which wants us hardened and by which we are forced to be hardened, whether we like it or not.

If Paul had not explained this question, or had not definitely laid it down that a necessity is imposed on us by the divine foreknowledge, what need was there for him to introduce those who murmur and plead that God's will cannot be resisted? For who would murmur or be indignant if he was not aware that this necessity was being asserted? The words are not obscure in which he speaks of resistance to the will of God. Is the meaning of "resist" ambiguous, or the meaning of "will," or what he means when he speaks of the will of God? Let countless thousands of the most reputable doctors be as blind here as they may, let them pretend that the Scriptures are not transparently clear, and let them panic at a difficult question. We for our part have the clearest possible words, which run as follows: "He has mercy upon whomever he wills, and he hardens whomever he wills," and: "You will say to me then, 'Why does he find fault? Who can resist his will?' " And it is not a difficult question; indeed, nothing is easier even for common sense to grasp than that this conclusion is certain, solid and true: "If God foreknows anything, it necessarily occurs," once it is presupposed on the basis of the Scriptures that God neither errs nor is deceived.

I admit that the question is difficult, and indeed impossible, if you wish to maintain at the same time both God's foreknowledge and man's freedom. For what could be more difficult, nay more impossible, than to insist that contradictories or contraries are not opposed, or to find a number that was at the same time both ten and nine? The difficulty is not inherent in our question, but is sought out and imported, precisely as the ambiguity and obscurity of the Scriptures is sought for and forcibly imported into them. Paul is thus putting a check on the ungodly, who are offended by this very plain speaking when they gather from it that the divine will is fulfilled by necessity on our part, and that very definitely nothing of freedom or free choice remains for them, but everything depends on the will of God alone. The way he checks them, however, is by bidding them be silent and revere the majesty of the divine power and will, in relation to which we have no rights, but which in relation to us has full right to do whatever it pleases. Not that any injustice is done to us, since God owes us nothing, has received nothing from us, and has promised us nothing but to do his will and pleasure.

This, then, is the place and the time for us to adore, not those Corycian caverns of yours, but the true Majesty in his awful wonders and incomprehensible judgments, and to say: "Thy will be done, on earth as it is in heaven." Yet we are nowhere more irreverent and rash than in probing into and arguing about these very mysteries and unsearchable judgments, though all the while we put on an air of incredible reverence in searching the Holy Scriptures that God has commanded us to search ⟨John 5:39⟩. Here we do not search, but there, where he has forbidden us to search, we do nothing but search, with never-ending temerity, not to say blasphemy. Or is there no temerity in the searching that tries to make the entirely free foreknowledge of God harmonize with our freedom, so that we are prepared to detract from the foreknowledge of God unless it allows freedom to us, or else, if it imposes necessity on us, to say with the murmurers and blasphemers: "Why does He still find fault? Who can resist his will? Where is the God who is by nature most merciful? Where is he who desires not the death of a sinner? Or has he created us in order that he may enjoy the torments of men?" and such like complaints, which will be howled out by the damned in hell forever. Yet natural reason itself is forced to admit that the living and true God must be one who by his freedom imposes necessity on us, since obviously he would be a ridiculous God, or idol rather, if he foresaw the future uncertainly, or could be proved mistaken by events, when even the heathen have given their gods an "ineluctable fate." [34] He would be equally ridiculous if he could not and did not do everything, or if anything took place without him.

But granted foreknowledge and omnipotence, it follows naturally by an irrefutable logic that we have not been made by ourselves, nor do we live or perform any action by ourselves, but by his omnipotence. And seeing he knew in advance that we should be the sort of people we are, and now makes, moves, and governs us as such, what imaginable thing is there, I ask you, in us which is free to become in any way different from what he has foreknown or is now bringing about? Thus God's foreknowledge and omnipotence are diametrically opposed to our free choice, for either

[34] Vergil, *Aeneid* viii.334: "*Fortuna omnipotens et ineluctabile fatum.*"

God can be mistaken in foreknowing and also err in action (which is impossible) or we must act and be acted upon in accordance with his foreknowledge and activity. By the omnipotence of God, however, I do not mean the potentiality by which he could do many things which he does not, but the active power by which he potently works all in all ⟨cf. I Cor. 12:6⟩, which is the sense in which Scripture calls him omnipotent. This omnipotence and the foreknowledge of God, I say, completely abolish the dogma of free choice. Nor can the obscurity of Scripture or the difficulty of the subject be made a pretext here; the words are quite clear and known even to schoolboys, and what they say is plain and easy and commends itself even to the natural judgment of common sense, so that it makes no difference how great a tally you have of centuries, times, and persons who write and teach differently.

Admittedly, it gives the greatest possible offense to common sense or natural reason that God by his own sheer will should abandon, harden, and damn men as if he enjoyed the sins and the vast, eternal torments of his wretched creatures, when he is preached as a God of such great mercy and goodness, etc. It has been regarded as unjust, as cruel, as intolerable, to entertain such an idea about God, and this is what has offended so many great men during so many centuries. And who would not be offended? I myself was offended more than once, and brought to the very depth and abyss of despair, so that I wished I had never been created a man, before I realized how salutary that despair was, and how near to grace. That is why there has been such sweating and toiling to excuse the goodness of God and accuse the will of man; and it is here the distinctions have been invented between the ordained and the absolute will of God, and between the necessity of consequence and consequent, and so forth, though nothing has been achieved by them except that the ignorant have been imposed upon by empty talk and "contradictions of what is falsely called knowledge" ⟨I Tim. 6:20⟩. Nevertheless, there has always remained deeply implanted in the hearts of ignorant and learned alike, whenever they have taken things seriously, the painful awareness that we are under necessity if the foreknowledge and omnipotence of God are accepted. Even natural Reason herself, who is offended by this necessity and makes such efforts to get rid of it, is compelled to admit it by the force of her own judgment, even if there were no Scripture at all.

For all men find these sentiments written on their hearts and acknowledge and approve them (though unwillingly) when they hear them discussed: first, that God is omnipotent, not only in power, but also in action (as I have said), otherwise he would be a ridiculous God; and secondly, that he knows and foreknows all things, and can neither err nor be deceived. These two points being granted by the hearts and minds of all, they are quickly compelled by inescapable logic to admit that just as we do not come into being by our own will, but by necessity, so we do not do anything by right of free choice, but as God has foreknown and as he leads us to act by his infallible and immutable counsel and power. Thus we find it written in the hearts of all alike, that there is no such thing as free choice, though this fact is obscured by the many arguments to the contrary and the great authority of all the men who for so many centuries have taught differently. It is the same as with every other law which (according to Paul) is written on our hearts ⟨Rom. 2:15⟩: it is recognized when it is rightly expounded, but obscured when mishandled by ungodly teachers and displaced by other opinions.

But to return to Paul. If in Rom., ch. 9, he is not explaining the question and definitely affirming our necessity on the basis of the foreknowledge and will of God, what need was there for him to introduce the simile of the potter, who out of one and the same lump of clay makes "one vessel for honor and another for dishonor? Yet what is molded does not say to its molder 'Why are you making me so?' " For he is speaking about men, and comparing them to the clay and God to the potter; which is surely a poor sort of comparison, or rather a quite inappropriate and irrelevant one, if he does not think that freedom for us simply does not exist. Why, in that case Paul's whole argument in defense of grace is meaningless. For the whole purpose of his epistle is to show that we can do nothing, even when we seem to be doing well, just as he says in the same chapter that Israel in pursuing righteousness did not attain to righteousness, while the Gentiles attained to it without pursuing it ⟨Rom. 9:30 f.⟩. With this I will deal at greater length when I bring up my own troops.

But Diatribe refuses to face the Pauline argument as a whole, so as to see what Paul is really driving at, and contents herself meanwhile with detached and distorted phrases. And it is no help to Diatribe that Paul later, in Rom., ch. 11, turns to exhortation again, and says: "You stand fast through faith; see that you do not become proud" and: "Even the others, if they believed, would be grafted in," etc. ⟨Rom. 11:20, 23⟩. For he says nothing there about the powers of men, but he uses imperative and subjunctive verbs, the import of which has been sufficiently stated above. Paul himself, moreover, in the same passage forestalls the supporters of free choice, for he does not say that the others are able to believe, but that God is able to graft them in again. In short, Diatribe proceeds with such trepidation and hesitancy in handling these passages of Paul that it looks as if in conscience she disagrees with what she herself says. For just when she ought above all to have gone on and produced proof, she almost always breaks off her discourse with "But that is enough of that," or "I will not now go into that," or "It is no part of our present purpose," or "The others would speak thus," or something of that kind, leaving the subject in midair, so that you do not know whether she wants it to appear that she is speaking in favor of free choice or merely parrying Paul with empty words. It is all typical of her attitude as one to whom there is nothing serious at stake in this dispute. We, however, ought not to be so uncommitted, so afraid of making a false move,[35] so easily swayed,[36] but should assert confidently, constantly, and fervently, and then demonstrate solidly, skillfully, and abundantly, what we teach.

Two Kinds of Necessity: The Case of Judas ⟨WA 720–722⟩

But now how beautifully she preserves freedom together with necessity when she says: "Not all necessity excludes free will, since God the Father necessarily begets the Son, and yet begets him freely and willingly, for he is not forced to do so" ⟨E., p. 68⟩. I ask you, are we now disputing about coercion and force? Have we not plainly stated in so many of our books that we are speaking of the necessity of immutability? We know that the Father begets willingly, and that Judas betrayed Christ by an act of will; [37] but we say this willing was certainly and infallibly going to occur in Judas himself if God foreknew it. Or if what I am saying is still not understood, let us have two sorts of necessity, one of force with reference to the work, the other of infallibility with reference to the time; and let anyone who listens to us understand that we are speaking of the latter, not of the former; that is to say, we are not discussing whether Judas became a traitor involuntarily or voluntarily,[38] but whether at a time preordained by God it was bound infallibly to happen that Judas by an act of his will should betray Christ.

But see what Diatribe says here: "If you look at the infallible

---

[35] "Super aristas incedere." See above, p. 126 n. 39.
[36] "Aut ventis velut arundo moveri."   [37] "Volendo."
[38] "Invitus aut volens."

foreknowledge of God, and his immutable will, Judas was necessarily going to turn traitor, and yet Judas could change his intention." [39] Do you really understand what you are saying, my dear Diatribe? Leaving aside the fact that the will can only will evil, as was proved above, how could Judas change his mind so long as the infallible foreknowledge of God remained? Could he change God's foreknowledge and make it fallible? Here Diatribe gives up; she deserts the standard, throws away her arms, and quits the field, making out that the discussion has to do with Scholastic subtleties about the necessity of consequence and consequent, and she has no desire to pursue such quibbles.

It is certainly prudent of you, just when you have brought the case into a crowded court [40] and there is now above all need of an advocate, to turn your back and leave to others the business of replying and defining. You should have taken this line from the start, and refrained from writing altogether, according to the saying: "Let him who has not learned to play,/From Marsfield contests keep away." [41] For it was not expected of Erasmus that he should solve the problem of how God can foreknow with certainty and yet things can happen contingently as far as we are concerned. This difficulty was in the world long before Diatribe. It was expected, however, that he should make some reply and give some definition. But instead, by availing himself of a rhetorical transition, he drags us who know nothing of rhetoric away with him, as if the matter at issue here were of no moment, but simply a lot of quibbling, and dashes bravely out of the crowded court, crowned with ivy and laurel.[42]

But not so, brother! No rhetoric has force enough to deceive an honest conscience; the sting of conscience is stronger than all the powers and resources of eloquence. We shall not allow a rhetorician to change the subject and confuse the issue here; this is not the place for that sort of trick. The turning point of the whole discussion, and the very heart of the matter, is in question here. And here either free choice is extinguished or it will triumph all along the line. Yet you, when you perceive the danger, or rather the certainty, of a victory over free choice, pretend that you perceive nothing but quibbles. Is this the way to play the part of a conscientious theologian? Can you have a serious interest in the case,

---

[39] *"Voluntas."*   [40] *"In medias turbas."*

[41] Horace, *Ars poetica* 379. "Marsfield" — the Campus Martius, used by the Romans for games, exercise and recreation, and military drill.

[42] Emblems of the scholar and the conqueror, sacred to Bacchus and Apollo respectively.

when you thus leave the audience in suspense and the argument in chaos and confusion, and yet wish to be regarded as having given honest satisfaction and carried off the palm? Such cunning and craftiness might be tolerable in secular affairs, but in theology, where the simple and undisguised truth is sought for the salvation of souls, it is utterly hateful and intolerable.

The Sophists too felt the invincible and irresistible force of this argument, and that is why they invented the necessity of consequence and consequent. But how completely useless this invention is, we have shown above. For they too fail to observe what they are saying and how much they admit against themselves. For if you grant the necessity of consequence, free choice is vanquished and laid low, and there is no help for it in either the necessity or the contingency of the consequent. What does it matter to me if free choice is not compelled, but does what it does willingly? It is enough for me that you grant that it must necessarily do what it does willingly, and that it cannot do anything else, if God has foreknown it. If God foreknows that Judas will turn traitor, or that he will change his will to betray, whichever God has foreknown will necessarily come about, or else God will be mistaken in his foreknowing and predicting, which is impossible.

For this is the result of the necessity of consequence, i.e., if God foreknows a thing, that thing necessarily happens. That is to say, there is no such thing as free choice. This necessity of consequence is not obscure or ambiguous, and even if the doctors of all the centuries were blind, they would be forced to admit it, since it is so manifest and certain as to be palpable. But the necessity of the consequent, with which they console themselves, is a mere phantom and diametrically opposed to the necessity of consequence. For example, there is a necessity of consequence if I say: God foreknows that Judas will be a traitor, therefore it will certainly and infallibly come about that Judas will be a traitor. In face of this necessity and consequence, this is how you console yourself: But because Judas can change his will to betray, there is therefore no necessity of the consequent. How, I ask you, do these two statements harmonize: "Judas can will not to betray" and "It is necessary that Judas should will to betray"? Do they not directly contradict and oppose one another? He will not, you say, be compelled to betray against his will. What has that to do with it? You have been speaking about the necessity of the consequent, and saying that it is not implied by the necessity of consequence, but you have said nothing about the compulsion [43] of the conse-

43 "Coactione."

quent. The question you were supposed to answer was about the necessity of the consequent, and you give an example about the compulsion of the consequent; I ask for one thing, you give me another. This comes of your being only half awake and not noticing how completely useless that device of the necessity of the consequent is.

Jacob and Esau ⟨WA 722–727⟩

So much for the first passage, which has been about the hardening of Pharaoh, but which has in fact involved all the passages and engaged a large part of our resources, invincible as they are. Now let us look at the second, about Jacob and Esau, of whom it was said before they were born: "The elder shall serve the younger" ⟨Gen. 25:23⟩. Diatribe gets round this passage by saying that it "does not properly apply to the salvation of man. For God can will that a man, willy-nilly, be a slave or a pauper, and yet not so as to be excluded from eternal salvation" ⟨E., p. 69⟩. I beg you to notice how many sidetracks and bolt-holes a slippery mind will seek out when it runs away from the truth; yet it does not succeed in escaping. Suppose this passage does not apply to the salvation of man (though more of this below), does this mean that Paul achieves nothing by quoting it ⟨Rom. 9:12⟩? Are we to make out that Paul is ridiculous or inept in so serious a discussion? That is the sort of thing that Jerome [44] does, who with a very superior air, but with sacrilege on his lips, dares in more than one place to say that things have a polemic force [45] in Paul which in their proper contexts they do not have. ⟨E., p. 70.⟩ This is as good as saying that when Paul is laying the foundations of Christian dogma, he does nothing but corrupt the Divine Scriptures and deceive the souls of the faithful with a notion hatched out of his own head and violently thrust upon the Scriptures. That is the way to honor the Spirit in Paul, that saint and elect instrument of God! And where Jerome ought to be read with discrimination, and this statement of his classed with a good many other impious things which (owing to his halfhearted and dull-witted way of understanding the Scriptures) that gentleman writes, Diatribe drags him in quite uncritically, and without deigning to make things easier by at least an explanatory comment, treats him as an infallible oracle

---

[44] See above, p. 70.
[45] A very pithy phrase in the Latin: *"Ea pugnare apud Paulum quae locis suis non pugnant,"* "Sayings do battle in Paul that do not in their proper places."

by which she both judges and modifies the Divine Scriptures. So it is that we take the impious utterances of men as rules and norms in interpreting Divine Scripture. And we are still surprised that Scripture should be obscure and ambiguous, and that so many Fathers should be blind with regard to it, when it is treated in this ungodly and sacrilegious manner!

Let him therefore be anathema who says that things have a polemic force in Paul which in their proper contexts are not in opposition. For this is only said, not proved, and it is said by those who understand neither Paul nor the passages cited by him, but are misled by taking the words in a sense of their own, that is, in an ungodly sense. For however truly this passage in Gen. 25⟨:21-23⟩ might be understood of temporal bondage only (which is not the case), yet it is rightly and effectively quoted by Paul to prove that it was not through the merits of Jacob and Esau, but through *him who calls* that Sarah [46] was told: "The elder will serve the younger" ⟨Rom. 9:11 f.⟩. Paul is discussing whether it was by the virtue or merits of free choice that these two attained to what is said of them, and he proves that it was not, but it was solely by the grace of "him who calls" that Jacob attained to what Esau did not. He proves this, however, by invincible words of Scripture, to the effect that they were not yet born, and had done nothing either good or bad ⟨Rom. 9:11⟩. And the whole weight of the matter lies in this proof; this is what our dispute is all about.

But Diatribe with her egregious rhetoric glosses over all that, and never discusses merits, although she undertook to do so and Paul's argument requires it; but she quibbles about temporal bondage, as if this had anything to do with the case, simply in order not to appear to be vanquished by the very potent words of Paul. For what could she have to yelp back at Paul in support of free choice? What help was free choice to Jacob, and what hindrance was it to Esau, when before either of them was born or had done anything it had already been settled by the foreknowledge and determination of God what should be the lot of each, namely, that the one should serve and the other rule. The rewards are decreed before the workmen are born and begin working. This is the point that Diatribe should have answered; it is this that Paul insists on, that they have so far done nothing either good or bad, and yet by divine decree one is ordained to be the master and the other the servant. The question is not whether that servitude has anything to do with salvation, but by what merit it is imposed on a man who had not merited anything. But it is very distasteful to

[46] Rebekah is meant.

have to contend with these low-down efforts to distort and evade Scripture.

Furthermore, that Moses is not concerned with their bondage only, and that Paul is quite right in understanding it as referring also to eternal salvation (which is not so important for our present purpose, but I will not allow Paul to be besmirched by the calumnies of sacrilegious persons), is clearly demonstrable from the text itself. The oracle in Moses runs thus: "Two peoples, born of you, shall be divided; the one shall be stronger than the other, the elder shall serve the younger" ⟨Gen. 25:23⟩. Here it is plain that two peoples are distinguished. One of them is received into the grace of God although he is the younger, so that he overcomes the elder, not indeed by his own strength, but by the favor of God. How else could the younger overcome the elder if God were not with him? Since, therefore, the younger is the future People of God, it is not only external dominion or servitude that is implied here, but everything that belongs to the People of God, i.e., the blessing, the Word, the Spirit, the promise of Christ, and the eternal Kingdom; a fact that Scripture even more fully confirms later when it describes how Jacob is blessed and receives the promises and the Kingdom ⟨Gen. 27:27 ff.⟩. All this Paul indicates in brief when he says that the elder will serve the younger, and thus sends us back to Moses who deals with the subject more fully. Hence, in answer to the sacrilegious opinion of Jerome and Diatribe, you can say that all the texts Paul quotes are more strongly polemical in their proper contexts than they are in Paul; and this is true not only of Paul but of all the apostles, who quote the Scriptures as witnessing to and asserting what they themselves are saying. But it would be ridiculous to cite as evidence something that has no evidence to give and has nothing to do with the case. For if among the philosophers those who try to prove the unknown by the still less known, or by something quite irrelevant, are regarded as ridiculous, how can we have the face to attribute this kind of thing to the chief champions and authors of Christian doctrine, on which the salvation of souls depends, especially when they are teaching fundamental articles of the faith? But such things are fitting for those who have no serious interest in the Divine Scriptures.

Now, with regard to the saying of Malachi that Paul adds on: "Jacob I loved, but Esau I hated" ⟨Mal. 1:2 f.; Rom. 9:13⟩, this she distorts with a threefold piece of ingenuity. ⟨E., p. 69.⟩ The first is: "If you press it literally, God does not love just as we love, nor does he hate anybody, since he is not subject to affections of this kind." What am I hearing? Is the question now how God loves and hates rather than why he loves and hates? By what merit of ours he loves and hates, that is the question. We know quite well that God does not love or hate as we do, since we are mutable in both our loving and hating, whereas he loves and hates in accord with his eternal and immutable nature, so that passing moods and feelings do not arise in him. And it is this fact that makes complete nonsense of free choice, because God's love toward men is eternal and immutable, and his hatred is eternal, being prior to the creation of the world, and not only to the merit and work of free choice; and everything takes place by necessity in us, according as he either loves or does not love us from all eternity, so that not only God's love but also the manner of his loving imposes necessity on us. Hence you see what an advantage Diatribe's subterfuges are to her, and how at every turn she finds herself more up against it the more she strives to escape, so little successful is she in resisting the truth.

But suppose your trope is valid, so that God's love is the effect of love and God's hatred the effect of hatred; are these effects produced apart from and independent of the will of God? Or will you say here also that God does not will as we do, and that no impulse to willing [47] arises in him? If, then, these effects occur, they occur only insofar as God wills. Now, what God wills he either loves or hates. Tell me, therefore, for what merit is Jacob loved and Esau hated before they are born and perform any act? Paul is therefore in an excellent position when he introduces Malachi in support of Moses' view, to the effect that God called Jacob before he was born because he loved him, not because he was first loved by Jacob or moved by any merit of his, in order to demonstrate in the case of Jacob and Esau what our free choice is capable of.

The second bit of ingenuity is that Malachi "does not seem to be speaking of the hate whereby we are damned eternally, but of temporal misfortune," for "those are reprimanded who thought to reestablish Idumaea." ⟨E., p. 69.⟩ This again [48] is said to the disparagement of Paul, as if he had done violence to the Scriptures. So completely are we lacking in reverence for the majesty of the Holy Spirit when we are intent on maintaining our own opinions. But let us for the moment put up with this disparagement, and see what the effect of it is. Malachi is speaking of temporal misfortune. What if he is? What has this to do with the present issue?

---

[47] "Affectum volendi."
[48] See n. 35, p. 69 (on the passage in Erasmus).

Paul is proving from Malachi that this misfortune was brought upon Esau without any merit and solely by the hatred of God, so as to draw the conclusion that there is no such thing as free choice. It is here that you are pressed, here that an answer should have been given.

We are disputing about merit, but you talk about reward, and talk in such a way that you cannot, after all, avoid what you wanted to avoid; for in fact when you talk of reward you admit merit. Yet you pretend you do not see this. Tell me, then, what cause had God for loving Jacob and hating Esau before either of them existed?

It is, however, false to say that Malachi is speaking only of temporal misfortune, nor has he any concern with the destruction of Edom, and you pervert the whole meaning of the prophet by this bit of ingenuity. The prophet shows in the plainest terms quite well what he means; that is to say, he reproaches the Israelites with ingratitude because, although God has loved them, they neither love him in return as their Father nor fear him as their Lord ⟨Mal. 1:6⟩. That God has loved them, he proves both by Scripture and by his acts, pointing out that although Jacob and Esau were brothers, as Moses writes in Gen. 25⟨:24⟩, yet he loved Jacob and chose him before he was born (as has been said a little earlier), but so hated Esau that he reduced his land to a wilderness. Moreover, he keeps on hating, with such pertinacity that when he has brought Jacob back from captivity and restored him, he still does not allow the Idumaeans to be restored, but even if they so much as express a wish to build, he threatens them with destruction. If these things are not contained in the plain text of the prophet itself, let the whole world accuse me of lying. It is therefore not the temerity of the Idumaeans that is reprimanded here, but (as I have said) the ingratitude of the sons of Jacob, who fail to see what he is conferring on them and taking away from their brothers the Idumaeans for no reason but because he hates in the one case and loves in the other.

How can it now be held that the prophet is speaking of temporal misfortune when in unmistakable terms he declares that he is speaking of two peoples, descendants of the two patriarchs, one of which was accepted as a people and preserved, whereas the other was abandoned and at length destroyed? To accept as a people and not to accept as a people is something that affects not temporal good or evil only, but everything. For our God is not the God of temporal things only, but of all things. Nor will he consent to be your God, or to be worshiped by you with half a shoulder or a limping foot, but with all your strength and all your heart, so that he may be God for you both here and hereafter, in all circumstances, cases, times, and works.

The third bit of ingenuity is the idea that according to the tropological [49] sense he neither loves all Gentiles nor hates all Jews, but only some of each. ⟨E., pp. 69 f.⟩ By the use of this trope it is brought about that "this testimony," as she says, "does not champion the cause of necessity, but is to repress the arrogance of the Jews." Then, having opened this way of escape, Diatribe reaches the point of saying that God "hates the unborn because he surely knows that they will commit deeds worthy of hatred"; and thus God's "hatred and love are in no way opposed to free choice." In the end she draws the conclusion that the Jews were plucked from the olive tree for the merit of unbelief, whereas the Gentiles were grafted in for the merit of faith—and this on the authority of Paul!—which gives to those plucked off a hope of being grafted in again, and to those grafted in the fear of being cut off.

May I perish if Diatribe herself knows what she is talking about. But perhaps here too there is a rhetorical device that teaches you to obscure the sense whenever there is any danger of your being caught by a word. We for our part see in this passage none of those tropological meanings which Diatribe dreams about but never proves. So it is not surprising if Malachi's testimony in its tropological sense is not opposed to her, when it has no such sense. Furthermore, we are not arguing about the cutting off and grafting in of which Paul speaks in his exhortation. We know that men are grafted in by faith and cut off by unbelief, and that they must be exhorted to believe lest they be cut off. But from this it does not follow and is not proved that they are able to believe or disbelieve by the power of free choice, which is the point at issue for us. We are not disputing about who are believers and who are not, who are Jews and who are Gentiles, and what the consequences of believing and disbelieving are; that is the business of an exhorter. What we are disputing about is this: By what merit or what work they attain to the faith by which they are grafted in or to the unbelief by which they are cut off; that is the business of a learned doctor. Describe this merit to us! Paul teaches that it comes about by no work of ours, but solely by the love and hate of God; though when it has come about, he exhorts them to persevere lest they be cut off. But an exhortation does not prove what we can do, but what we ought to do.

I am compelled to use almost more words in holding my oppo-

[49] *"Tropologico."*

nent and preventing him from wandering off and abandoning the issue than in dealing with the issue itself; although to have kept him to the point is to have vanquished him, so clear and invincible are the words, and that is why he does almost nothing but refuse to face them, hurrying to get out of sight and busying himself with something other than he set out to do.

The Potter and the Clay ⟨WA 727–730⟩

The third passage she takes up is from Isa. 45⟨:9⟩: "Does the clay say to him who fashions it, 'What are you making?' " and also Jer. 18⟨:6⟩: "Like the clay in the potter's hand, so are you in my hand." ⟨E., p. 70.⟩ Again she says that these passages have more polemic force in Paul ⟨Rom. 9:20 ff.⟩ than with the prophets from whom they are taken, since in the prophets they refer to temporal affliction, whereas Paul applies them to eternal salvation and reprobation; so that again she insinuates temerity or ignorance in Paul. But before we consider how she proves that neither of these texts excludes free choice, let me first say this, that Paul does not appear to have taken this passage out of the prophets, nor does Diatribe prove that he has. For Paul usually mentions the name of the writer or explicitly states that he is taking something from the Scriptures, and he does neither of these things here. So it is truer to say that Paul is taking this common simile, which others take for other purposes, and using it himself in his own spirit for a purpose of his own, just as he does with the saying, "A little leaven leavens the whole lump," which in I Cor. 5⟨:6⟩ he applies to corrupt morals and elsewhere uses against those who corrupt the Word of God ⟨Gal. 5:9⟩, in the same way as Christ refers to the leaven of Herod and of the Pharisees ⟨Mark 8:15⟩.

No matter, then, how much the prophets may be speaking of temporal affliction (and I refrain from discussing that now, so as to avoid being so often taken up and sidetracked by irrelevant questions), Paul nevertheless uses it in his own spirit against free choice. But as for the idea that freedom of choice is not lost if we are as clay in God's hands when he afflicts us, I do not see the point of it or why Diatribe contends for it, since there is no doubt that afflictions come upon us from God against our will, and put us under the necessity of bearing them willy-nilly, nor is it in our power to avert them, although we are exhorted to bear them willingly.

But it is worthwhile to listen to Diatribe prattling, by this simile, about how Paul's argument does not exclude free choice.

For she puts forward two absurd ideas, one of which she gathers from the Scriptures, the other from reason. ⟨E., p. 71.⟩ This is what she gets from the Scriptures: When Paul in II. Tim. 2⟨:20 f.⟩ has said that in a great house there are vessels of gold, silver, wood, earthenware, and some for noble use, some for ignoble, he at once adds: "If anyone purifies himself from these, then he will be a vessel for noble use," etc. Then Diatribe argues thus: "What could be more stupid than to address a Samian chamberpot, 'If you make yourself clean, you will be an honorable vessel'? Yet this could well be said to a vessel endowed with reason which, when admonished, can conform to the Lord's will." By this she means to say that the simile is not completely applicable, and is so far invalidated as to be ineffective.

Without caviling at this, I reply that Paul does not say, "If anyone purifies himself from his own filth," but "from these," that is, from vessels for ignoble use, so that the meaning is: If anyone remains separate and does not mix with the ungodly teachers, he will be a vessel for noble use, etc. Let us also grant that this passage of Paul's does precisely what Diatribe wants, i.e., that the simile is not applicable. But how will she prove that Paul's intention is the same here as in Rom., ch. 9, which is the passage in dispute? Is it enough to quote another passage, without any concern as to whether it is making the same point or a different one? There is no easier or commoner mistake with regard to the Scriptures, as I have often shown, than that of bringing together different passages from the Scriptures as if they were alike, with the result that the similarity of the passages—a point on which Diatribe prides herself—is more ineffective than our simile which she confutes. But not to be contentious, let us grant that in both passages Paul means the same thing, and—as is unquestionably true—that a simile does not always and in all respects apply, otherwise it would not be a simile or a metaphor but the thing itself. As the proverb says, a simile limps and does not always run on four feet.

Diatribe, however, errs and sins in this, that she neglects the reason for the simile, which ought to be particularly noticed, and captiously contends about words. For the meaning must be sought in the reasons for speaking, as Hilary says,[50] and does not lie in the words alone. Thus the effectiveness of a simile depends on the reason for the simile. Why, then, does Diatribe disregard the thing for the sake of which Paul uses this simile, and seize on something he says that is unconnected with the reason for the simile? My point is that it is a matter of exhortation when he says, "If anyone

[50] *De Trinitate* ix.2; quoted by Luther also in *WA* 50, 574, 18.

purifies himself," and of doctrine when he says, "In a great house there are vessels," etc., so that from the whole context of the words and the thought of Paul you can see that he is making a statement about the diversity and use of vessels. Hence the meaning is that since so many fall away from faith, there is no comfort for us but in being certain that "God's firm foundation stands, bearing this seal: 'The Lord knows those who are his,' and, 'Let everyone who names the name of the Lord depart from iniquity'" (II Tim. 2:19). Thus far we have the reason and the effectiveness of the simile, namely, that "the Lord knows those who are his." Then the simile follows, pointing out that there are different vessels, some for noble use, some for ignoble. With this the doctrine is proved, that the vessels do not prepare themselves, but the master prepares them. This is the meaning also in Rom., ch. 9, where the potter has power over the clay, etc. Thus Paul's simile stands unshaken as a most effective demonstration that freedom of choice is as nothing in the sight of God.

After this follows the exhortation, "If anyone purifies himself from these," etc., and its significance is plain enough from what has already been said. For it does not follow that anyone is therefore able to purify himself; though indeed, if anything is proved, it is proved that free choice can purify itself apart from grace, since he does not say, "If grace purifies anyone," but, "If anyone purifies himself." Now, concerning imperative and subjunctive verbs, quite enough has been said; but the simile is not expressed by subjunctive verbs, but indicative, thus: as there are elect and reprobate, so there are vessels for noble and ignoble use. In a word, if this way out is valid, the whole argument of Paul is worthless, for it would be pointless to introduce those who murmur against God the potter if the fault were seen to lie with the vessel and not with the potter. For who will complain if he hears that one deserving of damnation is being damned?

Her second absurdity Diatribe culls from Madam Reason, commonly called "human" reason, to the effect that the fault must be attributed not to the vessel, but to the potter, especially if He is such a potter as actually creates the clay as well as molds it. (E., p. 71.) "Here a vessel is thrown into eternal fire," she says, "which has been guilty of nothing but not being its own master." [51] Nowhere does Diatribe more obviously give herself away than in this passage. For what you hear said here—in other words, of course, but with the same meaning—is what Paul makes the

[51] Note the slight misquotation. Erasmus says: "which has been guilty of nothing because it is not its own master."

ungodly say: "Why does he find fault? Who can resist his will?"
This is what Reason can neither grasp nor endure, and what has
offended all those men of outstanding talent who have been received for so many centuries. Here they demand that God should
act according to human justice, and do what seems right to them,
or else cease to be God. The secrets of his majesty are no recom-
mendation; let him give a reason why he is God, or why he wills
or does what has no semblance of justice—much as you might summon a cobbler or girdle maker to appear in court.

Erasmus' Way of Reasoning Does Not Let God Be God
⟨WA 730–733⟩

Human nature [52] does not think fit to give God such glory as to
believe him just and good when he speaks and acts above and
beyond what the Code of Justinian has laid down, or the fifth
book of Aristotle's *Ethics*. The Majesty that is the creator of all
things must bow to one of the dregs of his creation, and the famed
Corycian cavern must reverse its role and stand in awe of the spec-
tators! Therefore, it is absurd that he should damn one who cannot help deserving damnation; and because of this absurdity,
it must be false that God has mercy on whomever he wills and
hardens whomever he wills. He must be brought to order, and
laws must be prescribed for him, so that he may damn none but
those who in our judgment have deserved it. In this way Paul and
his simile are satisfactorily dealt with: he must revoke it and allow it to be worthless, though he may modify it so that the Potter
(according to Diatribe's interpretation) makes the vessel for ignoble use on the ground of prior deservings, just as He rejected
some of the Jews on account of their unbelief and accepted the
Gentiles on account of their faith.

But if God works in such a way that he takes account of merits,
why do they murmur and protest? Why do they say: "Why does he
find fault? Who can resist his will?" Why is there need for Paul to
silence them? For who is surprised, let alone indignant or moved
to protest, when anyone who has deserved it is damned? Moreover, what becomes of the potter's power to make what he likes, if
he is subjected to merits and laws and not allowed to make what
he likes, but required to make what he ought? For the consideration of merits conflicts with the power and freedom to do what he
pleases, as is proved by the householder in the parable who, when
the workmen were murmuring and demanding their rights, op-

[52] *"Caro."*

posed them with his freedom of will in respect of his own goods ⟨Matt. 22:11-15⟩. These are the arguments that invalidate Diatribe's gloss.

But let us imagine, if you will, that God ought to be of such a character as to take account of merits in those who are to be damned. Must we not equally maintain and allow that he should take account of merits also in those who are to be saved? If we wish to follow reason, it is just as unfair that the undeserving should be rewarded as that the undeserving should be punished. Let us then conclude that God must justify men on the basis of preceding merits, or else we shall declare him unjust, since he takes pleasure in evil and ungodly men, and encourages and crowns their ungodliness with rewards. But alas then for us wretched mortals in the hands of that God! For who will be saved? Observe, therefore, the wickedness of the human heart! When God saves the unworthy without merits, or rather justifies the ungodly with their many demerits, it does not accuse him of injustice; it does not demand to know why he wills this, which in its judgment is most unjust, but because it is advantageous and pleasing to itself it deems it just and good. But when he damns those without merit, then since this is disadvantageous to itself, it is unjust, it is intolerable, and here there is protesting, murmuring, and blaspheming.

You see, then, that Diatribe and her friends in this case do not judge according to equity, but according as their own interest is affected. For if she had regard to equity, she would expostulate with God just as much when he crowns the unworthy as when he damns the undeserving. She would also praise and extol God just as much when he damns the undeserving as when he saves the unworthy; for there is equal unfairness in either case, judged by our standards. Or would it not be just as iniquitous to commend Cain for his murder and make him a king as to throw innocent Abel into prison or put him to death? When therefore Reason praises God for saving the unworthy, but finds fault with him for damning the undeserving, she stands convicted of not praising God as God, but as serving her own interests. That is to say, what she seeks and praises in God is herself and the things of self, not God or the things of God. But if God pleases you when he crowns the unworthy, he ought not to displease you when he damns the undeserving. If he is just in the former case, why not in the latter? In the former case he pours out grace and mercy on the unworthy, in the latter he pours out wrath and severity on the undeserving, and in both cases he is unprincipled and unjust by human standards, but just and true by his own. For how it is just that he crowns the unworthy is incomprehensible now, but we shall see it when we arrive there where it will no longer be a matter of believing but of seeing with unveiled face.[53] Similarly, how it is just that he damns the undeserving is incomprehensible now, except only to faith, until the Son of Man shall be revealed.

Diatribe, however, who intensely dislikes that simile of the potter and the clay, and is not a little annoyed at being so hard pressed by it, is at length reduced to producing different passages of Scripture, some of which seem to attribute everything to man, others everything to grace, and she pettishly insists that each case must be understood according to a sound interpretation and not taken literally.[54] ⟨E., pp. 71 ff.⟩ Otherwise, if we press this simile, she is prepared in return to press against us those imperative and subjunctive passages, especially that of Paul, "If anyone purifies himself from these." Here she makes out that Paul contradicts himself and attributes everything to man, unless a sound interpretation comes to the rescue. If, therefore, an interpretation is admitted here in order to leave room for grace, why should not the simile of the potter also admit of an interpretation in order to make room for free choice? My answer is that it does not matter to me whether you take it in a simple sense, a double sense, or a hundred senses. What I say is that by this "sound interpretation" nothing is gained, and what is wanted is not proved. For what ought to be proved is that free choice can will nothing good; but by that passage, "If anyone purifies himself from these," since it is a conditional statement, neither anything nor nothing is proved. Paul is merely exhorting. Or if you add Diatribe's inference, and say he is exhorting in vain if a man cannot purify himself, then it is proved that free choice can do everything without grace. And thus Diatribe disproves herself.

We are therefore still waiting for some passage of Scripture which teaches this interpretation; we put no faith in those who make it up out of their own heads. For we deny that there is any passage to be found which would attribute everything to man. We also deny that Paul contradicts himself where he says "If anyone purifies himself from these," and we affirm that the contradiction in Paul is as much a fiction as the interpretation which it extorts is an invention, and neither of them is proved. We do of course admit that if it is right to augment the Scriptures with Diatribe's

[53] Apparently a conflation of I Cor. 13:12 and II Cor. 3:18.
[54] *"Simpliciter"*—Erasmus' word—which is also rendered "as it stands" (E., p. 72) and "in a simple sense" (below).

inferences and appendages, as when she says that precepts are in vain if we are not able to fulfill them, then it is true that Paul contradicts himself; and so does the entire Scripture, for then Scripture is other than it was, and it even proves that free choice can do everything. And is it surprising if in that case it also contradicts what it says elsewhere, that God alone does everything? But a Scripture thus augmented is opposed not only to us but to Diatribe herself, who has laid it down that free choice can will nothing good. Let her therefore first clear herself and say how these two statements of hers agree with Paul: "Free choice can will nothing good" and "The words 'If anyone purifies himself' imply that he can purify himself or else there is no point in them."

You see therefore that Diatribe is baffled and beaten by that simile of the potter, and all she does is to try to get away from it, with never a thought of the harm her interpretation does to the cause she has undertaken, and of how she is refuting and making a fool of herself.

We, however, as we have said, have never aspired to an interpretation, nor have we said things like: "Stretch out your hand," i.e., "Grace will stretch it out" ⟨E., p. 73⟩. All these things Diatribe invents about us for the benefit of her own cause. What we have said is that there is no inconsistency in the statements of Scripture, and no need of an interpretation to remove the difficulty; but the supporters of free choice look for difficulties where there are none [55] and produce inconsistencies out of their own dreams. For example, there is no inconsistency between "If anyone purifies himself" and "God works all in all" ⟨I Cor. 12:6⟩; nor is it necessary, in order to remove the difficulty, to say there is something God does and something man does. For the former passage is a conditional statement, which neither affirms nor denies any work or virtue in man, but prescribes what work or virtue there ought to be in man. There is nothing figurative here, nothing needing interpretation; the words are simple and the sense is simple, so long as you do not add inferences and corrupting comments, as Diatribe does; for then the sense would become unsound, though not by its own fault but its corrupter's. The later passage, however, "God works all in all," is an indicative statement, affirming that all works and all virtue are in God. How, then, can the two passages conflict, when one of them says nothing about the virtue of man, and the other attributes everything to God? Do they not instead agree very well with one another?

But Diatribe is so overwhelmed, drowned, and corrupted by the

[55] "*Nodos in scirpo quaerunt,*" "Look for knots in bulrushes"—a proverb.

thought of this ungodly [56] idea that it is pointless to command impossibilities, that whenever she hears an imperative or subjunctive verb she cannot help appending her own indicative inferences, to the effect that if something is commanded, then we can do it, and we do it, otherwise the command is stupid. Then she bursts out and boasts on every hand of her victories, as if she could take it for granted that she has only to think of these inferences for them to be invested with something like divine authority. Hence she confidently lays it down that in some passages of Scripture everything is attributed to man, and that there is an inconsistency here which calls for an interpretation. She does not realize that this is all invented out of her own head, without an iota of Scripture anywhere to confirm it. What is more, she fails to see that it is the kind of thing which, if it were admitted, would confute no one more strongly than herself, since what she proves by it—if she proves anything—is that free choice can do everything, which is the opposite of what she set out to prove.

It is the same when she so often repeats that "if man does nothing, there is no room for merits; where there is no room for merits, there will be no room for either punishments or rewards" ⟨E., p. 73⟩. Again she fails to see how much more strongly she confutes herself by these ungodly [57] arguments than she confutes us. For what do these inferences of hers prove but that all merit rests with free choice? And in that case, what room will there be for grace? Furthermore, if free choice merits only a little, and grace does the rest, why does free choice receive the whole reward? Or are we to suppose it receives only a little reward? If there is room for merits so that there may be room for rewards, then the merit ought to be as great as the reward. But why am I wasting time and words on such rubbish? Even supposing that everything Diatribe wants were granted, and that our meriting was partly man's work and partly God's, they are still unable to define this work itself and show its content, its nature, and its extent; so that it is a dispute about something and nothing. [58]

The fact is, that since she proves none of the things she says, and can neither establish any inconsistency nor her own interpretation, nor produce any passage that attributes everything to man, but all these are figments of her own imagination, Paul's simile of the potter and the clay stands intact and invincible, showing that the sort of vessels into which we are shaped does not depend on our choice. And as for Paul's exhortations, such as "If anyone purifies himself," they are patterns to which we ought to be shaped,

[56] *"Carnalis."*   [57] *"Carnalibus."*   [58] *"Lana caprina"* (see p. 148 n. 8).

but not evidences of our work or endeavor. Let this be enough said about the hardening of Pharaoh and about Esau and about the potter.

Part V. Rebuttal of Erasmus' Critique of the *Assertio*

Genesis 6:3 and the Biblical Meaning of "Flesh" ⟨WA 733–736⟩

At length Diatribe comes to the passages cited by Luther against free choice, with the intention of confuting them too. ⟨E., p. 74.⟩ The first of them is Gen. 6⟨:3⟩: "My spirit shall not abide in man forever, for he is flesh." First, she argues that "flesh" here does not mean wicked desire, but weakness. Then she expands Moses' text, to the effect that "this saying does not apply to the whole human race, but only to the men of that day," and so it means "in these men." Moreover, it does not apply to all the men even of that age, since Noah is excepted. Finally, on the authority of Jerome,[59] she says that in Hebrew this saying gives a different impression, namely, of the clemency and not the severity of God—hoping perhaps to persuade us that since this saying does not apply to Noah but to the wicked, it is not the clemency but the severity of God that applies to Noah, while clemency and not severity applies to the wicked.

But let us leave these frivolities of Diatribe's, who never fails to make it clear that she regards the Scriptures as fables. With Jerome's trifling here we have no concern; it is certain he proves nothing, and we are not discussing Jerome's views but the meaning of Scripture. Let the perverter of Scripture pretend that the Spirit of God signifies indignation. ⟨E., pp. 75 f.⟩ We say he doubly lacks proof. First, he cannot produce a single passage of Scripture in which the Spirit of God stands for indignation, since on the contrary, kindness and sweetness are everywhere attributed to the Spirit. Secondly, if he did chance to prove that the Spirit stands for indignation in some place, he still could not prove it to be a necessary consequence that Spirit should be so understood in this passage also. Similarly, he may pretend that flesh stands for weakness, yet he proves just as little. For when Paul calls the Corinthians carnal ⟨I Cor. 3:3⟩, this certainly does not signify a weakness, but a fault, for he accuses them of forming sects and parties, which is not a matter of weakness or lack of capacity for more solid doctrine, but malice and the old leaven ⟨I Cor. 5:7 f.⟩, which he bids them cleanse out. Let us look at the Hebrew.

[59] *Lib. Hebraicarum quaest. in Gen. (MPL* 23.948).

"My spirit shall not judge in man forever, for he is flesh"—that is what Moses literally says. And if we would only get rid of our own dreams, the words as they stand are, I think, adequately plain and clear. That they are, moreover, spoken by God in wrath, is sufficiently shown by what precedes and follows, together with the resultant Flood. The reason for his speaking them was that the sons of men were marrying wives from the mere lust of the flesh, and then so filling the earth with violence that they compelled God in his wrath to hasten the Flood, and only delay for a hundred and twenty years ⟨Gen. 6:3⟩ what he would otherwise never have brought about at all. Read Moses attentively, and you will see plainly that this is what he means. But is there any wonder that the Scriptures are obscure, or that with them you can establish not only a free but even a divine choice, when you are allowed to play about with them as if you wanted to make a Vergilian patchwork [60] out of them? That is what you call solving problems, and removing difficulties by means of an "explanation." But it was Jerome and his master Origen who filled the world with such trifles, and set this pestilent example of not paying attention to the simplicity of the Scriptures.

For me it was enough to find proof in that passage that God himself [61] called men flesh, and so far flesh that the Spirit of God could not abide among them but at an appointed time was to be withdrawn from them. For what God means by saying that his Spirit will not judge among men forever, he goes on to explain when he sets a limit of a hundred and twenty years during which he will continue to judge. He contrasts "spirit" with "flesh," however, because men as being flesh give no admittance to the Spirit, while he himself as being Spirit cannot approve of the flesh, and that is why the Spirit is to be withdrawn after a hundred and twenty years. So you may take Moses' text to mean: "My Spirit, which is in Noah and other holy men, accuses the ungodly by means of the preached word [62] and the life of the godly—for to judge among men is to be active among them in the ministry of the word, convincing, rebuking, and exhorting, in season and out of season ⟨II Tim. 4:2⟩—but all in vain, because they are blinded and hardened by the flesh, and get worse the more they are judged, just as it aways happens when the word of God comes into the world, that men grow worse the more they are instructed. And this has the effect of hastening the wrath, just as the Flood was

---

[60] "*Vergilicentonas.*" Cf. Jerome, *Ep.* LIII.6 (*MPL* 22.544). A "cento" is a poem made up of verses of another poem.
[61] "*Divina auctoritas.*"   [62] "*Verbum praedicationis.*"

hastened then, for it not only means that sin is committed but also that grace is despised, and as Christ says: 'When the light comes, men hate the light ⟨John 3:19⟩.' "

Since, therefore, on the testimony of God himself, men are flesh and have a taste for nothing but the flesh, it follows that free choice avails for nothing but sinning. If, even when they have the Spirit of God among them to call and teach them, they go from bad to worse, what would they do if left to themselves without the Spirit of God? And it makes no difference when you say that Moses is speaking only about the men of that age, for the same applies to all men, since they all are flesh, as Christ says in John 3⟨:6⟩: "That which is born of the flesh is flesh." And how serious a defect this is, he himself shows in the same chapter, where he says that no one can enter the Kingdom of God unless he has been born again ⟨John 3:5⟩. So a Christian should know that Origen and Jerome and all their tribe are perniciously wrong when they deny that flesh stands for ungodly desire [63] in such passages. In I Cor. 3⟨:3⟩, for example, "You are still of the flesh" [64] refers to ungodliness. For Paul means that there are still some ungodly ones among them, and that even the godly, insofar as they have a taste for things carnal, are of the flesh,[64] although they are justified through the Spirit.

In short, what you will find in the Scriptures is this: Wherever flesh is treated as in opposition to spirit, you can generally take flesh to mean everything that is contrary to the Spirit, as ⟨in John 6:63⟩: "The flesh is of no avail." But where flesh is treated on its own, you may take it that it signifies the bodily constitution and nature, as for example: "They shall be two in one flesh" ⟨Matt. 19:5⟩; "My flesh is food indeed" ⟨John 6:55⟩; or "The Word became flesh" ⟨John 1:14⟩. In these passages you can drop the Hebraism and say "body" instead of "flesh," for the Hebrew language has only the one word "flesh" for what we express by the two words "flesh" and "body," and I wish this distinction of terms had been observed in translation throughout the whole canon of Scripture. My passage from Gen., ch. 6, will thus, I think, still stand firmly against free choice, when free choice is proved to be flesh, which Paul in Rom. 8⟨:7⟩ says cannot submit to God (as we shall see in that passage), and which Diatribe herself says can will nothing good.

[63] *"Impio affectu."*   [64] *"Carnales."*

*Other Old Testament Passages—the Universal Sinfulness and
Impotence of Man Under the Law ⟨WA 736–740⟩*

The second passage is Gen. 8⟨:21⟩: "The thought and imagination of man's heart are prone to evil from his youth," and also Gen. 6⟨:5⟩: "Every imagination of man's heart is intent on evil continually" ⟨E., p. 75⟩. She gets around this as follows: "The proneness to evil which is in most men does not take away free choice altogether." But I ask you, is God speaking of "most men" and not rather of all, when after the Flood he repents, as it were, and promises the survivors and their posterity that he will never again bring about a flood because of man, adding as the reason for this, that man is prone to evil—as if to say: "Should the wickedness of men be taken into account, there would never be any ending of the Flood; but from now on I will take no account of what they deserve," etc.? So you see that both before and after the Flood, God declares that men are evil, so that Diatribe's remark about "most men" is meaningless. Next, a proneness or proclivity to evil seems to Diatribe a matter of small moment, as if it were quite within our power to counteract or check it, whereas Scripture intends this proneness to signify the persistent attraction and drive of the will toward evil. Or why has she not consulted the Hebrew here too, where—to give you no cause to cavil—Moses says nothing about proneness? For this is what Gen. 6⟨:5⟩ says: *Chol Ietzer Mahescheboth libbo rak ra chol haiom,* that is, "Every imagination of the thoughts of his heart was only evil continually." It does not say "intent on" or "prone to" evil, but "altogether evil," and that nothing but evil is thought and imagined by man all his life. The nature of his wickedness is represented as such that it neither does nor can do otherwise, because it is evil; for an evil tree cannot bear other than evil fruit, as Christ testifies ⟨Matt. 7:17⟩. And as to Diatribe's pert question, Why is room given for repentance if no part of repentance depends on the will[65] but everything is done by necessity? I reply: You can say the same with regard to all the commandments of God, and ask why he gives commandments if everything is done by necessity. He gives commandments in order to instruct and admonish men as to what they ought to do, so that they may be humbled by the knowledge of their wickedness and attain to grace, as has been abundantly said. This passage too, therefore, still stands invincible against freedom of choice.

The third passage is Isa. 40⟨:2⟩: "She has received from the

---

[65] *"Arbitrio."* So also Erasmus, p. 75.

Lord's hand double for all her sins." Jerome (she says) interprets this in terms of the divine vengeance, not of grace given in return for evil deeds. ⟨E., p. 75.⟩ I see! Jerome says so, therefore it is true! I am discussing Isaiah, who speaks in the very plainest terms, and Jerome is thrown at me, who (to say no worse of him) is a man quite without either judgment or application. Where is that promise by which we bound ourselves to conduct our debate on the basis of the Scriptures themselves, not of men's commentaries? The whole chapter of Isaiah speaks of the forgiveness of sins proclaimed by the gospel, as the Evangelists show where they say "the voice of one crying" refers to John the Baptist. Can we let it pass, then, when Jerome in his usual way puts forward Jewish blindnesses as the historical sense and his own ineptitudes as the allegorical? Are we to let grammar be turned upside down, and to take a passage that speaks of forgiveness as speaking of vengeance? I ask you, what sort of vengeance is fulfilled through the preaching of Christ? But let us look at the words themselves in the Hebrew. "Comfort ye" (it says), "comfort ye, my people" [66] or "Comfort ye my people,[67] says your God." Now, he who orders "comfort" is not, I think, exacting vengeance! Then follows: "Speak to the heart of Jerusalem and preach to her." To "speak to the heart" is a Hebrew expression, and it means to speak good, sweet, and tender things, as in Gen. 34⟨:3⟩ Shechem speaks "to the heart" of Dinah whom he has corrupted; that is, he spoke tenderly to the unhappy girl, as our version puts it.

Now, the nature of the good and sweet things that are commanded to be preached for their comfort he explains by saying "that her warfare is ended, that her iniquity is pardoned, that she has received from the Lord's hand double for all her sins." The "warfare" (*militia*), for which our manuscripts wrongly read "wickedness" (*malitia*),[68] is taken by the bold Jewish grammarians as meaning "an appointed time," for that is how they understand Job 7⟨:1⟩: "The life of man is a warfare upon earth," that is, there is a set time for it. I prefer to take it simply, in the ordinary grammatical sense of "warfare," so that Isaiah is understood to be speaking of the toilsome course of the people under the law, as if they were engaged in military service. For Paul similarly loves to compare both preachers and hearers of the Word to soldiers, as for example when he bids Timothy be a good soldier ⟨II Tim. 2:3⟩ and fight the good fight ⟨I Tim. 6:12⟩. And he makes the Corinthians run in a race ⟨I Cor. 9:24⟩. He also says: "No

[66] *"Popule"* (in the vocative). [67] *"Populum"* (in the accusative).
[68] So the Vulgate.

one is crowned unless he competes according to the rules" ⟨II Tim. 2:5⟩. He equips the Ephesians and Thessalonians with arms ⟨Eph. 6:13-17; I Thess. 5:8⟩, and glories that he himself has fought the good fight ⟨II Tim. 4:7⟩; and there are similar instances elsewhere. So also in I Sam. 2⟨:22⟩ it is written in the Hebrew that the sons of Eli slept with the women who did military duty in the army [69] at the entrance to the Tent of Meeting, of whose service [70] Moses makes mention in Exodus ⟨38:8⟩. Hence the God of that people is called the Lord of Hosts, that is, the Lord of warfare or of armies.

Isaiah, therefore, is announcing that the service [71] of the people of the law [72] is to be brought to an end because under the law they have been oppressed by a burden too heavy to bear (as Peter says in Acts 15⟨:10⟩), and when they have been freed from the law they are to be transferred to a new service of the Spirit. Furthermore, this ending of their very hard service, and the exchanging of it for a new and most free service, will not be granted them on account of their merit, for they have not been able to sustain it; it will rather be on account of their demerit, since the way their service is brought to an end is by their iniquity being freely forgiven them. There are no obscure or ambiguous words here. He says the warfare is to be ended because the iniquity is pardoned, plainly indicating that as soldiers under the law they had not fulfilled the law, and could not fulfill it, but had been engaged in the service [73] of sin and were sinful soldiers. It is as if God said: "I am obliged to forgive them their sins if I want the law fulfilled by them; indeed, I must also put away the law, for I see that they are unable not to sin, especially when they are fighting, that is, when they are laboring to fulfill the law in their own strength." For the Hebrew expression "iniquity is pardoned" implies gratuitous goodwill; and it is by this that the iniquity is pardoned, without any merit and indeed with demerit. And this is the point of what follows: For "she has received from the Lord's hand double for all her sins." This includes, as I have said, not only the forgiveness of sins, but also the end of the warfare; and that means nothing else but that with the removing of the law, which was the power of sin ⟨I Cor. 15:56⟩, and the pardoning of sin, which was the sting of death ⟨ibid.⟩, they reign in freedom from both through the victory of Jesus Christ. This is what Isaiah means by "from the Lord's hand," for they have not obtained these things by their own powers or merits, but have received them from Christ the conqueror and the giver.

---

[69] *"Militantibus"* (Vulg.: *"quae observabant"*).   [70] *"Militia."*
[71] *"Militiam."*   [72] *"Legalis populi."*   [73] *"Militiam exercuisse."*

The Hebrew "in all sins" means the same as "for or on account of sins" in Latin; just as in Hos. 12⟨:12⟩, "Jacob did service in a wife" means "for a wife," and in Ps. 16⟨17:9⟩, "They have surrounded me in my life" means "for my life." Isaiah is thus showing what our merits are by which we obtain the twofold freedom that comes from the ending of our service of the law and the pardoning of our sin: they are all sins and nothing but sins. Ought we then to have let it pass when this splendid and invincible passage against free choice was so besmirched with the Jewish filth produced by Jerome and Diatribe? Impossible! However, my Isaiah still stands victorious over free choice, and makes it plain that grace is given, not to merits or the endeavors of free choice, but to sins and demerits, and that free choice with all its powers can do nothing but engage in the service of sin, so that even the law, which is supposed to be given as a help, becomes intolerable to a man and makes him a greater sinner while he serves under it.

Now, let us look at Diatribe's argument ⟨E., p. 75⟩ that, although sin abounds through the law, and where sin has abounded grace also abounds, "it does not necessarily follow that before that 'grace which makes acceptable' a man may not, with the help of God, prepare himself by morally good works for the divine favor." It would surprise me if that is Diatribe's own idea, and not rather one she has lifted out of some paper by somebody or other and put into her book. For she neither sees nor hears what these words mean. If through the law sin abounds, how is it possible that a man should be able to prepare himself by moral works for the divine favor? How can works help when the law does not help? What does it mean that sin abounds through the law, but that works done according to the law are sins?—But of this anon.

Then what does it mean that a man with the help of God can prepare himself by moral works? Are we arguing about divine assistance, or about free choice? For what might not be possible with divine assistance? The fact is, as I have said, that Diatribe has no respect for the cause she is pleading; that is why she snores and yawns through her speech like this. However, she cites Cornelius the centurion as an example of one whose prayers and alms pleased God ⟨Acts 10:4⟩, though he was not yet baptized and had not yet been inspired by the Holy Spirit. I, too, have read Luke on the Acts, but I have never found a single syllable to suggest that Cornelius' works were morally good without the Holy Spirit, as Diatribe dreams. On the contrary, I find that he was "an upright and God-fearing man"—for that is what Luke calls him ⟨Acts

10:22). But to call a man without the Holy Spirit "upright and God-fearing" is the same as calling Belial "Christ."

Moreover, the whole argument there turns on the fact that Cornelius was clean in God's sight, as is shown also by the vision sent from heaven with its rebuke to Peter; and it is obvious from the importance of what is said and done that Luke is making a special point of the uprightness and faith of Cornelius. Nevertheless, Diatribe and her Sophists are blind to all this, and though their eyes are open and the words could not be clearer nor the facts more evident, they see just the opposite; so careless are they in their reading and marking of Holy Writ, which they then have to brand as obscure and ambiguous. Granted he was not yet baptized and had not yet heard the word concerning the risen Christ, does it follow from this that he was without the Holy Spirit? In that case, you will have to say also that John the Baptist and his parents, and even Christ's mother and Simeon, were without the Holy Spirit. But let us take our leave of such deep gloom.

The fourth passage comes from the same chapter of Isaiah: "All flesh is grass, and all its glory is like the flower of the grass. The grass withers and the flower fades, because the Spirit of the Lord blows upon it," etc. ⟨Isa. 40:6 f.⟩. Dear Diatribe thinks it very forced to apply this to grace and free choice. ⟨E., p. 76.⟩ I wonder why? Because (she says) "Jerome takes 'spirit' to mean wrath, and 'flesh' to mean the natural weakness of mankind which avails nought against God." Once more I am presented with Jerome's trifling instead of Isaiah, and I have to put more effort into fighting against the weariness with which all this carelessness of Diatribe's is wearing me down than against Diatribe herself. But we have already expressed our opinion of Jerome's view, so let us compare Diatribe with herself. "Flesh," she says, is the weak nature of man, and "spirit" is divine wrath. Has divine wrath nothing else to wither, then, but this poor weak nature of man, which it ought rather to raise up? But here is something still better: the flower of the grass is "the glory which is born of the happiness of corporeal things. The Jews gloried in the Temple, in circumcision, in victims; the Greeks gloried in their wisdom." Therefore, the flower of the grass and the glory of the flesh is the righteousness of works and the wisdom of the world! How comes it, then, that righteousness and wisdom are called "corporeal things" in Diatribe? What, moreover, has this to do with Isaiah, who explains himself in his own words when he says: "Surely the people is grass"? He does not say: "Surely the weak nature of man is grass," but: "The people is grass," and he asserts this with an oath.

Now what is "the people"? Is it only the weak nature of man? Whether Jerome understands by "the weak nature of man" simply man's creatureliness or the wretchedness of his present lot, I do not know. But whichever it is, the divine wrath certainly gains high distinction and ample spoils from withering the poor creature or unhappy humanity, instead of scattering the proud and putting down the mighty from their seats and sending the rich empty away, as Mary sings ⟨Luke 1:51-53⟩. But let us banish these specters and follow Isaiah. "The people," he says, "is grass"; but "the people" is not merely the flesh or the weakness of man's nature, but it covers everything there is in "the people," including the rich, the wise, the righteous, the holy—unless the Jewish people does not include the Pharisees, elders, princes, nobles, the rich, etc. The "flower of the grass" is rightly called their glory, for they certainly gloried in their kingdom and government, and above all in their law, their God, their righteousness and wisdom, as Paul shows in Romans.[74]

When, therefore, Isaiah says "all flesh," what else does he mean but "all the grass" or "all the people"? (For he does not say simply "flesh," but "all flesh.") To a "people," however, belong soul, body, mind, reason, judgment, and whatever else can be named or found that is most excellent in man. For when he says, "All flesh is grass," he excepts none but the Spirit that withers it; and when he says, "The people is grass," he omits nothing. Take free choice, then, or take whatever may be regarded as the highest or the lowest in a people: Isaiah calls it all "flesh" and "grass." For these three terms, "flesh," "grass," and "people," as explained by the author of the book himself, all have the same meaning in this passage. Moreover, you yourself affirm that the wisdom of the Greeks and the righteousness of the Jews, which have been withered by the gospel, are grass or the flower of the grass. Do you perhaps think that their wisdom was not the most excellent thing the Greeks possessed, and that their righteousness was not the most excellent thing of which the Jews were capable? Then show us something more excellent!

The Whole Man—Body, Soul, and "Spirit"—Is "Flesh"
⟨WA 740–745⟩

Where is now the confidence with which you jeered (at Philip,[75] I believe), when you said: "If anybody should wish to argue that the most excellent part of human nature is none other than flesh,

[74] Rom. 2:17; 3:1; 9:4.   [75] Melanchthon.

that is to say, it is wicked, I would readily yield—if he proves his assertion by the testimony of Holy Scripture"? ⟨E., p. 76.⟩ You have here Isaiah, who cries aloud that the people devoid of the Spirit of the Lord is flesh, though even so you do not hear. You have your own confession, when (perhaps incautiously) you call the wisdom of the Greeks "grass or the glory of the grass," which is the same as saying "flesh"—unless you would argue that the wisdom of the Greeks does not pertain to reason, or the *hēgemonikon,* as you call it, which is the governing part of man. Though you pay no regard to us, do at least listen to yourself when you are overpowered by the force of truth and say things that are right. You have John: "That which is born of the flesh is flesh; that which is born of the Spirit is spirit" ⟨John 3:6⟩. This passage, which plainly shows that what is not born of the Spirit is flesh—otherwise the distinction made by Christ, who divides all men into the two classes of flesh and spirit, would not hold good—this passage, I say, you firmly put aside, as if it did not give you what you want, and you go off at a tangent in your usual way, after remarking that John says believers are born of God and become sons of God, yes, even gods and a new creature. You give no heed to what the distinction implies, but waste words in telling us who are in the second half of the distinction, relying on your rhetoric to prevent anyone from noticing such an artful transition and dissimulation as this.

It is difficult to believe that you are not being sly and deceitful in this passage. For anyone who treats the Scriptures with such artfulness and hypocrisy as you do may well have the face to profess himself as yet unlearned in the Scriptures, but desirous of being taught, although he desires nothing less, and only talks like this in order to discredit the plainest meaning of the Scriptures and to present his own pertinacity in a plausible guise. That is just how the Jews, down to the present day, say that the things taught by Christ, the apostles, and the whole Church, are not proved by the Scriptures. Heretics can be taught nothing by the Scriptures. The papists have not so far learned much from the Scriptures, though even the stones are crying out the truth ⟨Luke 19:40⟩.

Perhaps you are waiting for a passage to be produced from the Scriptures, consisting of these letters and syllables: "The governing part in man is flesh" or "That which is most excellent in man is flesh," in default of which you will be invincibly victorious— just as if the Jews should demand that a statement be produced from the Prophets, consisting of these letters: "Jesus, the carpenter's son, born of the Virgin Mary in Bethlehem, is the Messiah and the Son of God." Here, where you are hard pressed by the plain sense, you challenge us to produce the exact words; elsewhere, when you are vanquished by both words and sense, you have a supply of tropes, knotty problems, and "sound interpretations." Nowhere do you fail to find some means of contradicting the Divine Scriptures. And no wonder, when you do nothing else but look for something to contradict! Now you have recourse to the interpretations of the ancients, now to the absurdities of reason, and when neither of these helps, you discourse at a tangent on irrelevant matters, all in order to avoid being caught by the passage of Scripture in question. What can I say? Proteus is no Proteus [76] compared with you; yet even so you cannot escape. What victories the Arians boasted because the syllables and letters of *homoousios* [77] were not contained in the Scriptures, quite heedless of the fact that the same thing was most effectively proved by other words. But whether this is the mark of a good, not to say godly, mind and one desirous of being instructed, let impiety and iniquity itself be judge.

Hold on to your victory, then; we as the vanquished confess that these characters and syllables—"The most excellent thing in man is nothing but flesh"—are not to be found in the Sacred Scriptures. But see what your victory looks like when we show the wealth of evidence there is in the Scriptures, that not just one portion, or the most excellent thing, or the governing part of man is flesh, but that the whole man is flesh; and not only that, but the whole people is flesh, and as if that were not enough, the whole human race is flesh. For Christ says: "That which is born of the flesh is flesh" ⟨John 3:6⟩. Now untie your knots, invent your tropes, and look up the interpretation of the ancients—or else turn to another subject and fill in the time with a dissertation on the Trojan War so as to avoid seeing or hearing the present passage. We do not simply believe, but we see and experience, that the whole human race is *born of* the flesh. We are therefore obliged to believe what we do not see, namely, that the whole human race *is* flesh, as Christ teaches. Whether now the governing part of man is included in the whole man, the whole people, or the whole race of men, we give the Sophists leave to doubt and debate; as for ourselves, we know that in the whole human race are included body and soul with all their powers and works, all virtues and vices, all wisdom and folly, all righteousness and un-

[76] See above, p. 103 n. 7.
[77] The key word of the Nicene Creed, usually translated: "of one substance."

righteousness. They are all flesh, because they all savor of the flesh, that is, of the things that are their own, and they are devoid of the glory of God and the Spirit of God, as Paul says in Rom. 3⟨:23⟩.

Therefore, as to your saying ⟨E., p. 76⟩: "Yet not all human desire is flesh, but there is that part of man which is called his soul, and that which is called his spirit, with which we strive after virtue";[78] as the philosophers strove "who taught that we should sooner die a thousand deaths than commit evil, even though we knew that nobody would ever know of it, and that God would pardon it"—I reply that for one who believes nothing certainly, it is easy to believe and say anything. Your friend Lucian, not I, should ask you whether you can find one example in the entire human race (even though it were Socrates himself twice or seven times over) who has actually done what you speak of here, and what you say they taught. Why, then, do you tell such empty tales? Could men strive after virtue who did not even know what virtue was? Perhaps if I ask for a very outstanding example, you will say it was virtuous when they died for their country, their wives and children, their parents, or when they endured exquisite tortures rather than give way to lying or treachery—men like Q. Scaevola,[79] M. Regulus,[80] and others. Yet in all these instances, what can you show but the outward splendor of the works? Have you looked into their hearts?

Even so, their work made it at once apparent on the face of it that they did all these things for their own glory; so much so that they were not ashamed even to confess and boast that they were seeking their own glory. For it was with a consuming desire for glory that the Romans, on their own testimony, did whatever they did of virtue or valor, and so did the Greeks, so also the Jews, and so does the whole race of men. But although this may be honorable in the eyes of men, in the sight of God nothing is more immoral, indeed it is most impious and the height of sacrilege; and it is so because they did not act for the glory of God, nor did they glorify him as God, but by an act of most impious robbery they robbed God of his glory and attributed it to themselves, so that

---

[78] "Honesta."

[79] Probably Gaius Mucius Scaevola, who in 507 B.C. held his hand in the flames until it was charred, and by this evidence of Roman endurance persuaded the victorious Etruscan king Porsena to call off the war.

[80] Marcus Atilius Regulus, the Roman general who in 250 B.C., having been taken prisoner by the Carthaginians, was sent by them as the head of a peace mission to Rome, but advised against making peace and returned in accordance with his pledged word to Carthage, where he was put to death.

they were never more dishonorable and base than when they were resplendent in their most exalted virtues. Yet how could they act for the glory of God when they were ignorant of God and his glory—not because it was not apparent, but because the flesh did not allow them to see the glory of God, owing to their mad passion for their own glory.

There, then, you have that governing spirit, the principal part of man, which aspires to virtue: in other words, a usurper of divine glory and a pretender to divine majesty, above all when men are most honorable and most highly famed for their most exalted virtues. Now deny that these men are flesh and consigned to perdition by ungodly desire!

Now, I do not believe that what so much offends Diatribe is the idiom by which man is said to be flesh or spirit, where a Latin would say: "Man is carnal or spiritual." For this, like many other things, must be granted to the Hebrew language, that when it says man is flesh or spirit, it means the same as we mean when we say man is carnal or spiritual. It is just as when the Latins say: "A sad thing is the wolf in the fold, a sweet thing moisture to the standing corn," [81] or when they say: "The man yonder is a crime, and wickedness itself." So also Holy Scripture, stretching the point, [82] calls man flesh, as if he were carnality itself, because he savors too much of the things of the flesh and indeed of nothing but these; and it calls him spirit because he savors of, seeks, does, and endures nothing but the things of the spirit. But Diatribe may perhaps still have this question to ask: "Even if the whole man, and the most excellent thing in man, is said to be flesh, does it necessarily follow that whatever is flesh must also be called ungodly?"

We call ungodly anyone who is without the Spirit of God, for Scripture says it is to justify the ungodly that the Spirit is given. But when Christ distinguishes the Spirit from the flesh by saying: "That which is born of the flesh is flesh," and adds that what is born of the flesh cannot see the Kingdom of God ⟨John 3:6, 3⟩, it plainly follows that whatever is flesh is ungodly and under the wrath of God and a stranger to the Kingdom of God. And if it is a stranger to the Kingdom and Spirit of God, it necessarily follows that it is under the kingdom and spirit of Satan, since there is no middle kingdom between the Kingdom of God and the kingdom of Satan, which are mutually and perpetually in conflict with each other. These are the facts which prove that the loftiest virtues of the heathen, the best things in the philosophers, the most ex-

[81] Vergil, *Eclogues* III.80, 82.   [82] *"Per epitasin."*

cellent things in men, which in the eyes of the world certainly appear to be, as they are said to be, honorable and good, are nonetheless in the sight of God truly flesh and subservient to the kingdom of Satan; that is to say, they are impious and sacrilegious and on all counts bad.

But let us suppose that Diatribe's view is right, and that not every desire is flesh, i.e., ungodly, but that which is called spirit is good and sound. Notice what absurdity follows from this, though not of course as far as human reason is concerned, but with respect to the whole Christian religion and the supreme articles of faith. For if what is most excellent in man is not ungodly and lost or damned, but only the flesh, or the lower and grosser desires, what sort of redeemer do you think we shall make Christ out to be? Are we to rate the price of his blood so low as to say that it has redeemed only what is lowest in man, and that what is most excellent in man can take care of itself and has no need of Christ? Then in the future we must preach Christ as the redeemer, not of the whole man, but of his lowest part, namely the flesh, and man himself as his own redeemer in respect of his higher part. Choose which you please: if the higher part of man is sound, it does not need Christ as its redeemer, and if it does not need Christ, it triumphs with a glory above that of Christ, since in taking care of itself it takes care of the higher part, whereas Christ only takes care of the lower. Then the kingdom of Satan, too, will be as nothing, since it will rule only over the lower part of man, and in respect of the higher part will rather be ruled over by man.

So by means of this doctrine concerning the governing part of man, man will come to be exalted above Christ and the devil, or in other words, he will become Lord of lords and God of gods. What has now happened to that "probable opinion" which said that free choice could will nothing good? Yet here she contends that it is the principal part, and a sound and virtuous part, which does not even need Christ, but can do more than God himself and the devil can. I say this to let you see again how very perilous it is to venture into divine and sacred subjects without the Spirit of God and in the temerity of human reason. If Christ is the Lamb of God that taketh away the sin of the world ⟨John 1:29⟩, then it follows that the whole world is subject to sin, damnation, and the devil, and the distinction between principal and nonprincipal parts is of no use at all. For "world" means men, who savor of worldly things in all their parts.

"If the whole man," she says ⟨E., p. 76⟩, "even reborn in faith, is none other than flesh, where is the spirit which is born of the

Spirit? Where is the son of God? Where is the new creature? I wish to be instructed on these points." Thus Diatribe. But why? Why, my dearest Diatribe? What are you dreaming of? You ask to be informed how the spirit born of the Spirit is flesh. Oh, how gaily sure of victory must you be to crow over us here as vanquished foes, as if it were impossible for us to stand our ground. "Meanwhile" you seek to "make full use of [83] the authority of the Fathers who say that there are certain seeds of virtue implanted in the minds of men." First, if that is what you want, as far as we are concerned you may use or abuse [84] the authority of the Fathers; but you should take note of what you believe when you believe men who are expressing their own ideas without the word of God. But perhaps you are not so concerned for religion as to be much worried about what anyone believes, seeing you are so ready to believe men, regardless of whether what they say is certain or uncertain in God's sight. And we should like to be instructed on this point: When have we ever taught this thing you so freely and publicly impute to us? Who would be so crazy as to say that one born of the Spirit was nothing but flesh? We make a clear distinction between flesh and spirit as opposite realities, and we say with the oracles of God that a man who has not been born anew through faith is flesh. We then say that one who has been born anew is no longer flesh except as regards the remnants of the flesh that war against the firstfruits of the Spirit he has received ⟨Rom. 8:23; Gal. 5:17⟩. Yet I do not believe you have deliberately invented this in order to spite us; for if you had, what more scoundrelly trick could you have played on us?

But you either have no understanding of what we are about, or you show yourself unequal to the magnitude of the task, by which you are so overwhelmed and confounded that you are not sufficiently mindful of what you say either against us or for yourself. For when you say you believe, on the authority of the Fathers, that there are certain seeds of virtue implanted in the minds of men, you speak once more with a certain forgetfulness, since you have asserted earlier that free choice can will nothing good. How its inability to will anything good is compatible with certain seeds of virtue, I do not know. I am thus continually obliged to remind you of the real issue at stake, which you are continually forgetting and wandering off to discuss something other than you originally proposed.

[83] *"Abuti."*
[84] *"Abutaris":* Luther plays on the double sense of the word.

How Erasmus Persistently Evades the Issue ⟨WA 745–748⟩

Another passage is Jer. 10⟨:23⟩: "I know, O Lord, that the way of man is not in himself; that it is not in any man to walk and direct his steps." This passage, she says, refers rather to the outcome of joyous experiences than to the power of free choice. ⟨E., p. 77.⟩ Here again Diatribe confidently brings in a gloss to suit herself, just as if Scripture were under her complete control. As for considering the prophet's own meaning and intention, what need was there for a man of such authority to do that? All we need is: Erasmus says so, therefore it is so! If this passion for glossing is permitted in our adversaries, what point will they not be able to carry? Let him therefore prove this gloss from the train of the prophet's argument itself, and we will believe him. We, however, will prove from the same source that the prophet, when he saw that his teaching of the ungodly, for all his earnestness, was in vain, understood at once that his own word was of no avail unless God should teach it inwardly, and that therefore it was not within the power of man to hear and to will the good. Realizing this, and being in fear of the judgment of God, he beseeches God to correct him with judgment if in anything he needs to be corrected, and not to hand him over to the wrath of God along with the ungodly whom God permits to remain hardened in their unbelief.

However, suppose we do take the passage as referring to a sad or happy turn of events; what if this gloss itself proves a most powerful subverter of free choice? This new subterfuge is, of course, calculated to deceive the simple and innocent into thinking that the matter is settled. It is the same as with those who use that evasion about the necessity of consequence. For they do not see how much rather they are caught and trapped by these evasions, so diverted are they by these novel terms. If, then, the turn of events, in matters which are temporal and over which man has been given dominion ⟨Gen. 1:28⟩, is not in our hands, how, I ask you, can that heavenly reality, the grace of God, be under our control? Can the endeavoring of free choice lay hold of eternal salvation when it cannot keep hold of a farthing or even a hair of our head? If we have not the ability to lay hold of the creature, shall we have the ability to lay hold of the Creator? How crazy can we be? This applies much more to the issue of man's striving after good or evil, because in respect of both good and evil man is much more fallible and has much less freedom than when he strives after money or glory or pleasure. What a spendid piece of evasion, therefore, this gloss has proved to be, which denies man's freedom in relation to little, creaturely events, and asserts it in relation to supreme divine events! It is as if you said: "Codrus can't pay a sou, but he can pay thousands and thousands of pounds!" And I am surprised that Diatribe, who has hitherto so strongly denounced that saying of Wyclif's, that all things take place by necessity, now herself admits that for us the way things turn out is a matter of necessity.

Yet she goes on to say ⟨E., p. 77⟩: "Even if you so twist [this text] as to make it apply to free choice, nobody denies that apart from the grace of God, none can hold straight course in life. Nevertheless, we ourselves meanwhile also strive with all our powers, for we pray daily: 'O Lord my God, make my way straight in thy sight' ⟨Ps. 5:9⟩.[85] One who seeks help does not cease from trying." Diatribe thinks it does not matter at all what she replies, so long as she does not remain silent but says something; then she wants the matter to be regarded as settled, such confidence has she in her own authority. The point to be proved was whether we strive by our own powers, and she proves that one who prays attempts something. I ask you, is she laughing at us, or making fun of the papists? He who prays, prays in the Spirit, or rather the Spirit himself prays in us ⟨Rom. 8:15⟩. How then is the power of free choice proved by the striving of the Holy Spirit? Are free choice and the Holy Spirit the same thing for Diatribe? Are we now arguing about what the Holy Spirit can do? Diatribe therefore leaves me this passage of Jeremiah intact and invincible, and produces only this brainchild [86] of her own: "We too exert ourselves as we are able." And Luther will be forced to believe this, if only he will!

Again ⟨E., p. 77⟩, there is Proverbs ⟨16:1⟩: "It is for man to make ready the heart, but the government of the tongue is from the Lord." This too, she says, "refers to the outcome of events," as if it should be enough for us to have her word for it, without any other authority. And indeed it is more than enough, because granting the reference to "the outcome of events," we have plainly won the day; for as we have just said, when we have no freedom of choice in relation to our own affairs, much less have we any in relation to things divine. But notice her shrewdness: "How is a man to prepare his heart, since Luther says that all things happen by necessity?" I reply: Seeing that, as you say, "the outcome of events" is not under our control, how is a man to make things happen? The answer you give me, you can take as a reply to yourself. That is just the reason why we have to work, because everything future is uncertain for us, as Ecclesiastes ⟨Eccl. 11:6⟩ says:

[85] The Vulgate.   [86] "Sui capitis glossema," "this gloss out of her own head."

"In the morning sow your seed, and at evening withhold not your hand; for you do not know which will prosper, this or that." For us, I say, they are uncertain as regards our knowledge of them, but necessary as regards their happening. The necessity puts the fear of God into us that we may not be presumptuous and complacent, while the uncertainty occasions trust that we may not despair.

But Diatribe returns to her old song ⟨E., p. 77⟩, that a lot of things are said in the book of Proverbs which support free choice; for example: "Commit your work to the Lord." "You hear that?" she says, "your work!" In other words, there are in that book many imperative and subjunctive verbs, and also second person pronouns, and these are the foundations on which the proof of free choice rests, as for example: "Commit"—therefore you can commit; "work"—therefore you can do it. Similarly, you will take "I am your God" to mean: "You make me your God." "Your faith has made you well" ⟨Luke 17:19⟩—do your hear "your"? Explain it to mean "you produce faith"; then you have proved free choice. I am not jesting here, but showing that Diatribe does not take this subject seriously.

The verse in the same chapter: "The Lord has made everything for its purpose,[87] even the wicked for the day of trouble" ⟨Prov. 16:4⟩, she also modifies in her own words, acquitting God of having made any creature evil ⟨E., p. 77⟩; as if I had been speaking of creation and not rather of the unceasing activity of God in created things, an activity whereby he moves also the ungodly, as we said above concerning Pharaoh.

Nor does she think she is cornered by that verse in ch. 20: "The king's heart is in the hand of the Lord; he turns it wherever he will" ⟨Prov. 21:1⟩. ⟨E., p. 77.⟩ "He who 'turns,' "[88] she says, "does not immediately coerce"—as if we were speaking about coercion and not rather about the necessity of immutability. It is the latter that is signified by God's "turning," which is not such a snoring, indolent thing as Diatribe imagines, but is that most active working of God which a man cannot avoid or alter, but under which he necessarily has the sort of will that God has given him, and that God carries along by his own momentum, as I have said above.[89] Then, because Solomon speaks of the heart of a king, Diatribe thinks this passage cannot rightly have a general application, but means what elsewhere Job says: He "makes the hypocrite to reign, on account of the sins of the people" ⟨Job 34:30⟩.[90] Finally, she admits that the king is turned to evil by God, but in such a way that God permits the king to be driven by his passions for the

---

[87] *"Semetipsum"* (Vulg.), "for himself" (Douay).   [88] *"Inclinat."*
[89] See above, p. 140.   [90] The Vulgate.

punishment of his people. I reply: Whether God permits or turns, neither the permitting nor the turning takes place without God's willing and working; for the will of the king cannot escape the action of Almighty God, because everyone's will, whether it is good or evil, is impelled by it to will and to do.

As to our having made a general proposition out of the particular will of the king, I think what we did was neither inapt nor unscholarly. For if the heart of the king, which above all seems to be free and to have control over others, is nevertheless unable to will except in the direction in which God turns it, how much less is any of the rest of men able? And this inference would hold good, not only as drawn from the will of the king, but also from any other man's will. For if any one man, no matter how humble, is unable in the presence of God to will in any other direction than that in which God turns him, the same must be said about all men. Thus the fact that Balaam could not speak as he wished ⟨Num. 23:5 ff.⟩ is a plain argument from the Scriptures that man is not his own master nor the free chooser and doer of what he does; otherwise no Scriptural examples would hold good.

John 15:5, etc.: Free Choice Is "Nothing"—Coram Deo ⟨WA 748–753⟩

After this, and after remarking that the testimonies Luther collects out of Proverbs could be multiplied many times, and that suitably interpreted they could be made to stand either for or against free choice, she at length produces that Achillean [91] and unerring weapon of Luther's, John 15⟨:5⟩: "Apart from me you can do nothing," etc. ⟨E., p. 78.⟩ Even I must applaud the distinguished pleader for free choice who teaches us to adapt the testimonies of Scripture to our taste by suitable interpretations, so that they may truly stand on the side of free choice, or in other words, may serve to prove not what they ought but what pleases us. Next she pretends to be so afraid of one Achillean text that the simple reader, when he sees it overcome, will hold the rest in great contempt. However, I will keep an eye on Diatribe, with her big talk and heroic gestures, to see with what force she will bring down my Achilles, when hitherto she has never managed to hit a common soldier, not even a Thersites,[92] but she has shot her miserable self to pieces with her own weapons. She catches hold, then,

[91] See above, p. 78 n. 41.
[92] Homer, *Iliad* ii.211 ff.—the "barrack-room lawyer" of the Greek army before Troy, treated by Homer (and the noble chieftains) with great contempt.

of this word "nothing," and stabs at it with a multitude of words and examples, and by means of a suitable interpretation reduces it to this, that "nothing" can mean the same as "only a little thing" [93] or "an imperfect thing"; [94] she expounds in other words what the Sophists have hitherto taught regarding this passage: "Apart from me you can do nothing," that is to say, "nothing perfectly."

This long out-of-date and moth-eaten gloss she puts before us with her high-powered rhetoric as something new, insisting on it as if she were the first to think of it and it had never been heard of before, and seeking to display it to us as virtually a miracle; and all the while she is completely self-assured, never giving a thought to the text itself and what precedes and follows it, from which the meaning should be sought. I make no comment on the way she proves, with so many words and examples, that it is possible to take the word "nothing" to mean "only a little thing" or "an imperfect thing" in this passage, as if we were arguing about possibilities, when what should have been proved was whether or not it ought to be so taken. So the whole of this magnificent interpretation achieves nothing more—if it achieves anything at all—than to make that passage of John uncertain and ambiguous. Nor is this surprising, for it is Diatribe's one concern that the Scriptures of God should be everywhere ambiguous so that she may not be obliged to use them, and that the authority of the Fathers should be certain so that she may misuse them. Truly a wonderful religion, in which God's words are useless, men's words useful!

But what is most charming is to see how well she agrees with herself. ⟨E., p. 78.⟩ "Nothing" can be taken as "only a little"; and "in this sense," she says, "it is very true that without Christ we can do nothing, for he is speaking of the fruit of the gospel, which does not come except to those who abide in the Vine, that is, Christ," etc. ⟨John 15:4⟩. Here she herself admits that no fruit is produced unless we abide in the Vine, and she does this in just that "suitable interpretation" by which she proves that "nothing" means the same as "only a little" and "an imperfect thing." But perhaps the adverb "not" should also be "suitably interpreted," to mean that the fruit of the gospel is produced apart from Christ in some measure, or that "only a little" or "an imperfect specimen" of it is produced. In that case, we may preach that the ungodly, apart from Christ, and with Satan reigning in them and fighting against Christ, can produce something of the fruits of life, or in other words, the enemies of Christ can act for Christ—but no more of that.

[93] *"Modicum."*   [94] *"Imperfectum."*

Here I should like to be told how the heretics are to be resisted, who will apply this rule everywhere in the Scriptures, maintaining that "nothing" and "not" are to be taken as signifying "imperfection." For instance: "Without him was not anything made" ⟨John 1:3⟩, i.e., "very little"; or "The fool says in his heart, 'There is no God'" ⟨Ps. 14:1⟩, i.e., there is an imperfect God; or "It is he that hath made us, and not we ourselves" ⟨Ps. 100:3⟩, i.e., we did only a little toward making ourselves. And who knows how many more passages there are in the Scriptures, where "nothing" and "not" occur? Are we to say here: "A suitable interpretation must be sought"? But there is no heretic for whom his own interpretation is not suitable. Really, is this the way to solve knotty problems, by opening a door to such license for corrupt minds and lying spirits? For you who do not give a tinker's curse for the certainty of Holy Scripture, I can well believe such license of interpretation to be convenient; but for us who labor to establish consciences, there can be nothing more inappropriate, nothing more injurious, nothing more pestilential than such convenience.

Listen, therefore, great conqueror of the Lutheran Achilles: Unless you prove that "nothing" in this passage not only can but ought to be taken as "a very little," you will have done nothing with all your profusion of words and examples but fight a fire with dry straw. What have we to do with your "can" when what is required is that you should prove "ought"? And unless you do so, we shall abide by the natural, grammatical meaning of the word, and laugh at both your armies and your triumphs.

What now remains of the "probable opinion," which stated that free choice can will nothing good? But perhaps an appropriate interpretation is finally brought in here, to the effect that "nothing good" means "something good," by a quite novel kind of grammar and logic, according to which what is something is nothing, which for logicians would be impossible because they are contradictories. What has become also of our belief that Satan is the prince of this world, who according to Christ [95] and Paul [96] reigns in the wills and minds of men who are his captive slaves? Is it likely that that roaring lion ⟨I Peter 5:8⟩, that implacable and never-resting foe of the grace of God and of man's salvation, would ever let it come about that man, who is his slave and a part of his kingdom, should strive toward the good with any motion or momentum whereby he might escape his tyranny? Will he not rather spur and urge him on both to will and to do with all his powers what is contrary to grace? Why, even the righteous, who are led by the

[95] John 12:31; 14:30.   [96] Eph. 2:2; 6:12.

Spirit of God, are hard put to resist him and to will and do the good, so savage are his assaults on them.

You, who imagine the human will as something standing on neutral ground [97] and left to its own devices, find it easy to imagine also that there can be an endeavor of the will in either direction, because you think of both God and the devil as a long way off, and as if they were only observers of that mutable free will; for you do not believe that they are the movers and inciters of a servile will, and engaged in most bitter conflict with one another. Let only this be believed, and our thesis stands secure, while free choice is laid low, as we have shown above. For either the kingdom of Satan in man means nothing, and then Christ must be a liar, or else, if his kingdom is as Christ describes it, free choice must be nothing but a captive beast of burden for Satan, which can only be set free if the devil is first cast out by the finger of God ⟨Luke 11:20⟩. From this I think you will sufficiently understand, dear Diatribe, what meaning and importance to attach to the frequent remark of your author (who detests Luther's obstinate habit of asserting), that although Luther supports his case with a mass of quotations from Scripture, these can be dealt with in a single word. For who does not know that all the Scriptures can be dealt with in a single word? We knew this quite well before we ever heard of Erasmus. But the question is whether it is good enough that Scripture should be dealt with in a word. Whether it is rightly dealt with, and whether it ought to be so dealt with—that is the point at issue. Let a man consider this, and he will find out how easy it is to deal with the Scriptures, and how detestable Luther's obstinacy is. He will find, however, not only that words accomplish nothing, but that neither do all the gates of hell ⟨Matt. 16:18⟩.

What therefore Diatribe is unable to do for her affirmative, let us do for the negative—though we are under no obligation to prove a negative; and let us extract an admission from her by the force of the arguments that in this passage "nothing" not only can but ought to be taken, not as "a very little," but as what the word naturally means. And we will do this over and above that invincible argument by which we have already carried the day, namely, that words are always to be used in their ordinary, natural meaning, unless we have proof to the contrary, which Diatribe has neither given nor can give.

We will start operations,[98] then, from the very nature of the case or from the plain fact, which is evidenced by Scriptures that are

[97] *"In medio libero."*   [98] *"Extorquemus autem id primum."*

neither ambiguous nor obscure, that Satan is by far the most cunning and powerful ruler of this world (as we have said), and as long as he reigns the human will is not free nor under its own control, but is the slave of sin and Satan, and can only will what its master wills. Nor will he permit it to will anything good—though even if Satan were not in command of it, sin itself, of which man is the slave, would press heavily enough on him to make him unable to will the good. Moreover, the very next words in the context enforce the same point, though Diatribe treats them with great contempt, despite my having commented on them at considerable length in my *Assertions*. For this is how Christ proceeds in John 15⟨:6⟩: "If anyone does not abide in me, he is cast forth as a branch and withers; and they gather him up and cast him into the fire and he burns." This, I say, Diatribe in her most rhetorical manner has passed over, hoping that her doing so would not be noticed by the dull Lutherans. You see here, however, that Christ himself interprets his own simile of the branch and the Vine, and quite clearly explains what he wishes to be understood by the word "nothing," namely, that a man apart from Christ is cast out and withers. And what else can it mean to be cast out and to wither, but to be consigned to the devil and become continually worse? But to become worse is not the same as being able or endeavoring to do something. A withering branch grows more and more ready for the fire, the more it withers. If Christ himself had not thus expanded and applied this simile, no one would have ventured to expand and apply it so. It is therefore clear that in this passage "nothing" must be taken in the strict sense which the nature of the word suggests.

Now let us look at the passages by which Diatribe proves that "nothing" sometimes stands for "a very little," so that in this connection too we may show that Diatribe is and achieves nothing, and even if she did, it would still be nothing, so thoroughly and completely is she herself nothing. ⟨E., p. 78.⟩ "In common parlance," she says, "that man is said to do nothing who does not achieve the end for which he strives. But he who strives has generally made some progress." I reply: I have never heard this said "in common parlance"; you have taken the liberty of inventing it. Words should be looked at, as they say, from the point of view of the subject matter and the intention of the speaker. No one calls it "nothing" that he does when he endeavors, and if he speaks about "nothing," he is not speaking of the endeavor, but of its result; for this is what a person has in mind when he says: "So and so is doing nothing, or getting nothing done," that is to say,

he is achieving nothing, has not succeeded. Furthermore, supposing your example were valid, which it is not, it makes for us rather
than for you. For what we are contending for, and want firmly
established, is that free choice does many things, but these are
nonetheless "nothing" in the sight of God. What advantage to it
is its endeavoring, if it does not succeed in reaching its goal? So
whichever way she turns, Diatribe runs into trouble and confutes
herself, as is usually the case with those who support a bad cause.

She is similarly unforunate in quoting that example from Paul:
"Neither he who plants nor he who waters is anything, but only
God who gives the growth" ⟨I Cor. 3:7⟩. "That which is of least
moment and in itself useless," she says, "he calls 'nothing.' " ⟨E.,
p. 78.⟩ Who does? Do you, Diatribe, venture to say that the ministry of the Word is in itself useless and of least moment when Paul
everywhere gives it such high praise, and especially in II Cor.
3⟨:6-9⟩, where he calls it the dispensation of life and glory? Once
more you fail to consider either the subject matter or the intention of the speaker. As regards the giving of the growth, the
planter and waterer are nothing, but as regards planting and wa-
tering they are not nothing, seeing that the supreme work of the
Spirit in the Church of God is to teach and to exhort. That is
what Paul means, and that is what his words plainly enough convey. But suppose this absurd example also is valid, again it will
stand on our side. For our contention is this, that free choice is
"nothing," that is, as you expound it, in itself useless, in the sight
of God; for it is this order of being we are speaking about, though
we are not unaware that even an ungodly will is something and
not a mere nothing.

There is also I Cor. 13⟨:2⟩: "If I have not love, I am nothing."
I cannot see why she brings this example in, unless she simply
wants to lengthen her list—or thinks we are short of weapons with
which to run her through. For it is strictly true that a man is nothing in the sight of God if he is without love. And that is precisely
what we teach about free choice; therefore, this example too
stands for us against Diatribe—unless Diatribe still does not know
what we are disputing about. For we are not discussing "being by
nature," but "being by grace" [99] (to put it in current terms) .[1]
We know there are things free choice does by nature, such as eating, drinking, begetting, ruling, so that Diatribe cannot laugh us
out of court with her shrewdly idiotic remark that if we press the
word "nothing," it would not be possible even to sin without
Christ, although Luther has admitted that free choice avails only

[99] *"De esse naturae . . . de esse gratiae."*   [1] *" (Ut vocant) ."*

for sinning. Such is the nonsense Diatribe in her wisdom is pleased to talk, even on a serious subject. For our contention is that man apart from the grace of God remains nonetheless under the general omnipotence of God, who does, moves, and carries along all things in a necessary and infallible course, but that what man does as he is thus carried along is nothing, in the sense that it is worth [2] nothing in the sight of God, and is not reckoned as anything but sin. So in the realm of grace, anyone who is without love is nothing. Why, then, since Diatribe herself admits that in this passage we are concerned with the fruit of the gospel, which is not produced apart from Christ, does she at once shy away from the question at issue and start playing a different tune, with quibbles about natural work and human fruit—unless because no one is ever consistent who is devoid of the truth?

Then there is John 3⟨:27⟩: "A man cannot receive anything unless it is given him from heaven" ⟨E., p. 79⟩. John is speaking of a man, who already surely was something, and he denies that this man receives anything, namely, the Spirit and his gifts—for it was of this he was speaking, not of nature. For he had no need of Madam Diatribe to teach him that a man already has eyes, nose, ears, mouth, hands, mind, will, reason, and everything there is in a man—unless Diatribe thinks the Baptist was so raving that when he used the word "man," he had in mind Plato's chaos, or Leucippus' void, or Aristotle's infinity, or some other nothing which by a gift from heaven might at length become something.[3] This is indeed the way to bring forward examples from the Scriptures, this deliberate tomfoolery in so important a matter! To what purpose, then, is that profusion of words with which she teaches us that fire, our shrinking from evil and inclining toward the good, and the rest, are from heaven, as if anyone did not know these things or denied them? ⟨E., p. 79.⟩ We are talking about grace and, as she herself has said, about Christ and the fruit of the gospel, yet she whiles away the time with stories about nature, dragging out the case and befogging the simple reader. Meanwhile, she not only produces no instance where "nothing" stands for "a very little," as she proposed to do, but she also plainly shows that she neither understands nor cares what Christ or grace may be, or how grace is something other than nature, although even the least intelligent Sophists knew that and made free and constant use of the distinction in their schools; and at the same time she quite fails to see that all her examples support us against her. For the Baptist's

---

2 "*Valere*."
3 The reference is to the cosmogonies of the philosophers named.

saying, that a man can receive nothing unless it is given him from heaven, certainly implies that free choice is nothing. That is how my Achilles is vanquished, when he is furnished by Diatribe with weapons by which she herself, unarmed and defenseless, is dispatched. That is how "in one little word" the Scriptures are explained, with which that obstinate assertor, Luther, supports his case.

Divine Grace and Human Cooperation ⟨WA 753–756⟩

After this she lists a large number of similes, with which she only succeeds as usual in drawing the undiscerning reader's attention to irrelevant matters while completely ignoring the real issue. ⟨E., p. 79.⟩ For instance, God indeed preserves the ship, but the sailor brings it into port; hence the sailor does not do "nothing." This simile implies a division of labor, attributing to God the work of preserving, and to the sailor that of navigating; and if it proves anything, it proves that the whole work of preserving is God's, and the whole work of navigating is the sailor's. Yet it is a beautifully apt simile! It is the same with the farmer who reaps the harvest, when God has given it. Again there are different works for God and man—unless she makes the farmer also the Creator who gives the harvest. But suppose for the moment that the same works are given to God and man, what do these similes achieve? Only that as God works, the creature cooperates with him. But are we now disputing about cooperation, and not rather about the power and the operation that belong to free choice in itself?

Where, then, is our orator running off to, who was going to speak about a palm, but talks of nothing but a gourd? [4] "It started as a wine jar, why does it end as a water jug?" [5] We too know that Paul cooperates with God in teaching the Corinthians ⟨I Cor. 3:9⟩, inasmuch as he preaches outwardly while God teaches inwardly, each doing a different work. He also cooperates with God when he speaks by the Spirit of God ⟨I Cor. 12:3⟩, and both do the same work. For what we assert and contend for is this, that when God operates without regard to the grace of the Spirit, he works all in all, even in the ungodly, inasmuch as he alone moves, actuates, and carries along by the motion of his omnipotence all things, even as he alone has created them, and this motion the creatures can neither avoid nor alter, but they necessarily follow and obey it, each according to its capacity as given it by God; and thus all

---

[4] Apuleius, *Metamorphoses* I.15.   [5] Horace, *Ars poetica* 21 f.

things, even including the ungodly, cooperate with God. Then, when he acts by the Spirit of grace in those whom he has justified, that is, in his Kingdom, he actuates and moves them in a similar way, and they, inasmuch as they are his new creation, follow and cooperate, or rather, as Paul says, they are led ⟨Rom. 8:14⟩. But that is not our subject here.

We are not discussing what we can do through God's working, but what we can do of ourselves; that is to say, whether, created as we are out of nothing, we do or attempt to do anything under the general motion of omnipotence to prepare ourselves for the new creation of the Spirit. Here an answer should have been given, instead of changing the subject. For the answer we give is this: ⟨1⟩ Before man is created and is a man, he neither does nor attempts to do anything toward becoming a creature, and after he is created he neither does nor attempts to do anything toward remaining a creature, but both of these things are done by the sole will of the omnipotent power and goodness of God, who creates and preserves us without our help; but he does not work in us without us, because it is for this he has created and preserved us, that he might work in us and we might cooperate with him, whether outside his Kingdom through his general omnipotence, or inside his Kingdom by the special virtue of his Spirit. (2) In just the same way (our answer continues), before man is changed into a new creature of the Kingdom of the Spirit, he does nothing and attempts nothing to prepare himself for this renewal and this Kingdom, and when he has been recreated he does nothing and attempts nothing toward remaining in this Kingdom, but the Spirit alone does both of these things in us, recreating us without us and preserving us without our help in our recreated state, as also James says: "Of his own will he brought us forth by the word of his power, that we might be a beginning of his creature" ⟨James 1:18⟩—speaking of the renewed creature. But he does not work without us, because it is for this very thing he has recreated and preserves us, that he might work in us and we might cooperate with him. Thus it is through us he preaches, shows mercy to the poor, comforts the afflicted. But what is attributed to free choice in all this? Or rather, what is there left for it but nothing? And really nothing!

Read Diatribe here for five or six pages, where she brings in the above-mentioned sort of similes, and also some very fine texts and parables from the Gospels and Paul, with no other aim than to teach us that there are in the Scriptures (as she says) innumerable passages that speak of the cooperation and help of God. ⟨E., p. 85.⟩

Now, if I gather from these "that man can do nothing without the help of the grace of God, therefore no works of man are good," she by a rhetorical inversion gathers rather the contrary, "that there is nothing man cannot do with the help of the grace of God, and that therefore all the works of man can be good. Hence, all the passages in the Divine Scriptures which speak of help serve also to establish free choice, and they are innumerable. So I have already won the day if the issue is settled by the number of testimonies." So says Diatribe.

Do you think she was quite sober or in her right mind when she wrote this? For I am loath to put it down to her malice and wickedness—unless perhaps she has wanted me to die of unrelieved boredom while she keeps on discoursing, so very characteristically, about subjects other than those she proposed. But if she has been pleased to play the fool in a matter of such importance, we shall be pleased to expose her voluntary fooleries to public contempt.

First, we neither dispute nor are unaware that all the works of man can be good if they are done with the help of the grace of God, and also that there is nothing man cannot do with the help of God's grace. But we cannot get over our amazement at the carelessness with which, after setting out to write about the power of free choice, you write about the power of the grace of God. Then, as if men were stocks and stones, you dare to say in public that free choice is established by the passages of Scripture which commend the help of the grace of God; and not only that, but you even sing your own praises as victor in the most gloriously triumphant tones. Now, I really know from this very word and deed of yours what free choice is and is capable of, namely, madness. What, I ask you, can it be in you that talks like this but free choice itself? Just listen to your inferences: Scripture commends the grace of God, therefore it proves free choice; it commends the help of the grace of God, therefore it establishes free choice. By what sort of logic did you learn to draw these conclusions? Why not the contrary: Grace is preached, therefore free choice is abolished; the help of grace is commended, therefore free choice is destroyed? For what purpose is grace conferred? Is it in order that free choice, which possesses of itself all the vigor it needs, may proudly posture and disport with grace like a superfluous gewgaw at a fair? [6] I therefore invert your conclusion, and though I am no orator, mine is the better rhetoric. However many passages there are in the Divine Scriptures that speak of help, they all abolish free choice; and they are innumerable. So I have won, if the issue is settled by

[6] *"Diebus bacchanalibus."*

the number of testimonies. For the reason why grace is needed, and why the help of grace is given, is that free choice by itself can do nothing, or, as Diatribe herself has put it in that "probable opinion" of hers, it cannot will good. When grace is commended, therefore, and the help of grace is preached, the impotence of free choice is preached at the same time. This is a sound conclusion and a valid inference, against which not even the gates of hell will prevail ⟨Matt. 16:18⟩.

Here we will bring to an end the defense of those arguments of ours which Diatribe has attacked, lest the book grow to an immoderate length. Any that remain, if they are worth noting, will be dealt with among the things we have to assert. For as to what Erasmus repeats in his Epilogue ⟨E., p. 87⟩—that if our view stands, then all the precepts, all the threats, all the promises, are in vain and there is no room left either for merits or demerits, rewards or punishments; and it is difficult to defend the mercy or even the justice of God if God damns those who cannot help sinning,[7] besides other unfortunate consequences, which have so disturbed the greatest minds as to throw them quite off balance—with all these we have already dealt above. We neither accept nor approve that middle way [8] which (in all sincerity, I believe) he recommends to us ⟨E., p. 89⟩, suggesting that we should concede "a tiny bit" [9] to free choice, so that the contradictions of Scripture and the above-mentioned difficulties might be the more easily removed; for by this middle way, not only is the issue not settled, but we are no farther forward. For unless you attribute absolutely everything to free choice, as the Pelagians do, the contradictions of Scripture remain, merit and reward are abolished, the mercy and justice of God are done away, and all the difficulties remain which we seek to avoid by means of a tiny, ineffectual power of free choice, as we have sufficiently shown above. We must therefore go all out and completely deny free choice, referring everything to God; then there will be no contradictions in Scripture, and the difficulties, if not cured, can be endured.

I beg of you, however, my dear Erasmus, not to believe that I am pursuing this case more out of passion than principle. I will not let myself be accused of such hypocrisy as to think one way and write another, and it is not true, as you suggest ⟨E., p. 90⟩, that I have grown so heated in defense of my views as to be now for the first time denying free choice altogether, after having

---

[7] "Necessario peccantes."   [8] "Mediocritatem."   [9] "Perpusillum." (E., p. 90.)

previously attributed something to it—you can show me no such thing in my books, I know. There are theses and treatises of mine in print, in which I have continually asserted, down to the present moment, that free choice is nothing: it is a reality—I used that word then [10]—only in name. It is under conviction of the truth, and as challenged and compelled by the debate, that I have thought and written as I have. As to my having gone about it with some vehemence, I acknowledge the fault, if fault it is; or rather, I greatly rejoice that this testimony is borne to me in the world in the cause of God. And may God himself confirm this testimony at the last day! For no one would be happier than Luther to be commended by the testimony of his time that he had been neither slack nor deceitful in maintaining the cause of truth, but had shown quite enough and even too much vehemence. I should then be blessedly out of reach of Jeremiah's word: "Cursed is he who does the work of the Lord with slackness" ⟨Jer. 48:10⟩.

However, if I seem to be rather too hard on your Diatribe, you must forgive me; for I do it in no malicious spirit, but out of concern because by your authority you have been seriously damaging the cause of Christ, though for all your erudition you have as a matter of fact made out no case at all. Now, who can always so control his pen that it never grows warm? Even you, who in your zeal for moderation are almost frigid in this book, not infrequently hurl fiery and bitter darts, so that unless your reader is very patient and well disposed, you may well seem virulent. But all this has nothing to do with the case, and we ought gladly to pardon one another for such things; for we are human beings, and nothing human is strange to us.[11]

Part VI. A Display of the Forces on Luther's Side

We have come to the last part of this book, in which, as we promised, we must produce our forces against free choice. But we shall not produce all of them; for who could do that in one small book, when the whole of Scripture, every jot and tittle of it, is on our side? Nor is it necessary; on the one hand, because free choice is already vanquished and prostrate by a twofold conquest —once where we prove that everything Diatribe thought to be in its favor is actually against it, and again where we show that the arguments she sought to refute still stand invincible. On the other

---

[10] In the Heidelberg Disputation of 1518 (*WA* 1, 354, 13).
[11] Terence, *Heautontimoroumenos* I.i.25.

hand, even if free choice were not already vanquished, no more than a couple of missiles would be required to lay it low, and that would be enough. For what need is there, when an enemy has been killed by any one shot, to riddle his dead body with a lot more? Now, therefore, we shall be as brief as the subject will allow. And out of our numerous armies we will bring forward two high commanders with a few of their battalions, namely, Paul and John the Evangelist.

St. Paul: Universal Sinfulness Nullifies Free Choice ⟨WA 757–763⟩

This is how Paul, writing to the Romans, enters into an argument against free choice and for the grace of God: "The wrath of God is revealed from heaven against all ungodliness and wickedness of men who in wickedness hold back the truth of God" ⟨Rom. 1:18⟩. Do you hear in this the general verdict of all men, that they are under the wrath of God? What else does this mean but that they are deserving of wrath and punishment? He gives as the reason for the wrath, the fact that they do nothing but what deserves wrath and punishment, because they are all ungodly and wicked, and in wickedness hold back the truth. Where now is the power of free choice to attempt anything good? Paul represents it as deserving the wrath of God, and pronounces it ungodly and wicked. And that which deserves wrath and is ungodly, strives and prevails against grace, not for grace.

There will be smiles here at sleepy old Luther, who has not looked carefully enough at Paul; and someone will say that Paul is not there speaking about all men, nor about all their doings, but only about the ungodly and wicked and, as is expressly stated, those who in wickedness hold back the truth, so that it does not follow that all men are like that. To this I reply that for Paul it makes no difference whether you say "against all ungodliness of men" or "against the ungodliness of all men"; for Paul almost everywhere uses Hebraisms, so that the meaning is: "All men are ungodly and wicked, and in their wickedness they suppress the truth, hence they are all deserving of wrath." Furthermore, in the Greek there is no relative, "of men who," but an article, like this: "The wrath of God is revealed against all ungodliness and wickedness of men the suppressors of the truth in wickedness"; so that the clause translated "who in wickedness hold back the truth" is, as it were, adjectival to "all men," just as the relative clause is adjectival in "our Father who art in heaven," for which an alternative rendering would be "our heavenly Father" or "our Father in

heaven." The objection, on the other hand, is designed to separate out those who believe and are godly.[1]

But all this would be mere empty talk were it not so compellingly confirmed by the drift of Paul's argument itself. For shortly
before, he has said: "The gospel is the power of God for salvation to everyone who has faith, to the Jew first and also to the
Greek" (Rom. 1:16). Here are no obscure or ambiguous words;
"to Jews and Greeks" means that to all men the gospel of the
power of God is necessary in order that they may have faith and
be saved from the wrath that is revealed. I ask you, when he declares that the Jews, rich as they are in righteousness, the law of
God, and the power of free choice, are without distinction destitute
and in need of the power of God to save them from the wrath
that is revealed, and when he makes this power necessary for them,
does he not deem them to be under wrath? What men will you
pick out, then, as not liable to the wrath of God when you are
obliged to believe that the finest men in the world, the Jews and
the Greeks, were in that condition? Again, what exceptions will
you make among the Jews and Greeks themselves when Paul
without any distinction puts them all into one category and brings
them all under the same judgment? Must we suppose that among
these two most distinguished peoples there were not any who aspired to virtue? Did none of them strive with all the might of
their free choice? But Paul pays no attention to this; he puts them
all under wrath, declares them all ungodly and wicked. And must
we not believe that in similar terms the rest of the apostles, each
in his own sphere, consigned all the other nations also to this
wrath?

This passage of Paul's, therefore, stands unyielding in its insistence that free choice, or the most excellent thing in men—even
the most excellent men, who were possessed of the law, righteousness, wisdom, and all the virtues—is ungodly, wicked, and deserving of the wrath of God. Otherwise, Paul's whole argument is
valueless; but if it is not, then the division he makes leaves no
one on neutral ground,[2] when he assigns salvation to those who
believe the gospel, and wrath to all the rest, or takes believers as
righteous and unbelievers as ungodly, wicked, and subject to
wrath. For what he means is this: The righteousness of God is revealed in the gospel as being of faith, so it follows that all men

---

[1] *"Dicitur enim ad differentiam eorum qui credunt et pii sunt."* Unless *"is
qui dicit"* here is the same as *"is qui ridet"* at the beginning of the paragraph, this sentence makes nonsense of its context.
[2] *"Nullum medium."*

are ungodly and wicked. For it would be foolish of God to reveal righteousness to men if they either knew it already or possessed the seeds of it. But seeing that God is not foolish, and yet he reveals to them the righteousness of salvation, it is evident that free choice, even in the highest type of men, neither possesses nor is capable of anything, and does not even know what is righteous in the sight of God—unless perhaps the righteousness of God is not revealed to the highest type, but only to the lowest, despite Paul's boasting that he is under obligation both to Jews and Greeks, wise and foolish, barbarians and Greeks ⟨Rom. 1:14⟩.

Therefore, Paul in this passage lumps all men together in a single mass, and concludes that, so far from being able to will or do anything good, they are all ungodly, wicked, and ignorant of righteousness and faith. And this conclusion indisputably follows from the fact that God reveals to them, as ignorant and sitting in darkness, the righteousness of salvation; for this means that in themselves they are ignorant, and being ignorant of the righteousness of salvation, they are certainly under wrath and damnation, from which in their ignorance they can neither extricate themselves nor even try to. For how can you try, if you do not know what there is to try about, or how, why, and wherefore to try?

With this conclusion, plain fact and experience agree. For show me any one of the whole race of mortals, even if he is the holiest and most righteous of them all, to whom it has ever occurred that the way to righteousness and salvation is the way of faith in One who is both God and man, who for the sins of men both died and rose again and is seated at the right hand of the Father; or show me any who has even dreamed of this wrath of God which Paul here says is revealed from heaven. Look at the greatest philosophers; what have been their thoughts about God, and what have they left in their writings about the wrath to come? Look at the Jews, constantly instructed by so many signs, so many prophets; what do they think of this way? Not only have they not accepted it, but they so hate it that no nation under heaven has more fiercely persecuted Christ, down to the present day. But who would venture to say that among so great a people there was not one who cultivated his free choice and endeavored all he could by its power? How is it, then, that they all endeavor in the opposite direction, and that the most excellent thing in the most excellent men has not only not followed this method of righteousness, and has not only been ignorant of it, but since it has been published and revealed, has actually rejected it with the greatest hatred and sought to destroy it? So much so that Paul in I Cor. 1⟨:23⟩ says that this way is a stumbling block to Jews and folly to Gentiles.

Now, whereas he names Jews and Gentiles without distinction, and it is certain that the Jews and the Gentiles were the principal peoples under heaven, it is at the same time certain that free choice is nothing else but the supreme enemy of righteousness and man's salvation, since there must have been at least a few among the Jews and Gentiles who toiled and strove to the utmost of the power of free choice, yet just by doing so they did nothing but wage war against grace. Now go and say that free choice inclines [3] toward the good, when goodness and righteousness themselves are a stumbling block and foolishness to it! And you cannot say that it applies to some but not to all, for Paul speaks of all without distinction when he says "to Gentiles folly and to Jews a stumbling block" and excepts none but believers. "To us," he says, meaning those who are "called" and "saints" ⟨I Cor. 1:2⟩, it is "the power and wisdom of God" ⟨I Cor. 1:18⟩. He does not say "to some Gentiles and some Jews," but simply "to Gentiles and Jews" who are not of "us"; and thus he separates believers from unbelievers by a clear line of division, leaving no one in between.[4] But we are discussing the Gentiles as they act apart from grace, and it is these to whom Paul says the righteousness of God is a folly that they abhor. So much for the laudable endeavor of free choice toward the good!

Consider, moreover, whether Paul himself is not citing the most outstanding among the Greeks when he says it was the wiser among them who became fools and whose minds were darkened, or who became futile in their reasonings, that is, in their subtle disputations ⟨Rom. 1:21 f.⟩. Tell me, does he not here touch the sublimest achievement of Greek humanity—their reasonings? For this means their best and loftiest ideas and opinions, which they regarded as solid wisdom. But this wisdom, which he elsewhere calls foolish ⟨I Cor. 1:21⟩, he here calls futile, as having succeeded by its many endeavors only in becoming worse, so that at length with darkened minds they worshiped idols and perpetrated the consequent enormities which he records. If, therefore, the noblest effort and achievement of the noblest of the Gentiles is evil and ungodly, what must we think of the rest, the common herd or the lower orders (so to say) of the Gentiles? For even here among the noblest he makes no distinction, but condemns their devotion to wisdom without any respect of persons. And when the achievement or the attempt at it is itself condemned, then all who devote themselves to it are condemned, even though they exercise

---

[3] *"Nititur."*   [4] *"Nullo relicto medio."*

the utmost power of free choice in doing so. Their very best endeavor itself, I say, is asserted to be vicious, so how much more those who engage in it?

In a similar way, he goes on to reject without any distinction the Jews who are literally but not spiritually Jews ⟨Rom. 2:29⟩: "You," he says, "with the letter and circumcision dishonor God" ⟨v. 27⟩. Also: "For he is not a Jew who is one outwardly, but he is a Jew who is one inwardly" ⟨vs. 28 f.⟩. What could be plainer than this division? The outward Jew is a transgressor of the law! Yet how many Jews do you think there were, who though not having faith were most wise, religious, and virtuous men, and men who strove with might and main to attain to righteousness and truth? Why, he frequently bears them testimony, that they have a zeal for God ⟨Rom. 10:2⟩, that they pursue the righteousness of the law ⟨Rom. 9:31⟩, that they earnestly seek night and day to attain to salvation ⟨Acts 26:7⟩, that they live blamelessly ⟨cf. Phil. 3:6⟩. Even so they are transgressors of the law, because they are not Jews spiritually, and they stubbornly resist the righteousness of faith. What then remains but that free choice is worst when it is best, and the more it endeavors the worse it becomes and behaves? The words are plain, the division is certain, there is nothing to contradict it.

But let us hear Paul himself as his own interpreter! In the third chapter, in a sort of peroration, he says: "What then? Are we better off than they? Not at all. For we have argued that Jews and Greeks are all under sin" ⟨Rom. 3:9⟩. Where is free decision now? All, he says, all Jews and Greeks are under sin. Are there any "tropes" or "knots" here? What is the whole world's interpreting worth in face of this clear as possible statement? When he says "all" he excepts none, and when he declares that they are under sin, or in other words, are slaves of sin, he leaves nothing of good in them. But where has he stated this case, that Jews and Gentiles are all under sin? Nowhere but the place we have shown, where he says: "The wrath of God is revealed from heaven against all ungodliness and wickedness of men" ⟨Rom. 1:18⟩. And he goes on to prove this from experience, pointing out that in God's displeasure they have been given up to so many vices, as though these fruits of their own ungodliness convict them of willing and doing nothing but evil.

Then he judges the Jews separately, when he says that the Jew according to the letter [5] is a transgressor, and proves this similarly

---

[5] *"Judaeum litera"*—one who has the outward marks but not the inward spirit of his religion. Cf. Rom. 2:28 f.; II Cor., ch. 3.

by fruits and experience, saying: "You preach against stealing, yet you steal; you abhor idols, yet you commit sacrilege" (Rom. 2:21 f.); and he excepts none at all but those who are Jews according to the Spirit (cf. Rom. 9:6 ff.; Gal. 4:22 ff.). Nor can you get away from this by saying that although they are under sin, yet what is best in them, such as their reason and will, has a bias toward the good. For if a good tendency remains, it is false when he says that they are under sin. For when he names Jews and Gentiles, he includes everything there is in Gentiles and Jews, unless you are going to turn Paul upside down and insist that he wrote: "The flesh of all Jews and Gentiles, that is to say, their lower passions, are under sin." But the wrath that is revealed from heaven against them is going to damn their whole being, unless they are justified through the Spirit; and that would not be the case if they were not with their whole being under sin.

However, let us see how Paul proves his point from Holy Writ, and whether "the words have more polemic force in Paul than in their own context." [6] "As it is written," he says, " 'None is righteous, no, not one, no one understands, no one seeks for God. All have turned aside, together they have become worthless'; no one does good, not even one," and so forth (Rom. 3:10 ff.). Here give me a "suitable interpretation" if you can! Invent tropes, allege that the words are obscure and ambiguous, and defend free choice against these damning sentences if you dare! Then I, too, will willingly yield and recant, and will myself be a confessor and assertor of free choice. It is certain that these things are said of all men, for the prophet represents God as looking down on all men and passing this judgment on them. For so it says in Ps. 13⟨14:2 f.⟩: "The Lord looks down from heaven upon the children of men, to see if there are any that understand or that seek after God; but they have all gone astray," etc. And lest the Jews should think that this did not apply to them, Paul forestalls them with the assertion that it applies above all to them: "We know," he says, "that whatever the law says, it speaks to those who are under the law" (Rom. 3:19). He meant just the same where he said: "To the Jew first, and also to the Greek" (Rom. 2:9 f.). You hear, therefore, that all the children of men, all who are under the law, Gentiles and Jews alike, come under this judgment in the sight of God, that not even one of them is righteous, understands, or seeks after God, but all have turned aside and become worthless. Now, I imagine that among the children of men and those who are under the law there are included also the best and noblest of them, who by the power

---

[6] See above, p. 70.

of free choice strive after virtue and the good, concerning whom Diatribe loudly proclaims that they have an awareness of the good and certain seeds of virtue implanted in them—unless perhaps she maintains that they are children of angels!

How, then, can they strive after the good, when they are totally ignorant of God and neither seek after God nor pay any regard to him? How can they have a power worth anything as a means to the good when they have all turned aside from the good and are altogether worthless? Are we ignorant of what it means to be ignorant of God, not to understand, not to seek after God, not to fear God, to turn aside and become worthless? Are not the words entirely clear, and do not they teach us just this, that all men are devoid of the knowledge of God and full of contempt for him, and they all turn aside to evil and are worthless as regards the good? For it is not a question here of ignorance about where to find food or of contempt for money, but of ignorance and contempt for religion and godliness. And such ignorance and contempt are beyond doubt not in the flesh and the lower and grosser passions but in the highest and most excellent powers of men, in which there ought to reign righteousness, godliness, the knowledge of God and reverence for God. In other words, they are in the reason and the will, and therefore in the power of free choice itself, or in the very seeds of virtue and the most excellent thing there is in man.

Where are you now, friend Diatribe, with the promise you gave earlier that you would willingly agree that the most excellent thing in man is flesh, i.e., ungodly, if this were proved from the Scriptures? Agree now, then, when you hear that the most excellent thing in all men is not only ungodly, but ignorant of God, contemptuous of God, inclined to evil and worthless as regards the good. For what does it mean to be wicked but that the will—which is one of the most excellent things—is wicked? What does it mean to be without understanding of God and the good but that reason —which is another of the most excellent things—is ignorant of God and the good, or is blind to knowledge of godliness? What does it mean to turn aside and become worthless but that men have simply no ability in any part of themselves, and least of all in their most excellent parts, to turn to the good, but only to evil? What does it mean not to fear God, but that in all their parts, and especially the higher ones, men are despisers of God? But to be despisers of God is to be at the same time despisers of all the things of God—his words, works, laws, precepts, and will, for example. What now can reason dictate that is right when it is it-

self blind and ignorant? What can the will choose that is good
when it is itself evil and worthless? Or rather, what choice has the
will when reason dictates to it only the darkness of its own blind
ignorance? With reason in error, then, and the will misdirected,
what can man do or attempt that is good?

But someone will perhaps venture the sophistry that although
the will goes astray and reason is ignorant in actual fact, yet it is
inherently possible for the will to make some attempt at the good
and for reason to know something of the right, since there are
many things we can do which we do not do; and after all, we are
discussing here what is possible, not what actually happens. I
reply that the words of the prophet include both actuality and
potentiality, and to say that a man does not seek for God is the
same as saying that he cannot seek for God. You may gather this
from the fact that if there were a power or ability in man to will
good, then since no inaction or idleness is permitted by the motion of divine omnipotence, as we have shown above, it would be
impossible for it to avoid being set in motion and, at least in one
instance if not more, displayed in some employment. But this is
not what happens, for God looks down from heaven and does not
see even one who seeks or attempts to seek him; hence it follows
that there is nowhere any power which might attempt or wish to
seek him, but instead they all turn aside. Besides, if Paul were not
understood as implying man's impotence, his argument would lose
its point. For his whole concern here is to make grace necessary for
all men. But if they were able to initiate anything of themselves,
there would be no need of grace. As it is, however, they are not
able and therefore they do need grace.

So you see that free choice is completely abolished by this passage, and nothing good or virtuous is left in man, since he is flatly
stated to be unrighteous, ignorant of God, a despiser of God,
turned aside from him, and worthless in the sight of God. The
prophet's words are weighty enough, and not less in their own context than in Paul's quotation of them. It is no small matter to say
that man is ignorant of God and despises God, for these are the
sources of all crimes, the sink of all sins, nay, the hell of all evils.
Could any evil not be there where there is ignorance and contempt of God? In short, the reign of Satan in men could not have
been described in fewer or more expressive terms than by his
saying that they are ignorant of God and despisers of God. That
betokens unbelief, it betokens disobedience, sacrilege, and blasphemy toward God; it betokens cruelty and lack of mercy toward
our neighbor; it betokens love of self in all the things of God and

men. There you have a picture of the glory and power of free choice!

However, Paul goes on to state explicitly that he is speaking of all men, and especially of the best and noblest among them when he says: "So that every mouth may be stopped, and the whole world may be held accountable to God. For no human being will be justified in his sight by works of the law" ⟨Rom. 3:19 f.⟩. Tell me, how can every mouth be stopped if there still remains a power by which we can do something? For we shall be able to say to God: "There is not absolutely nothing here; there is something you cannot condemn, a measure of ability you yourself have given; this at least will not be silenced, and will not be accountable [7] to you." For if the power of free choice is sound and valid, it is not true that the whole world is accountable and guilty before God; for that power is no insignificant affair in an insignificant part of the world, but most conspicuous and most common throughout the whole world, and its mouth ought not to be stopped. Or else, if its mouth ought to be stopped, it must be accountable to God and guilty, together with the whole world. But by what right can it be said to be guilty unless it is unrighteous and ungodly, or in other words, deserving of punishment and retribution? Show me, please, by what interpretation this power of man can be absolved of the guilt with which the whole world is charged before God, or by what device it can be exempted from inclusion in the whole world.

These words of Paul: "All have turned aside, the whole world is guilty, there is none righteous," are mighty rolls of thunder and piercing lightning flashes, and in truth the very "hammer that breaks the rocks in pieces," as Jeremiah calls it ⟨Jer. 23:29⟩, by which everything that exists is shattered, not only in one man or some men or some part of them, but in the whole world and all men without a single exception, so that at these words the whole world ought to tremble, fear, and take to flight. What stronger or graver terms could have been used than that the whole world is guilty, all the children of men are turned aside and worthless, no one fears God, no one is not wicked, no one understands, no one seeks for God? Nevertheless, such was and is the hardness and insensate obstinacy of our hearts that we have neither heard nor felt these thunderings and lightnings, but have set up and extolled free choice and its powers in spite of them all, so that we have truly fulfilled the saying in Mal. 1⟨:4⟩: "They build, but I will tear down."

7 *"Obnoxium."*

Free Choice May Do the Works of the Law but
Not Fulfill the Law ⟨WA 763-769⟩

In similarly grave terms, this also is said: "No human being will be justified in his sight by works of the law" ⟨Rom. 3:20⟩. This is strong language—"by works of the law," just as is also "the whole world" and "all the children of men." For it should be observed that Paul refrains from mentioning persons and speaks of pursuits,[8] which means that he involves all persons and whatever is most excellent in them. For if he had said that the common people of the Jews, or the Pharisees, or certain ungodly people are not justified, it might have been thought that he had left out some who by the power of free choice and the help of the law were not altogether worthless. But when he condemns the works of the law themselves and makes them impious in the sight of God, it is clear that he is condemning all those whose strength lay in their zeal for the law and its works.

But it was only the best and noblest that were zealous for the law and its works, and that only with the best and noblest parts of themselves, namely, their reason and will. If, therefore, those who exerted themselves in respect of the law and works with the utmost zeal and endeavor both of reason and will—in other words, with the whole power of free choice, and were assisted besides by the law itself as with divine aid, finding in it instruction and stimulation—if these, I say, are condemned for ungodliness and, instead of being justified, are declared to be flesh in the sight of God, what is there now left in the whole race of men that is not flesh and not ungodly? For all are alike condemned who rely on works of the law.[9] For whether they have exercised themselves in the law with the utmost zeal or with only moderate zeal or with no zeal at all does not matter in the least. None of them could do anything but perform works of law, and works of law do not justify; and if they do not justify, they prove their doers ungodly and leave them in this condition; and the ungodly are guilty and deserving of the wrath of God. These things are so clear that no one can utter one syllable against them.

But they are in the habit of trying to get round Paul here, by making out that what he calls works of the law are the ceremonial works, which since the death of Christ are deadly. I reply that this is the ignorant error of Jerome,[10] which in spite of Augustine's strenuous resistance—God having withdrawn and let Satan pre-

---

[8] "Studia."   [9] Cf. Gal. 3:10.
[10] Ep. LXXXII.2, 18 (MPL 33.283).

vail—has spread out into the world and persisted to the present day. It has consequently become impossible to understand Paul, and the knowledge of Christ has been inevitably obscured. Even if there had never been any other error in the Church, this one alone was pestilent and potent enough to make havoc of the gospel, and unless a special sort of grace has intervened, Jerome has merited hell rather than heaven for it—so little would I dare to canonize him or call him a saint. It is, then, not true that Paul is speaking only about ceremonial laws; otherwise, how can the argument be sustained by which he concludes that all men are wicked and in need of grace? For someone could say: Granted we are not justified by ceremonial works, yet a person might be justified by the moral works of the Decalogue, so you have not proved by your syllogism that grace is necessary for these. Besides, what is the use of a grace that liberates us only from ceremonial works, which are the easiest of all, and which can at the lowest be extorted from us by fear or self-love? It is, of course, also untrue that ceremonial works are deadly and unlawful since the death of Christ; Paul never said that, but he says they do not justify and are of no advantage to a man in the sight of God as regards setting him free from ungodliness. Once this is accepted, anyone may do them without doing anything unlawful—just as eating and drinking are works that do not justify or commend us to God ⟨I Cor. 8:8⟩, yet a man does nothing unlawful when he eats and drinks.

They are also wrong in that the ceremonial works were as much commanded and required in the old law as was the Decalogue, so that the latter was neither more nor less important than the former. And as Paul is speaking primarily to Jews, as he says in Rom. 1⟨:16⟩, no one need doubt that by works of the law he means all the works of the entire law. For it would be meaningless to call them works of the law if the law were abrogated and deadly, since an abrogated law is no longer a law, as Paul very well knew. He is therefore not speaking of an abrogated law when he speaks of the works of the law, but of the law that is valid and authoritative. Otherwise, how easy it would have been for him to say: "The law itself is now abrogated!"—then we should have had a clear and unambiguous declaration.

But let us appeal to Paul himself as his own best interpreter, where he says in Gal. 3⟨:10⟩: "All who rely on works of the law are under a curse; for it is written, 'Cursed be everyone who does not abide by all things written in the Book of the Law, and do them.' " You see here, where Paul is making the same point in the same words as in the epistle to the Romans, that every time he mentions the works of the law he is speaking of all the laws written in the Book of the Law. And what is more remarkable, he actually quotes Moses, who curses those who do not abide by the law ⟨Deut. 27:26⟩, although he himself preaches that those are accursed who rely on the works of the law. He thus makes two contrary statements, the one being negative, the other affirmative. He can do this, however, because the fact is that in the sight of God those who are most devoted to the works of the law are farthest from fulfilling the law, because they lack the Spirit that is the true fulfiller of the law, and while they may attempt it by their own powers, they achieve nothing. So both statements are true and both types are accursed—those who do not abide by the law, as Moses puts it, and those who rely on works of the law, as Paul puts it; for they each lack the Spirit, without whom the works of the law, no matter how much they are done, do not justify, as Paul says ⟨Rom. 3:20⟩, and therefore they do not abide in all the things that are written, as Moses says ⟨Deut. 27:26⟩.

In short, Paul's division is confirmation enough of what we teach, for he divides men as doers of the law into two classes, putting those who work according to the Spirit in one, those who work according to the flesh in the other, and leaving none in between. For this is what he says: "No flesh will be justified by works of the law" ⟨Rom. 3:20⟩; and what else does this mean but that those of whom he is speaking do the works of the law without the Spirit, because they are "flesh," or ungodly and ignorant of God, and that these works are of no help to them at all? He draws the same distinction in Gal. 3⟨:2⟩, where he says: "Did you receive the Spirit by works of the law, or by hearing with faith?"; and again in Rom. 3⟨:21⟩: "But now the righteousness of God has been manifested apart from law"; and again: "We hold that a man is justified by faith apart from works of law" ⟨Rom. 3:28⟩.

From all this it is unmistakably plain that for Paul the Spirit is opposed to works of law in just the same way as he is to all other unspiritual things and to the whole gamut of powers and pretensions of the flesh. It is thus clear that Paul takes the same view as Christ, who in John 3⟨:6⟩ says that everything not of the Spirit is of the flesh, no matter how splendid, holy, and exalted it may be, even including the very finest works of God's law, no matter with what powers they are performed. For there is need of the Spirit of Christ, without whom all our works are nothing else than damnable. It can be taken as settled, then, that by works of the law Paul means not simply ceremonial works, but all the works of the law in its entirety. With this it will also be settled that everything connected with the works of the law is condemned if it is without the Spirit. And one of the things without the Spirit is that very power of free choice—for this is the matter at issue— which is held to be the most outstanding thing a man has. Now, nothing more excellent can be said of a man than that he is en- gaged in works of the law; and Paul is speaking not of those who are engaged in sins and impiety contrary to the law but of these very ones who are engaged in works of the law, that is to say, the best of men, who are devoted to the law, and who, besides the power of free choice, have the help of the law itself to instruct and inspire them. If, therefore, free choice, assisted by the law and oc- cupying all its powers with the law, is of no avail and does not justify, but remains in the ungodliness of the flesh,[11] what may we suppose it is able to do by itself, without the law?

"Through the law," he says, "comes knowledge of sin" (Rom. 3:20). He shows here how much and how far the law helps. In other words, he shows that free choice by itself is so blind that it is not even aware of sin, but has need of the law to teach it. But what effort to get rid of sin will anyone make who is ignorant of sin? Obviously, he will regard what is sin as no sin, and what is no sin as sin. Experience shows this plainly enough by the way in which the world, in the persons of those whom it regards as the best and most devoted to righteousness and godliness, hates and persecutes the righteousness of God proclaimed by the gospel, call- ing it heresy, error, and other abusive names, while advertising its own works and ways, which in truth are sin and error, as righ- teousness and wisdom. With this text, therefore, Paul stops the mouth of free choice when he teaches that through the law sin is revealed to it as to someone ignorant of his sin. That is how far he is from conceding to it any power of striving after the good.

Here we have also the answer to that question which Diatribe so often repeats throughout her book: "If we cannot do anything, what is the point of so many laws, so many precepts, so many threatenings and promises?" Paul here replies: "Through the law comes knowledge of sin." He replies to this question very differ- ently from the way man or free choice thinks. He denies that free choice is proved by the law and cooperates with it to produce righteousness; for what comes through the law is not righteousness but knowledge of sin. It is the task, function, and effect of the law to be a light to the ignorant and blind, but such a light as reveals sickness, sin, evil, death, hell, the wrath of God, though it affords no help and brings no deliverance from these, but is content to

[11] *"In impietate et carne."*

have revealed them. Then, when a man becomes aware of the disease of sin, he is troubled, distressed, even in despair. The law is no help, much less can he help himself. There is need of another light to reveal the remedy. This is the voice of the gospel, revealing Christ as the deliverer from all these things. It is not reason or free choice that reveals Christ; how should it when it is itself darkness and needs the light of the law to reveal its disease, which by its own light it does not see, but believes to be health?

So also in Galatians ⟨3:19⟩, dealing with the same question, he says: "Why then the law?" He does not, however, reply as Diatribe does, that it proves the existence of free choice, but he says: "It was added because of transgressions, till the offspring should come to whom the promise had been made." It was because of transgressions, Paul says; not meaning, however, that it was in order to put a stop to them, as Jerome dreams,[12] since Paul is arguing that a promise had been given to the future offspring that God would take away and put a stop to sins by the gift of righteousness; but it was in order to increase transgressions, as he says in Rom. 5⟨:20⟩: "Law came in to increase sin." Not that sins were not committed or did not abound without the law, but that they were not known to be transgressions or sins of such grave consequence; on the contrary, most of them and the greatest of them were regarded as righteousness. Now, when sins are unrecognized, there is no room for a remedy and no hope of a cure, because men will not submit to the touch of a healer when they imagine themselves well and in no need of a physician. Therefore, the law is necessary to make sin known so that when its gravity and magnitude are recognized, man in his pride who imagines himself well may be humbled and may sigh and gasp for the grace that is offered in Christ.

Notice how simple the words are: "Through the law comes knowledge of sin"; yet they alone are powerful enough to confound and overthrow free choice. For if it is true that when left to itself it does not know what sin and evil are—as he says both here and in Rom. 7⟨:7⟩: "I should not have known that covetousness is sin if the law had not said, 'You shall not covet,'"—how can it ever know what righteousness and goodness are? And if it does not know what righteousness is, how can it strive toward it? If we are unaware of the sin in which we were born, in which we live, move, and have our being, or rather, which lives, moves, and reigns in us, how should we be aware of the righteousness that reigns outside of us in heaven? These statements make complete

12 *Comment. in Ep. ad Gal.* lib. II.c.3 (*MPL* 26.366).

and utter nonsense of that wretched thing, free choice.

\This being so, Paul speaks with full confidence and authority when he declares: "But now the righteousness of God is manifested apart from law, although the law and the prophets bear witness to it; the righteousness of God, I say, through faith in Jesus Christ for all and upon all who believe in him. For there is no distinction; since all have sinned and fallen short of the glory of God, they are justified by his grace as a gift, through the redemption which is in Christ Jesus, whom God put forward as an expiation by his blood," etc. ⟨Rom. 3:21-25⟩. Paul's words here are absolute thunderbolts against free choice.

First: "The righteousness of God is manifested apart from law." This distinguishes the righteousness of God from the righteousness of the law; for the righteousness of faith comes from grace apart from law. The phrase "apart from law" cannot mean anything else but that Christian righteousness exists apart from the works of the law, in the sense that works of law are utterly useless and ineffective for obtaining it, as he says immediately below: "We hold that a man is justified by faith apart from works of law" ⟨Rom. 3:28⟩, and as he has said above: "No human being will be justified in his sight by works of the law" ⟨Rom. 3:20⟩. From all of which it is very clearly evident that all the devoted endeavors of free choice are worth absolutely nothing. For if the righteousness of God exists apart from law and the works of law, must it not much more exist apart from free choice? Especially as the highest aspiration of free choice is to practice moral righteousness, or the works of the law, with the help afforded by the law to its own blindness and ignorance. This expression "apart from" excludes morally good works; it excludes moral righteousness; it excludes preparations for grace. In a word, imagine whatever you may as being within the power of free choice, Paul will still persist in saying that the righteousness of God remains [13] "apart from" that kind of thing. And suppose I allow that free choice can by its own endeavor achieve something—good works, let us say, or the righteousness of the civil or moral law—yet it does not attain to the righteousness of God, nor does God regard its efforts as in any way qualifying it for his righteousness, since he says that his righteousness functions [14] apart from the law. But if it does not attain to the righteousness of God, what will it gain if by its own works and endeavors (if this were possible) it achieves the very sanctity of angels? The words are not, I think, obscure or ambiguous here, nor is there room for any kind of tropes. For Paul clearly dis-

[13] *"Constat."*   [14] *"Valere."*

tinguishes the two righteousnesses, attributing one to the law and the other to grace, maintaining that the latter is given without the former and apart from its works, while the former without the latter does not justify or count for anything. I should like to see, therefore, how free choice can stand up and defend itself against these things.

A second thunderbolt is his saying that the righteousness of God is revealed and avails for all and upon all who believe in Christ, and that there is no distinction ⟨Rom. 3:21 f.⟩. Once more in the plainest terms he divides the entire race of men into two, giving the righteousness of God to believers and denying it to unbelievers. Now, no one is crazy enough to doubt that the power or endeavor of free choice is something different from faith in Jesus Christ. But Paul denies that anything outside this faith is righteous in the sight of God; and if it is not righteous in the sight of God, it must necessarily be sin. For with God there is nothing intermediate between righteousness and sin, no neutral ground, so to speak, which is neither righteousness nor sin. Otherwise, Paul's whole argument would come to nothing, since it presupposes this division, namely, that whatever is done or devised among men is either righteousness or sin before God: righteousness if faith is present, sin if faith is absent. With men, of course, it is certainly a fact that there are middle and neutral cases, where men neither owe one another anything nor do anything for one another. But an ungodly man sins against God whether he eats or drinks or whatever he does, because he perpetually misuses God's creatures in his impiety and ingratitude, and never for a moment gives glory to God from his heart.

It is also no small thunderbolt when he says: "All have sinned and fall short of the glory of God" and "There is no distinction" ⟨Rom. 3:23, 22⟩. I ask you, could he put it more plainly? Show me a worker of free choice and tell me whether in that enterprise of his he also sins. If he does not sin, why does not Paul make an exception of him? Why does he include him "without distinction"? It is certain that one who says "all," excepts no one in any place, at any time, in any work or endeavor. Hence if you except any man for any kind of effort or work, you make Paul a liar, because the subject of such work and endeavor of free choice is also included in "all," and Paul ought to have had enough respect for him not to place him so freely and without qualification among sinners.

Then there is the statement that they lack the glory of God. You can take "the glory of God" here in two senses, active and passive.

This is an example of Paul's habit of using Hebraisms. Actively, the glory of God is that by which God glories in us; passively, it is that by which we glory in God. It seems to me, however, that it ought to be taken passively here—like "the faith of Christ," which suggests in Latin the faith that Christ has, but to the Hebrew mind means the faith we have in Christ. Similarly, "the righteousness of God" in Latin means the righteousness that God possesses, but a Hebrew would understand it as the righteousness that we have from God and in the sight of God. So we take "the glory of God" not in the Latin but in the Hebrew sense as that which we have in God and before God, and which might be called "glory in God." Now, a man glories in God when he is certain that God is favorable to him and deigns to look kindly upon him, so that the things he does are pleasing in God's sight, or if they are not, they are borne with and pardoned. If, then, the enterprise or endeavor of free choice is not sin, but good in God's sight, it can certainly glory and say with confidence as it glories: "This pleases God, God approves of this, God counts this worthy and accepts it, or at least bears with it and pardons it. For this is the glory of the faithful in God, and those who do not have it are rather put to shame before him." But Paul here denies this, saying that they are completely devoid of this glory. Experience proves that he is right; for ask all the exercisers of free choice to a man, and if you are able to show me one who can sincerely and honestly say with regard to any effort or endeavor of his own, "I know that this pleases God," then I will admit defeat and yield you the palm. But I know there is not one to be found.

Now, if this glory is lacking, so that the conscience dare not say for certain or with confidence that "this pleases God," then it is certain it does not please God. For as a man believes, so it is with him; and in this case he does not believe with certainty that he pleases God, although it is necessary to do so, because the offense of unbelief lies precisely in having doubts about the favor of God, who wishes us to believe with the utmost possible certainty that he is favorable. We thus convict them on the evidence of their own conscience that free choice, when it is devoid of the glory of God, is perpetually guilty of the sin of unbelief, together with all its powers, efforts, and enterprises.

"Congruous" and "Condign" Merit ⟨WA 769–771⟩

However, what will the patrons of free choice say in the end to what follows: "justified by his grace as a gift"? What does "as a gift" mean? What does "by his grace" mean? How do endeavor and merit accord with a righteousness freely bestowed? [15] Perhaps they will say here that they attribute to free choice as little as possible, and by no means condign merit.[16] But these are empty words. For what is sought by means of free choice is to make room for merits. Diatribe has shown this all along by her insistent demand: "If there is no freedom of choice, what room is there for merits? If there is no room for merits, what room is there for rewards? To what are we to ascribe it if a man is justified without merits?" Paul here replies that there is no such thing as merit, but all who are justified are justified freely (*gratis*), and this is to be ascribed to nothing but the grace of God. With the gift of righteousness, moreover, there are given also the Kingdom and eternal life. What about "enterprise" now? What about "earnest striving" and "works"? What about the merits of free choice? What use are they? You cannot complain of obscurity and ambiguity; the facts and the words are very clear and very simple.

For suppose they do attribute as little as possible to free choice, nevertheless they teach that by means of this minimum we can attain to righteousness and grace. Nor have they any other way of solving the problem of why God justifies one man and abandons another than by positing free choice, and inferring that one has endeavored while the other has not, and that God respects the one for his endeavor but despises the other, and he would be unjust if he did anything else. And although they protest both in speech and writing that they do not seek to obtain grace by condign merit,[17] and in fact do not use the term, yet they are only playing a trick on us with the word, and holding on to the thing it signifies just the same. For what excuse is it that they do not call it condign merit, when they attribute to it everything that belongs to condign merit? When they say that the man who endeavors finds favor with God, while the one who does not endeavor does not find favor, is not this plainly a case of condign merit? Are they not making God a respecter of works, merits, and persons? They say that one man lacks grace by his own fault, because he has not striven after it, while the other, because he has striven, obtains grace, as he would not have done if he had not striven. If this is not condign merit, I should like to know what there is that deserves the name. You could play about with any word in this fashion, and say: It is not, of course, condign merit, but it has the

---

[15] "*Gratuita et donata.*"
[16] "*Meritum condignum.*" On these terms, see Introduction, p. 25, and cf. below, p. 321.
[17] "*Condigno merito.*"

same effect as condign merit; the thorn is not a bad tree, but only produces the fruit of a bad tree; the fig is not a good tree, but it produces what a good tree usually does.[18] Diatribe is not indeed ungodly, though she speaks and acts only as an ungodly person does.

For these advocates of free choice, it turns out as the proverb says: "In avoiding Charybdis he runs into Scylla." [19] For in their anxiety not to agree with the Pelagians, they start denying condign merit, and by their very denial they establish it more firmly than ever. They deny it in the words they speak and write, but affirm it in fact and in their hearts, and they are on two accounts worse than the Pelagians. First, because the Pelagians confess and assert condign merit, simply, candidly, and ingenuously, calling a spade a spade [20] and a fig a fig, and teaching what they really believe. These friends of ours, however, though they believe and teach the same, make dupes of us with deceptive words and a false pretense, as if they dissented from the Pelagians, though this is the last thing they do; so that if you go by their hypocrisy, they seem to be the bitterest foes of the Pelagians, while if you look at the facts and their real opinion, they themselves are Pelagians double-dyed. The second reason is that by this hypocrisy they both value and purchase the grace of God for far less than the Pelagians. For the latter do not assert that there is a tiny little something in us by which we can attain to grace, but that there are whole, full, perfect, great, and many efforts and works. But our friends say that it is a very little thing, and almost nothing, by which we merit grace.

If we must have error, then, there is more honesty and less pride in the error of those who say that the grace of God costs a great deal, and so hold it dear and precious, than of those who teach that it costs only a trifling amount, and so hold it cheap and contemptible. But Paul kills both these birds with one stone when he says that all are justified freely, or again, are justified apart from law and works of law. For when he asserts that justification is freely bestowed on all who are justified, he leaves no one to work, or earn, or prepare himself, and he leaves no work that can be called congruous or condign; and thus by a single stroke of this thunderbolt he shatters both the Pelagians with their total merit, and the Sophists with their little scrap of merit. Free justification allows of no workers, because there is an obvious contradiction between "freely given" and "earned by some sort of work." Be-

---

[18] Cf. Matt. 7:16 f.

[19] Gualtherus ab Insulis, *Alexandreis* i.301: *"Incidis in Scyllam, cupiens vitare Charybdim."*

[20] *"Scapham scapham,"* literally: "a boat a boat."

sides, justification by grace excludes consideration of anyone's personal worthiness, as he says below in ch. 11: "If it is by grace, it is no longer on the basis of works; otherwise grace would no longer be grace" ⟨Rom. 11:6⟩. He says the same in ch. 4: "Now to one who works, his wages are not reckoned as a gift, but as his due" ⟨Rom. 4:4⟩. Thus my Paul, unconquerable conqueror of free choice that he is, wipes out two armies with a single word. For if we are justified "apart from works," then all works are condemned, whether small or great, for he makes no exception but thunders equally against all.

You will notice here how unobservant all these friends of ours are, and what good it does to rely on the venerable old Fathers, who have been approved through such a long succession of ages. Were not they too all equally blind, or rather, did they not simply overlook the clearest and most explicit statements of Paul? Can anything, I ask you, be said clearly and explicitly in defense of grace against free choice if Paul's language here is not clear and explicit? He first extols grace by contrasting it with works, and then in the clearest and simplest terms he states that we are justified freely, and that grace would not be grace if it were earned by works, so that he quite unmistakably excludes all works in the matter of justification in order to establish grace alone and free justification. Yet with all this light we still search for darkness, and when we cannot claim large and all-inclusive things for ourselves, we try to claim little modest things, just to ensure that justification by the grace of God shall not be free and apart from works. As if he who denies us all the important things will not even more deny that the little modest things help us in any way toward justification, when he has laid it down that we are justified only by his grace apart from all works, and therefore apart from the law itself, in which all works, great and small, congruous and condign, are included. Now go and boast of your ancient authorities, and rely on what they say, when you see that they have one and all overlooked the clearest and plainest teaching of Paul as if they deliberately shunned this morning star, or rather this sun, because of the carnal notion they doubtless entertained that it would be absurd to have no place left for merits.

The Righteousness of Works and of Faith; and a Summary of St. Paul's Testimony Against Free Choice ⟨WA 771–776⟩

Let us take a look here at what Paul says later about the example of Abraham ⟨Rom. 4:1-3⟩. "If Abraham," he says, "was justified by works, he has something to boast about, but not before God. For what does the Scripture say? 'Abraham believed God, and it was reckoned to him as righteousness.' " Please notice here too the distinction Paul makes by referring to a twofold righteousness of Abraham.

First, there is the righteousness of works, or moral and civil righteousness; but he denies that Abraham is justified in God's sight by this, even if he is righteous in the sight of men because of it. With this righteousness, he has indeed something to boast about before men, but like the rest he falls short of the glory of God. Nor can anyone say here that it is the works of the law, or ceremonial works, that are being condemned, seeing that Abraham lived so many years before the law was given. Paul is speaking simply about the works Abraham did, and the best ones he did. For it would be absurd to argue as to whether anyone is justified by bad works. If, therefore, Abraham is not righteous because of any works, and if both he himself and all his works remain in a state of ungodliness [21] unless he is clothed with another righteousness, namely, that of faith, then it is plain that no man is brought any nearer to righteousness by his works; and what is more, that no works and no aspirations or endeavors of free choice count for anything in the sight of God, but are all adjudged to be ungodly, unrighteous, and evil. For if the man himself is not righteous, neither are his works or endeavors righteous; and if they are not righteous, they are damnable and deserving of wrath.

The other kind of righteousness is the righteousness of faith, which does not depend on any works, but on God's favorable regard and his "reckoning" on the basis of grace. Notice how Paul dwells on the word "reckoned," how he stresses, repeats, and insists on it. "To one who works," he says, "his wages are not reckoned as a gift but as his due. And to one who does not work but has faith in him who justifies the ungodly, his faith is reckoned as righteousness, according to the plan of God's grace" ⟨ Rom. 4:4 f.⟩.[22] Then he quotes David as saying the same about the "reckoning" of grace: "Blessed is the man against whom the Lord will not reckon his sin," etc. ⟨Rom. 4:6 ff.⟩. He repeats the word "reckon" nearly ten times in this chapter. In short, Paul sets the one who works and the one who does not work alongside each other, leaving no room for anyone between them; and he asserts that righteousness is not reckoned to the former, but that it is

[21] *"Sub impietate."*
[22] The phrase "according to the plan of God's grace" is the reading of the Clementine Vulgate.

reckoned to the latter provided he has faith. There is no way of escape for free choice here, no chance for it to get away with its endeavoring and striving. It must be classed either with the one who works or with the one who does not work. If it is classed with the former, so you are told here, it does not have any righteousness reckoned to it, whereas if it is classed with the latter—the one who does not work but has faith in God—then it does have righteousness reckoned to it. But in that case it will no longer be a case of free choice at work, but of a being created anew through faith.

Now, if righteousness is not reckoned to the one who works, then clearly his works are nothing but sins, evils, and impieties in the sight of God. Nor can any impudent Sophist break in here with the objection that a man's work need not be evil, even if the man himself is evil. For Paul purposely speaks, not simply of the man as a man, but of the man as a worker, in order to make it unmistakably plain that the man's works and endeavors themselves are condemned, no matter what their nature, name, or sign may be. It is, however, with good works that he is concerned, since he is arguing about justification and merit. Hence although with the phrase "one who works" he refers quite generally to all workers and all their works, it is particularly of their good and virtuous works that he is speaking. Otherwise, there would be no point in his distinction between the "one who works" and the "one who does not work."

I will not here elaborate the very strong arguments that can be drawn from the purpose of grace, the promise of God, the meaning of the law, original sin, or divine election, any one of which would be sufficient by itself to do away completely with free choice. For if grace comes from the purpose or predestination of God, it comes by necessity and not by our effort or endeavor, as we have shown above. Moreover, if God promised grace before the law was given, as Paul argues here and in Galatians, then grace does not come from works or through the law; otherwise the promise means nothing. So also faith will mean nothing—although Abraham was justified by it before the law was given—if works count for anything. Again, since the law is the power of sin ⟨I Cor. 15:56⟩ in that it serves only to reveal and not to remove sin, it makes the conscience guilty before God, and threatens it with wrath. That is what Paul means when he says: "The law brings wrath" ⟨Rom. 4:15⟩. How, then, could there be any possibility of attaining righteousness through the law? And if we receive no help from the law, what help can we expect from the power of choice alone?

Furthermore, seeing that through the one transgression of the one man, Adam, we are all under sin and damnation, how can we attempt anything that is not sinful and damnable? For when he says "all," he makes no exception either of the power of free choice or of any worker, but every man, whether he works or not, endeavors or not, is necessarily included among the "all." Not that we should sin or be damned through that one transgression of Adam if it were not our own transgression. For who could be damned for another's transgression, especially before God? It does not, however, become ours by any imitative doing of it ourselves, for then it would not be the one transgression of Adam, since it would be we and not Adam who committed it; but it becomes ours the moment we are born—a subject we must deal with some other time. Original sin itself, therefore, leaves free choice with no capacity to do anything but sin and be damned.

These arguments, I say, I will not elaborate, both because they are so very obvious and so very substantial, and also because we have already said something about them earlier in the book. But if we wished to list all the points made by Paul alone by which free choice is overthrown, we could not do better than make a running commentary on the whole of Paul, showing how the much vaunted power of free choice is refuted in almost every word. I have already done this with the third and fourth chapters,[23] on which I have chiefly concentrated in order to expose the inattentiveness of all these friends of ours who have a way of reading Paul that enables them to find, even in his clearest passages, anything but these very strong arguments against free choice. I also wanted to show the foolishness of the confidence they repose in the authority and writings of the ancient doctors, and to leave them to consider what the effect of these most evident arguments must be if they are treated with due care and judgment.

For my own part, I confess to being greatly astonished. Paul again and again uses these universal terms, "all," "none," "not," "nowhere," "apart from"—for example: "All have turned aside"; "None is righteous"; "No one does good, not even one"; "All are sinners and damned through one man's transgression"; "We are justified by faith, apart from law, apart from works"—so that although one might wish to put it differently, he could not speak more clearly and plainly. Hence I am, as I say, astonished that in face of these universal words and sentences, contrary and even contradictory ideas have come to prevail, such as: "Some have not turned aside, are not unrighteous, not evil, not sinners, not damned," and "There is something in man that is good and strives

[23] Of the epistle to the Romans.

after the good"—as if the man that strives after the good, whoever he may be, were not included in the words "all," "none," "not"!

I should not myself find it possible, even if I wished, to make any objection or reply to Paul, but should have to regard my power of free choice, endeavors and all, as included in those "alls" and "nones" of which Paul speaks, unless a new kind of grammar or a new use of language were introduced. It might have been possible to suspect a trope and give a twist to the words I have cited if Paul had used this kind of expression only once or in only one passage; but in fact he uses it continually, both in the affirmative and the negative form, treating his theme through a polemical partition of categories which on both sides have universal application.[24] In consequence, not only the natural sense of the words and the actual statement he makes, but both the immediate and wider context and the whole purpose and substance of his argument lead alike to the conclusion that what Paul means to say is that apart from faith in Christ there is nothing but sin and damnation—it was in this way that we promised we would refute free choice, so that all our opponents would be unable to resist; and I think I have done it, even though they will neither admit defeat and come over to our view, nor yet keep silence. That is not within our power; it is the gift of the Spirit of God.

However, before we hear John the Evangelist, let us add a crowning touch from Paul—and if that is not enough, we are prepared to bring out the whole of Paul against free choice, commenting on him verse by verse. In Rom. 8⟨:5⟩: where he divides the human race into two types, namely, flesh and spirit (just as Christ does in John 3⟨:6⟩) , he says: "Those who live according to the flesh set their minds on the things of the flesh, but those who live according to the Spirit set their minds on the things of the Spirit." That Paul here calls carnal all who are not spiritual is evident both from this very partition and opposition between spirit and flesh, and from his own subsequent statement: "You are not in the flesh but in the Spirit if the Spirit of God really dwells in you. Anyone who does not have the Spirit of Christ does not belong to him" ⟨Rom. 8:9⟩. What else is the meaning of "You are not in the flesh if the Spirit of God is in you" but that those who do not have the Spirit are necessarily in the flesh? And if anyone does not belong to Christ, to whom else does he belong but Satan? Clearly, then, those who lack the Spirit are in the flesh and subject to Satan.

[24] *"Sententiam per contentionem et partitionem utrobique universalium partium—tractat."*

Now let us see what he thinks of the endeavor and power of free choice in those he calls carnal. "Those who are in the flesh cannot please God" ⟨Rom. 8:8⟩. And again: "The mind of the flesh is death" ⟨v. 6⟩. And again: "The mind of the flesh is enmity toward God" ⟨v. 7⟩. Also: "It does not submit to God's law, indeed it cannot" ⟨v. 7⟩. Here let the advocate of free choice tell me this: how something that is death, displeasing to God, hostility toward God, disobedient to God, and incapable of obedience can possibly strive toward the good? For Paul did not choose to say simply that the mind of the flesh is "dead" or "hostile to God," but that it is death itself, hostility itself, which cannot possibly submit to God's law or please God, just as he had said a little before: "For what was impossible to the law, in that it was weak because of the flesh, God has done," etc. ⟨v. 3⟩.

I, too, am familiar with Origen's fable about the threefold disposition of flesh, soul, and spirit, with soul standing in the middle and being capable of turning either way, toward the flesh or toward the spirit. But these are dreams of his own; he states but does not prove them. Paul here calls everything flesh that is without the Spirit, as we have shown. Hence the loftiest virtues of the best of men are in the flesh, that is to say, they are dead, hostile to God, not submissive to the law of God and not capable of submitting to it, and not pleasing to God. For Paul says not only that they do not submit, but that they cannot. So also Christ says in Matt. 7⟨:18⟩: "A bad tree cannot bear good fruit," and in ch. 12⟨:34⟩: "How can you speak good when you are evil?" You see here not only that we speak evil, but that we cannot speak good. And although he says elsewhere that we who are evil know how to give good gifts to our children ⟨Matt. 7:11⟩, yet he denies that we do good even when we give good gifts, because although what we give is a good creation of God, we ourselves are not good, nor do we give these good things in a good way; and he is speaking to all men, including his disciples. Thus the twin statements of Paul are confirmed, that the righteous live by faith ⟨Rom. 1:17⟩, and that whatsoever is not of faith is sin ⟨Rom. 14:23⟩. The latter follows from the former, for if there is nothing by which we are justified but faith, it is evident that those who are without faith are not yet justified; and those who are not justified are sinners; and sinners are "bad trees" and cannot do anything but sin and "bear bad fruit." Hence, free choice is nothing but a slave of sin, death, and Satan, not doing and not capable of doing or attempting to do anything but evil.

Take also the example in ch. 10 ⟨Rom. 10:20⟩, quoted from

Isaiah: "I have been found by those who did not seek me; I have shown myself to those who did not ask for me" (Isa. 65:1). He says this with reference to the Gentiles, because it has been given to them to hear and to know Christ, though previously they could not even think of him, much less seek him or prepare themselves for him by the power of free choice. From this example it is clear enough that grace comes so freely that no thought of it, let alone any endeavor or striving after it, precedes its coming. It was the same also with Paul when he was Saul. What did he do with his wonderful power of free choice? He certainly gave his mind to very good and virtuous things from the point of view of reason. But observe by what endeavor he finds grace! Not only does he not seek it, but he receives it even while raging furiously against it. On the other hand, he says concerning the Jews in ch. 9 (Rom. 9:30): "Gentiles who did not pursue righteousness have attained it, that is, righteousness through faith; but Israel who pursued the righteousness which is based on law did not succeed in fulfilling that law." What murmur can any defender of free choice raise against this? The Gentiles, just when they are full of ungodliness and every kind of vice, receive righteousness freely by the mercy of God, while the Jews, who devote themselves to righteousness with the utmost zeal and endeavor, are frustrated. Does not this simply mean that the endeavoring of free choice is in vain, even when it strives after the best, and that of itself it rather "speeds toward the worse, and backward borne glides from us"? [25] Nor can anyone say that they did not strive with the utmost power of free choice. Paul himself bears them witness in ch. 10, "that they have a zeal for God, but it is not enlightened" (Rom. 10:2). Therefore, nothing is lacking in the Jews that is attributed to free choice, and yet nothing comes of it, or rather, the opposite comes of it. In the Gentiles there is nothing to be found of what is attributed to free choice, and yet the righteousness of God results. What is this but a confirmation by the unequivocal example of the two nations and the clearest possible testimony of Paul that grace is given freely to those without merits and the most undeserving, and is not obtained by any efforts, endeavors, or works, whether small or great, even of the best and most virtuous of men, though they seek and pursue righteousness with burning zeal?

[25] Vergil, *Georgics* i.200.

St. John: Free Choice Is of "the World," "the Flesh"; Grace Is of Christ, by Faith. The Two Are Opposites ⟨WA 776–783⟩

Let us now come to John, who is also an eloquent and powerful devastator of free choice. At the very outset, he represents free choice as so blind that it cannot even see the truth, let alone be able to strive toward it. For he says: "The light shines in the darkness, but the darkness does not comprehend it" ⟨John 1:5⟩; and shortly afterward: "He was in the world, and the world knew him not. He came to his own, and his own received him not" ⟨vs. 10 f.⟩. What do you think he means by "world"? Will you exempt any man from this description unless he has been recreated by the Holy Spirit? It is characteristic of this apostle to use this word "world" to mean precisely the whole race of men. Hence, whatever he says about the world applies also to free choice as the most excellent thing in man. Thus according to this apostle, the world does not know the light of truth ⟨v. 10⟩, the world hates Christ and those who are his ⟨John 15:18 f.⟩, the world neither knows nor sees the Holy Spirit ⟨John 14:17⟩, the whole world is in the power of the evil one ⟨I John 5:19⟩, all that is in the world is the lust of the flesh and the lust of the eyes and the pride of life ⟨I John 2:16⟩. "You," he says, "are of the world" ⟨John 8:23⟩. "The world cannot hate you, but it hates me because I testify of it that its works are evil" ⟨John 7:7⟩. All these and many similar passages proclaim the glories of free choice, that principal part of the world and that which governs it under the overlordship of Satan.

For John too speaks of the world antithetically, so that "world" means everything that has not been taken out of the world into the Spirit, as Christ says to the apostles: "I took you out of the world and appointed you," etc. ⟨John 15:16, 19⟩. If now there were any in the world who were endeavoring toward the good (which should be the case if free choice were able to do anything), John ought surely to have limited the word out of respect for these people, so as not to implicate them, by using a general term in all the evils of which he accuses the world. As he does not do this, it is evident that he makes free choice guilty of all the charges brought against the world, since whatever the world does, it does by the power of free choice, or in other words, by means of reason and will, which are its most notable components.

He goes on: "To all who received him, who believed in his name, he gave power to become children of God; who were born, not of blood nor of the will of the flesh nor of the will of man, but of God" ⟨John 1:12 f.⟩. By this absolute distinction he drives out of the Kingdom of Christ "blood," "the will of the flesh," "the will of man." I think "blood" means the Jews, that is, those who claimed to be sons of the Kingdom because they were sons of Abraham and the Patriarchs, and thus gloried in their blood. The "will of the flesh" I take to mean the zeal with which the people devoted themselves to the law and works. For "flesh" here means those who are carnal and without the Spirit, so that although they certainly have the ability to will and endeavor, they do so, in the absence of the Spirit, in a carnal way. The "will of man" I understand as the strivings of all men generally, whether under the law or without the law, Gentiles or whatever they may be, so that the meaning is: "They become sons of God neither by natural birth [26] nor by zeal for the law nor by any other human doing,[27] but only by a divine birth." If therefore they are not born of the flesh, nor trained by the law, nor prepared by any human discipline, but are born anew from God, it is plain that free choice counts for nothing here. For I think the word "man" [28] in this passage is to be taken in the Hebrew sense as meaning any and every man, just as "flesh" is understood in contrast with Spirit to mean the people without the Spirit; and the "will" I take to be the highest power in men, as the principal element in free choice.

But supposing we do not so understand the individual terms, the matter itself as a whole is quite clear. For by his division John rejects everything that is not born of God, inasmuch as he says we do not become sons of God except by being born of God; and this takes place, as he himself explains, by believing in the name of Christ. In this rejection, moreover, the will of man, or free choice, being neither a birth from God nor faith, is necessarily included. But if free choice were worth anything, the will of man ought not to be rejected by John, nor should men be drawn away from it and directed to faith and the new birth alone; otherwise, the word of Isaiah would apply to him: "Woe to you who call good evil" ⟨Isa. 5:20⟩. As it is, since he rejects equally blood, the will of the flesh, and the will of man, it is certain that the will of man can no more do anything toward making men sons of God than can blood or carnal birth. But no one doubts that carnal birth does not make men sons of God. As Paul says in Rom. 9⟨:8⟩: "It is not the children of the flesh who are the children of God," and he proves this by the example of Ishmael and Esau.

The same John introduces the Baptist speaking thus of Christ: "And of his fullness we have all received, grace for grace" ⟨John 1:16⟩. He says that grace has been received by us from the fullness

---

[26] *"Nativitate carnis."*   [27] *"Studio humano."*   [28] *"Virum."*

of Christ; but for what merit or effort? "For grace," he says, meaning Christ's grace; just as Paul also says in Rom. 5⟨:15⟩: "The grace of God and the free gift in the grace of that one man Jesus Christ abounded for many." Where is now the endeavor of free choice by which grace is obtained? John says here, not only that grace is not received by any effort of ours, but that it is received through another's grace or another's merit, namely, that of the one man Jesus Christ. It is therefore either false that we receive our grace in return for another's grace, or else it is evident that free choice counts for nothing. For we cannot have it both ways; the grace of God cannot be both so cheap as to be obtainable anywhere and everywhere by any man's puny endeavor, and at the same time so dear as to be given us only in and through the grace of one Man and so great a Man. I wish the defenders of free choice would take warning at this point, and realize that when they assert free choice they are denying Christ. For if it is by my own effort that I obtain the grace of God, what need have I of the grace of Christ in order to receive it? Or what do I lack when I have the grace of God?

Now, Diatribe has said, and all the Sophists say, that we secure grace and prepare ourselves to receive it by our own endeavor, even if not "condignly," yet at least "congruously." [29] This is plainly a denial of Christ, when it is for his grace that we receive grace, as the Baptist testifies. For I have already exposed that fiction about "condign" and "congruous," showing that these are empty words, and that what they really have in mind is the merit of worthiness, [30] and this to a more ungodly degree than the Pelagians themselves, as we said. [31] The result is that the ungodly Sophists and Diatribe alike deny the Lord Christ who bought us, more than the Pelagians or any heretics ever denied him. So little can grace tolerate the power of free choice or even the slightest hint of it. The fact that the defenders of free choice deny Christ is proved, moreover, not only by this Scripture but also by their very way of life. For they have turned Christ from a kindly Mediator into a dreaded Judge for themselves, whom they strive to placate by the intercessions of his mother and the saints, and by a multitude of invented works, rites, religious orders, and vows, in all of which their aim is to placate Christ so that he may give them grace. They do not believe that Christ is their advocate with God, and obtains grace for them by his own blood, and as it says here, "grace for grace" ⟨John 1:16⟩. And as they believe, so it is with

[29] "Non de condigno, sed de congruo." Cf. above, p. 51.
[30] "Condignum meritum."   [31] On p. 311.

them. Christ is truly and deservedly an inexorable Judge to them, inasmuch as they abandon him as a Mediator and most merciful Savior, and count his blood and his grace of less value than the efforts and endeavors of free choice.

Let us look also at an example of free choice. Nicodemus (John 3:1 ff.) surely is a man who leaves nothing to be desired as regards the capabilities of free choice; for what is there that he fails to do in the way of effort or endeavor? He confesses that Christ is true and has come from God; he praises His signs, he comes by night to hear Him and converse with him. Does he not seem to have sought by the power of free choice the things that belong to godliness and salvation? Yet see how he comes to grief. When he hears the true way of salvation by means of a new birth as taught by Christ, does he recognize it or profess that it is what he himself has been seeking? On the contrary, he is so shocked and perturbed that he not only says he cannot understand it, but he rejects it as impossible. "How," he says, "can this be?" (John 3:9). Nor indeed is it surprising, for whoever heard that a man must be born anew of water and the Spirit in order to be saved? (v. 5). Whoever thought that the Son of Man would have to be lifted up, that whosoever believes in him should not perish but have eternal life? (vs. 14 ff.). Did the greatest and most discerning philosophers ever make mention of this? Did the princes of this world ever possess this knowledge? Did any man's free choice ever strive toward this? Does not Paul confess it to be "wisdom hidden in a mystery" (I Cor. 2:7), which though foretold by the prophets and revealed by the gospel, has yet from eternity been kept secret and unknown to the world (Rom. 16:25)?

What can I say? Let us ask experience. The whole world, human reason itself, indeed free choice itself, is obliged to confess that it never knew Christ nor heard of him before the gospel came into the world. And if it did not know him, much less did it seek after him, or even could seek after him or make any endeavor to come to him. Yet Christ is the way, the truth, the life, and salvation (John 14:6). It must therefore confess, willy-nilly, that by its own powers it has been unable either to know or to seek after the things that pertain to the way, the truth, and salvation. Nevertheless, despite this confession and our own experience, we insanely argue with empty words that there still remains in us a power capable of both knowing and applying itself to the things that pertain to salvation. That is as good as saying it can know Christ the Son of God lifted up for us, although no one has ever known or been able to think of such a thing. So ignorance here is no longer ignorance, but knowledge of Christ, that is, of the things that pertain to salvation. Do you still not see and feel that the assertors of free choice are clearly mad when they call a thing knowledge that they themselves admit to be ignorance? Is not this putting darkness for light, as Isaiah says ⟨Isa. 5:20⟩? To think that God so mightily stops the mouth of free choice by its own confession and experience, yet not even so can it keep silence and give God the glory!

Furthermore, when Christ is called the way, the truth, and the life ⟨John 14:6⟩, and that antithetically, so that whatever is not Christ is not the way but error, not the truth but a lie, not the life but death, then it necessarily follows that free choice, since it is neither Christ nor in Christ, is included in the error, the lie, and the death. Where and whence, then, have we that intermediate and neutral thing, the power of free choice, which although it is not Christ or the way, the truth, and the life, must still not be error, or a lie, or death? For unless everything said about Christ and grace were said antithetically, so as to be set over against its opposite—for instance, that outside of Christ there is nothing but Satan, apart from grace nothing but wrath, apart from light only darkness, apart from the way only error, apart from the truth only a lie, apart from life only death—what, I ask you, would be the point of all the discourses of the apostles and of Scripture as a whole? They would all be in vain, because they would not insist on the absolute necessity of Christ, which in fact is their chief concern; and they would not do so because some intermediate thing would be found, which of itself would be neither evil nor good, neither Christ's nor Satan's, neither true nor false, neither alive nor dead, perhaps even neither something nor nothing, and that would be called "the most excellent and exalted thing in the whole race of men"!

Choose then which you please. If you grant that the Scriptures speak antithetically, you will be able to say nothing about free choice but what is contrary to Christ, namely that error, death, Satan, and all evils reign in it. If you do not grant that they speak antithetically, then you enervate the Scriptures, so that they lose their point and fail to prove that Christ is necessary. Hence, inasmuch as you maintain free choice, you cancel out Christ and ruin the entire Scripture. Moreover, although verbally you may make a show of confessing Christ, yet in reality and in your heart you deny him. Or if the power of free choice is not wholly in error or damnable, but sees and wills what is virtuous and good and what pertains to salvation, then it is in sound health and has no need of Christ the physician ⟨Matt. 9:12⟩, nor has Christ redeemed that part of man; for what need of light and life is there where there is light and life? And if that part has not been redeemed by Christ, the best thing in man has not been redeemed, but is good and is saved by itself.[32] But then God is unjust if he damns any man, because he damns what is best and soundly healthy in man, or in other words, he condemns the innocent. For there is no man who does not have the power of free choice; and although a bad man may misuse it, this power is not thereby destroyed, we are told, but still strives or can strive after the good. And if that is so, then it is undoubtedly good, holy, and righteous, and ought not to be damned but separated from the man who is to be damned. This, however, cannot be done; and if it could, a man no longer possessed of free choice would not be a man at all. He would have neither merits nor demerits, nor could he be saved, but would be simply a brute and no longer immortal. It therefore remains that God is unjust if he damns, along with the evil man, that good, righteous, and holy power which even in an evil man has no need of Christ.

But let us proceed with John. "He who believes in him," he says, "is not judged; he who does not believe is judged already, because he has not believed in the name of the only Son of God" ⟨John 3:18⟩. Tell me, is free choice counted among those who believe, or is it not? If it is, then again it has no need of grace, since of itself it believes in Christ, though of itself it neither knows him nor gives him a thought. If it is not, then it is already judged; and what does that mean but that it is damned in the sight of God? But God damns none but the ungodly, so therefore it is ungodly. And what godliness can the ungodly aspire to? We cannot, I think, make an exception of the power of free choice here, since John is speaking of the *whole man*, who he says is damned. Besides, unbelief is not one of the grosser passions, but sits and holds sway at the summit—the citadel of the will and reason, just like its opposite, faith. Now, to be unbelieving is to deny God and make him a liar, as I John 1⟨:10⟩ says: "If we do not believe God, we make him a liar" ⟨cf. ch. 5:10⟩. And how can a power that is contrary to God and makes him a liar strive toward the good? If this power were not unbelieving and ungodly, John should not have said of the *whole man* that he is judged already, but rather that with regard to his grosser passions man is already judged, but with regard to what is best and most excellent in him he is not judged, because this strives after faith, or rather, already believes.

[32] *"Per sese bonum et salvum."*

Hence where Scripture says, as it so often does, that every man is a liar, we must say on the authority of free choice that, on the contrary, it is rather the Scripture that lies, because man is not a liar in the best part of him, his reason and will, but only in his flesh, blood, and bones, so that the whole of that which entitles man to be called man, namely reason and will, is soundly healthy and holy. Again, there are the words of the Baptist: "He who believes in the Son has eternal life; but he who does not believe in the Son shall not see life, but the wrath of God rests upon him" ⟨John 3:36⟩. This will have to be understood as follows: "Upon him" means that whereas the wrath of God rests upon the grosser passions of man, upon his power of free choice, that is to say, his will and reason, there rests grace and eternal life. On this model, in order that free choice may be maintained, you can twist anything that is said in the Scriptures against ungodly men, to apply by synecdoche [33] to the brute part of man, so that the rational and truly human part may be left untouched. I shall then return thanks to the assertors of free choice, and shall sin with confidence, safe in the knowledge that reason and will, or free choice, cannot be damned, since it is never extinguished but remains forever sound, righteous, and holy. And with will and reason thus beatified, I shall rejoice that the filthy, brutish flesh is separated from them and damned; so far shall I be from wishing to have Christ as its Redeemer. Do you see what the dogma of free choice leads us to, how it denies all things divine and human, temporal and eternal, and with all these monstrous notions makes itself a laughingstock?

Again, the Baptist says: "No one can receive anything except what is given him from heaven" ⟨John 3:27⟩. Diatribe may here stop that parading of her forces where she enumerates all the things we have from heaven. ⟨E., p. 79.⟩ We are not disputing about nature but about grace, and we are not asking what we are on earth, but what we are in heaven before God. We know that man has been constituted lord over the lower creatures, and in relation to them he has authority and free choice, so that they obey him and do what he wills and thinks. What we are asking is whether he has free choice in relation to God, so that God obeys man and does what man wills, or rather, whether God has free choice in relation to man, so that man wills and does what God wills and is not able to do anything but what God wills and does. The Baptist says here that a man can receive nothing except what is given him from heaven; consequently, free choice must be noth-

[33] A figure of speech in which a part is used to express the whole, or vice versa.

ing. Also, "He who is of the earth belongs to the earth, and of the earth he speaks; he who comes from heaven is above all" ⟨John 3:31⟩. Here again he makes all men earthly who do not belong to Christ, and says they savor and speak of earthly things; and he leaves no room for any in between. Free choice, therefore, which is not in any event "he who comes from heaven," must necessarily be of the earth and must savor and speak of the earth.

But if ever at any time, in any place or work, there was any power in any man that did not savor of earthly things, the Baptist ought to have made allowance for this man and should not have said of all men generally that apart from Christ they are of the earth and speak of the earth. So also below, in ch. 8, Christ says: "You are of the world, I am not of the world; you are from below, I am from above" ⟨John 8:23⟩. Now those to whom he was speaking possessed free choice, or reason and will, yet even so he says they are of the world. But what new thing would he be telling us, to say they were of the world as regards the flesh and the grosser passions? Did not the whole world know this already? Besides, what need is there to say that men are of the world as regards the brute part of them, when in this respect even beasts are of the world?

Now take the saying of Christ in John 6⟨:44⟩: "No one comes to me unless my Father draws him." What does this leave to free choice? For he says that everyone needs to hear and learn from the Father himself, and that all must be taught by God. He plainly teaches here, not only that the works and efforts of free choice are fruitless, but that even the message of the gospel itself (which is what this passage is about) is heard in vain unless the Father himself speaks, teaches, and draws inwardly. "No one can come," he says, "no one"; and thus that power by which a man is able to make some endeavor toward Christ, or in other words, toward the things that pertain to salvation, is asserted to be no power at all. Nor is free choice helped by Diatribe's attempt to depreciate this clear and most powerful passage by quoting from Augustine to the effect that God draws us in the same way as we draw a sheep, by holding out a green twig to it.[34] By this simile she claims it is proved that there is in us a power to follow the drawing of God. But this simile is valueless in connection with this passage. For God holds out not only one of his good things, but all of them, and even Christ his Son himself, yet not a man follows unless the Father inwardly does something else and draws in some other way; instead, the whole world persecutes the Son whom he holds out to

[34] *Tract. in Ioan. Evang.* XXVI.5 (*MPL* 35.1609).

it. The simile fits very well the case of the godly, who are already sheep and know God their Shepherd; for they, living in the Spirit and moved by him, follow wherever God wills and whatever he holds out to them. But the ungodly does not come even when he hears the Word, unless the Father draws and teaches him inwardly, which He does by pouring out the Spirit. There is then another "drawing" than the one that takes place outwardly; for then Christ is set forth by the light of the Spirit, so that a man is rapt away to Christ with the sweetest rapture, and rather yields passively to God's speaking, teaching, and drawing than seeks and runs himself.

Let us take one more passage from John, where he says: "The Spirit will convince the world of sin, because they have not believed in me" ⟨John 16:8 f.⟩. Here you see that it is sin not to believe in Christ. And this sin is surely not seated in the skin or the hair, but precisely in the reason and the will. But when he makes the whole world guilty of this sin, of which experience shows that the world is as ignorant as it is of Christ until the convincing Spirit reveals it, then it is evident that in the sight of God free choice, with its will and its reason alike, is reckoned as a captive of this sin and as damned by it. Therefore, so long as it is ignorant of Christ and does not believe in him, it cannot will or strive after anything good but necessarily serves this sin without knowing it.

In a word, since Scripture everywhere preaches Christ by contrast and antithesis, as I have said, putting everything that is without the Spirit of Christ in subjection to Satan, ungodliness, error, darkness, sin, death, and the wrath of God, all the texts that speak of Christ must consequently stand opposed to free choice; and they are innumerable, indeed they are the entire Scripture. If, therefore, we submit the case to the judgment of Scripture, I shall win on all counts, and there will not be a jot or a tittle left that will not damn the dogma of free choice. Moreover, the fact that Scripture preaches Christ by contrast and antithesis, even if the great theologians and defenders of free choice are or pretend to be ignorant of it, is nevertheless known and commonly confessed by all Christians.

The Two Kingdoms, of Christ and of Satan. The Assurance of Faith ⟨WA 782–783⟩

For Christians know there are two kingdoms in the world, which are bitterly opposed to each other. In one of them Satan reigns, who is therefore called by Christ "the ruler of this world" ⟨John

12:31⟩ and by Paul "the god of this world" ⟨II Cor. 4:4⟩. He holds captive to his will all who are not snatched away from him by the Spirit of Christ, as the same Paul testifies, nor does he allow them to be snatched away by any powers other than the Spirit of God, as Christ testifies in the parable of the strong man guarding his palace in peace ⟨Luke 11:21⟩. In the other Kingdom, Christ reigns, and his Kingdom ceaselessly resists and makes war on the kingdom of Satan. Into this Kingdom we are transferred,[35] not by our own power but by the grace of God, by which we are set free from the present evil age [36] and delivered from the dominion of darkness.[37]

The knowledge and confession of these two kingdoms perpetually warring against each other with such might and main would alone be sufficient to confute the dogma of free choice, seeing that we are bound to serve in the kingdom of Satan unless we are delivered by the power of God. These things, I say, the common people know, and they confess them abundantly in their proverbs and prayers, their attitudes and their whole life.

I leave aside that truly Achillean text of mine, which Diatribe has bravely passed over and left intact. I mean, where Paul in Rom. 7⟨:14 ff.⟩ and Gal. 5⟨:16 ff.⟩ teaches that there is in the saints and the godly a battle between the Spirit and the flesh, so fierce that they cannot do what they would. From this I argued thus: If human nature is so evil that in those born anew of the Spirit it not only does not endeavor after the good but actually strives and fights against it, how should it endeavor after the good in those who are not yet born anew but are still "in the old man" and in bondage to Satan? For even here Paul is not speaking only of the grosser passions, in which Diatribe commonly takes refuge when she wants to evade the Scriptures, but he lists among the works of the flesh heresy, idolatry, dissension, strife, which undoubtedly have their seat in those highest faculties, the reason and the will. If, therefore, the flesh wages war against the Spirit with such passions as these in the saints, it will fight against God all the more in the ungodly and in free choice. That is why in Rom. 8⟨:7⟩ he calls it hostility to God. I should like to see *this* argument pulled to pieces, and free choice defended against it.

For my own part, I frankly confess that even if it were possible, I should not wish to have free choice given to me, or to have anything left in my own hands by which I might strive toward salvation. For, on the one hand, I should be unable to stand firm and keep hold of it amid so many adversities and perils and so many assaults of demons, seeing that even one demon is mightier than

[35] Col. 1:13 f.   [36] Gal. 1:4.   [37] Col. 1:13.

all men, and no man at all could be saved; and on the other hand, even if there were no perils or adversities or demons, I should nevertheless have to labor under perpetual uncertainty and to fight as one beating the air,[38] since even if I lived and worked to eternity, my conscience would never be assured and certain how much it ought to do to satisfy God. For whatever work might be accomplished, there would always remain an anxious doubt [39] whether it pleased God or whether he required something more, as the experience of all self-justifiers proves, and as I myself learned to my bitter cost through so many years. But now, since God has taken my salvation out of my hands into his, making it depend on his choice and not mine, and has promised to save me, not by my own work or exertion but by his grace and mercy, I am assured and certain both that he is faithful and will not lie to me, and also that he is too great and powerful for any demons or any adversities to be able to break him or to snatch me from him. "No one," he says, "shall snatch them out of my hand, because my Father who has given them to me is greater than all" (John 10:28 f.). So it comes about that, if not all, some and indeed many are saved, whereas by the power of free choice none at all would be saved, but all would perish together. Moreover, we are also certain and sure that we please God, not by the merit of our own working, but by the favor of his mercy promised to us, and that if we do less than we should or do it badly, he does not hold this against us,[40] but in a fatherly way pardons and corrects us. Hence the glorying of all the saints in their God.

The Mercy and Justice of God in the Light of Nature, Grace, and Glory ⟨WA 784–785⟩

Now, if you are disturbed by the thought that it is difficult to defend the mercy and justice of God when he damns the undeserving, that is to say, ungodly men who are what they are because they were born in ungodliness and can in no way help being and remaining ungodly and damnable, but are compelled by a necessity of nature to sin and to perish (as Paul says: "We were all children of wrath like the rest," [41] since they are created so by God himself from seed corrupted by the sin of the one man Adam) — rather must God be honored and revered as supremely merciful toward those whom he justifies and saves, supremely unworthy as they are, and there must be at least some acknowledgment of his divine wisdom so that he may be believed to be righteous where

[38] I Cor. 9:26.   [39] "Scrupulus."   [40] "Non imputet."   [41] Eph. 2:3.

he seems to us to be unjust. For if his righteousness were such that it could be judged to be righteous by human standards, it would clearly not be divine and would in no way differ from human righteousness. But since he is the one true God, and is wholly incomprehensible and inaccessible to human reason, it is proper and indeed necessary that his righteousness also should be incomprehensible, as Paul also says where he exclaims: "O the depth of the riches of the wisdom and the knowledge of God! How incomprehensible are his judgments and how unsearchable his ways!" [42] But they would not be incomprehensible if we were able in every instance to grasp how they are righteous. What is man, compared with God? How much is there within our power compared with his power? What is our strength in comparison with his resources? What is our knowledge compared with his wisdom? What is our substance over against his substance? In a word, what is our all compared with his?

If, therefore, we confess, as even nature teaches, that human power, strength, wisdom, substance, and everything we have, is simply nothing at all in comparison with divine power, strength, wisdom, knowledge, and substance, what is this perversity that makes us attack God's righteousness and judgment only, and make such claims for our own judgment as to wish to comprehend, judge, and evaluate the divine judgment? Why do we not take a similar line here too, and say, "Our judgment is nothing in comparison with the divine judgment"? Ask Reason herself whether she is not convinced and compelled to confess that she is foolish and rash in not allowing the judgment of God to be incomprehensible, when she admits that everything else divine is incomprehensible. In all other matters we grant God his divine majesty, and only in respect of his judgment are we prepared to deny it. We cannot for a while believe that he is righteous, even though he has promised us that when he reveals his glory we shall all both see and feel that he has been and is righteous.

I will give an example to confirm this faith and console that evil eye which suspects God of injustice. As you can see, God so orders this corporal world in its external affairs that if you respect and follow the judgment of human reason, you are bound to say either that there is no God or that God is unjust. As the poet says: "Oft I am moved to think there are no gods!" [43] For look at the prosperity the wicked enjoy and the adversity the good endure, and note how both proverbs and that parent of proverbs, experience, testify that the bigger the scoundrel the greater his luck.

[42] Rom. 11:33.   [43] Ovid, *Amores* iii.8.36.

"The tents of the ungodly are at peace," says Job ⟨Job 12:6⟩, and Psalm 72⟨73:12⟩ complains that the sinners of the world increase in riches. Tell me, is it not in everyone's judgment most unjust that the wicked should prosper and the good suffer? But that is the way of the world. Here even the greatest minds have stumbled and fallen, denying the existence of God and imagining that all things are moved at random by blind Chance or Fortune. So, for example, did the Epicureans and Pliny; while Aristotle, in order to preserve that Supreme Being of his from unhappiness, never lets him look at anything but himself, because he thinks it would be most unpleasant for him to see so much suffering and so many injustices. The prophets, however, who did believe in God, had more temptation to regard him as unjust—Jeremiah, for instance, and Job, David, Asaph, and others. What do you suppose Demosthenes and Cicero thought, when after doing all they could they were rewarded with so tragic a death?

Yet all this, which looks so very like injustice in God, and which has been represented as such with arguments that no human reason or light of nature can resist, is very easily dealt with in the light of the gospel and the knowledge of grace, by which we are taught that although the ungodly flourish in their bodies, they lose their souls. In fact, this whole insoluble problem finds a quick solution in one short sentence, namely, that there is a life after this life, and whatever has not been punished and rewarded here will be punished and rewarded there, since this life is nothing but an anticipation, or rather, the beginning of the life to come.

If, therefore, the light of the gospel, shining only through the Word and faith, is so effective that this question which has been discussed in all ages and never solved is so easily settled and put aside, what do you think it will be like when the light of the Word and of faith comes to an end, and reality itself and the Divine Majesty are revealed in their own light? Do you not think that the light of glory will then with the greatest of ease be able to solve the problem that is insoluble in the light of the Word or of grace, seeing that the light of grace has so easily solved the problem that was insoluble in the light of nature?

Let us take it that there are three lights—the light of nature, the light of grace, and the light of glory, to use the common and valid distinction. By the light of nature it is an insoluble problem how it can be just that a good man should suffer and a bad man prosper; but this problem is solved by the light of grace. By the light of grace it is an insoluble problem how God can damn one who is unable by any power of his own to do anything but sin and be guilty. Here both the light of nature and the light of grace tell us that it is not the fault of the unhappy man, but of an unjust God; for they cannot judge otherwise of a God who crowns one ungodly man freely and apart from merits, yet damns another who may well be less, or at least not more, ungodly. But the light of glory tells us differently, and it will show us hereafter that the God whose judgment here is one of incomprehensible righteousness is a God of most perfect and manifest righteousness. In the meantime, we can only *believe* this, being admonished and confirmed by the example of the light of grace, which performs a similar miracle in relation to the light of nature.

CONCLUSION

That the Case Against Free Choice Is Unanswerable Let Erasmus Be Willing to Admit ⟨WA 786–787⟩

I will here bring this little book to an end, though I am prepared if need be to carry the debate farther. However, I think quite enough has been done here to satisfy the godly and anyone who is willing to admit the truth without being obstinate. For if we believe it to be true that God foreknows and predestines all things,[1] that he can neither be mistaken in his foreknowledge nor hindered in his predestination, and that nothing takes place but as he wills it (as reason itself is forced to admit), then on the testimony of reason itself there cannot be any free choice in man or angel or any creature.

Similarly, if we believe that Satan is the ruler of this world, who is forever plotting and fighting against the Kingdom of Christ with all his powers, and that he will not let men go who are his captives unless he is forced to do so by the divine power of the Spirit, then again it is evident that there can be no such thing as free choice.

Similarly, if we believe that original sin has so ruined us that even in those who are led by the Spirit it causes a great deal of trouble by struggling against the good, it is clear that in a man devoid of the Spirit there is nothing left that can turn toward the good, but only toward evil.

Again, if the Jews, who pursued righteousness to the utmost of their powers, rather ran headlong into unrighteousness, while the Gentiles, who pursued ungodliness, attained righteousness freely and unexpectedly, then it is also manifest from this very fact and

[1] Rom. 8:29.

experience that man without grace can will nothing but evil.

To sum up: If we believe that Christ has redeemed men by his blood, we are bound to confess that the whole man was lost; otherwise, we should make Christ either superfluous or the redeemer of only the lowest part of man, which would be blasphemy and sacrilege.

My dear Erasmus, I beg you now for Christ's sake to do at last as you promised; for you promised you would willingly yield to anyone who taught you better ⟨E., p. 97⟩. Have done with respecting of persons! I recognize that you are a great man, richly endowed with the noblest gifts of God—with talent and learning, with eloquence bordering on the miraculous, to mention no others—while I have and am nothing, unless I may venture to boast that I am a Christian. Moreover, I praise and commend you highly for this also, that unlike all the rest you alone have attacked the real issue, the essence of the matter in dispute, and have not wearied me with irrelevancies about the papacy, purgatory, indulgences, and such like trifles (for trifles they are rather than basic issues), with which almost everyone hitherto has gone hunting for me without success. You and you alone have seen the question on which everything hinges, and have aimed at the vital spot; for which I sincerely thank you, since I am only too glad to give as much attention to this subject as time and leisure permit. If those who have attacked me hitherto had done the same, and if those who now boast of new spirits and new revelations would still do it, we should have less of sedition and sects and more of peace and concord. But God has in this way through Satan punished our ingratitude.

Unless, however, you can conduct this case differently from the way you have in this Diatribe, I could very much wish that you would be content with your own special gift, and would study, adorn, and promote languages and literature as you have hitherto done with great profit and distinction. I must confess that in this direction you have done no small service to me too, so that I am considerably indebted to you, and in this regard I certainly respect and admire you most sincerely. But God has not yet willed or granted that you should be equal to the matter at present at issue between us. I say this, as I beg you to believe, in no spirit of arrogance, but I pray that the Lord may very soon make you as much superior to me in this matter as you are in all others. There is no novelty in it, if God instructs Moses through Jethro [2] and teaches Paul through Ananias.[3] For as to your saying ⟨E., p. 97⟩ that you

[2] Ex. 18:13 ff.   [3] Acts 9:10 ff.

have wandered very far from the mark if you are ignorant of Christ, I think you yourself see what it implies. For it does not follow that everybody will go astray if you or I do. God is preached as being marvelous in his saints,[4] so that we may regard as saints those who are very far from sanctity. And it is not difficult to suppose that you, since you are human, may not have rightly understood or observed with due care the Scriptures or the sayings of the Fathers under whose guidance you think you are attaining your goal; and of this there is more than a hint in your statement that you are asserting nothing, but have only "discoursed." [5] No one writes like that who has a thorough insight into the subject and rightly understands it. I for my part in this book *have not discoursed, but have asserted and do assert,* and I am unwilling to submit the matter to anyone's judgment, but advise everyone to yield assent. But may the Lord, whose cause this is, enlighten you and make you a vessel for honor and glory.[6]

Amen.

[4] *"Mirabilis in sanctis suis"* (Ps. 67:36, Vulg. EVV tr.: "terrible in his sanc- tuary").
[5] See p. 28.
[6] Rom. 9:21.

Appendix: On the Adagia of Erasmus

For the last thirty years of his life Erasmus was continually revising and reissuing a large work on the *Adagia*, or proverbs, of classical antiquity. Into successive editions of this work he poured more and more of his erudition, extending his comparisons over the whole field of ancient learning. Most of the proverbs were accompanied by pleasant discursive essays in Erasmus' inimitable blend of chattiness and wit, and occasionally these essays developed into treatises of over a score of pages, so that in addition to being what might be called the bedside book of the Renaissance the *Adagia* became a kind of scholarly confessional for Erasmus himself. The first *Collectanea* of these sayings, issued in Paris in 1500, contained 808 proverbs and was reprinted 26 times; by 1508 when the Aldine Press at Venice printed what Erasmus now called *Adagiorum Chiliades*, "Thousands of Proverbs," the number had risen to 3,260. In 1515, Frobenius at Basle took over the printing of successive editions of the work, of which there were seven more between 1517 and 1536, the final total of sayings being . 4,251. The references here are to the 1520 edition published by Frobenius, it being the nearest in time to the *De libero arbitrio;* a copy of this edition is in the John Rylands Library in Manchester.

It will be seen that there are at least two places (pp. 54 and 83) where a proper understanding of Erasmus' meaning is extremely difficult without the key provided by his remarks in the *Adagia*. In particular his reference to *Diomedea necessitas* (p. 83) shows the extent to which he was dominated by books, for it only introduces obscurity where none existed. The first edition of the *De libero arbitrio* prints "*praeter casam*" (p. 54), but in several subsequent editions ignorance of the allusion here has led to the easier reading "*praeter causam*" appearing in the text.

The following are the more noteworthy proverbial phrases employed by Erasmus:

Page 54: "*Ita fugias ne praeter casam.*"

This is the full form of the proverb, found in Terence, *Phormio*, V.ii.3, and it seems to refer to passing a safe retreat or hiding place. Perhaps the allusion is to a child's game. The following is the comment of Erasmus:

Adagia I. v. 4;

Extat apud Ter. in Phormione cum primis venustum adagium Ita fugias ne praeter casam, quo quidem admonemur ne sic aliquod vitium fugiamus, ut in aliud maius incauti devolvamur. Nostrapte culpa facimus, inquit, ut malos expediat esse, dum dici nimium bonos studemus et benignos. Ita fugias, ne praeter casam, ut aiunt. Verba sunt Demophonis senis semet accusantis, quod dum avari famam plus satis cupide studeret effugere, stulti reprehensionem incurrisset. Donatus adagii metaphoram hunc ad modum enarrat, si modo commentum hoc Donati videtur esse. Ita fugito, ne tuam casam praetermittas, quae sit tibi tutissimum exceptaculum. Aut ita fugias, ne praeter casam, ubi custodiri magis et prehendi fur et mulctari verberibus potest. Aut verbum erat, inquit, furem exagitantis, et interea providentis, ne ante casam transeat ne in praetereundo etiam inde aliquid rapiat. Hanc veluti divinationem, incerta ac varia coniectantum quis ferret, nisi videremus et iuris interpretibus, et Graecorum adagiorum enarratoribus hunc eundem esse morem. Primum interpretamentum mihi magis arridet. Quidam enim calore fugiendi, etiam ea praetercurrunt, ubi commode poterant quiescere. Quod unica voce Graeci παραφέρεσθαι vocant, id est, perperam praeterire ac praetervehi, ab eo, quod amplectandum erat, aberrantem. Opinor ad hoc adagium respexisse Lucianum in Nigrino, cum scribit, καὶ τοῦτο δὲ ἐν ταῖς τραγῳδίαις καὶ κωμῳδίαις λεγόμενον, ἤδη καὶ παρὰ θύραν βιαζόμενοι, id est, et hoc quod in tragoediis et comoediis dicitur, Iam et praeter casam incitati.

"There is in the *Phormio* of Terence a very attractive proverb, 'See that you don't flee past your own dwelling,' which warns us not to flee from one vice with such vehemence that we incautiously fall into a greater. It is our own fault, it says, that we should naturally fall into the criticism of being evil through striving to be thought overkind and good. So flee, but not past your dwelling, as they say. The words are those of the old man Demophon, who accuses himself of incurring the charge of folly while endeavoring too eagerly to avoid that of avarice. Donatus, if indeed the commentary is by Donatus, interprets the figure of speech in the proverb thus: In flight do not pass by your own dwelling, which is your safest refuge. Or, Pass not by your dwelling, where the thief can best be seized and guarded and flogged. Or, he says, the word is spoken by a man driving away a thief and taking care that the thief does not pass his dwelling, lest even in passing he should snatch something. No one could tolerate this sort of divination, the result of wild and fanciful guesswork, if we did not see that interpreters of Greek proverbs and expounders of legalistic niceties had exactly the same characteristics. The first interpretation attracts me most. There are some who in the heat of flight pass by those places where they could rest in safety. The Greeks express this idea by the one word παραφέρεσθαι, that is, in one's wandering to be carried and pass fruitlessly past the point which was to be grasped. I think Lucian in his *Nigrinus* is glancing at this proverb when he writes, καὶ τοῦτο δὲ ἐν ταῖς τραγῳδίαις καὶ κωμῳδίαις λεγόμενον, ἤδη καὶ παρὰ θύραν βιαζόμενοι, that is, this too which is said in tragedies and comedies, 'Now they are driven past their own dwelling.' "

Page 58: *"Per mare quaerat aquas"* ("Seek water in the sea.")

Adagia I. ix. 75:

ἐν θαλάσσῃ ζητεῖς ὕδωρ, id est, in mari quaeris aquam. Ibi quaeris, perinde quasi difficile inventu, ubi nihil aliud occurrat; veluti, siquis in moribus scelestissimi hominis, unum aut alterum admissum vestigat, cum tota vita sit contaminata, aut siquis in scriptoribus indoctis, pauca captet quae reprehendat, cum nihil occurrat non reprehendendum.

Martialis:
Si memini, per mare, inquit, quaeris aquam.

Item Propertius Elegiarum libro primo:
Nunc tu
Insanus medio flumine quaeris aquam.

"ἐν θαλάσσῃ ζητεῖς ὕδωρ, that is, you are looking for water in the sea. You are seeking something as though it were difficult to find, in a place where nothing else occurs. Just as if one were in the character of an utter scoundrel to investigate one or other particular crime, when in fact his whole life is polluted; or as if one were to cavil at a few mistakes in the work of illiterate authors, where everything is faulty. Martial writes, 'If I remember,' he said, 'you are looking for water in the sea,' and likewise Propertius in the first book of his *Elegies:* 'Now you madly seek for water in midstream.' "

Page 83: *"Diomedea, ut aiunt, omnium rerum necessitatem."*

Adagia I. ix. 5:

Διομήδειος ἀνάγκη, id est, Diomedea necessitas. De iis qui, vi adacti, non sponte, quid faciunt. Quidam originem adagii referunt ad Thracium illum Diomedem, qui solitus fertur, hospites suos compellere, ut cum filiabus suis deformissimis rem haberent. Quo facto, eosdem interimebat. Unde fabula sparsit, Diomedis equas homines pabuli vice esitare solitos, videlicet filias a viris agitatas equas appellans. Alii referunt ad Diomedem ducem Graecorum huiusmodi commentum adferentes, cum Diomedes & Ulysses communi opera, sublato Palladio, redirent, noctu, Ulysses quo facti gloriam in se unum transferret, destinabat occidere Diomedem praecedentem, ac Palladium secum portantem. Itaque cum ensem in caput illius a tergo vibrasset, Diomedes animadversa ad lunae lumen gladii umbra, subtraxit se plagae, correptumque Ulyssem, vinctis manibus praecedere compulit, gladio lato subinde caedens illius Tergum. Hinc Diomedea necessitas.

"Διομήδειος ἀνάγκη, that is, Diomedean necessity. Of those who act not of their own will but through compulsion. Some refer the origin of the proverbs to the Thracian Diomede, who is said to have been in the habit of compelling his guests to have intercourse with his hideous daughters, after which he would murder them. And so the fable threw off another, that the mares of Diomede were accustomed to human flesh as food, of course referring to women mounted by men as mares. Others refer to Diomede the Greek chieftain, quoting an anecdote that when Diomede and Ulysses were returning from their nocturnal exploit of capturing the shield of Pallas, Ulysses with the idea of transferring all the glory of the deed to himself, determined to kill Diomede as he walked in front carrying the shield of Pallas. But as he brandished the sword from behind above Diomede's head Diomede caught sight of the shadow in the moonlight, avoided the blow, seized Ulysses, bound his hands and compelled him to walk ahead, while he ceaselessly beat him behind with his broad sword. Hence Diomedean necessity."

No further comment is needed except on the roundabout medieval way of expressing a perfectly simple notion by a grotesque piece of mythology.

Page 95: "*Veluti malum nodum malo cuneo propelleret.*"

This seems to be an injunction against chopping wood with a razor.

Adagia I. ii. 5:

> *Malo nodo, malus quaerendus cuneus.*

Ad hanc sententiam accedit & illud: Malo nodo, malus est quaerendus cuneus. Ita divus Hieronymus ad Oceanum: Interim iuxta vulgare proverbium: Malo arboris nodo, malus cuenus requirendus est. Eo licebit uti: Quoties malum, simili malitia retundimus. Sumptum a sectoribus roborum, qui siquando durior in ligno nodus inciderit, nolunt in eo periclitari securim, verum cuneum quempiam durum magis bonum inserunt. Congruit huic Sophoclis apud Menandrum,

> πικρὰν χολὴν κλύσουσι [sic] φαρμάκῳ πικρῷ,

id est, Remedio amaro, bilem amarem diluunt.

> "*Malo nodo, malus quaerendus cuneus.*
> (For a tough knot take a blunt wedge.)

"To this saying one might add the following: For a tough knot, a blunt wedge must be sought. So St. Jerome to Oceanus: Meanwhile it is very like the common proverb: For a tough knot of wood, a blunt wedge must be sought. We can employ this metaphor whenever we strike down an evil by a similar evil [i.e., homoeopathically]. It is taken from the practice of woodcutters who whenever they encounter a harder knot in wood refuse to risk an ax upon it but insert a hard wedge as being better. In agreement with this is the saying of Sophocles in Menander,

> πικρὰν χολὴν κλύσουσι φαρμάκῳ πικρῷ,

that is, 'They dissolve bitter bile with a bitter remedy.' "

In this section of the *Adagia*, Erasmus comments on two or three similar proverbs, *Clavo clavum, paxillo paxillum, Malum malo medicari*, and then goes on to those which have a similar ring, such as *Morbum morbo addere, Igni ignem addere, Oleum camino addere*, etc.

There are other proverbial phrases scattered up and down the *Discourse:* "*musca cum elephanto*" (p. 36), "*qui vel equum claudum sanare potuerit*" (p. 45), "*velut ignis ex collisione silicum*" (p. 47), "*baculum curvum ut rectum facias*" (p. 96), which are not the texts of essays in the *Adagia* but show how readily Erasmus' command of proverbial lore came to his aid as he wrote.

Luther too is fond of proverbs, and in his *De servo arbitrio* there are nearly as many as in Erasmus. One might quote "*Aiunt, aio, negant, nego*" (p. 108), which is a line from Terence that had become a proverb; "*super aristas graderis*" (p. 126), "*in suggesto declamare*" (p. 135), "*nodum in scirpo quaerere*" (p. 144), "*vox et praeterea nihil*" (p. 145), all from a short section of the text.

A. N. MARLOW

INDEXES

GENERAL INDEX

For the main themes of these works, such as "faith," "grace," "predestination," "righteousness," the reader is referred to the main table of contents.

The works of each author are under that author's name, e.g., *Adagia* will be found under the heading "Erasmus."

341

BIBLICAL REFERENCES